WATER

Original manuscript revised and updated by:

W. Sherman Gillam
Assistant Director, Research
Office of Saline Water
Department of the Interior

W. H. McCoy
Chief, Division of Chemical Physics
Office of Saline Water
Department of the Interior

WATER

The Fountain of Opportunity

H. G. Deming

Late Professor of Chemistry
University of Nebraska

New York

Oxford University Press

1975

Copyright © 1975 by Oxford University Press, Inc.
Library of Congress Catalogue Card Number: 74-16657

Printed in the United States of America

Foreword

From the dawn of civilization, ever since there has been an association of men which could be called "society," water has been one of society's concerns. The earth's water resources, in the form of rainfall or snow, in the streams and lakes, in the oceans, and in aquifers have shaped the development of peoples and nations.

Early nomadic societies shaped their wanderings and their customs to fit the vagaries of the naturally occurring precipitation. As permanent agricultural settlements emerged, the management of water resources for irrigation and domestic supplies were among the first technologies.

The earliest codes of law reflect the involvement of government in problems of water management and water rights. References can be found in the Code of Hammurabi and in the Old Testament. The Roman Empire developed an elaborate system of water law along with its extensive aqueducts. Free use of the waterways for commerce was assigned significance in both the Magna Carta and in the Northwest Ordinance enacted by our Continental Congress.

The importance of water resources to society and to government is not diminished today. Our complex, metropolitan civilization and advanced technologies have generated new demands for water. Sophisticated industrial processes, central power stations, and advanced sanitation systems are major modern demands. The ancient uses, too, are still important. Agriculture still represents the predominant consumptive use of our national water supplies, and waterborne commerce remains a major mode of transportation and the lifeline of many large cities.

Our culture also increasingly values water in its natural state. Outdoor recreation, fish and wildlife conservation, and simply the aesthetic appreciation of unspoiled lakes and streams are competing with traditional developmental purposes.

Water is a fundamental resource. In most regions it is a finite and scarce resource. Its importance to man can never diminish and the claims upon it seem destined to increase both in complexity and in quantity.

The management of water resources, therefore, will continue to pose a challenge worthy of whatever talent, knowledge and technology society commands. It will pose a challenge to leaders and citizens; to legislators, lawyers, scientists, engineers, and farmers; to water resource planners and managers as well as to those whose needs they seek to serve.

Dr. Deming in this book has presented the broadest perspective of water, its nature, and its uses. It can be an enlightening book for the curious student who wants to know something about an important aspect of the world he lives in. It can be a useful book for the generalist who has discovered that water influences his work or his leisure and who wants to be informed in his judgments. Most importantly, for some readers it may be the beginning of a lifelong interest and a life's work.

In my own work in the United States Senate, I have devoted many days to the consideration of policy decisions involving water resources. Some of these decisions rank among the most complex and perhaps the most significant which the Senate has addressed. They affect the welfare and prosperity of vast regions and of millions of citizens.

For the interested student, water resources management offers a variety of career opportunities. Thy can be opportunities for the most satisfying kind of work; work which taxes the best efforts of the individual and which is of vital importance to himself, his community, and to the nation.

Henry M. Jackson, Chairman
Senate Committee on Interior and
Insular Affairs

Washington, D.C.
August 1974

Author's Preface

The radiant energy of the sun evaporates water from the oceans, lakes, rivers, leaves, and moist soils of the world and lifts the vapor to the level of the clouds. Here it is recondensed to liquid and poured back over nearly all the earth as an eternal cascade of fresh water. Fresh water would everywhere be in satisfying abundance were it only more evenly distributed. Yet so unevenly do the waters of the great cascade fall back upon the earth that there are deserts, in which there is practically never any rain, and tropical forests, in which rainfall almost never ceases.

The abundance or scarcity of fresh water is one of the chief factors that determine the density of human population in different parts of the earth. One is tempted to believe that the destiny of every nation was determined, long before modern man appeared on the earth, by accidents of climate or geology, which allotted to each land a generous or scant portion of earth's eternal fountain. Yet is this really so? May not the great outpouring of fresh water actually be a fountain of opportunity? Difficulties to overcome may just be nature's way of making us a little smarter than earthworms.

Man's efforts to distribute water more evenly over the surface of the earth has often permitted dense populations to exist in areas that otherwise would have been sparsely tenanted. In regions of abundant rainfall this benefit is often won at the cost of polluted water. Water-borne disease is often the unsuspected source of high infant mortality, which may keep human population nearly stationary, even in lands in which food is abundant.

Deserts have had a very different history from the rain-drenched lands of the tropics. They have often delayed or prevented settlement by human beings. Yet deserts do have some advantages. They are often immune to the floods that damage or destroy settlements in wetter locations. They offer some protection against being surprised by raids of hostile neighbors. Arid lands are also more sanitary places of residence than river banks, since human wastes are decently buried, instead of being discarded into streams. It is thus no wonder that human groups have often preferred to settle in relatively arid places. At about the dawn of recorded history great empires arose in lands that then, as still today, had limited supplies of fresh water.

For arid lands to be settled, there had to be considerable advance in the control, conveyance and storage of water—items of what is today called *hydraulic engineering*. Dams, thrown across small streams, diverted water for irrigation. In many places (as still in California today) irrigation resulted in a dramatic increase in the food supply. Gradually, as cities increased in size, men had to learn how to construct aqueducts, tunneled through solid rock or built of blocks of stone, for bringing water from great distances.

In the dispersal of the human race over every habitable isle or continent, water was important for another reason. Rivers, streams, and lakes have always been the easiest routes for wandering human tribes to reach the interior of continents. Other wanderers, moving in the opposite direction, encountered a great blue barrier—the earth-encircling ocean. Faced with this, some tribes just sat down for ten thousand generations and never ventured out of sight of land nor dreamed a sail. Others, on arriving at the ocean's edge, found behind them a great desert, which seemed to offer permanent protection from other human groups. In the end, they found this protection inadequate, and so built a Great Wall, equally ineffective. They, too, failed to explore the ocean.

Still other human groups, more venturesome or inventive than the rest, developed outrigger canoes. In these, they ventured from island to island, far out of sight of land, until they had discovered and settled every habitable island in the vast Pacific.

The earliest of these small migrant groups were perhaps impelled to wander by no more important a motive than a desire for adventure or curiosity about what lay beyond the horizon. They gave primitive men a foothold on three of the earth's seven continents. Those coming afterward found the land already taken, hence there were conflicts—

brief and extended. Waves of mounted horsemen battered down old empires, burning cities, crumbling palaces and aqueducts, destroying irrigation systems, and leaving death and destruction everywhere. The most recent of the numberless tragedies was the most widespread and perhaps the saddest. Adventurers from Europe wrested the whole Western Hemisphere from men whose ancestors had possessed it for more than ten thousand years.

The causes of most of the great migrations of history have been forgotten. Perhaps they were not clearly understood by many who participated in them. Yet there is no doubt that changes in the quality or abundance of fresh water were often their chief cause. Perhaps all the wells went dry during a sequence of years of poor rainfall. Perhaps, on the contrary, rainfall was so abundant that every year brought a disastrous flood. Or it may be that epidemic disease carried off so many people that even before the dawn of science it became evident to everyone that the tribe had picked a poor place to settle. In any case, fresh water brought the signal to sally forth and seize better lands, no matter who controlled them.

In the present century men have at last become more conscious of how often the fertility of the soil has been destroyed by salt brought in by the irrigation water. When this happens, it is migrate or starve.

Today, technical knowledge ensures that ruining of land by salt shall not go on indefinitely. The remedy is often merely to make sure that the irrigation water never has more than a specified, very slight concentration of salt. There is good protection, too, against the destruction of soil fertility by salt if better water or rainwater, with good drainage, is available after the irrigation season, to leach accumulated salts from the soil and drain them away to lower depths.

In many salt-ruined areas the accumulation of salt and alkali in the soil has been going on for centuries. Such soils may sometimes be improved, but the process is slow and costly. Lands gradually ruined during more than a thousand centuries cannot usually be redeemed in a few decades.

A needless but often fatal impediment in reclaiming desert regions is in political rivalries and long-nurtured hatreds—so full of grievances is history, so slow are men to forgive, and so intolerant and unrelenting are human hearts toward men of another race or creed.

Countries that receive only a scant portion of earth's eternal fountain are sometimes the very ones that lack important deposits of coal, natural gas, or petroleum. Importing these fuels in sufficient quantity to ensure the industrial development of such countries would often cost as much as the resulting improvement in their economy would produce. Desert-based "have-not" countries are likely to remain in that condition until, after a century or two, men have learned to exploit more efficiently the motive power behind the great fountain of opportunity—the radiant energy of the sun.

In the long run, the only *destiny* that seems inescapable is that bequeathed us by our ancestors; for the wealth of nations does not reside in mineral deposits, fossil fuels, or abundant fresh water resources, but in the ability to use these resources intelligently. It is *human quality* that counts. The great contest between the two opposing worlds of the twentieth century is actually a contest between opposing views of what qualities a state should cultivate in its citizens.

H.G.D.

Lincoln, Neb.
1972

Editors' Preface

The great importance of water to mankind is generally recognized, but most of us are not really aware of the many specific influences of this vital and pervasive liquid. This book is the product of the mind—and heart—of a distinguished author and professor of chemistry, whose career spanned more than sixty years; whose breadth of knowledge was combined with a remarkable gift for communication; and whose passing even at age eighty-five was much too soon.

No significant aspect of water's environmental influence is omitted: from molecular structure to flood control, from cells of living things to the influences on continental populations, from crop growth to industrial pollution; presented where necessary in historical context. In our years of involvement with the Federal desalination program, we have seen quite a number of books on water but none that approaches the breadth and value of this one. It is a privilege to be associated with its publication, even in such a small way, and we firmly believe that it will be of deep interest and benefit to anyone wanting to know more about the mechanism of operation of our world and its people.

W.S.G.
W.H.McC.

Washington, D.C.
August 1974

Acknowledgments

The editors are much indebted to Mrs. Betty Edwards for the cheerful and capable way in which she did the hard work of typing and re-typing the manuscript.

Contents

1
Fresh Water Resources in Nature   3

Water Is a Permanent Resource, 3; Glaciers and Polar Icecaps, 4; Resources of Underground Water, 5; A System of Aquifers, 6; Water Table and Hydrostatic Balance, 8; Flow of Water in Aquifers, 9; Ground Water in Desert Areas, 12; Tracing and Measuring Underground Flow, 13; How Limestone Caves Are Formed, 16; Springs and Wells, 17; Wells and the Settlement of the West, 19; Fresh Water in Lakes and Ponds, 21; The American Great Lakes, 22; The World's Giant Lakes, 26; Rivers as Fresh Water Resources, 26.

2
Fresh Water and the Land   29

Exploitation, Then Conservation, 29; Land Capability, 31; Erosion Control, 32; Watershed Management, 33; Soil Components and Soil Types, 35; The Penetration of Surface Soil by Water, 36; The Water-Holding Capacity of Soils, 38; The Availability of Soil Moisture, 40; Irrigation Methods, 41; Salt in Irrigation Water, 43; How Much Water Does a Crop Need?, 44; Profits and Pitfalls in Irrigation, 45; Drainage for Wet Lands, 46; Water Withdrawal for Different Uses, 48; Water Economy, 49; Depleted Aquifers, 51; Artificial Replenishment, 52.

3
The Return of the Rivers   54

Our Dwindling Powerhouse: The Sun, 54; The Earth's Gaseous Ocean, 56; Rate of Evaporation, 59; Vapor Pressure, 61; Moisture in the Atmosphere, 63; Evaporation and Precipitation Statistics, 64; The Cooling Effect of Evaporation, 65; The Transport of Energy by Water Vapor, 67; Incoming and Outgoing Radiant Energy, 68; Ocean Currents, 69; Ascending and Descending Air, 70.

4
Climates, Winds, and Weather   72

The Earth's Primary Climatic Zones, 72; The Coriolis Effect, 74; Prevailing Winds, 78; Secondary or Minor Air Circulations, 80; Stable and Unstable Air Masses, 81; What Determines Wind Direction, 83; Weather Forecasting, 86; Conditions for Rainfall, 86; Rain-making, 89; Rain Forests, Deserts, and Swamps, 90; Fresh Water and the World's Food Supply, 93.

5
Water Molecules Account for Water's Behavior   96

Chemical Changes, 96; Elements and Compounds, 97; The Formula of Water Vapor, 99; Electron Pairing, 100; Assembling a Molecule of Water Vapor, 101; Polar Molecules, 102; Water Is an Associated Liquid, 105; The Conductivity of Water, 106; Physical Properties of Liquid Water, 107; The Transparency of Water, 109; Dissolved Oxygen in Water; What Happens When Water Freezes, 112.

6
Water as the Vehicle of Life   114

Water and Protoplasm, 114; A Plant Cell—a Bag Within a Bag Within a Box, 115; Contrasting Dead with Living Membranes, 117; Organelles: Nucleus and Ribosomes, 118; DNA and the Pattern of Heredity, 119; Stages in the Development of a Plant Cell, 122; More About Photosynthesis, 122; The Formation of Insoluble Carbohydrates, 124; Amino Acids and Proteins, 125; How Root Tips Penetrate the Soil, 127; Root Systems, 128; Contest for Water Between Plant and Soil, 131; Water Channels in Higher Plants, 132; Transpiration, 134;

Transpiration rates, 136; What Goes on in Lakes and Ponds, 138; Comparing Plants with Animals, 141; Water Balance and Water Economy, 143; Water Content of Animals at Different Ages and for Different Species, 144; Osmotic Equilibrium, 146; Water for Livestock, 147; Desert Animals, 148; A Look at Ourselves, 149.

7
The Conveyance and Storage of Water   115

Water Supplies in Ancient Times, 151; Victims of Warfare, Sand, and Silt, 153; Sources of Water for Modern Cities, 154; Cities in Competition with Agriculture, 155; The Penalty of Size, 156; Quick Construction by Earth-Moving Machinery, 158.

8
Water as a Carrier of Energy   161

Water Wheels and Hydraulic Turbines, 161; Pressure Within Water at Various Depths, 162; Pressure as a Measure of Energy, 163; Streamline vs. Turbulent Flow, 165; The Potential and Kinetic Energy of Flowing Water, 166; Mathematics Provides a Key, 167; Energy from the Controlled Descent of Water, 169; Artificial Reservoirs and High Dams, 171; Energy for the Future, 174.

9
Remaking a Continent   178

Hydraulic Engineering, 178; Scale Models, 179; Flood Control on the Lower Mississippi, 181; River Traffic Then and Now, 183; The Improvement of Northern Rivers, 185; The Civil Works Program of the Corps of Engineers, 186.

10
Water and Energy from the Pacific States   189

California's Central Valley project, 189; The Earthquake Threat, 193; A Continental Idea: NAWAPA, 194; Water from the Far North, 195; Water and Power from the Great Trench, 197; Tragedy on the Yukon, 198.

11
A Horrid Word for a Horrid Deed: Pollution 200

Contamination vs. Pollution, 11; Sanitation Zero, 201; Water-Borne Disease, 202; Modern Sewage Disposal, 204; Septic Tanks, 206; The Problem of the Liquid Effluents, 207; Pollution from Long Ago Claims Victims Today, 208; The Results of Pollution of Lakes and Ponds, 209; Dead and Dying Great Lakes, 210; Chemistry Intervenes To Control the Sea Lamprey, 212; Restocking the Lakes, 214; The Menace of Aquatic Weeds, 215.

12
Industrial Pollution 217

Contamination or Pollution by Salt, 218; Pollution by the Iron and Steel Industries, 219; How Streams Are Endangered by the Paper Industry, 212; The Threat to Dissolved Oxygen, 223; The Rebirth of the Sacramento, 225; Pollution by Detergents, 227; Pollution by Pesticides, 229; Sex Interference and Sex Attractants in the War Against Insects, 232; Effects of the Thermal Alteration of Water by Industry, 234; Let's Save the Tidal Flats, 236; Pollution by Oil, 238; Legal Measures To Control Pollution, 239; National Pollution Control, 240.

13
The Worldwide Menace of Salt 243

Sources of the Ocean's Salt, 243; Salt Accumulation in Soils, 244; Plant Growth in the Presence of Salt, 245; Damage Done by Toxic Elements, 246; The Sensitivity of Different Crops to Salt, 247; Salt Tolerance, 249; How the Soil Itself May Be Ruined by Salt, 251; Irrigation with Saline Water, 251; Salt-Laden Zones of the United States and Canada, 253; A Glance at Mexico, 254; India and Pakistan, 255; Salt Balance and the Fate of Nations, 256.

14
Making Water Fit To Use 257

Chlorine and Hypochlorites in Water Purification, 257; Coagulation and Filtration, 258; Final Disinfection by Chlorine or Chlorine Dioxide, 259; Disinfection by Ozone or Ultraviolet Light, 260; Water Discolored by Plant Residues, 261; Fluoridation, 261; Simple Ways To Get Rid of Hardness, 262; Standards of Water Quality, 264; Bacteriological Examination, 265; Victims of the Old Oaken Bucket, 265; Water Testing, 266; Iron and Manganese in Water, 267; Getting Rid of Hydrogen Sulfide, 268.

15
Fresh Water from the Ocean   269

Fresh Water for Mariners, 269; Dissolved Salts in the Ocean, 270; Treasure from the Ocean, 271; Special Properties of Salt Water, 274; Desalination Methods, 277; Why Desalination Is Expensive, 278; Least Demand for Energy in Desalination, 279; Solar Stills, 281; Multiple Effect Distillation, 283; Ways to Economize on Heat, 285; Vacuum Flash Distillation, 286; How Corrosion and the Deposition of Scale Are Prevented, 288; Vapor Compression Distillation, 289; Desalting by Freezing, 290; Electrolysis and Electrodialysis, 292; Reverse Osmosis, 295; Desalination in Dual Purpose Plants, 296; The Transport of Ions by Living Plants and Animals, 299; The Office of Saline Water, 301; Statistics, 304.

16
Conclusion   305

The Wildlife: This Is Their Continent, Too, 305.

Appendix   307

A. Heat, Work, and Energy, 307; B. Temperature and Latent Heat, 309; C. Radiant Energy, 310; D. Operation with Very Large and Very Small Numbers, 313; E. Ions and Ionic Equations, 314; F. The Conductivity Test for Salt, 317; G. Measures of Concentration and Weight Composition, 319; H. The pH Scale of Acidity or Alkalinity, 322; I. Colloids and High Polymers, 323; J. Diffusion, Dialysis, Osmosis, and Osmotic Pressure, 325; K. Atomic Weights of a Few Important Elements, 332; L. Handy Conversion Factors, 33.

Index   335

WATER

Fresh Water Resources in Nature

Water Is a Permanent Resource

Mountain brooks, rushing streams, roaring cataracts, and rivers in full flood must give everyone the impression that fresh water, after falling on the land as rain or snow, is lost for human use when it mingles with the salt-laden, earth-encircling ocean. Actually, the amount of surface water is almost negligible in comparison with the amount of water that is trickling silently and invisibly downhill, deep underground. Sometimes a drop of water in this slow-moving dark and silent stream needs thousands of years to complete its journey to the sea or to some place where it issues once more as a well or spring. An extremely long time may be needed, too, for rain or snow that has fallen on icefields or polar icecaps to be carried out by glaciers, to melt, and so at length to reach the sea.

If it were not for this long delay in the mingling of fresh water with the ocean, our planet's resources of fresh water would be very limited. Most of the earth's fresh water is locked up in polar icecaps, quite beyond human reach. Such currently unavailable fresh water is estimated to be about 9,000,000 cubic miles, as compared with about 1,050,000 cubic miles of available fresh water. The latter includes (in cubic miles):

Available underground water	1,000,000
Lakes and ponds	30,000
Soil moisture	16,000
Atmospheric moisture	3100
Rivers (water in transit at any moment)	300

In comparison, the volume of salt water in the ocean is about 317,000,000 cubic miles. This is nearly 97 per cent of earth's available water.

Water vapor is the lightest of the chief components of the earth's atmosphere. If it did not freeze, it would accumulate in the rarefied upper atmosphere, at heights of more than ten miles, and thence gradually be lost into space. Yet, because the upper atmosphere is very cold, water there freezes into solid particles of ice or snow, which slowly drift earthward. Thus the earth tends to retain its supply of water indefinitely. Indeed, it may be slowly gaining available water by two different processes: (1) molecules of water are captured from space as the earth moves around the sun; and (2) water is freed by volcanic heat from hydrated (water-holding) rocks and minerals that are apparently dry.

The combustion of fuels, the respiration of animals, and the decay of dead plant and animal materials are three closely related processes in which vast quantities of water are produced; but they tend to be offset by photosynthesis (a process in which green plants, with the aid of the energy of sunlight, convert carbon dioxide and water into living plant tissue). The net result of all these processes may conceivably be slowly to increase the earth's store of uncombined water. Yet this store is so enormous that it has long been and will long remain for all intents and purposes constant. The mass and temperature of the earth join to make this planet unique in our solar system in having a plentiful supply of water.

Glaciers and Polar Icecaps

Almost three-fourths of all the fresh water on the earth is locked up in icecaps and glaciers. About 90 per cent of this great volume of solidified water (which is actually compacted snow) is in the mile-deep icecap of the Antarctic continent, which has three times the area of the continental United States, excluding Alaska. This is about six million cubic miles of ice. If slowly melted, it would keep the Mississippi River flowing for about 50,000 years, and all the rivers of the earth for about 830 years. Poured into the ocean, such a great volume of fresh water would raise the ocean's level about 250 feet.

Polar icecaps are so inaccessible that they are not counted as resources of fresh water. Yet they influence climate tremendously. The relatively small icecap of Greenland largely determines wind and weather in the United States, Europe, and other temperate regions of the Northern Hemisphere. The glaciers and ice sheets of past ages sculptured and remodeled a large part of this portion of the earth and thus determined the course of many of the rivers of today. Geologists have identified sources of places in which ice sheets, creeping toward the sea, scoured great troughs in the mountain slopes and filled valleys with rubble. Thus many horizon-wide landscapes were given nearly their present form. Chiefly by scouring, glaciers and ice sheets accomplished in a few thousand years what would have taken running water millions of years to bring about.

Coast lines change as land and ocean contend for mastery of the earth's surface. Whatever land gains by retreat of melting ice into the ocean is partly lost by a rise in the ocean's level. Conversely, whenever ice sheets advance, the land partially regains the area that is lost, because the land is a little farther advanced toward the sea by the fall in the ocean's level.

So much water was deposited as ice on the continents during the most recent ice age, which ended about 10,000 years ago, that the ocean's level was lowered about 460 feet. This lowering brought to light many peaks that have subsequently been submerged. A famous example is Cobb's seamount, about 316 miles west of Gray's Harbor, Washington. It rises steeply from a depth of about 10,000 feet to within about 120 feet of the present surface of the ocean.

An important result of the lowering of the ocean's level during the most recent ice age was that the central part of the bottom of the Bering Sea was left high and dry. Thus was created what is often called a land bridge, but which was actually a broad expanse of nearly level tundra. Over this, during the prolonged ice age, a great many species of plants and animals, and eventually man, passed from Asia into North America.

Resources of Underground Water

The *aquifers* (underground water channels) of the earth have been estimated to contain about one million cubic miles of water, within reach of wells not over half a mile deep. This is about ten times the rain that falls the world around in any one year, and about forty times the rain that falls on the land.

North America has approximately a proportionate share of the world's supply of underground water, or about 170,000 cubic miles. If all of it were pumped to the surface, the continent would be about 100 feet under water. This would give each of the present 250,000,000 inhabitants of the continent about 750,000,000 gallons, which would supply agriculture, industry, and rural and urban water supply systems for about 1400 years, at present rates of withdrawal.

Below the half-mile depth that may be tapped economically by wells, there is perhaps another million cubic miles of fresh water, beneath the surface of all the continents, yet so inaccessible that it might as well be on the moon. Many crystalline rocks, such as granite, from the earth's surface down to a depth of many miles, contain vast quantities of water, chemically combined with the rock. This water would be expelled only if the rock were heated in a furnace. What we call underground water resources constitute the only available part of the water that is actually underground.

Unfortunately, the underground water that is less than half a mile beneath the surface is not evenly distributed. However, 10 per cent of North America's underground waters are in sand or gravel or in fractured limestone, sandstone, or basalt—the kinds of strata that most readily yield water to wells. The ones that do yield water are not all continuously replenished by rainfall or by the seepage from streams, and the water that they yield is not always a good quality. Finally, the supply of water underground is often seriously contaminated or its availability is diminished by prolonged misuse.

A System of Aquifers

Wells sunk in any locality may encounter no aquifer or only one; or, at different depths, they may encounter several or many (Figure 1-1). Water carried by aquifers or drawn from shallow wells is called ground

Figure 1-1. A System of Aquifers

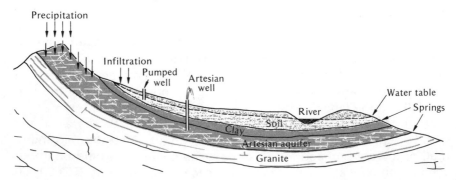

water. That flowing in surface streams or stored in ponds, lakes, or reservoirs is surface water.

A system of aquifers is a little like dishes stacked in a kitchen sink, with a large platter at the bottom, then smaller and smaller plates above, then saucers of diminishing size. The platter represents an aquifer that descends to the deepest "geologic horizon" and brings water from the greatest distance, perhaps hundreds of miles.

The quality of water delivered by an aquifer depends on the kind of soil through which the water has seeped after falling as rain or snow, on the duration of its underground journey, and on the character of the underground strata through which it has moved. It may be almost as pure as rain water or so loaded with impurities as to be almost unfit for any use. Deep-lying aquifers, not subject to active circulation, are most likely to yield water that is highly mineralized or saline (too salty for most uses).

When a well penetrates an aquifer in which the water is under considerable pressure, pumping may be unnecessary. This is a flowing artesian well. When such a well is deep its rate of flow is usually steady. The water within it moves very slowly if its zone of replenishment is only a little higher than its zone of discharge (a well field). Yet this water often moves over a broad front. A thousand artesian wells may scarcely diminish its rate of flow.

Because deep artesian water moves very slowly it is often very old. In the Alban artesian basin, in the Sahara, the water has taken thousands of years to travel 180 miles. The Romans—and others, down to the present—tapped this supply with artesian wells. Today, it furnishes water for a new development—a petroleum well field in the Sahara. In Greenland, water used now in some American military posts has been accumulating as snow for thousands of years.

Figure 1-2. How Pumping Lowers the Water Table

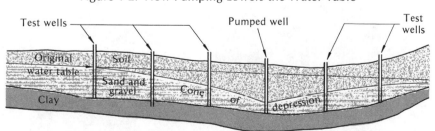

Water Table and Hydrostatic Balance

The water table is the top of the zone of complete saturation in permeable rock and soil near the earth's surface. It is the level at which water stands in a shallow well, or the level of water in a nearby pond, lake, or slow-moving stream (Figure 1-1). It fluctuates with the seasons, rising a little after a heavy rain and falling during periods of prolonged drought. Pumping water for irrigation may seriously lower the water table. Ditching to drain a swamp may bring disaster when land improvement by drainage was intended.

Above the water table, water percolates downward and is steadily incorporated into the ground water reservoir and is transported through permeable deposits to springs and wells. Liquid water usually does not move laterally through the layer of unsaturated soil that overlies the water table and is in contact with it. This is partially because its passage through wet soil is interrupted at innumerable points by trapped air.

The water table slopes at a moderate rate to the nearest lake, pond or river. The slope depends on rate of recharge and permeability. As more and more wells are sunk in a given locality, or as more and more water is pumped from them, the water table is lowered. A "cone of depression," shown in Figure 1-2, is created about each well.

When the water table is at the same level at two places less than a quarter of a mile apart, and when the levels in both places rise and fall together, one may assume that there is an underground connection between them. This condition is called hydrostatic balance (Figure 1-3).

Figure 1-3. Hydrostatic Balance Near a Seacoast

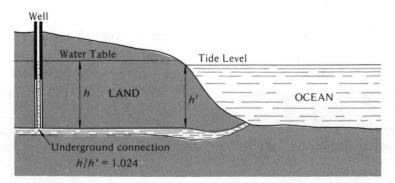

The level of water in wells near a seacoast often rises and falls with the tides. This suggests hydrostatic balance.

Yet sea water is 2.5 per cent denser than fresh water. The vertical distance from the surface of fresh water in a well to a water-filled underground passage from the well into the ocean is therefore 1.025 times that from the ocean's surface, whatever the stage of the tide. The water in the well nevertheless remains fresh if the underground current of fresh water is moving seaward with sufficient velocity to prevent the intermingling of fresh water and sea water by *diffusion* (see section J, Appendix).

The Flow of Water in Aquifers

The water in aquifers almost always occupies cracks or pores in underground rock or the open spaces between particles of sand or gravel. If the surface of the earth is ordinary soil, this is a zone of aeration into which both air and water penetrate. After a heavy rain, there is very little air in this zone, which is almost saturated with water; but in periods between rains much of the water drains away into the lower depths, and its place is taken by air. Below the water table, all of the crevices and pores in fractured or porous rock are completely filled with water. This part of the ground water is free to drain laterally into wells, ponds, lakes, or streams.

Water moves through aquifers under the pull of gravity. The zone of replenishment, in which water enters an aquifer, is normally at a higher

Figure 1-4. Zones of an Aquifer

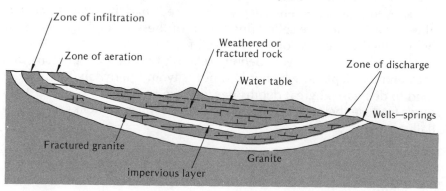

elevation than the zone of discharge, where the water again reaches the surface, after passage underground (Figure 1-4). The volume of water contained in aquifers, at depths of not over a half-mile, is estimated to be at least 3000 times the volume that is visible in rivers. Much of this underground flow comes to the surface before it reaches the sea. It is then incorporated into lakes and rivers; but some of it issues from fresh water springs in shallow oceans, not very far from the shore.

The rate of movement of water through an aquifer depends in part on the difference in elevation between the zones of replenishment and discharge and their distance apart—in other words, on the average slope of the water table, or pressure surface in a confined aquifer. It also depends on the size and shape of the intervening pores, fissures, or channels through which the water flows, since they determine the friction that the water must overcome, underground.

When the rocks through which the water is moving are porous (limestone, for example), the friction is small and the flow may be rapid. In granular materials the rate of flow is greatest when the particles between which the water flows are "well sorted" (nearly of the same size). If they are "poorly sorted," much of the space between the larger particles is filled by smaller ones and the water movement is impeded. Thus poorly sorted strata deliver the water much more slowly.

Some kinds of rocks (granite, for example) contain few pores and are practically not penetrated by water except where they are cracked or fissured. Yet most rocks near the surface of the earth are penetrated thoroughly by cracks that at first may be no thicker than a hair. These fractures (termed "joints" by geologists) are gradually widened by changes in temperature, the prying action of repeated freezing, and the solvent action of water in the presence of air and carbon dioxide. Thus, even granite, where deeply weathered, may become as permeable as sandstone. The splintering action of these natural agencies may be observed at the base of any rocky cliff.

Although there is no very definite relation between the porosity of a rock and the depth at which it lies, porosity and permeability to water tend to decrease at great depths because the weight of overlying strata tends to close the pores. At depths of several miles, all rocks are essentially non-porous.

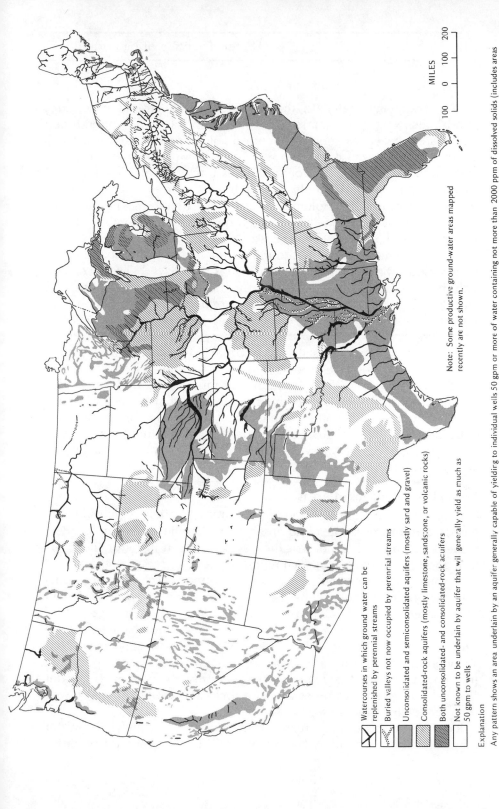

Figure 1-5. Ground Water Areas in the Conterminous United States

From *The Conservation of Ground Water* by H. E. Thomas (McGraw-Hill, 1951), Plate I. Used by Permission.

MILES

200

100

0

100

Note: Some productive ground-water areas mapped recently are not shown.

Watercourses in which ground water can be replenished by perennial streams

Buried valleys not now occupied by perennial streams

Unconsolidated and semiconsolidated aquifers (mostly sand and gravel)

Consolidated-rock aquifers (mostly limestone, sandstone, or volcanic rocks)

Both unconsolidated- and consolidated-rock aquifers

Not known to be underlain by aquifer that will generally yield as much as 50 gpm to wells

Explanation

Any pattern shows an area underlain by an aquifer generally capable of yielding to individual wells 50 gpm or more of water containing not more than 2000 ppm of dissolved solids (includes areas where more highly mineralized water is actually used).

Among granular materials, the best bearers of ground water are gravel beds. Next come coarse sand, fine sand, sandstone, limestone, and basalt (a heavy, dark, easily fractured volcanic rock). Clay is a poor carrier of water, because it is composed of extremely fine particles; and because it is so plastic that it does not easily fracture, forming joints.

Granite and similar insoluble rock yield very little dissolved material to water. Limestone and dolomite (a limestone rich in magnesium carbonate) dissolve more readily, but often deposit a considerable part of what has been dissolved when the water emerges into open air, hence is no longer under pressure. Ground water is often almost saturated with minerals dissolved from rocks, since it may have been in contact with the rocks for centuries. Fortunately, most minerals are silicates of very slight solubility. Since ground water remains very nearly constant in composition, its quality may be controlled by very infrequent chemical analyses.

A few of our American states (Wisconsin, Michigan, Nebraska, and all of the Gulf states except Texas) are almost completely underlain by aquifers capable of yielding 50 gallons per minute to a well; but in the Dakotas, Texas, and the eleven continental states that lie west of them, most aquifers are of limited extent, their distribution is spotty, and more than half the total area of the state is usually without known subterranean supplies that will yield to a well a flow of at least 50 gallons per minute (Figure 1-5).

Ground Water in Desert Areas
Ground water in desert or semidesert areas is often replenished by penetration of fresh water into an aquifer at some distant point. Permanent streams or lakes or irrigation systems (as in Egypt or India) afford good opportunities for such replenishment.

In some desert or semidesert regions, ground water from local rains is important because it may be the only fresh water in that area. In still other desert areas, rainfall is of less importance because a large part of the scanty rain evaporates before the next one. The character of the surface on which a rain falls determines how much good it will do. Truly porous rocks (such as sandstone) may offer less of an opportunity for penetration by water than rocks that are merely fissured. The water that gets into very small pores wets the rocks as it would a paper towel, then gradually evaporates.

Rain in an arid area may create a freshet down a dry gully. This water may collect in a temporary lake or pond. This gives a better opportunity for the replenishment of ground water, should soil permeability be adequate. The deeper the pond, the less surface it has from which water may evaporate and the greater the pressure is at the bottom of the pond, to force the water into or through whatever lies below. Eventually, every pond in a desert area is likely to go dry, to await refilling at the next freshet. Stockmen who use the pond to water their animals must then find what comfort they can from knowing that some of the water that has disappeared may still be reached by shallow wells.

Tracing and Measuring Underground Flow

It is usually easy to determine whether an underground formation is permeable to water, or whether there is direct underground connection between two points on the surface. A solution of an easily detectible substance (a tracer) is injected into the underground stream at an upstream point and samples of the water are tested for the tracer at the downstream point. One useful chemical tracer is the dichromate ion, $Cr_2O_7^=$. It is detected in a concentration as little as one part by billion by weight in water by a chemical reagent, diphenylcarbazole. Dyes, spores, chemicals, and radioactive substances all can be used, depending on the situation.

Radioactive substances are detected with a Geiger counter. Water is a public resource, which would be injured by the introduction of an improper tracer. For this reason, the tracing of an underground stream should be done only under proper technical supervision.

Under favorable conditions a trained observer may not only trace an underground stream but also estimate its volume rate of flow. The key to this is in the observation that when water is flowing through a many-branched channel its average velocity is never more than half the maximum velocity and may be only a third. One injects a tracer at a known rate into the underground stream at any upstream point (Figure 1.6), and notes how long it takes for the tracer just to begin to arrive at a convenient downstream point. To find the average elapsed time, multiply the observed time by 2 if the flow is through fractured rock and by 2.5 or 3 if it is through porous rock, such as sandstone. From the average elapsed time and the distance traversed one might find the average linear velocity, v, of the underground stream. When this is multiplied by the cross-section, a, of the aquifer (often known from geological explorations), one has the volume rate of flow (cubic feet or cubic meters per second).

Although not generally applicable, there are occasions when the thickness of the aquifer may be roughly inferred from the maximum concentration finally attained by the tracer at a sufficiently distant downstream point of test (Figure 1-6, C), when the tracer is being injected at a steady rate, r (weight units per second). The tracer spreads both vertically and horizontally, from its point of injection, A, through a slender, tapering cone, until its vertical spread is arrested at some point B by overlying and underlying impervious strata. Thereafter, it spreads only laterally. The concentration at any point C, beyond B, is inversely proportional to AC. In brief,

$$\text{Conc. at B} \,/\, \text{conc. at C} = \text{AC}/\text{AB}$$

Water advancing through the tapering cone spreads laterally so slowly that the distance AB, from the point of injection to the point at which the vertical spread is arrested, is about ten times the thickness of the aquifer. Thus for AB, in the equation above, we might write 10t.

The circular area at the base of the tampering cone is $0.7854\, t^2$. If this area is multiplied by the velocity of the underground stream, v, and by the concentration at B found above, the result is the rate of injection, r, of the tracer, in weight units per minute, whenever the tracer is being injected at a measured steady rate. In brief,

$$r = 0.7854t^2 \times v \,(\text{conc. at C}) \times \text{AC}/10t$$

then,

$$t = 12.73\, r/v \times (\text{conc. at C}) \times \text{AC}$$

By making several such tests, along a line that is perpendicular to AC, one may find an average value for the thickness of the aquifer. This

Figure 1-6. Estimating the Rate of Flow in an Aquifer

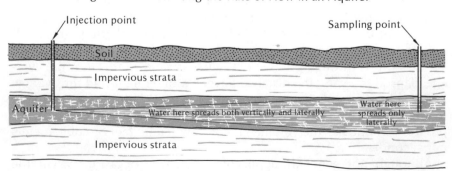

when multiplied by the width of the aquifer and by its average linear rate of flow, gives the volume rate of flow of the underground stream.

Another interesting technique, though rarely used due to practical difficulties, is tracing via infrared radiography. Objects that are slightly warm emit invisible, infrared light (section C, Appendix). On a photographic film that is sensitized to infrared they may appear to be actually incandescent. A more recent method is to fly over the area to be surveyed in an airplane or traverse it with a satellite, with the equipment continuously focused on the terrain beneath. By scanning the radiographic image with an infrared sensor, a record may be obtained that resembles a succession of "photographs." (A similar method was used to obtain a succession of "photographs" of the planet Mars in the summer of 1969.) Often, an underground stream that is only slightly warmer or colder than the earth surrounding it and that is not very far beneath the earth's surface may thus be clearly traced.

In other instances, the course of an underground stream may conceivably be betrayed by an extra density of bushes or trees, growing in the earth above it; and these, because of the evaporation of water from their leaves, are revealed as a dark area on an infrared radiogram. Though the ability of infrared radiography to detect slight differences

Figure 1-7. Stages in the Formation of a Limestone Cave

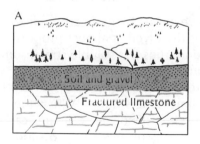
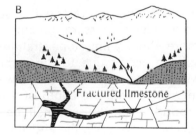
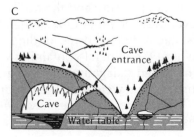

in temperature is remarkable, a Florida rattlesnake, the "pit viper," can do as well. It is able to detect its prey—small, warm blooded animals—at distances of several feet, with the aid of infrared sensors, located in depressions just behind the reptile's eyes.

How Limestone Caves Are Formed

Underground water has produced innumerable limestone caves wherever limestone is abundant (Figure 1-7). Scouring by underground streams is not involved, for most underground water moves very slowly. Instead, dissolving limestone is a chemical action, brought about by the remarkable ability of carbon dioxide, in the presence of water, to dissolve limestone.

Carbon dioxide gas is produced by the decay of plant residues in the soil or by the action of organic or mineral acids on limestone. It dissolves in water to form a solution whose faintly acid taste is in bottled carbonated drinks and familiar to everyone. (Some of these drinks also contain dilute phosphoric acid, and others, citric acid.)

Although limestone (largely calcium carbonate) dissolves but little in pure water, it is readily attacked by water containing carbon dioxide according to this equation:

$$CaCO_3 + CO_2 + H_2O \rightleftarrows Ca(HCO_3)_2$$
solid   dissolved in water

At 20°C, a liter of water will dissolve about 1.7 g of carbon dioxide, but under higher pressure the amount dissolved is almost proportionately more. When a limestone stratum underlies less soluble strata, some dissolving occurs due to the carbon dioxide content of ground water. Most solution occurs near the water table; but pressure is also a factor, increasing with the depth of the limestone stratum. When the underground water thus containing excess dissolved calcium carbonate reaches a dry cave, the above reaction is reversed due to sudden lowering of pressure and the availability of space into which the water can evaporate. Solid $CaCO_3$ is, therefore, deposited on the roof of the cave (stalactites) and corresponding formations build up from the cave floor where the mineral-containing water drips from the roof, the latter being called stalagmites. Growing slowly for tens of millennia they sometimes attain weights in the hundreds of tons.

Most American caves have been carved out of limestone by the process just described. In addition, a few have been formed by wave action along precipitous coasts. In volcanic eruptions, lava flows sometimes solidify externally, then drain free of liquid, forming caves or tunnels called lava tubes.

More than 12,000 caves have been found and explored in the United States. The chief risks in cave exploration are light failure and being trapped by flash floods. Companions on the watch, above and below ground, give the needed protection. Vertical drops of over 400 feet are sometimes encountered in caves (Fern Cave, in northern Alabama, for example).

The living creatures within limestone caves bear witness to the wonderful persistence of life under adverse circumstances and to the resourcefulness of nature. Fish that spend their lives in total darkness have no need for eyes, which in some species have dwindled to rudimentary vestiges of organs of sight. As a substitute, they have acquired filament-like vibration sensors, which can detect motion in their watery environment at considerable distances. Though sightless, they move about and find their food with seeming ease.

Springs and Wells

Intermittent "flash floods" and the steady work of streams and rivers gradually wear away the surface of the earth, creating and deepening valleys everywhere. Thus aquifers that originally were deeply buried may finally be laid bare. Underground water then reaches the surface at that spot as a natural spring. (Springs may, of course, arise in other environments.) Spring water is sometimes surprisingly pure if it has percolated through practically insoluble material such as quartz (white sand). In other instances it is laden with dissolved calcium bicarbonate, or other dissolved minerals, and in consequence is exceedingly "hard." Spring water that has come from a great depth is usually free from harmful bacteria, though of course there is always danger that in reaching the surface it may pass through soil that is being contaminated with human wastes.

The deeper the earth's crust, the hotter it is. Water penetrating to considerable depths may be heated almost to the boiling temperature, then upon reaching a large vertical crevice may rise up to the surface and issue as a hot spring. Since hot water dissolves silica much more readily than cold water does, the deposits of this material (SiO_2) around hot springs and geysers in the Yellowstone National Park and elsewhere are quite spectacular.

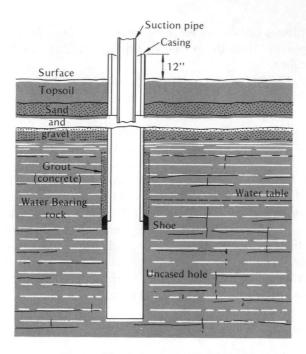

Figure 1-8. A Properly Cased Well

A well is actually only an artificial spring. Those dug by hand and lined with brick and stone (to prevent cave-ins) may descend only a few feet below the water table, and may yield only 1 or 2 gal/min. They are sometimes dangerous because they are subject to contamination. Deeper wells are dug with a plunging or rotating bit, and are cased with pipe (Figure 1-8). Inside this casing hangs a smaller pipe, through which water is pumped to the surface.

A spring or well may contain water that has fallen as rain or snow in a neighboring place and then has trickled downward through the soil until it has come to rest on a layer of nearly impervious material, such as compacted clay or impenetrable, unfractured rock; or it may contain water that has seeped through a deep-lying aquifer and which may therefore have come from far away. Water from nearby is more likely to be free from dissolved mineral impurities, but it may still be unfit to drink because it has been polluted by human beings or domestic animals or by industries.

Do not get the idea that water that is polluted can ordinarily be purified by being filtered through underground strata. The only result of an effort to purify water in this way would be, in most cases, to pollute the aquifer and perhaps render it incapable of delivering safe water for many years. Once polluted, water in an aquifer usually remains polluted, until the source of pollution is removed; then contact with air during many years gradually kills bacteria and decreases the amount of oxidizable waste material that the water at first contained.

Whether a well sunk in a given spot will strike water, and if so at what depth, is usually difficult to determine. The needed depth depends in part on the contours of the surface terrain, which in most parts of the earth are determined by erosion. For deep wells, it is more important to know something about the slope, thickness, and character of each of several buried strata. In lack of such information, most wells in newly settled regions are located "by pure guess," although there are still people who believe in "water-witching"—the location of underground water with the aid of a forked stick or "divining rod."

Wells and the Settlement of the West

From Missouri and Iowa westward to the Pacific Coast, the order in which different parts of the land were settled was often determined by the development of means for finding, pumping, and conveying water. The earliest settlers in this generally arid region went to live near rivers, which furnished both water and wood (from trees that chiefly grew on islands in the rivers). Large rivers also furnished transportation, though sometimes undependably.

Homesteads had to be located far enough away from the rivers to be safe from flooding in winter, and hundreds of little communities were abandoned because their founders underestimated the frequency and magnitude of floods. Each new decade brought new emigrants from the eastern states and Europe. They settled in locations that were farther from the rivers. First they sought out natural springs; then they sank wells.

The first wells were dug by hand, by the settlers themselves, at considerable risk from cave-ins, breaking well ropes, and falling buckets, hammers, wrenches, chisels, and stones.

In addition there was the danger of gases that collect in wells. Carbon dioxide lingers indefinitely in wells because it is 50 per cent heavier than air. A digger descending into a well filled with carbon dioxide was dead within a minute. Hydrogen sulfide was in wells dug in regions rich in "sulfur springs." And if a well was sunk near coal seams, or if a fracture in the earth let combustible gases (chiefly methane) escape and mix with the air, the first candle or lantern lowered into the well often caused an explosion.

At first, buckets were used to lift water from shallow wells, hand over hand, without benefit of windlass. Then horses, walking round and round, pumped water for small fields or even a village. In 1854 the American windmill was invented. It was as important to the settlement of the West as the cotton gin to the growing of cotton in the South. Because its speed was automatically controlled, a windmill could be left by itself for weeks at a time. Once a tank at the surface of the ground had been filled, all the water thereafter pumped spilled back into the well.

The small wood-burning locomotives of the late nineteenth and early twentieth century stopped frequently for water, which was pumped by a windmill beside the tracks, then softened in twin tanks (as described in Chapter 14).

The water used in those early days did not all come from wells. The rain barrel under the eaves yielded not only water but frogs, dead leaves, and lost toys. Yet its water was sometimes quite safe to drink. Water that had collected in the hollows dug in dry gullies, to catch and hold the last trickles of spring freshets, was important too. Once the green scum, insects, mosquito larvae, and pollywogs were strained out of the water, it was drinkable. It became less safe for the early inhabitants, however, after others settled upstream from them: the more people there were upstream, the more wastes there were in the water when it reached them.

Such a simple sanitary precaution as boiling suspected water was rarely practiced in pioneer days. During the gold rush to California in 1849 and 1850 ox teams, accompanied by mounted horsemen and driven livestock, traveled over the trails leading westward from St. Joseph and Council Bluffs to the Pacific Coast. Journals kept by these emigrants tell how the trails were marked by newly dug graves. It has been estimated that between 10,000 and 20,000 wayfarers rest today in unmarked graves along the Old West's favorite trails. Typhoid and dysentery were taking their toll, while hundreds of oxen and horses died from water taken from alkaline water holes.

During all these years water was so scarce that every drop not actually drunk was passed on from its first use to others more and more degraded. It finally went to hogs and chickens or to irrigate a forlorn little box of flowers beside the settler's front door. Yet the agony of scarce water was often needless. Along the Platte and its tributaries, where hundreds died of polluted water during the days of the great westward migration—and in other locations that the reader can identify from present-day maps (Figure 1-5) of water resources—an aquifer, deep underground, was all the while carrying such a generous flow of water that thousands of pumped wells scarcely diminished its flow. The development of this resource had to await not merely the discovery of the aquifer but also the invention of centrifugal pumps (capable of lifting water more than the 34-foot limit of old-fashioned suction pumps) and modern diesel engines.

Fresh Water in Lakes and Ponds

The ocean contains so much salt that we scarcely count it as a natural resource until we recall that it is, after all, the source of the earth's fresh water. "Available" surface water for the entire earth is only 55,000 cubic miles, and about half of this contains so much salt that its use is limited. About an equal amount of fresh water is at present unavailable because it is locked up in small glaciers on high mountain tops, on every continent except Australia.

The surface fresh water of the earth probably amounts to only 3 per cent of the available underground water, yet it is far more important as a source of water for human use. Today, as when human communities first appeared, man obtains most of his municipal water supplies from rivers, lakes, and ponds, rather than from wells; and still today, waste water is permitted to flow back into the surface water resource, often polluting it dangerously.

The ponds and lakes of the world have been estimated to contain 100 times as much fresh water as is found at any given moment in all of the earth's flowing streams. In some regions (Minnesota, Canada, Finland) there are thousands of little lakes and ponds, occupying hollows in a ground moraine, a rock debris deposited by a prehistoric glacier; or they may be tarns, basins scooped out of rocks during glacial periods.

Small lakes also sometimes occupy sink holes, where ceilings have collapsed over caves, or they may have been impounded by lava flows or landslides, or may fill the crater of an extinct volcano (Crater Lake, Oregon, for example). Lake Okeechobee, in Florida, is the largest fresh water lake that is wholly contained in any single American state. It was once part of an ancient shallow sea, but is now just a wide place in the Kissimmee River.

There must be hundreds of thousands of such relatively small lakes and ponds. Yet their total capacity is insignificant, compared with a few giant lakes, presently to be described. Even the smallest lake or pond helps to delay the return of fresh water to the ocean, thus providing a better opportunity for recharging fresh water aquifers.

Fresh water lakes and ponds are just temporary phenomena. They are all doomed to disappear. The channels through which they discharge are gradually deepened by outflowing streams, and silt from higher ground gradually fills them. They can be saved only by dams or landslides.

Successive stages in the extinction of a lake are easily recognized. Streams bring in suspended particles of clay and fine sand. If the lake is salty, or if the river discharges into the ocean, salt causes aggregation and precipitates the clay particles, and settling is rapid. In fresh water, settling is much slower and may require months. Silt is then deposited rather uniformly over a wide area, or throughout a lake of moderate size. The margins of the lake finally become so shallow that oxygen from the air readily penetrates to the bottom. Water-loving plants can then take root along the margins, and a thick growth of swamp vegetation is produced—cattails, other reeds or rushes, mosses, grasses, blueberries, and other shrubs, willows, and eventually water-tolerant conifers. This vegetation slows the rate of flow of water through the lake, hastens the deposition of silt, and creates vast quantities of decaying plant material. Thus the lake gradually becomes a marsh—a mere wet spot in the landscape. In the end, the marsh, too, disappears and is replaced by forest or farmland.

The dead storage of a lake is the volume of water that can never be drained away because it lies beneath the level of the lake's outlet. At normal rates of flow, most artificial reservoirs can be filled or emptied within a few weeks. A natural lake could take many years to be refilled, if once completely emptied.

The American Great Lakes

North America's Great Lakes contain 5460 cubic miles of fresh water—roughly one-fifth of the total capacity of all the world's fresh water lakes. The Great Lakes (Figure 1-9) provide access for ocean commerce

Figure 1-9. The Great Lakes

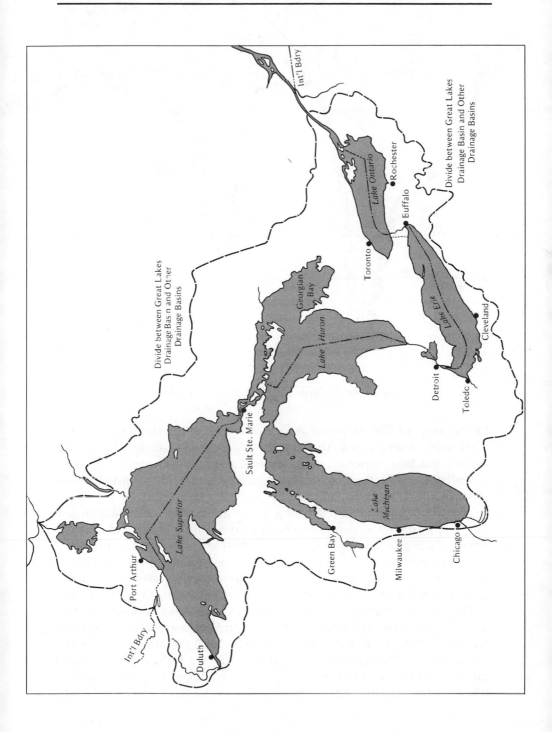

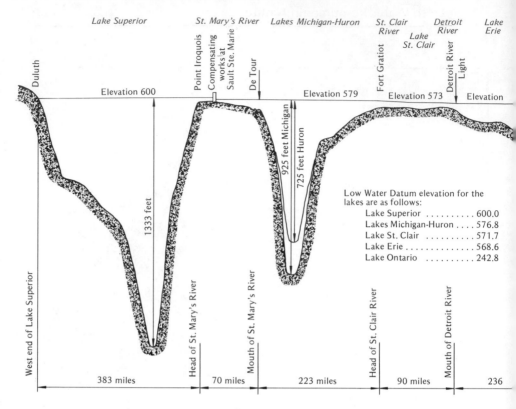

Figure 1-10. Great Lakes, St. Lawrence Profile

to the heart of the continent as far west as Duluth, Minnesota, nearly 2000 miles from the sea. Through the "Soo" locks, leading from Lake Huron into Lake Superior, pass barges that carry iron ore, grain, coal, petroleum, and lumber. The tonnage is greater than that of the Panama Canal.

The Great Lakes supply drinking water and water for industrial use to the most highly industrialized parts of the United States and Canada. Their falls and rapids supply a noteworthy part of North America's demand for energy. Their fisheries have long been an important source of food. They are the world's most valuable fresh water playground, which affords recreation to millions in boating, fishing, and swimming.

The general structure of the American Great Lakes is shown in Figure 1-10. Observe that Lakes Michigan and Huron are actually a single lake, with a common level. The surface of Lake Ontario is well below the bottom of Lake Erie. In consequence, Niagara Falls, slowly receding upstream (4 or 5 feet per year), after a few centuries may become a series of rapids, like those now existing below the falls, and so may seri-

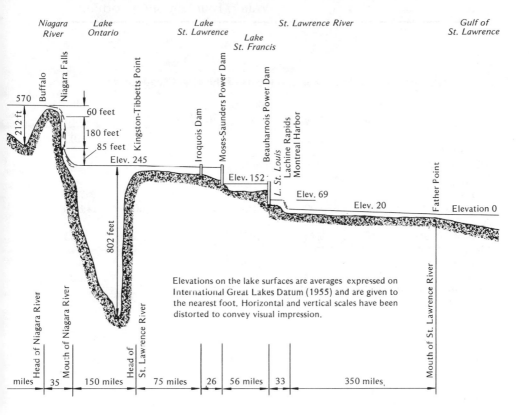

Niagara Lake Lake St. Lawrence River   Gulf of
River Ontario St. Lawrence   St. Lawrence
        Lake
        St. Francis

570 60 feet

212 ft 180 feet

85 feet

Elev. 245

Elev. 152

Elev. 69

Elev. 20 Elevation 0

802 feet

Elevations on the lake surfaces are averages expressed on
International Great Lakes Datum (1955) and are given to
the nearest foot. Horizontal and vertical scales have been
distorted to convey visual impression.

miles 35 150 miles 75 miles 26 56 miles 33 350 miles

ously lower the level of Lake Erie, which eventually could drain dry.
This natural cycle can, of course, be easily altered by constructing artificial outlet works.

Lake Superior has the largest area of any of the world's fresh water
lakes (see Table 1-1). Lake Huron ranks fourth in area and Lake Michigan fifth. Lake Erie and Lake Ontario are much smaller, ranking only
eleventh and thirteenth. The importance of the Great Lakes to North
America is shown by the fact that although only 3.5 per cent of the area
of the 48 first admitted states lies within the drainage basin of the Great
Lakes, this area has nearly a seventh of the population of the United
States and about a third of that of Canada.

The World's Giant Lakes

Only two other continents have more than one lake that ranks as a
giant. Two in Asia—the Caspian Sea and Aral Sea in Russia—have no
outlet into the ocean. Every stream that enters a lake brings in dissolved

Table 1-1.
Data on the Great Lakes and the Rivers of the Great Lakes System

	Lake Superior	Lake Michigan	Lake Huron	Lake St. Clair	Lake Erie	Lake Ontario
Length (miles)	350	307	206	26	241	193
Breadth (miles)	160	118	183	24	57	53
Area (miles^2)	31,800	22,400	23,000	490	9,910	7,600
Drainage basin* (miles^2)	80,000	67,900	72,600	7,420	32,600	34,800
Average depth (feet)	487	276	195	10	58	283
Maximum depth (feet)**	1,333	923	750	21	210	802
Volume (miles^3)	2,935	1,170	849	1	110	393

	St. Marys	St. Clair	Detroit	Niagara	St. Lawrence
Length (miles)	70	27	32	37	502

* Total land and water.
** Maximum natural depth. The dredged channel in Lake St. Clair is 27.5 ft. deep.

salts, whereas evaporation removes only water. Land-bound lakes are therefore salty, and many are even more saline than the ocean itself.

Among the world's fresh water lakes, Lake Baikal, in eastern Siberia, ranks only sixth in area, but it is so deep (over a mile, in most places) that its capacity (6300 cubic miles) is about 15 per cent greater than the combined capacity of the American Great Lakes.

Africa has three Lakes (Victoria, Tanganyika, and Nyassa), each with about the same capacity or area as an American Great Lake. Only North America, Asia, and Africa have lakes as large as Ontario, the smallest of the major American Great Lakes.

The giant lakes are so large that they moderate the climate of their surroundings, to an extent matched only by the ocean itself and by the great icecaps of Greenland and Antarctica. In being cooled or frozen as winter approaches, the giant lakes delay the cooling of the neighboring land areas. Afterward, since heat is absorbed in melting the ice, they delay the coming of spring. The fluctuation of the air temperature above a giant lake is always less than that above neighboring land areas.

The giant lakes of the Northern Hemisphere owe their existence to

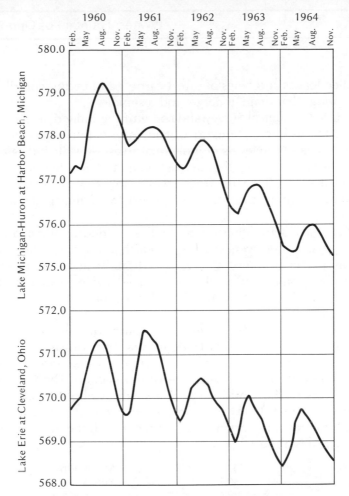

Figure 1-11. Fluctuating Levels in the Great Lakes

glacial scouring action. Those of Africa occupy part of a great rift system—a rent in the earth's crust—which extends for more than two thousand miles down the valley of the Jordan River, through the Red Sea, thence southward to Kenya in Africa. Many lakes, including the Dead Sea, occupy downdropped segments of the earth's crust along this rift.

Rivers as Fresh Water Resources

Rivers are just spillways through which water that is in momentary local surplus drains away downhill. Their flow is usually maintained, year after year, by melting snows and the runoff from rains, reinforced by the slow seepage of water through grasslands and meadows or through the fallen leaves and twigs of forest carpets and by the contributions of small springs that drain underground reservoirs.

The U.S. Geological Survey and some of the individual states operate about 8000 gaging stations to obtain information about the volume rate of flow and the levels of individual rivers. Results indicate that the discharge rate of even the largest rivers and the levels of even the largest lakes do fluctuate from season to season (Figure 1-11) and sometimes have a downward or upward trend that persists for many years.

Similar gaging by other countries has yielded approximate rates of discharge for other rivers and for the earth as a whole. Their combined capacity (water in transit at any given time) is about 300 cubic miles. This is a very small part of the earth's fresh water resources, although from the standpoint of utility for the human race, it is the most important part.

Rivers have always been important routes of commerce and settlement, and have done much to determine the course of history. They have permitted parts of the earth that possessed great rivers to be quickly settled, leaving deserts almost untenanted. The total discharge of the rivers of the world, large and small, is about 8400 cubic miles per year, of which the world's six largest rivers deliver nearly half. For a few of the most important rivers of the world, the yearly discharge in cubic miles[1] is about:

Amazon	1330	Mississippi	133.0
Congo	300	Yukon	39.6
Nile	28	Columbia	42.7
Ganges	141	St. Lawrence	107.0
Yangtze	165	Colorado	1.18
Mekong	84	Rio Grande	0.59

It will probably surprise most readers to note that the flow of the Amazon is ten times that of the Mississippi, and that the latter is outranked by several of the other great rivers of the earth. Another surprise, for most North Americans, is that the flow of the St. Lawrence is about 80 per cent of that of the Mississippi. Observe also that the Colorado River and the Rio Grande, which are important to irrigation in the arid Southwest, are very small in comparison with the Columbia and Yukon (and several other western rivers discussed in Chapter 10), whose waters still chiefly go to waste, except as they are made to develop electrical energy.

1. To convert cubic miles per year into cubic feet per second, multiply by 4605.

2

Fresh Water and the Land

Exploitation, Then Conservation

Well before the human race appeared or became very numerous, the slow forces of geology, biology, and chemistry, molded all the continents and left almost everywhere a sufficient layer of soil to support the growth of plants in marsh, meadow, wooded thicket, and forest. Plant growth, by impending the runoff from rainfall or snowfall, protected the land from erosion. Gradually, over centuries, vegetation produced soils rich in humus, the partially decayed remains of plant life.

For a long time, damage to the earth's natural resources was slight, for the earth was large and its human burden light. The first settlers on every continent were hunters, rather than tillers of the soil. They began the destruction of the soil by setting fires in grasslands in the hope that a fresh, new growth of grass, after the fires, might invite deer and so provide better hunting. The pace of destruction quickened as man became civilized, since he then began to cut down forests to obtain wood or charcoal, and cleared hillsides for the cultivation of crops.

In the Western Hemisphere, the first settlers found a vast expanse of virgin forest, rich soil, and unplowed prairie. These intruders were rugged individualists, each taking what he needed for himself. Few noted that when forests were cut down the soil was quickly eroded; when swamps were ditched and drained the wildfowl quickly disappeared; where game was slaughtered it often never came back; where a light prairie soil was deeply plowed it often all blew away at the first long hot summer or prolonged drought. With forests gone or depleted, wild animals disappeared or became extinct, fish perished in polluted streams, wild fowl were no longer plentiful in pond, meadow, or thicket at the settler's very door. The world of Daniel Boone seemed destined to vanish forever.

When the first American explorers penetrated beyond the Mississippi, in the early years of the nineteenth century, they were confronted by what Zebulon Pike called the Great American Desert, which extended from the middle reaches of the Missouri River, beyond the vast expanse of prairie, apparently endlessly, toward the Pacific. To many it must have seemed that the Louisiana Purchase was no great bargain.

Yet seventeen states have since then been developed west of Iowa and Missouri in the vast, arid domain that the United States acquired from France and Mexico or won by exploration. In 1964 one of them, California, became the most populous state in the Union, with a population of 18,000,000—more than 4½ times the total population of the 13 Atlantic states in 1790. Yet water is still in short supply in all this vast region. The 17 western states include one of the great arid regions of the world. Their rapidly increasing population makes water scarcity ever more acute.

Europeans had been in North America for nearly four hundred years, the bison herds and the Indians of the plains both faced extinction, and the twentieth century had arrived before it was generally sensed that the natural resources of the expanding North American republic were neither limitless nor indestructible. Too many of Daniel Webster's contemporaries had taken his call to develop the resources of our land to be just a reminder that the resources were there for anyone to exploit. Yet, by the twentieth century, observation had shown that damage to natural resources may to some extent be repaired. "Conservation" became the watchword of the new century's early decades. This implies not merely economy in the use of resources, but their management and protection to ensure maximum use in the public interest.

Important problems in conservation are management of watersheds, best use of the land, prevention of soil erosion, preservation of wildlife, protection of forests, development of river navigation, prevention of floods, and development of hydroelectric energy. These problems are all interrelated; hence, all of them may need to be mentioned in any book dealing with fresh water. They overleap state and provincial boundaries and tend to become national and international problems. They have gradually led to the creation of national (United States and Canadian) agencies devoted to natural resources. Under the direction of the United States Department of the Interior are Bureaus of Land Management, Reclamation, Sport Fisheries and Wildlife, Outdoor Recreation, National Parks, the Geological Survey, and the Offices of Saline Water, Water Resources Research, and Oil and Gas. In addition, the Department of the Interior has administrations devoted to electric power development in the Southeastern, Southwestern, and Bonneville districts. The government is spending several billion dollars each year on such projects. Thus the importance of water is brought home to every taxpayer.

Land Capability

Diverse climates and geological origins have created many different kinds of soil, the world around. India and Australia, for example, have some soil types not found in the United States.

Water and soil must jointly be conserved. The best use for land, often referred to as land capability, depends on the type and depth of soil, the steepness of the land, the total rainfall or snowfall, the time of year in which it comes, the length of the growing season, the temperature during this season, and other factors.

Unfortunately, the best use for land was largely disregarded in the early development of our continent. Even today, expanding cities take over the surrounding countryside with little regard for the conservation of water, soil, or forests. Vast areas, once the abode of gentle wild animals, are being buried beneath a concrete canopy, as suburban developments strip the hillsides of their verdure, as tennis courts and swimming pools replace sylvan glades, and as four-laned highways cut through hills, linking city with distant city. Such "improvements" gradually efface even the memory of the narrow old dusty, muddy, or snow-encumbered road that wound over the river and through the woods to grandfather's farm. Concrete-covered areas today account for almost as many acres as the state of Indiana.

Eight classes of land capability are recognized by the Soil Conservation Service in the United States. Types I, II, III, and IV are suitable for growing different crops and permit cultivation to control weeds or aid root development. Type V is suitable for pasture or even for trees if enough water is available. Types VI and VII are lands close to hillsides and thus are subject to erosion but still suitable for trees. Type VIII is land not suitable for agriculture of any kind, though it is still often of value for recreational areas, wildlife preservation, and watershed protection. This is the sort of land that is most often set aside for national parks.

Even a small area often has several distinct land capabilities, which may have been noted and recorded on land survey maps. Yet a fairly large area, several square miles of prairie land, for example, may be of a single land capability type, easily recognized.

Erosion Control

Erosion was the first and for nearly three centuries the most important cause of land destruction. Its results were often more serious than they first appeared to be. The underlying rock was rarely stripped completely bare, yet the rich surface soil was often carried away and deposited as silt on the lowlands of a distant state or as mud at the outlet of a river into the sea. The land behind might appear uninjured to the uninformed passerby, yet deep plowing had often caused most of its humus to be lost by oxidation. Loss of humus decreased the soil's capacity for holding water and hence increased the rate of erosion. A vicious sequence had begun which sometimes soon caused the land to be so cut up by gullies that even city-dwellers realized it would never yield another crop. Still another feature often appeared in lands that had been close-cropped for years. The soil was sometimes deprived of minerals needed for the growth of plants that satisfactory crops could not be grown without the application of fertilizers.

The conservation of soil, water, and land all begin by the control of splashdown. Ideally, each raindrop should penetrate the earth in the very spot where it falls and should remain underground until it is absorbed by the roots of growing crops, discharges at springs, or is put to use by industry or serves humanity in some other way. This ideal is, of course, never attained. If rain is falling rapidly, the small cracks, crevices, and tunnels through which the first drops plunge underground soon disappear by collapse of their walls. Surface runoff, from that moment onward, persists until the rain ceases.

The first step in preventing land erosion is to stop trenches from deepening. The threatened areas may be planted with tufts of firm-rooted grasses, and later with bushes or young trees, among which cut weeds or other vegetable trash may be scattered. You may see examples of this practice wherever cuts have been made through hills in the construction of concrete highways.

Whether the purpose is to conserve farmland or protect highways, the effort is always to provide stable spillways, through which excess water may run, under such good control that there is very little erosion. Several different methods of controlling erosion are used: Strip cropping, in which strips of grass or legumes are planted between strips of other crops, is practiced on slopes that are not very steep and on level areas (e.g. the Great Plains) to reduce wind erosion. Mulch tillage is cultivation that leaves most of the straw, stalks, overturned roots, and stubble on the land, where they impede runoff and gradually increase the humus content, hence improve the water-holding capacity of the soil. On steeper slopes, contour plowing or terracing may be needed.

Soil is made more permeable to water and at the same time is enriched in humus and nitrogen by incorporating clover and other leguminous crops into the soil by "plowing under." A vast program of soil conservation, involving millions of acres, is under the supervision of the United States Soil Conservation Service, which cooperates with many local soil conservation districts. It has sometimes managed to reclaim whole districts that previously seemed permanently ruined by land misuse. In public lands reserved for grazing or forestry, the United States Bureau of Land Management and the Forest Service are entrusted with the conservation of the soil.

In some places the problems of erosion control seem practically insoluble. Northwest of Los Angeles, for example, the scant rainfall permits only grass, sagebrush, greasewood, manzanita, and trash trees to grow on steep hillsides. Devastating fires, almost every summer, destroy even this inadequate soil covering. Sudden rains, a few months later, may plunge down the bare hillsides, bringing landslides that sweep away homes, bury automobiles, and take human lives.

Watershed Management

A watershed or drainage basin is an area from which water drains into a single river. Many small watersheds make up the great Missouri River watershed. This joins with the Ohio-Tennessee River watershed, then (still farther south) with the watersheds of the Arkansas, Red, Yazoo, and many smaller rivers to form the great Mississippi watershed, which drains an area of about 1,250,000 square miles, or 41 per cent of the area of the first 48 states.

Water and soil conservation and the protection of forests, grazing lands, and wildlife are part of watershed management, which should exercise supervision over the whole area of a watershed to see that the surface resources of water are not seriously depleted. It is important that total outflow from the watershed through the stream that drains it (ultimately, into the ocean) does not decrease indefinitely. If the natural flow, averaged over a period of a few years, has a downward trend, this is evidence that the water is being used consumptively beyond the capacity of the ground water system for replenishment. Good watershed management seeks to preserve or improve the land capacity of the whole area. The Muskingum Water Conservancy District in Ohio, the Brandywine Valley in Pennsylvania and Delaware, and the Delaware River watershed program are examples of local efforts in watershed management. The Delaware Valley improvement is a good example of what can be accomplished by the joint efforts of several states and the Federal Government.

Preventing soil erosion may conserve water. For effective prevention of soil erosion, however, plant growth must be encouraged—an intervention that consumes a certain quantity of water, in transpiration from plants. So the total runoff from a small watershed may actually be diminished by good soil conservation practices. The beneficial result is that surface runoff will be less subject to flooding. For this reason the protection of forest and grazing lands is an important part of every soil and water conservation program. The preservation of fish and wildlife and the development of recreation areas are just extra benefits that come from intelligent watershed management.

In addition to the agencies already mentioned, the United States Forestry Service has contributed a great deal to our knowledge of how watersheds should be managed. One of their most important studies is that of the Coweata Hydrologic Laboratory in western North Carolina. A concrete dam at the outflow is provided with a weir (an outlet of definite shape and size, through which water flows at a volume rate that may be inferred from the depth). In this way, the outflow from the whole area may be precisely measured. This project has confirmed what one would expect: cutting down a forest increases the rate of outflow of water from the watershed, since there is then no loss of water by transpiration (evaporation from the leaves of plants). Nevertheless, if every tree is left on the ground in the very spot where it falls, even steep hillsides are protected by the rubbish that covers them.

Some of the results of the intensive study of forests were entirely unexpected. Moderate rainfall, for example, whenever it comes fairly late in the summer, helps create a vigorous forest. Yet heavy downpours in early summer encourage the growth of grass, which may become shoulder high to a man on horseback before the summer is over. After that, if the rains slacken, the grass may lose 75 per cent of its moisture and become a grave menace to the forest because of the risk of fire. If a heavy snowfall occurs the following winter, the weight of the snow on branches may break many of them off, and add fuel to any fires that may start thereafter.

As if that were not bad enough, spring freshets from the melting snow may wash out access roads, so that fire-fighters find it difficult to get into any area where a fire is raging. Fires are now often fought with helicopters, which fly over the burning woods and dump loads of water or ammonium phosphate solution. This, like some other soluble phosphates, is a good fire-retardant because it coats the burning wood with a glossy, incombustible film of metaphosphoric acid, HPO_3, which excludes oxygen. After ammonium phosphate has subdued a fire, the next rain washes it into the soil, where it brings mineral nutrients (N and P) to seedling trees. If a forest has been neglected for several years, it may become impossible to control any fire that gets started until several square miles of valuable timber have been burned over.

On another watershed the Forest Service has shown that very steep hillsides should never be grazed or plowed, since severe erosion is then inevitable. In Colorado, the Service has shown that small clearings in forests may conserve water, in part by permitting snow to be deposited on the ground instead of on the branches of trees, where a good part of it may be lost by evaporation before it melts. By contrast, cutting an extensive area of a forest and removing the product exposes everything by destruction by erosion. Good timber-cutting practices aid in conserving both soil and water. The poet's plea: "Woodman, spare that tree!" was backed by good reasons.

Soil Components and Soil Types

Different types of soils differ greatly in their capacity for holding water, hence differ in the kinds of crops they will support. Soils consist of varying mixtures of sand, silt, or clay, or of mixtures of sand and clay, with decaying plant remains.

Sand consists of irregular, rounded mineral fragments, not greatly altered by weathering, and ranging from about .02 to 2 mm (0.0008 to 0.08 in.) in diameter. If sand is shaken with water, it will settle to the bottom of the container in a few moments.

Silt consists of rock particles of intermediate size (0.002 to 0.02 mm) between those of sand and clay. They usually contain both these soil components. The character of good soil is often determined by its proportion of silt.

Clay particles are much finer (less than 0.002 mm in thickness). Instead of being rounded, they are usually flat flakes. Ions (section E, Appendix) and water molecules can penetrate between the still finer flakes that compose the microscopically visible particles of clay. Clay owes to this fact its capacity for being swollen by water, and the ability of some kinds of clay to exchange cations (positively charged ions) with salt solutions. Clay shaken with water may need many days to settle out. In settling, it may separate into distinct bands or layers that reveal the presence of different kinds of material of different particle sizes.

Plant residues, in various stages of decay, may be of any size, from visible fragments downward. Living organisms are responsible for their gradual disintegration. Rodents, insects, and earthworms begin it. Simpler organisms carry on from there—algae, fungi, protozoa, bacteria. The final result is an indefinite, structureless, colloidal residue—humus. Humus, like clay, absorbs water readily, but for a different reason.

If to the preceding we add water and trapped air, our list of important soil components is complete. As water increases in the soil, trapped air decreases. Waterlogged soil is soil in which the water table is so close to the land surface that evaporation is direct. Many plants will not survive waterlogging.

Soil character is very largely determined by the identity and proportions of the materials that compose it. They in turn do much to determine the size of the soil particles, the capacity of the soil for holding water and being penetrated by air, and arability (capacity for being ploughed). In different parts of the world, many different soil types are recognized. Your agricultural adviser or county agent can tell you whether the soil types of your own district have been determined and are perhaps shown on a soil map. The percentages of sand, silt, and clay determine the texture of the soil: a sandy soil contains roughly less than 20 per cent silt and clay; loam contains roughly equal quantities of sand and clay, or of clay + silt + organic matter; generally, the best for cultivation; and clay soils over 30 per cent clay.

The Penetration of Surface Soil by Water

The ability of a soil to absorb water is partly determined by its recent history. Rodents and earthworms are often important in creating openings for the penetration of water. Intelligent farmers do all in their power to preserve the work of these small engineers. Freely branching roots (corn, many vegetables) and especially the decay of roots after death, improve soil structure by separating particles that otherwise would become closely packed and especially by interposing particles of a different size to prevent separated particles from falling again into close-packing. We can readily understand that cultivation sometimes injures soil texture.

When soils are irrigated or when rain falls upon them, the surface soil usually soaks up water very rapidly for a few minutes, as little streams run down into pores between the grains and the miniature tunnels of earthworms and insects and root channels. Without such openings, raindrops or the mistlike droplets of sprayed irrigation water may fail to penetrate the surface, almost as if the soil particles were waxed.

The first drops of every rain enter crevices, cracks, and fissures in the earth. They cause underground creatures to scurry or quiver and chirp and expel air from the soil. Then what began as a steady downward trickle of water becomes the sluggish creep of a film of water, which engulfs soil particle after soil particle, driving air before it. Meanwhile, the cracks and fissures through which the first raindrops plunged underground disappear by collapse of their walls or by the swelling of particles of clay or humus. Runoff then begins: water that is worth money to the farmer on whose land it has fallen departs in haste to benefit someone else, often tearing great rents in the earth on its way to the nearest river.

Time is gained for the absorption of water, and runoff and erosion are decreased by any of the methods for conserving moisture and soil that were described in the early part of this chapter. Cultivation commonly increases erosion, except on very level lands. When the risk of erosion is great, the landowner should examine his land, acre by acre, with something like the care with which generals, on the eve of a battle, are supposed to take note of the topography of a battlefield.

The penetration of soil by water is not altogether owing to the force of gravity. Subsoil distillation (evaporation, followed by the removal of the vapor by diffusion to another place and recondensation there) is often found to play a part, and so does capillarity (the tendency for a liquid to penetrate into narrow channels between wetted surfaces).

Although the molecules of a liquid cling very tightly to the surface of any solid that they can wet, they do vibrate with an energy that increases with temperature (section B, Appendix). So they gradually wander away over any wettable surface, displacing absorbed water vapor and air as they go. Because the molecules of water strongly attract one another, those leading the advance over any surface that is being wetted drag others after them. So every liquid that can wet a surface creeps away into every nook and cranny, seeking out crevices not revealed by powerful microscopes and penetrating deeply where one might expect no penetration at all.

If a wetted channel leads upward, the ascending film of liquid may drag a continuous column of liquid after it that fills the channel. Thus we account for the rise of liquids in wicks and the rise of water through porous soil from an underground source of water. Penetration of crevices by a liquid is most pronounced with liquids which, like water, have a high surface tension (a measure of the cohesive strength of a surface film on liquid).

Once within a narrow tube or crevice, water vapor is even more firmly held than liquid water. The surface of ordinary glass holds water vapor so tenaciously that a temperature of at least 110°C is needed to expel most of it. In addition, glass holds internally considerable water that is released only at temperatures at which the glass begins to soften.

If the mutual attraction of the molecules of a wall and molecules of a liquid is less than the attraction of the molecules of the liquid for one another, the liquid will not wet the wall. The surface of the liquid then shrinks and is turned downward where it meets the wall. There the liquid descends to a lower level. The wall surface, exposed by the retreat of the liquid, is taken over by adsorbed air and vapor.

In summary: the penetration of water into soil and its movement underground is chiefly owing to the force of gravity, which moves it downhill; yet this movement is supplemented by subsurface distillation, which moves water from warmer to cooler locations, or to those in which the vapor pressure of water is less, because of the presence of dissolved salts. Capillarity, too, is important, since it moves water from crevices that are wide into those that are narrow, and from surfaces that are hard to wet to those wet more easily.

The Water-Holding Capacity of Soils

The removal of surplus water by drainage, after a rain or irrigation, must take place within one to three days or most crops will suffer. The damage is chiefly owing to the destruction of roots by a lack of oxygen. Slow drainage may be caused by a water table near the surface, by recent deep saturation, or by a water-blocking layer of impermeable material such as clay or hardpan. Too much sodium (the ion Na^+) in irrigation water will displace calcium (the ion Ca^{++}) from a clay soil, will cause clay particles to swell, and thus will decrease drainage. Even the use of sodium nitrate instead of calcium nitrate or ammonium sulfate in nitrogenous fertilizers may decrease a soil's drainage.

Sandy soils hold water so loosely that it will drain away by gravity to a moisture content of up to 10 to 12 per cent of the weight of the soil in an oven-dried condition. A very fine sand will retain more water than a coarse one because there is more surface to hold water; it will also draw water up farther and more rapidly by capillarity from a subterranean source. Humus and clay, and about equally, hold water much more tenaciously than sand ever does, and they may contain twice as much water as sand holds. Clays commonly have moisture content of 50 per cent by weight, and sometimes even more.

The water drained from soil is sometimes called gravitational water. Water then remaining is the field capacity for water, usually expressed as a percentage by weight of complete dry soil. The field capacity includes capillary water, which wets the surfaces of the soil particles and is readily available to plants, together with some of the water in soil colloids, chiefly clay and humus, which is less readily available because colloids retain it rather strongly. There is also in soils a little completely unavailable hygroscopic water (that still remaining in air-dried soil but removed by drying the soil in an oven at 105°C). Soils also contain water vapor, which sometimes contributes to the movement of water in soils, particularly in arid regions.

Figure 2-1 shows successive stages of removal of water from a sandy loam, in comparison with its removal from a clay loam. The curves are simply illustrative and do not represent actual experiments. However, it is a fact that the successive stages in the loss of water do not disclose any sharp changes in the direction of the curves showing dehydration (loss of water). From this we may conclude that different kinds of soil water grade imperceptibly into one another and that our classification of soil water is a purely arbitrary one.

The water-holding capacity of a soil is largely determined by the sizes and gradations in size of its particles, its content of clay and humus, and the kind of clay.

The total surface of the particles of a soil, hence the capacity of the

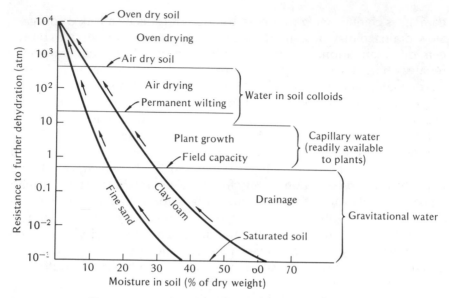

Figure 2-1. Dehydration Curves for Different Soils

soil for holding capillary water, increases in proportion as their size is reduced. For example, particles having one-tenth of a specified area have ten times the total surface in the same weight of soil. The top 6.5 inches of sandy soil may have a total surface of 5000 acres, for each acre of land. For a sandy loam the total surface may be 50,000 acres, and for a clay soil may be 500,000 acres.

The percentage porosity of a soil is of less importance to water-holding capacity than is the size of the pores. Sand has a considerable percentage of very large pores from which water drains rapidly. Its water content at saturation is large, but its water-holding capacity is small. Sand does have one advantage in comparison with clay: unless waterlogged, it is much better aerated.

The Availability of Soil Moisture

The ability of a well-drained soil to resist further loss of moisture increases very rapidly as drying proceeds. This resistance to dehydration is called moisture tension. It may be inferred from measurements of the vapor pressure of the water still remaining in the soil, and in other ways. It is usually expressed in atmospheres. From a third to a half of the field capacity of a soil for moisture can usually be removed before the moisture tension rises above two atmospheres. It is about 15 atmospheres when the soil is so dry that there is permanent wilting (wilting that persists overnight). For an air-dried soil it may be over 500 atmospheres, and 10,000 atmospheres for an oven-dried soil. In Figure 2-1, the moisture tension of two different types of soil is compared at different stages of drying. This diagram is merely suggestive and does not present the results of an actual experiment. A slow rise in the moisture tension as drying proceeds represents a stage in the drying in which colloidal material (chiefly humus and clay) still hold a considerable quantity of moisture and are slowly releasing it. Further along in the drying process, when the colloids have lost most of their water, the moisture tension of the soil once more rises rapidly.

Moisture in a well-drained field may migrate upward or downward, almost without regard to gravity, because of differences in moisture tension. By incorporating humus into a soil we give it a supply of moisture that is only slowly released as it passes in the form of water vapor to neighboring places, where the moisture tension is lower. The migration of water vapor within soils is of course also dependent on differences in temperature or differences in salinity (since dissolved salts decrease vapor pressure). Though these movements are sometimes important, there is little that can be done to alter or control them or change the direction of the movement of water vapor through a soil.

Irrigation Methods
There are four chief ways for getting irrigation water onto land:

1. Irrigation by flooding is possible only on flat lands, such as the rice fields of Arkansas and Louisiana and the cranberry bogs of several northern and eastern states. It looks simple, but is apt to be complicated and expensive when applied to large areas. The soil must be carefully leveled and have sufficient porosity and depth everywhere for the water to be absorbed within a few hours; otherwise, the root systems of most crops may die for lack of oxygen. (There are a few exceptions —notably, paddy rice and cranberries.)

2. Irrigation by ditching and furrows is the most common method for getting water onto the land in the 17 western states. In the 31 eastern and southern states it is much less frequently used. It can be wasteful of water, since there is loss by seepage and by transpiration from the leaves of non-crop vegetation, along all the main distribution canals and laterals.

3. Irrigation by spraying or sprinkling has been growing very rapidly during the past few years, in the vegetable farms of the eastern seaboard and the citrus groves of Florida. Quick-coupling aluminum pipe or stiff-walled plastic pipe, perforated or fitted with spray nozzles, may easily be moved from one part of a field or orchard to another. This type of irrigation calls for a larger initial investment than irrigation by flooding. Yet soil erosion is avoided, almost regardless of slope, uniform application of water is possible with every type of soil, and the amount of water applied may be varied to suit the needs of the growing crop. All the land may be used, weeds are easily controlled, and water-soluble fertilizers may be applied directly through the sprinklers. This method calls for water that is free from sediment. Otherwise the spray nozzles will quickly be clogged.

In windy locations, water thrown into the air by sprinklers may be distributed very unevenly. Sometimes the trouble is overcome by a moderate increase in the rate of application of water.[1] In most localities, there are fortunately hours during which the wind slackens perceptibly. Soils that take moisture poorly because they are very dry and full of trapped air may usually be dealt with by a short preliminary application of water. As the water absorbed, the air is displaced. The soil is then ready for more water.

Another type of spray irrigation has been introduced into Florida and Texas citrus groves. Its distinguishing feature is a rotating sprinkler head, 19 ft above the ground. Water delivered upward and outward through this under a pressure of 75 to 85 lb/in^2 sprinkles a circle with a radius of at least 220 ft, in the absence of wind. The sprinkler straddles and grasps a small (6/16 in.) galvanized steel cable, which it reels in, driven by water pressure; thus it is slowly moved toward and beyond the source of its water. Water is delivered to it through a 600-ft length of 4-in. or 6-in. synthetic rubber hose, coupled in 100-ft lengths.

Moving 1 to 3 ft/min, the sprinkler may take 7.5 to 24 hr to arrive at the end of its quarter-mile traverse, where the water is automatically cut off. Although the water issues through the sprinkler in a continuous stream, it encounters an oscillating interceptor, which breaks it into a fine spray. The rate of delivery is about 500 gal/min.

As the sprinkler moves, the hose is dragged through mud behind it,

1. The rate of flow through a small hole or nozzle varies as the fourth power of the radius, provided that the pressure can be maintained at its former value in spite of an increase in the size of the opening. For example, a 25 per cent increase in the radius of the opening will multiply the rate of flow by about 2.4 and a 50 per cent increase will multiply it by 5 (since $1.25^4 \cong 2.4$, and $1.5^4 \cong 5$).

like an alligator's tail. (A one-eighth mile of 6-in. hose holds about four tons of water.) A much larger area is irrigated than was formerly ever possible between successive calls for labor and a tractor in resetting the sprinklers. A 20-acre grove may be given a 1.3-in. depth of irrigation in 24 hours allowing for time lost in resetting the sprinkler. The foregoing describes, of course, only one of several possible sprinkler systems.

4. Subsurface irrigation, often called controlled drainage, seeks to maintain the water table at a constant level, sufficiently low to permit good aeration of the roots of the crop, yet sufficiently high to permit water to rise to the roots by capillarity. This type of irrigation calls for land that is characterized by a shallow water table such as land brought into use by draining a swamp. The river delta area, northeast of San Francisco, and the Everglades area of Florida are the most important examples in the United States of this type of irrigation.

Salt in Irrigation Water

Even when water is abundant and fairly pure, its use in irrigation may be prevented by damage that may be done to crops by dissolved minerals in the soil or water. Water that contains so much salt that it is quite unfit for irrigation may not taste salty. Fortunately, the amount of salt in irrigation water or soil may be estimated by a measurement of the electrical conductivity of the water or a saturated soil extract.

The more salt, that is, the more ions, in any given volume of the water or saturated soil extract, the greater is the conductivity. Section F of the Appendix tells something about this test and explains what is meant by the unit of conductivity, the mho-per-centimeter (mho/cm). A thousandth part of this conductivity is the millimho-per-centimeter (mmho/cm). It corresponds approximately to a solution containing 470 weight units (grams) of sodium chloride to a million of water (470 ppm). This is roughly 0.05 per cent by weight.

Water whose electrical conductivity is less than 1 mmho/cm is sufficiently free from salt for the irrigation of crops having only slight salt tolerance. As a rough rule, irrigation water of good quality should have a conductivity of not over 1.5 mmho/cm, corresponding to 0 to 700 ppm of common salt; fair quality, 700 to 2000 ppm; poor quality, over 2000 ppm. (The U.S. Public Health Standard for salt in drinking water is less than 500 ppm.) The salt tolerance of individual crops is discussed in Chapter 13.

It is important to see that the salt content of irrigation water not exceed the salinity tolerance of crops grown. Water from deep wells is of stable quality unless contaminated by the deepening of canals near the seacoast or the intrusion of salt water into a fresh water aquifer in drilling for petroleum. Water from a river or lake of fair capacity should be tested at least once a year to be sure that it remains uncontaminated.

Water of a small lake or stream may be contaminated by water draining from salt-laden lands, which can ruin garden lands or an orchard within a few months. In salt-threatened districts, anyone who neglects to have his irrigation water tested at frequent intervals risks having to abandon his land. Destruction of a farm or orchard by salt is less spectacular than a fire that destroys a home; but it is more ruinous because insurance will not cover it.

How Much Water Does a Crop Need?

An important question for any practical farmer or group of farmers planning an irrigation project relates to the total volume of water needed. An agricultural experiment station in their own neighborhood may have determined the water consumed by representative crops, irrigated under ideal conditions. Even if the test station is somewhat distant and the climate is not quite identical, one may assure that the need of different crops for water is in the same ratio as at the test station. If it has been found that alfalfa, at the test area, needs 20 per cent more water for irrigation than is needed for citrus, the same ratio may be assumed wherever in that general latitude both crops may be grown. This estimate makes allowance for the fact that the crops have very different root systems.

Another method takes note of the ratio of water consumed in growing a crop to the weight of dry matter produced and assumes that the same ratio holds under ideal conditions in neighboring areas. If the only available data are for a latitude, climate, and soil type very different from the one for which irrigation is planned, one is nevertheless not without recourse. Formulas have been found that will permit allowance to be made for these factors in estimating the need for water of the projected crop.

When such estimates have been made, some engineering questions must still be answered. What irrigation system will be used, and what fraction of the water it conveys will be consumed by the crop in transpiration? (One may not count on more than 40 per cent being delivered in irrigation by ditching and not more than 80 per cent in irrigation by sprinklers.) How frequently will the irrigation water need to be applied, and how much at each application?

What will be the effect of rain during the irrigation period? One should not regard rainwater as a cost-free substitute for irrigation water (secured by diverting a river or delivered by artesian wells or pumped wells). The catch-rain system needs to be carefully planned and the cost of rain water established for different amounts of precipitation. What capacity must the reservoir have to provide for the heaviest downpour likely to be observed in the next 25 years? What will prevent it from quickly being filled with sand or rubble washed down from higher land in its rear?

Profits and Pitfalls in Irrigation

In the 17 continental states between Iowa and the Pacific Ocean, irrigation has brought many areas into cultivation that otherwise would have remained uncultivated or been left to "dry farming." Although the total area irrigated is only about 5 per cent of the farmland in these western states, it is at least 15 to 20 per cent of the land in cultivated crops. Nearly half of the money value of crops in these states comes from irrigated acres; and in California, irrigated acres have sometimes yielded 85 per cent of the money value of crops. Irrigation in these western states results in larger crops and better crop quality and permits many crops to be grown that without irrigation would not be grown at all. Examples are California cotton, grapes, and artichokes, Washington apples, Colorado alfalfa, Nebraska sugar beets, and Idaho potatoes. Irrigation makes dense planting possible, and this in turn makes mechanization possible, which greatly decreases labor costs. Unfortunately, there are pitfalls, too, in irrigation. Most crops require 1 to 4 inches of water at every irrigation and irrigation may be needed every 8 to 14 days during the growing season. That amounts to 7 to 10 gallons per acre per minute, day and night, until the need for water is past. Is that much water, or good quality, actually available? Can a clear legal title be secured to use it? Is the soil of a type well suited to irrigation farming? Will the water supply last, or will it dwindle away during prolonged droughts? Will the land itself, if irrigated, gradually be ruined by the accumulation of salt? Many other questions arise, calling for expert advice at every stage of planning and development of an irrigation project. The advice of a hydrologist will be needed, of an irrigation engineer, of experts in soils, crops, and marketing, and, perhaps especially, legal advice. The first person to practice irrigation in any locality runs the same sort of risks as are encountered by the first to prospect for minerals or drill for oil!

Drainage for Wet Lands

The living parts of every plant, and even resting seeds, need oxygen to carry out oxidative processes associated with life. Organic matter is oxidized in successive steps that finally lead to water and carbon dioxide, while energy is released as heat. This is respiration. It takes place in living plants, around the clock, day and night, although during daylight hours it is obscured by photosynthesis, the process by which water and carbon dioxide are converted, with the aid of the energy of sunlight, into living organic matter and oxygen. Oxygen in the soil is also necessary for decay, in which dead plant tissue is converted, first into the structureless and ambiguous product called humus and at length into carbon dioxide and water—the ultimate products of respiration. Oxygen is also used by the bacteria of the soil in oxidizing sulfur to sulfate and ammonium salts to nitrate (the source of nitrogen for most species of plants).

Wet soils are not readily penetrated by oxygen, hence all the processes of oxidation are impeded. Paddy rice, growing with roots submerged, fails to find enough nitrate nitrogen for building organic nitrogen compounds. The rice makes a chemical adaptation in which it uses ammonium salts instead of nitrate. The wetness of a soil, either directly by the control of oxygen or indirectly by the control of bacteria, joins with temperature and the supply of mineral nutrients in the soil to determine what species of plants—the native vegetation—will thrive in a particular locality.

The lack of oxygen in waterlogged soil is just the beginning of many evils, which even chance passers-by may notice. Wet pasture land supports only coarse grasses, moss, and aquatic plants, which are unfit for grazing. The soil is cold, and such pasturage as it does yield comes late in spring and fails at the first touch of autumn. Animals that have the misfortune to be pastured on such soil are often more prone to disease. Grazing sheep quickly ruin the land itself by close-cropping, or by perforating its upper layer by trampling.

If wet land is drained well enough to be arable, it may nevertheless become unworkable with each shower. Crops are often poor because the best time for planting may be missed on account of rain. Root crops, corn, and other crops that call for deep tillage must be given up and the land either indefinitely left fallow or sold as "acreage" to people who are so foolish as to buy land, sight unseen, by mail. Wet land may be "surface drained" by plowing it into convex ridges from which the water flows into intervening furrows, thence into ditches that convey it to lower levels. Most expensively, but usually much more effectively drainage is provided by "underground drains" in which surface water finds its way through beds of small stones (3 inches) into cylindrical drains of porous tile. The effect of drainage is to lower the water table, but considerable water is held by capillarity, above the water table to a height of 2 feet, in sandy soils, and as much as 4 feet in clay soils.

In draining any area, one must first determine whether sufficient slope is available, and where the outflowing water will finally be delivered. One must also take note of legal restrictions, reasonable or not, that have been set up for the protection of other landowners. In the United States, drainage became commonplace only after the development of ditch-digging and tile-making machines. Even today it is profitable only with crops whose dollar return per acre is high.

If a swampy area is overdrained and underirrigated there may be sudden disaster in time of prolonged drought. The topsoil in a drained swamp is not soil at all but peat or muck, which may consist of as much as 60 to 90 per cent organic matter (partially decayed vegetation). This shrinks so much on being exposed to the air that the land subsides. Under cultivation, drained peat or muck soils are destroyed by oxidation and dehydration at the rate of half an inch to a full inch per year. To prevent this, such lands are often flooded when not occupied by crops. In the San Francisco Bay area, the land has subsided so much that dikes had to be built and pumping undertaken to prevent inundation by tide water. In Florida, a different sort of disaster has had to be faced. The dried peat of the overdrained Everglades proved to be almost as combustible as coal. Fires, often spontaneous, repeatedly spread over many square miles, wiping out every living thing, clawing deeply into the earth, burning unchecked for months, and leaving behind an ash-covered, smoking wilderness, uninhabitable as the throat of Vesuvius. The cities of southeastern Florida and its agricultural industries are in competition with its wildlife for the water of the Everglades. After such a disaster as that just described it may be many years before the delightful wild creatures reappear in something like their former abundance.

Water Withdrawal for Different Uses

The largest use of water in the United States, and nearly everywhere the most rapidly growing use, is in industry. The total estimated rate of withdrawal of water from surface and underground sources in 1970 was about 370,000 million gallons a day (mgd). About 51 per cent of that total was for industry, about 40 per cent for irrigation, 8 per cent for urban water supplies, and only 1 per cent for rural use, exclusive of irrigation. Water is used in great quantities in the manufacture of paper and rayon and as a cooling agent in the manufacture of steel and in canning fruit.

The use of water in any locality is determined by its cost, the capacity of the area for agriculture, industrial development, and the density of the population. The U.S. Geological Survey recognizes 17 regions in each of which the kind of water use is fairly uniform. It has published data on the kind and amounts of use in these regions, as well as in separate states in 1960.[2]

Self-supplied water for industry is 100 mgd in steam-driven electric power plants and about 40 mgd for other purposes. About 40 per cent of all water used in industry is surface water that is taken from lakes and rivers and largely returned, with or without contamination.

In sharp contrast to irrigation, most of the industrial use of water is in the eastern states, and only 2 per cent of the water used is consumed. It is consumed chiefly in cooling, because during this process some of the water evaporates. Almost all of the water used for cooling can be re-used if it has not been contaminated. About a third of it is saline water, hardly fit for any other use.

Irrigation water is usually measured in acre-feet. (An acre-foot is enough water to cover an acre of land a foot deep—325,850 gallons.) Over 90 per cent of the 39,000,000 irrigated acres are in the 17 arid continental states west of Iowa. These states actually used 90,000,000 acre-feet for crops in 1960, and about 26,000,000 additional acre-feet were lost by evaporation and seepage during conveyance through canals and ditches. (In the eastern states this loss is much less, since water for irrigation is often conveyed through pipes. Most of the demand for irrigation water occurs during a few weeks of the growing season.)

About a third of the water used in irrigation in the United States is

2. U.S. Geological Survey, Circular 456.

obtained from wells and springs. The rest comes from rivers, lakes, and ponds. The most important fact about water for irrigation is that under the best conditions about 60 per cent of it is consumed (permanently lost) by evaporation from the leaves of plants. In fact, the only important way that water can be moved through a plant is by being pulled up in coherent little threads or filaments of liquid as the water ahead of it evaporates from the leaves.

The loss and consumption of water in irrigation in the United States is about 4 times the "once-and-for-all" use of water by private and public utilities, and about 25 times that of industries whose water is self-supplied.

Municipal water systems (publicly or privately owned) supply 140 million people and thousands of industrial plants. This includes water lost by seepage and evaporation, as well as that actually used in the home or in street flushing, fire fighting, or in washing and humidifying air in air conditioning. Industry and commerce account for about a third of the water supplied by municipal water systems.

The non-irrigation rural use of water (70 per cent from wells) is a little over half for human use, and most of the rest for livestock. If livestock are watered from ponds, loss by evaporation may be five times that actually used by the animals themselves. If there is running water in a home about 100 to 150 gallons are used per person per day. If there is none, each person averages 10 gallons. Americans traveling abroad often complain about the lack of running water in the home. It does not indicate the need for more spirit of progress but simply shows that not many countries are ready to multiply their water supplies ten- to fifteen-fold, simply to permit water to be used as wastefully as it is in the United States.

Water Economy

The conservation of every natural resource involves not only protection against contamination and destruction, but also economy in use. The best incentive to economy is to compel every user to pay a fair price for all he withdraws or consumes. If this were done with water, lawns in water-scarce localities would soon be replaced by strips of gravel or green concrete; stock-watering ponds would give way to automatic dispensers, operated by the weight of drinking animals; and irrigation, in many places, might be discontinued, because it would be cheaper to import food than to grow it so expensively. Water for irrigation, which has often been available for less than a cent for a thousand gallons ($3.26 an acre-foot), is likely to command many times that price when thirsty cities and industries, growing like mushrooms, compete with farmers for a larger share of available water.

Linings for canals, ditches, and small streams may almost completely prevent loss of water by seepage. Canals have sometimes been sealed by floating dispersed clay or (better) a mixture of clay and organic material (waxes, resins, lignin, or ethylcellulose), in the form of an emulsion, down the canal. Concrete is the preferred lining.

Canal linings not only decrease loss by seepage but also discourage the growth of water-loving "trash trees" along the water courses. Trash trees line every major watercourse and waste water in a reckless way.

When water lies stagnant in storage ponds, a trace of a wetting agent (an organic compound that spreads on the surface of water in a layer only one molecule thick) may decrease evaporation spectacularly. Otherwise, loss by evaporation, in arid areas of the western states, may sometimes be as much as 5 to 6 feet per year. Where feasible a better way to prevent evaporation is by storage of water underground, i.e. to recharge an aquifer.

Since the chief use of water in industry is in cooling, an important need is to improve the efficiency of heat transfer in cooling. More efficient cooling towers are needed in the manufacture of gasoline or in the condensation of exhaust steam in generating fuel-derived electric energy. They might easily reduce the per-kilowatt-hour demand for water in cooling to a third of that now needed.

The use of salt water in cooling calls for expensive, corrosion-resistant equipment. But when stainless steel in cooling equipment is replaced by aluminum, the superior heat conductivity may permit cooling by compressed air instead of by water. Chapter 13 discusses the long overlooked but spectacular possibilities of irrigation by saline water of soil that is pure sand, free from clay.

Water may often be re-used. Instead of being wasted in flushing away sewage (thus perhaps polluting the water supplies of cities downstream), it can be saved for better uses. Sewage can be converted into fertilizer, as described in Chapter 11. The liquid effluent from a sewage treatment plant, free from odor but loaded with discarded plant nutrients, has usually just been chlorinated and discharged into the nearest stream. "Let the downstream neighbors worry!" There are better ways than that.

The need for economy in the use of water is sure to increase. It will determine what areas in the world shall be thickly populated, and how their inhabitants shall live. If water were used only for drinking, cooking, and bathing, a few gallons a day for each person would be enough. In the great arid regions of the world, such economy in the use of water has been a way of life for ages. At present, the total use of water in the United States for all purposes, including industry and irrigation, is about 1500 gallons per person per day.

Depleted Aquifers

A modern turbine driven by an electric motor or a diesel engine may deliver hundreds of gallons a minute (Figure 2-2). In a state like Nebraska, which has an abundant supply of underground water, there may be thousands of pumped wells. In the San Joaquin Valley, California, there are 50,000. If the total rate of removal of water from an aquifer is

Figure 2-2. Depleted Aquifers
From *The Conservation of Ground Water* by H. E. Thomas (McGraw-Hill, 1951), Plate II.

greater than the rate at which water re-enters through surrounding porous strata, the water table is perceptibly lowered. This decline in head is roughly proportional to the rate of water withdrawal. The specific capacity of a well (usually expressed in gallons per minute per foot of drawdown) is the discharge rate divided by the drawdown. *Drawdown* is the decline in head of a well due to pumping. Hydrologists, studying the possibility of a continuous water supply from a well, can use this figure, in connection with other data, to predict what will happen to the water supply in the future. One need not wait until the well runs dry to take steps to prevent it from doing so.

Drainage of swamps or too many wells in a given area may seriously lower the water table before anyone realizes what is happening. In the Central Valley of California, so much water was pumped from the aquifer between 1943 and 1953 that the land subsided: the 4 million acre feet of water withdrawn from the aquifer were taken at the expense of a permanent loss of about 2 million acre feet of the aquifer's capacity.

A good part of the water resources of the world have been surveyed or are actively being studied by hydrologists, although development and proper management, even in the United States, in some areas is no more than well begun. In the United States at large, the water table is not being systematically lowered. In many regions the natural replenishment is sufficient to ensure a steady water supply at the present rate of use. There are areas, however, especially in the arid Southwest, in which water levels are being steadily lowered. This calls for artificial replenishment, since natural replenishment might take many centuries. The abandoned homes of cliff dwellers in these regions bear witness to the uncertainty of water supplies. Years of cloudless skies; watercourses all gone dry; then the inevitable sad and fatal culmination: empty buckets falling into empty wells!

Artificial Replenishment

In regions in which the depletion of aquifers is already occurring at an alarming rate, some attempts at replenishment are being made. In the Central Valley of California and around Peoria, Illinois, water confined by ditches and dikes gradually seeps through the soil or enters wells, and replenishes an aquifer. Obviously, such water can be recovered only by pumping, or sometimes by sinking artesian wells at suitable locations.

In a few places—for example, on Long Island—an aquifer is being successfully recharged through wells that are sunk to the water-bearing strata for the express purpose of recharge. Such wells run the risk of clogging by sediment, precipitated salts, algae, and bacterial growth. In consequence, they may need to be pumped out periodically or otherwise cleaned.

Water used for recharge is always water that is in surplus supply at a given moment. Although recharging by wells is expensive, it may be cheaper than storage in surface reservoirs, particularly when land is valuable. Loss of water by evaporation is of course prevented when water is stored underground. Recharging an aquifer can occur incidentally with irrigation in that when salts have accumulated in an irrigated soil sometimes it is necessary to flush them out by a considerable input of irrigation water during the season in which crops are not growing. The surplus water tends to replenish the aquifer at all downstream points at which water is withdrawn.

Recharge of an aquifer through the surface layers of sand or gravel results in a certain amount of purification, since the sand acts as a filter. Yet salts, viruses, bacteria, and detergents are never entirely filtered out, hence recharging an aquifer should always be under the control of trained hydrologists. If an aquifer is once penetrated by bacteria or salt it is likely to remain contaminated for years or generations, in spite of all efforts.

The recharging of an aquifer is a little like the practice of storing natural gas underground, where it serves not only to conserve a supply of gas for future use but also to maintain the pressure that is needed to keep petroleum wells flowing.

3

The Return of the Rivers

All the rivers run into the sea, yet the sea is not filled; unto the place from which the rivers come, thither they return again.
(Ecclesiastes 1:7).

The men of ancient times were well aware that water poured into the sea by the rivers of the earth in some way found its way back to the sources of the rivers. Just how it did this was never quite clear. The fleecy clouds of an average day seemed inadequate to the task of returning all the water that the earth's rivers delivered. Were there perhaps underground streams, flowing *uphill* from the sea to the river sources? Was sea water, during this magical journey, in some equally magical way freed from salt? Such ideas might have been acceptable when the earth itself was believed to be flat and so thin that the sun, passing beneath the earth at night, warmed the water of a desert spring.

Actually, the waters that the rivers of the earth pour into the sea are evaporated by the energy of the sun and returned to the river sources as invisible water vapor, riding the winds. Clouds are just an incident and play only a minor and momentary part in the eternal cycle: ocean, water vapor, clouds, rain or snow, rivers draining back into the ocean (Figure 3-1). When ocean water evaporates the salt and other mineral impurities that the rivers have taken from the land remain in the ocean. Thus the reborn rivers remain forever fresh.

Our Dwindling Powerhouse: The Sun

All the springs, wells, and fountains of the earth are sustained by the fiery fountains of the sun. The sun is a gigantic "nuclear reactor," within

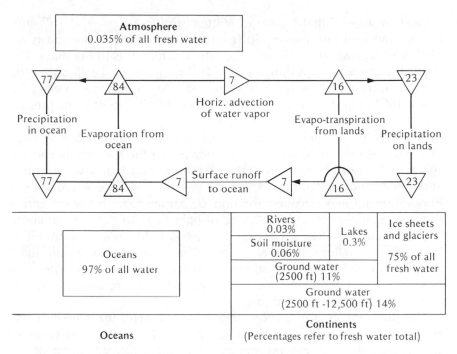

Figure 3-1. The Hydrological Cycle
From *Atmosphere, Weather and Climate* by R. G. Barry and R. J. Chorley
(Holt, Rinehart and Winston, 1970), Figure 2.1. Used by permission.

which matter is converted into energy. From the rate of outpouring of energy by the sun one may calculate the rate at which the sun is losing mass. Let us follow such a calculation through.

Satellites in orbit or observers on mountain tops have measured the solar constant (the rate at which the sun's energy is received by the earth). It amounts to about 1.36 ergs per second over each square centimeter of the earth's surface, whenever the sun's rays fall vertically.

The sun, for all we know, is pouring out its energy impartially in all directions. To find its total rate of emission of energy one must multiply the solar constant, 1.36 ergs per second, by the number of square centimeters in the surface of a sphere whose radius is the earth's average distance from the sun—1.49×10^{13}cm (about 93 million miles). That works out as 3.8×10^{33} erg/sec or about 5×10^{23} horsepower. (See section D, Appendix, for the use of powers of 10 in expressing very large or very small numbers.)

Einstein showed that 1 gram of matter produces $c^2 = 9 \times 10^{20}$ ergs, when converted into energy. So from the rate at which the sun is radiating energy we may calculate the rate at which it is losing mass. The result is somewhat disturbing—4.2×10^{12} g, or about 4 million metric tons per second. Yet the sun is so enormous that, at this rate, it will take about 1660 million years for the sun to lose 0.01 per cent of its present mass.

The energy set free by the sun is not carried through space as heat. This must be evident to anyone who recalls that the space between the sun and the earth is nearly a perfect vacuum, and that a vacuum is a very poor conductor of heat. The sun's energy is set free as radiant energy, often termed radiation (section C, Appendix). This leaps across the intervening space with the speed of light (3×10^{10} cm/sec, or about 186,000 mile/sec). Radiant energy in fact is light, visible or invisible. Whatever the nature of the radiation—X rays, ultraviolet, visible light, infrared, or radio waves—it almost certainly has the same speed in empty space. It takes about eight minutes for the radiant energy set free by the sun to reach the earth.

The sun's energy is of a wide range of frequencies (explained in section C of the Appendix). Only a small part of it is within the range of frequencies that the eye recognizes as visible light. Radiation of the next lower frequency range is termed infrared and that of next higher range, ultraviolet. Different frequencies behave in different ways as they pass through the atmosphere, encounter objects at the earth's surface, and are finally changed into heat.

The sun's staggering outpouring of energy is, from humanity's point of view, almost all energy wasted. The earth intercepts only about one part of the sun's energy in 540 million. A considerable part of this is immediately lost by being reflected back into space. Some of what remains is used to evaporate water from oceans, lakes, rivers, moist soil, and the leaves of plants. This still leaves a surplus of energy, which creates the winds and ocean currents that determine climate in every part of the earth and is used by green plants in photosynthesis.

The Earth's Gaseous Ocean

The people of ancient times greatly underestimated the capacity of earth's "gaseous ocean," the atmosphere, for carrying water from the liquid ocean back to the river sources. They did not realize that water vapor is invisible, and that more of it was carried by every breeze than anyone thought possible. They knew nothing about *air*, the gaseous mixture that composes the atmosphere, except that men and animals breathe it and that it is sometimes moist and sometimes dry. The philosophers of ancient Greece were not even sure that air is a material thing or that it has weight. Did the atmosphere extend upward to the sun, moon and stars? Perhaps no one ever asked.

We now know that the atmosphere covers the whole earth with a continuous thin blanket which establishes different climates in different parts of the earth and allots very unevenly to each land a portion of fresh water. Since the atmosphere is gaseous, it is compressible. Indeed, it is so much compressed by its own weight that half of it lies below a height of about 3½ miles. Consequently, the barometer (which measures the pressure created by the part of the atmosphere that lies above the barometer's own location) stands at only about 15 inches (38 cm) at an elevation of 3½ miles, as compared with 30 inches (76 cm) at sea level. Above that height, the barometric pressure continues to fall, and finally becomes immeasurably small.

Not only the barometric pressure, but also the temperature of the atmosphere decreases as one ascends, until a height of about 8 miles is reached, a little more than twice the height of Mount Everest. Below the 8 mile level is the part of the atmosphere called the troposphere (Figure 3-2). This is a zone of turbulence: winds, ascending and descending air currents, cloud formation, precipitation as rain or snow, re-evaporation, storms—all the details of weather.

Above the troposphere lies a quiet zone, the stratosphere, in which the temperature remains nearly constant (−70°F) to a height of about 12 miles, and above that increases, attaining the freezing point (32°F) at about 30 miles. The stratosphere influences the kind and intensity of radiation that penetrates through it from the sun to the earth's surface or is reradiated from the earth into space. It contains only a trace of moisture.

Above the stratosphere, students of the upper atmosphere recognize a mesosphere, in which both temperature and pressure decrease again. From the surface of the earth to a height of about 55 miles the atmosphere shows no very noticeable tendency to separate into layers. This part of the atmosphere, which includes the three zones already mentioned, is called the homosphere because its properties and composition are homogeneous. Yet the atmosphere at a height of 55 miles is only about one-tenth as dense as at the earth's surface.

Above the 55-mile level, where the air is not only very thin but quiet,

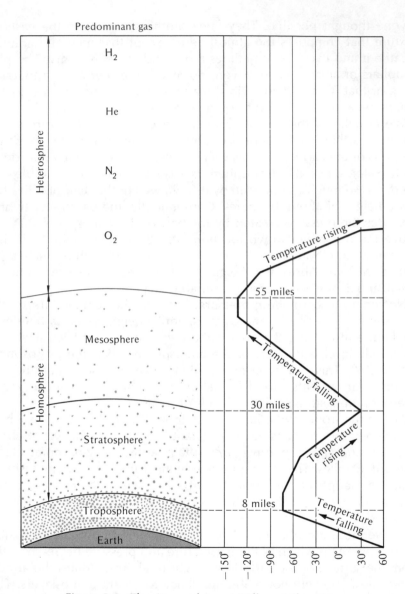

Figure 3-2. The Atmosphere at Different Elevations

is the thermosphere. There is here some separation of the atmosphere into layers of somewhat different composition: first, a layer in which nitrogen predominates; above that, a layer that is chiefly oxygen; above that, a layer in which helium is predominant; and, finally, a layer of hydrogen. This, the order of decreasing density, is also the order of decreasing molecular weight.

In the end, altitudes are reached at which molecules of atmosphere escape from the earth's attraction and take their departure, one by one, to become miniature satellites about the earth or planetoids about the sun.

The upper thermosphere, which has almost zero density, finally merges with the atmospheres of the other planets and the sun. To give temperatures or sound velocities at the extreme altitudes (above 110 miles) at which astronauts "walk in space" would be deceptive. There are not enough atmospheric molecules at these altitudes to make temperature stable or definite. Exchange of energy, between bodies under such conditions, is by radiation rather than by heat conduction. The whiteness or brightness of an astronaut's suit or space vehicle is consequently of more importance than its heat-insulating qualities. Sound, too, fails in extremely rarefied air—high-pitched sounds first, then those of lower pitch.

Rate of Evaporation

A liquid that will evaporate will do so at temperatures far below its boiling point. Figure 3-3 shows why. The closely packed molecules that compose every liquid are especially closely packed in a surface film a few molecules thick. All molecules are in constant motion—the more vigorous, the higher the temperature. Those from beneath the surface of a liquid, arriving at the surface film, are usually just turned back (as at a and b). Yet, now and then, a molecule arrives at the surface with sufficient kinetic energy to burst through the surface film. Even then, it is sometimes dragged back into the surface by the attraction of molecules beneath it (as at c and d). At other times, it makes good its escape and goes wandering off into the space above it, as at e. It is then a molecule of vapor.

A vapor or a gas, under low or moderate pressure differs from the same substance in the liquid state in having a much lower density and in filling its container completely, instead of having a definite upper

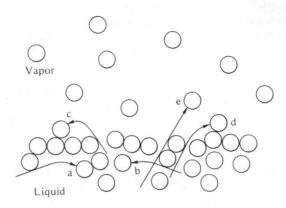

Figure 3-3. Details of Evaporation

surface. We conclude that the molecules of a gas or vapor are so far apart that they attract one another only very slightly, hence scatter indefinitely through whatever space is offered. We thus also account for gases being much more readily compressible than liquids.

The rate at which water or any other liquid evaporates increases, more and more rapidly, with increasing temperature. This indicates that an increased temperature rapidly increases the number of molecules that have sufficient speed to break through the surface film of the liquid and escape as vapor. Evaporation is still more rapid if a current of air removes the vapor as fast as it is formed. The air current sweeps away the escaping molecules of vapor and prevents them from re-entering the liquid.

Evaporation from the surface of a continuous liquid is more rapid than that from moist soil at the same temperature. Yet land is usually warmer than water in the same locality; and a rain forest in the tropics, because of tremendous leaf surface, presents an extra area for evaporation and hence leads to evaporation that is often more rapid than that from a fresh water pond of the same temperature.

Evaporation from the land areas of the earth is much more irregular and variable than that from the surface of water. As the temperature is lowered or as the land becomes drier, evaporation decreases toward zero. There is some evaporation from snowfields and icecaps, though it is very slow.

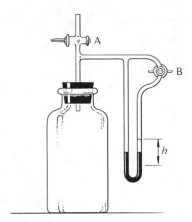

Figure 3-4. Demonstrating Vapor Pressure
With the stopcocks A and B open, air is pumped from the apparatus. Then B
is closed and a droplet of a volatile liquid is admitted through A. Evaporation
of the liquid promptly displaces mercury in the gage tube through a distance
h. Even without the removal of air, almost the same difference of level is attained at equilibrium if B is open into the air instead of connecting with A,
but more time is needed because evaporation is slower.

Vapor Pressure

Water will not evaporate indefinitely into a vacuum or a confined or
stagnant sample of air. After a time, some of the vapor molecules that
have escaped from the liquid begin to find their way back into it. Finally, as many molecules re-enter the liquid during each second as escape from it. There is then equilibrium (a condition of balance) between evaporation and recondensation. The escaping vapor sets up a
pressure—easily demonstrated, as in Figure 3-4. When equilibrium is
reached, this pressure reaches a maximum and thereafter remains constant, so long as the temperature remains unchanged.

The term vapor pressure usually refers to the maximum or equilibrium
pressure set up by the vapor escaping from a liquid, at a specified temperature. One may expose water to evaporation in a deep or shallow
layer or pour it over straw. The quantity of vapor that it will yield to a
cubic foot of air or vacuum and the maximum pressure that the vapor
will create at each temperature will be the same in all cases.

As the temperature is raised, evaporation becomes more and more
rapid, hence the vapor pressure increases, too—slowly at first, then

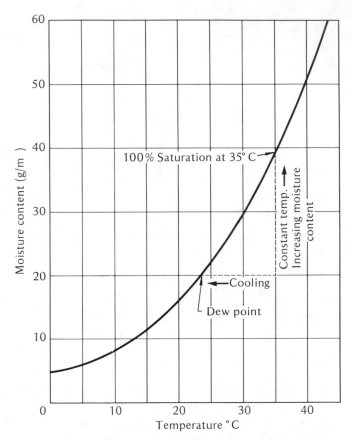

Figure 3-5. Vapor Pressure Curve for Water
Dotted lines show that vapor may be condensed to liquid by cooling or compression, while temperature is held constant by removing heat.

more and more rapidly, as shown in Figure 3-5. In the end, the pressure of the escaping vapor is great enough to overcome the pressure
of the atmosphere—to push back the atmosphere. The liquid then boils
—evaporates freely, not only from its original surface but from the surface of bubbles forming within the liquid. Steam is water vapor formed
at the boiling point of water.

Figure 3-5 shows that the boiling point of a liquid is raised by increasing the pressure upon it and that it is lowered by decreasing the
pressure. "Pressure cooking" of tough meats and vegetables is cooking

under increased pressure, to gain increased temperature; whereas vacuum drying of milk or other liquids is drying under reduced pressure (a partial vacuum) in order to get rid of water quickly without raising the temperature very much.

Vapor pressure, when it is not very large, is usually expressed in millimeters of mercury. This is the difference in level, h, that pressure of the vapor will support in the U-tube (see Figure 3-4) when it contains mercury.

Moisture in the Atmosphere

Dry air may be so dry that it takes a good desiccant (drying agent) to show that it contains any moisture at all. Moist air may contain so much moisture that this moisture exerts the maximum or equilibrium pressure for water at that temperature. It is then said to be saturated.

If saturated air is free from dust particles or ions (electrically charged particles) it may usually be cooled a few degrees without depositing any liquid moisture. It is then supersaturated. The best way to express the moisture content of air is as a weight ratio—the weight of water contained in a unit weight of air (1 pound of 1 kilogram of air, weighed dry). Less convenient is the absolute humidity (the weight of moisture in 1 liter or 1 cubic meter of air). Since the volume of an air sample varies with the temperature, the absolute humidity does, too.

Weather observers, in reporting the humidity of the atmosphere, usually state the relative humidity—the moisture in it, expressed as a percentage of that in an equal volume of fully saturated air at the same temperature. At inland locations, all day long, the weight ratio of moisture in the air remains very nearly constant. By contrast, the relative humidity—because it is always reckoned in comparison with what the air could contain if fully saturated at the increased temperature—always falls off rapidly as the day advances. It is least at the hottest part of the day—usually in the early afternoon. Air that is 100 per cent saturated in the early morning at 65°F is only 50 per cent saturated when the temperature has risen to 85°F.

The most accurate measurements of relative humidity are made with a wet-and-dry bulb thermometer. This is actually two thermometers, one which (the dry bulb) measures the temperature of the surrounding air. The other (the wet bulb) measures the temperature of air that is continuously cooled by evaporation of water from a wick. To ensure rapid evaporation, the wet bulb is exposed to a brisk breeze (at least 10 feet per second), or the two bulbs are swung in a circle at the end of a string.

The drier the air the more rapidly water evaporates from the wet bulb, withdrawing heat from it; hence, the greater the difference in temperature, the more rapidly heat flows back into the wet bulb from the surrounding air. Finally, the rate at which heat flows back equals the rate at which heat is withdrawn by evaporation. The temperature difference remains constant, no matter how long the whirling continues.

Evaporation and Precipitation Statistics

From measurements of evaporation rates under different conditions, it is possible to estimate the total rate at which water evaporates over the earth as a whole. This is in fairly close agreement with the total net rate of precipitation, as given by rainfall and snowfall measurements. (Every raindrop or snowflake that falls through unsaturated air is diminished by evaporation as it falls—hence, only net rates of precipitation can be measured.)

Evaporation from the ocean is about 83,700 cubic miles a year. This would lower the ocean's level about 3 inches every month, were this water not continuously recondensed and returned to the ocean. In addition, about 16,000 cubic miles of fresh water are evaporated every year, from lakes and rivers, moist soils, and (most important of all) the leaves of vegetation.

One might perhaps expect evaporation from the ocean to be most rapid at the Equator. However, equatorial regions are usually blanketed with clouds, which reflect a good part of the incoming solar energy. Most rapid evaporation is, therefore, not at the equator itself but 15° to 30° on either side of it. In the Red Sea and Arabian Sea, which are nearly landlocked, evaporation is so rapid that their water is much more saline than the neighboring Indian Ocean.

Indeed, the rate that the Red Sea loses water by evaporation is such that its level would decrease over 11 inches in an average month if it were completely cut off from the adjoining ocean. This compares with an evaporation of only 1 to 3 inches a month from fresh water lakes and ponds of the North Temperate Zone. This is in spite of the fact that the fresh water has a higher vapor pressure than salt water, hence evaporates about 10 to 40 per cent more rapidly than sea water at the same temperature and with the same wind velocity.

If precipitation were uniform, over land and sea alike, every part of the earth would receive about 8 inches of rainfall a month the year around. This would be sufficient for every human need. Yet nature so disregards human needs that about three-fourths of the total precipitation is over the ocean, where there is water enough already; and the rainfall that the land receives ranges from zero in a few desert regions to an average of about 40 inches a month in isolated regions of excessive rainfall (the Amazon Valley, equatorial Africa, and a good part of Southeast Asia). In addition, the great Antarctic continent, Greenland, and a few widely scattered areas in mountainous regions have a burden of snow and ice that steadily increases wherever glaciers do not remove it at a more than compensating rate.

Precipitation may vary even more than evaporation does, with very slight changes in conditions. Within the city limits of Honolulu, visitors are amazed by the lush vegetation and abundant rainfall of mountain valleys through which moisture-laden breezes ascend, depositing moisture as they go; yet, only a few miles away, are semi-desert areas, dominated by coarse grass, cactus, and scrub trees.

Precipitation varies unpredictably from year to year in any given place. Even in areas like the American central and eastern states, in which rainfall in an average year is satisfactory, in some years there may be a disastrous drought, in which cities run short of water, and later in the same year there may be floods, which sweep away roads and bridges, ruin farmlands, bury villages and towns in mud, waist deep, and destroy in a few moments engineering works that took men and machines months or years to construct.

The Cooling Effect of Evaporation

The cooling effect of evaporation is familiar to everyone and has been put to use since prehistoric times. A farmer or yachtsman raises a wet finger to determine the direction of the wind. Natives of desert and semi-desert lands cool drinking water by suspending it in a breezy place in porous-walled earthen jugs. Water seeping through the pores evaporates from the outer surface of the jugs, cooling the water that still remains. If the air is dry enough (as in Palm Springs, California, for example) one may even cool a house by trickling water onto straw or excelsior that is exposed to a blast from an electric fan.

Almost exactly 100 calories of heat are needed to heat 1 gram of liquid water from its freezing point (0°C) to its boiling point (100°C). Then 540 more calories are needed in changing the water into vapor, without increasing its temperature in the least. In brief, the evaporation of water causes heat to disappear—about 5.4 times as much heat as is needed to heat liquid water from the freezing to the boiling temperature.

It is easy to explain why heat disappears when water or any other liquid is evaporated: a molecule within the liquid can burst through the surface layer of molecules and escape into the vapor only if it has more than the average speed, hence more than the average kinetic energy at that temperature. Its departure leaves the molecules that remain with less than the former average energy, that is to say, with less than the former temperature. (Section D of the Appendix explains that temperature is a measure of the energy of an average molecule.)

The heat that disappears in the evaporation of a liquid was formerly said to become "latent" because it seemed to lie hidden, to reappear as heat if the water vapor recondensed to liquid water. Actually, latent heat is not heat, but a form of potential energy—energy that depends on a force (in this case, the force of mutual attraction between the molecules of water vapor). This force increases very rapidly as the vapor molecules approach one another more and more closely and finally condense into liquid water.

The heat that disappears when water evaporates is greater than for an equal number of molecules of any other liquid. The force of mutual attraction between the molecules of liquid water must therefore be unusually strong. As evaporation takes place at higher and higher temperatures, the heat that disappears in evaporation continuously decreases. It becomes zero at the liquid's critical temperature—the temperature at which a heat-expanded liquid is indistinguishable from (identical with) compressed vapor, in equilibrium with it.

Every year 96,000 to 100,000 cubic miles of water are evaporated from the earth. The process requires about a fifth of all the radiant energy that reaches the earth from the sun, and nearly half of all that the earth temporarily retains. (Some radiant energy immediately reradiates into space by reflection from clouds or dust or the molecules of the gases of the earth's atmosphere.)

The mantle of liquid water and water vapor that surrounds the earth acts as a great thermostat, decreasing temperature differences and moderating climates the world around. Temperatures are prevented from mounting too high by the disappearance of heat in evaporation; and the lowering of the temperature of an air mass as it passes over a mountain is kept within bounds if the mass contains moisture that is precipitated as rain or snow, thus releasing heat.

The energy output of the sun fluctuates a little (about 2 to 5 per cent on either side of its average value). Nevertheless, an increase in solar activity increases the rate at which heat disappears in the evaporation of water from the earth's store of liquid water. Thus the earth has a fair degree of immunity from damage that might otherwise have come from the erratic behavior of the sun.

The Transport of Energy by Water Vapor

The winds that carry water from evaporation sites to the ends of the earth are also carriers of energy. A one-inch rain over a square mile of area deposits about 72,000 tons of liquid water. The heat released in the condensation of this much water from water vapor is roughly that released by burning 6500 tons of anthracite coal (about 9 per cent of the weight of the water precipitated). Both water and energy—and both, for the most part, invisibly—are adrift with every breeze.

When heat is released in the recondensation of water vapor to liquid water, it helps to determine the force and direction of the very wind that transports it. During the torrential rains that accompany every tropical hurricane, the heat set free increases the uplift and rouses the circling winds as though a gigantic top were being lashed by a whip. Energy pours into the hurricane as insolation (radiant energy, received directly from the sun) and as heat, released in precipitation. This input becomes kinetic energy (section A, Appendix) in rousing winds, and gravitational potential energy, in lifting air to a higher elevation.

When a low-pressure air that is connected with a hurricane passes from tropical into temperate latitudes, especially after it becomes cloud-capped, energy input by insolation almost ceases. Afterward, when precipitation begins to slacken because the air mass is running out of moisture, the release of heat by precipitation begins to slacken too. The hurricane then just coasts to a stop, like a car that has run out of gas. Its life, from its moment of maximum energy, depends on the character and roughness of the surface over which it is passing, while its kinetic energy is being dissipated (converted into heat). Over the ocean, a moderate hurricane may last more than a week after it begins to fade: but over mountainous land, it may be largely dissipated in a single day.

A hurricane of moderate size (diameter, 100 miles) whirls 235 billion tons of air with an average speed of perhaps 50 miles an hour and may continue about two weeks. This represents 1.483×10^{10} kilowatt hours of energy. If such a hurricane could be harnessed to generate electrical energy, it would duplicate the hydroelectric output of Niagara Falls, which is determined by present international agreements, during about four months. The energy of even an ordinary thunderstorm is that of a small (120 kiloton) atomic bomb; and the earth's atmosphere spawns and dissipates about 10,000 such storms during an average day.

In a leisurely way, during the course of ages, running water has scoured away mountains and uplands and deposited the resultant particles as loamy soil in distant valleys or as silt in forming deltas at the mouths of rivers, or as ooze and precipitated salts over ocean bottoms. The weight of these transported mountain ranges irresistibly depresses the ocean beds, while the continents, relieved of their titanic burden, spring upward. Thus the solid and apparently rigid crust of the earth, as ages pass, appears to ripple.

We tend to ascribe the gradual wearing away of the mountains and uplands to the disintegrating chemical effects of air and moisture, supplemented by scouring and grinding by running water and ice. Yet it was energy from the sun that elevated water in the first place and carried it to distant locations, where it was deposited as rain or snow wherever the ground was not level. All these processes, endlessly remolding the surface of the earth, are accomplished by energy brought in by water vapor and transported by winds that the water vapor itself helped to rouse.

Incoming and Outgoing Radiant Energy

About 40 per cent of the energy that reaches the earth from the sun is at once reflected back into space, almost unaltered in frequency, by high-flying clouds, or is scattered by dust particles or molecules of the gases of the atmosphere, or is expended in creating ozone in the upper atmosphere. About 15 per cent of the energy that reaches the earth is absorbed (changed into heat) in passing through the atmosphere. This part heats the atmosphere directly. The rest (about 40 to 45 per cent of the incoming solar energy) gets through to the surface of the earth and heats the lands or ocean and evaporates water.

Thus the lower atmosphere is not only heated but is mingled with water vapor. Both of these changes make air less dense, because water vapor weighs only about 62 per cent as much as an equal volume of dry air under the same conditions. Decreased density makes the atmosphere unstable: its lower layers rise, winds are created, and there is world-wide air circulation.

If the upper atmosphere absorbed more solar energy than penetrated to the earth beneath, the earth's surface would be as if submerged in a hot vapor bath and might be uninhabitable by human beings. A stagnant atmosphere may be one reason why our sister planet, Venus, is so unlike the earth.

Winds, roused in an unstable atmosphere by the incoming energy of the sun, transport energy as heated air and especially as moist air. (When air that has been saturated with water vapor at 70°F is cooled to 32°F, a little more than half the heat set free comes from the condensation of water vapor into liquid water.)

Ocean Currents

Winds also move heat indirectly by creating surface currents in the ocean. Prevailing winds, blowing ceaselessly over the ocean, yield a part of their kinetic energy to the water beneath. Prevailing ocean currents, thus produced, flow in directions that are in part determined by prevailing winds; yet they are always deflected by the earth's rotation in the direction that the sun appears to move—toward the right (clockwise) in the Northern Hemisphere and toward the left (counterclockwise) in the Southern Hemisphere. The course of the surface currents in the ocean is also in part determined by the contours of the continents and the location and depths of seas.

Each of the earth's seven oceans has its own surface current, circling endlessly "with the sun" about a quiet area, while constantly yielding a part of its flow to mingle with that of neighboring oceans. Thus a bottle tossed into the mid-Atlantic may turn up on the shores of Madagascar or China. Each of these circling "rivers in the sea" branches, meanders, and alters its direction and speed from moment to moment and from season to season.

The most famous surface current is the Gulf Stream, which has been estimated to transport about 75 times the volume of water carried by all of the earth's fresh water rivers, or about 500 times the flow of the Mississippi. It moves from the Gulf of Mexico an accumulation of heat that might otherwise make Florida as tropical as Yucatan; and it delivers this heat on the other side of the Atlantic, permitting palms to grow in southwest Ireland, and giving England, Holland, and France an earlier and more balmy springtime than is enjoyed by New England.

The great ocean currents do much to determine climate. A cubic mile of warm surface ocean current, for each degree Fahrenheit above the temperature of the surrounding ocean, transports as much heat as would be set free by burning 350,000 tons of anthracite coal. Yet the annual flow of the Gulf Stream is about 650,000 cubic miles and it begins with a temperature surplus (beyond that of the surrounding ocean) of about 20°F.

Many surface currents have a profound effect on the distribution of marine species. The frigid sub-surface Humboldt current, flowing northward along the coast of Chile from its origin in the Antarctic, upwells off the coast of Peru, bringing in plankton that serves as food for a wonderful profusion of marine life, from cuttlefish to whales. Fish-eating sea birds have inhabited these waters for ages, in such myriads that a seemingly inexhaustible deposit of guano has accumulated on all the neighboring shores.

No matter what form energy takes, as it circles the earth in wind, wave, or ocean current, it is all finally converted into heat. Yet every object, hot or cold, is constantly exchanging radiant energy with its surroundings, at a rate that increases rapidly with increasing temperature. The earth not only absorbs radiant energy from the sun, but re-radiates it into space, chiefly as longwave infrared (radiant energy with twenty- to twenty-five-fold increased wavelength, as compared with incoming solar energy. This increase in wavelength comes from the fact that the temperature of the earth is so much lower than that of the sun (section C, Appendix).

Income and outgo of radiant energy, for the earth as a whole, nearly balance. Any net loss is in part made good by energy set free by radioactive minerals and heat set free as the friction of the tides very gradually slows down the earth's rotation. The earth, moreover, doubtless still has part of its original store of heat. It has probably remained very near its present temperature during the uncounted ages since life first appeared upon it.

Ascending and Descending Air

In ascending, air is cooled because it does work (expends energy) in expanding, pushing back the overlying or surrounding air. The cooling may be sufficient to bring the ascending air to its dew point. Thus a cloud is formed. A flat-bottomed cloud shows that air with a nearly uniform temperature and humidity is rising, so that the dew point is reached at a definite elevation. Descending air is heated, potential energy being changed into heat. Clouds then tend to disappear.

A column of air is stable when it tends neither to fall nor rise. It is then neither gaining nor losing energy by radiation, and has at every level a temperature that remains steady. In a stable air column, air at every level is in equilibrium with that at a slightly lower or higher level. Any molecule of air that descends in such a column loses potential energy, which is converted into heat. The reverse is true of any molecule that ascends. Thus the lowest part of the earth's atmosphere tends to be the warmest.

Air that contains no liquid or solid particles (in brief, air that is free from clouds or mist) has a lapse rate (rate of temperature decrease) of about 5.5°F for each 1000-feet increase in elevation. Dry air having a temperature of 70°F at sea level is likely to be at about 15°F at 10,000 feet, and —40°F at 20,000 feet.

The lapse rate for a rising mass of air is usually less than that just stated, because the kinetic energy of the updraft supplies force that would otherwise have to come from heat. For that contains suspended droplets of liquid water or particles of ice, the lapse rate is still less— usually 2° to 3°F for each 1000 feet. The air then has no great tendency toward convection (bodily mixing by updrafts and downdrafts).

4

Climates, Winds, and Weather

The Earth's Primary Climatic Zones

The relative sizes of the earth's primary climatic zones are determined by the angle (about 23½°) that the earth's axis makes with the plane in which the earth moves around the sun. The equatorial or Torrid Zone extends from 23½° north to 23½° south of the Equator, which is about 40 per cent of the earth's surface. About 70 per cent of the Torrid Zone is ocean. The sun moves north or south with changing seasons, but the limits of its travel are the limits of the Torrid Zone. Thus the sun shines vertically over some part of this zone every minute of the year.

In consequence of the sun being directly above, a good part of the Torrid Zone is covered the year around, by a belt of moisture-laden rising air—the doldrums. This is a realm of cloud-capped oceans, prolonged calms, light, indecisive breezes, and sudden squalls. In the days of sailing ships, vessels would often lie becalmed for weeks, while their crews ran short of drinking water or were decimated by scurvy. Then, in an instant would come the threat of a squall. Everyone able to stir would be summoned into the rigging to take in every shred of sail.

The doldrums shift north and south with the sun, as season follows season. The Equator is crossed, twice each year, by the sun, at the time of the equinoxes (Figure 4-1). Thus there are two rainy seasons near the Equator, each beginning several weeks after an equinox. As one goes farther and farther from the Equator, the two rainy seasons fall closer and closer together and finally merge.

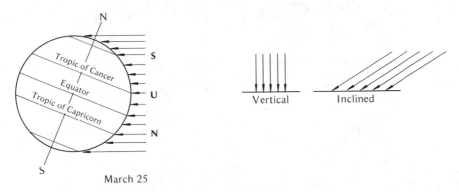

Figure 4-1. The Earth in Orbit, Spring Equinox

Adjoining the Torrid Zone, north and south, are the two temperate zones. Each of these extends to within 23½° of the North or South Pole. Each accounts for 26 per cent of the earth's surface. The sun never shines vertically on any part of the temperate zones, though it does shine at a slant, continuously on some part of them, every moment of the year. Observe (Figure 4-1) that the effect of slanting rays is to spread the incoming rays over a greater area of the earth's surface, hence to make the heating less intense.

The Arctic and Antarctic zones surround the earth's poles at a distance of 23½° of latitude. The sun is visible in each of them for only a part of the year, and at most only six months in any year. Each of these zones accounts for only 4 per cent of the earth's surface. Nevertheless, the Arctic Zone plays an important part in determining the climate of the Northern Hemisphere, since it is the site of a downpouring of cold air, which it seems to deliver in a series of giant puffs, almost the year around.

In the two temperate zones and especially in the two arctic zones, less heat is received from the sun over each square mile of the earth's surface, hence less water is evaporated into the atmosphere than in the Torrid Zone. Do not conclude, however, that the farther a locality is from the equator the less heat it gets from the sun. Latitudes more than 23½ degrees from the equator never have the sun directly overhead. This is a handicap in getting energy from the sun; but it is more than offset by the extra length of the day in sufficiently high latitudes, during all of the summer months.

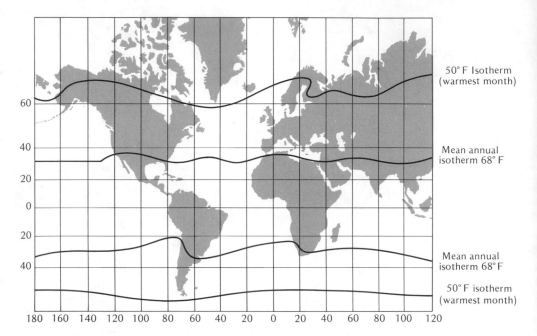

Figure 4-2. Climatic Zones (based on average temperatures)

The greatest input of solar energy during the summer is at about the latitude of New York. The solar input falls off rapidly as one passes northward into Canada. Yet even the borders of the Arctic Zone get enough heat and rainfall, every summer, to support an amazing flora and fauna.

Although the zones into which the earth is divided in Figure 4-1 are called climatic zones, one should not conclude that climate is chiefly determined by the angle at which the sun's rays reach the earth. A better representation of climate is shown in Figure 4-2, in which the lines that separate the different zones are mean annual isotherms—lines that connect points of equal average temperature. Observe that mountain ranges sometimes cause isotherms to take a north-south direction.

The Coriolis Effect

The ancients believed that the earth stood still and that the sun circled around it once in every 24 hours. If this were actually true the principal movements of the earth's atmosphere would be very simple; upward

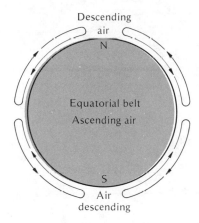

Figure 4-3. Primary Air Circulation Over a Non-rotating Earth

in a broad belt of calms near the Equator; poleward at high elevations; downward in the polar regions, in both the Northern and Southern hemispheres; thence, due north and south, except as deflected by mountain ranges, in returning to the tropics over the surface of the earth. This simple pattern of flow is shown in Figure 4-3. The rotation of the earth changes the simple pattern into the complicated one shown in Figure 4-4.

The angular rate of rotation of the earth is everywhere once in 24 hours; but the linear rate, in miles per hour or feet per second, is greater at the Equator and dwindles away to zero at the poles. We have spoken of the steadily rising air of the doldrums. Adjoining the doldrums, north and south, descending air comes over parts of the earth's surface that are all rotating toward the east, but each with a little higher linear velocity than the preceding one. The descending air is left behind; in other words, is deflected toward the west. Thus we account for the trade winds, whose steady and undeviating urge brought dismay and near panic to the crews of Columbus' ships.

For the same reason, when ocean currents approach the Equator, they too are deflected toward the west. When they approach the poles the effect of the earth's rotating is felt even more strongly, but deflection is in the opposite direction, i.e., toward the east.

Coriolis, a French engineer, perceived (1835) that the earth's rotation appears to deflect every object moving over the earth's surface as if the object at any point were acted upon by an imaginary force proportional

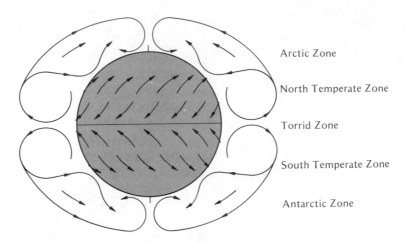

Figure 4-4. Effects of the Earth's Rotation on Primary Air Circulation
Central circle: directions of prevailing winds near surface. Outside central
circle: trends at different elevations.

to the velocity of the body and to the sine of the latitude (the ratio
o/h in Figure 4-6). Deflection is toward the right (clockwise) in the
northern and toward the left (counterclockwise) in the Southern Hemisphere. It is greatest near the poles, and zero at the Equator.

The Coriolis force arises from the fact that the movement of masses
over the earth's surface is usually referred to a moving coordinate system (that is, the latitude and longtitude grid which rotates with the
earth). The simplest way to begin to visualize the manner in which this
deflecting force operates is to picture a rotating disc on which moving
objects are deflected. Figure 4-5 shows the effect of such a deflective
force operating on a mass moving outward from the center of a spinning disc. The body follows a straight path in relation to a fixed frame
of reference (for instance, a box which contains a spinning disc), but
viewed relative to coordinates rotating with the disc the body swings
to the right of its initial line of motion. This effect is readily demonstrated if a pencil line is drawn across a white disc on a rotating turntable. Figure 4-5 illustrates a case where the movement is not from the
center of the turntable and the object passes an initial momentum in
relation to its distance from the axis of rotation. In the analogous case
of the rotating earth (with rotating reference coordinates of latitude
and longitude), there is apparent deflection of moving objects to the
right of their line of motion in the Northern Hemisphere and to the left

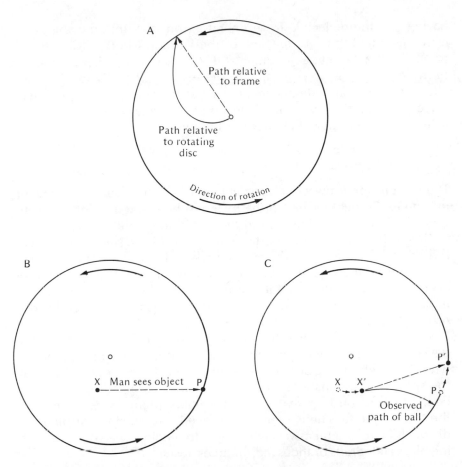

Figure 4-5. Coriolis Force
From *Atmosphere, Weather and Climate* by R. G. Barry and R. J. Chorley (Holt,
Rinehart and Winston, 1970), Figures 3-1 and 3-2. Used by permission.

in the Southern Hemisphere, as viewed by observers on the earth. The
deflective force (per unit mass) is expressed by:

$$-2\omega V \sin \phi$$

where ω = the angular velocity of spin ($15°$/h or $2\pi/24$ radians/h for
the earth = 7.29×10^{-5} radians/sec); ϕ = the latitude and V = the
velocity of the mass. $2\omega\sin\phi$ is referred to as the Coriolis parameter (f).

The magnitude of the deflection is directly proportional to: (a) the
horizontal velocity of the air (that is, air moving at 11 m/sec (25 mph)

having half the deflective force operating on it as that moving at 22 m/sec (50 mph); and (b) the sine of the latitude (sin $0° = 0$; sin $90° = 1$). The effect is thus a maximum at the poles (that is, where the plane of the deflecting force is parallel to the earth's surface) and decreases with the sine of latitude becoming zero at the Equator (that is, where there is no component of the deflection in a plane parallel to the surface). Values of f vary with latitude as follows:

Latitude	0°	10°	20°	43°	90°
f (10^4/sec)	0	0.25	0.50	1.00	1.458

The Coriolis force always acts at right angles to the direction of the air motion to the right in the Northern Hemisphere and at right angles to the direction of the air motion to the left in the Southen Hemisphere.

The Coriolis force is of importance in meteorology, since it influences the primary circulation of the atmosphere and joins with other factors to determine the direction of every breeze. It also helps to control every tidal and nontidal ocean current. It must be taken into account in ballistics (the flight of projectiles) and in launching lunar and earth-orbiting satellites.

Some biologists believe that homing birds and bees can sense the deviating effect of the Coriolis force and use it (perhaps in conjunction with the height of the sun or the length of daylight) to find their way toward distant destinations. The most remarkable fact about migrating eels, fish, and birds is that young members of the species, making the trip for the first time, seem not to need the guidance of older individuals in finding their way, unerringly, to feeding, spawning, or nesting places hundreds or thousands of miles away.

Prevailing Winds

The prevailing winds of the Northern Hemisphere are here summarized. Winds from the west are represented by → and winds from the east by ←. Descending and ascending air masses are represented by ↓ and ↑, respectively.

Arctic Zone (northern Alaska and Canada, Siberia)	Polar high pressure area ↓
Temperate Zone (southern Canada, the United States, most of Europe).	Winds at all elevations →
Tropical Zone	Winds over 25,000 feet →
	Winds near the surface ←
Equatorial Belt	The doldrums ↑

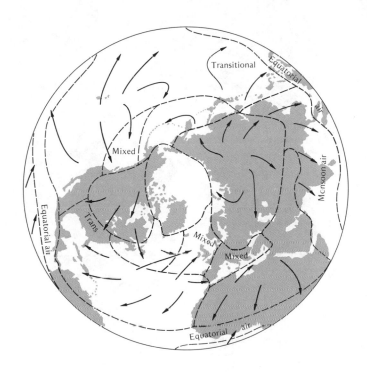

Figure 4-6. Air Masses in Winter
From *Atmosphere, Weather and Climate* by R. G. Barry and R. J. Chorley (Holt,
Rinehart and Winston, 1970), Figure 4-1. Used by permission.

The winds of the Southern are like those of the Northern Hemisphere, except that the greater expanse of ocean makes them somewhat less complicated. The only places in which the winds at all elevations are from the west are parts of the temperate zones in both the Northern and Southern hemispheres. This fact tends to simplify the weather patterns of the United States and Europe.

The prevailing winds of the earth's primary climatic zones are the primary circulation of the earth's atmosphere. Figures 4-6 and 4-7 display them in some detail. They join with the contours of elevated land areas and rates of evaporation in each climatic zone to fix the general distribution of snowfall or rainfall, over all the surface of the earth. These all join to determine what part of earth's fresh water shall fall upon or drain away through each nation.

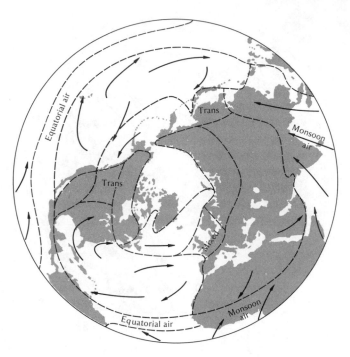

Figure 4-7. Air Masses in Summer
From *Atmosphere, Weather and Climate* by R. G. Barry and R. J. Chorley (Holt, Rinehart and Winston, 1970), Figure 4-4. Used by permission.

Secondary or Minor Air Circulations

There are regions in which a secondary air circulation is important or even dominant, at least at certain seasons of the year. An example is India and its neighbors in Southeast Asia. Cold, dry air, descending in a high pressure area in central Siberia, flows southward through passes of the Himalayan Mountains, and even overrides many of their peaks, and in January spreads out over the Indian plains. By its descent it is warmed, so that clouds rarely form, while those that do appear are quickly dispersed and do not release very much rain.

Six months later, conditions are reversed. During July, the bare rocks of the mountain peaks and passes heat the air above them, creating a vigorous updraft. Warm, moist air flows in from the Indian Ocean and replaces the air that is rising. Thus we account for the warm "monsoon breeze," which brings abundant rain. In Vietnam and its neighbors there is also a monsoon season, usually a few weeks later than the one in India.

Other local air circulations may be determined by warm or cold ocean currents or by the contours of the land. During the hot part of every day, land along a seacoast heats up rapidly, heats the air above it, and creates an updraft. Cool, moist air from over the neighboring ocean flows in to replace the uplifted air and we have a "sea breeze," flowing landward. After sunset, as the land continues to radiate heat, it is likely to become colder than the water in the ocean. Air over the ocean then rises and its place is taken by air brought in by a "land breeze," blowing toward the ocean.

In much the same way, rocky and bare mountain peaks heat the air above them, and air flows toward them, all day long. At night, conditions are reversed and so, too, is the wind direction.

Something rather different is observed when air ascending a mountain valley is cooled and begins to deposit moisture. The heat set free in the precipitation makes the air warmer than it otherwise would be, but there is less uplift because dry air is denser than moist air. The air, having lost part of its moisture, may continue right up over the crest of the range and descend through the valleys beyond it. Clouds on the lee side of a rainy summit usually just fade away, and aircraft find safe landing places. Sometimes the lee side of a rainy summit is so dry that it supports only a sparse desert vegetation. Thus we account for the near-desert conditions of a good part of the states of Nevada and Arizona.

Stable and Unstable Air Masses

A set of conditions or a group of bodies is said to be stable if it automatically returns to its former condition after being slightly disturbed. Thus a pendulum at rest at the lowest point of its swing is in a stable condition, and so is a floating log. An air mass is stable when its temperature and humidity are uniform over a considerable area at every elevation. The rate of temperature decrease with increasing elevation is then always normal for air of that temperature and humidity.

Stable air masses are rainless, relatively quiet, and not subject to mixing by updrafts or downdrafts. They are formed whenever air, losing energy by radiation, descends in a high pressure area and spreads out over an ocean or a wide continental plain of nearly uniform temperature. They are formed in five different geographical locations (Figures 4-6 and 4-7): Arctic (A), maritime Polar (mP), continental Polar (cP), maritime Tropical (mT), and continental Tropical (cT). The temperate zones do not form stable air masses, seemingly because the shape of the continents or the existence of mountain ranges or warm or cold ocean currents does not favor the formation of a quiet atmosphere over a sufficiently wide area.

The colder an air mass is the less moisture it contains, regardless of its place of origin. Yet as it wanders away from its place or origin it gradually changes its character by gaining or losing moisture or radiant energy. The rate at which this happens depends on many factors, the most important of which are the climatic zone, the season of the year, whether the air mass is moving over land or water, the difference in temperature between it and the land or water beneath it, the upslope or downslope of the terrain, and whether land over which it is passing is forested or bare. Changes in the temperature or humidity of an air mass begin at the surface of the earth and progress upward until the whole mass has changed its character and has perhaps become unstable.

Stable air masses meet along fronts that appear to advance or recede as they exchange energy with their surroundings or with one another. A cold front is one in which descending cold air underruns and lifts adjacent warm air, often rendering the latter unstable. Sometimes warm air moves into a region in such quantities that it overwhelms a mass of colder air, thus creating a warm front. A stationary front is one that for the moment neither advances nor recedes.

In the temperate zones stable air masses nearly always move from west to east, in the same direction as the prevailing winds. Your morning weather map may show a maritime polar air mass that has just moved in from the Pacific Ocean in the latitude of Oregon, bringing plenty of moisture with it. Several days afterward, the same air mass, moving eastward, may have become unstable in passing over the Rocky Mountains, and may be depositing snow or rain, from Colorado through Idaho and Montana into adjoining southern Canada. Later yet, the air mass (still cold, but with regained stability) may be in contact with uplifting warm, moist air that has moved inland from the Gulf of Mexico. The result may be rain and tornadoes in the northern borders of the Gulf States, then floods in the Ohio Valley. Finally, an air mass that originally came into existence in the Pacific Ocean may pass out over the New England States into the Atlantic, and there may lose its identity.

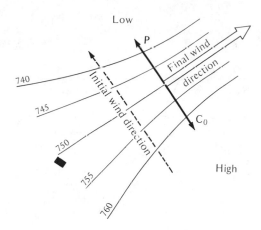

Figure 4-8. Pressure Gradient Force

What Determines Wind Direction

Until about three hundred years ago everyone believed that a steady force must be applied to an object to keep it moving with unchanging speed. Then Newton perceived how wrong this idea is. To make anything move with unchanging speed a force needs to be applied only where there is friction, and then there need be only enough force to overcome the friction. With friction absent or overcome by a force, unchanging speed shows that no force is being applied to the moving object or that applied forces balance.

The most evident force acting on the moving air is that owing to a difference of pressure. This is proportional to the change in pressure that occurs in traversing unit distance, in the direction in which pressure is most rapidly changing. For this reason it is called the pressure gradient force. It is represented by P in Figure 4-8.

The outlined white arrows in this figure indicate the direction and speed of a steady breeze. When the air begins to move, it is more and more deflected by the rotation of the earth toward the right (clockwise) in the Northern Hemisphere and toward the left (counterclockwise) in the Southern Hemisphere. We may think of this deflection is being caused by a Coriolis force, C_0, as applied at the tip of the white arrow and blending the arrow toward the right or left, according to the hemisphere. Since the wind finally blows with constant speed

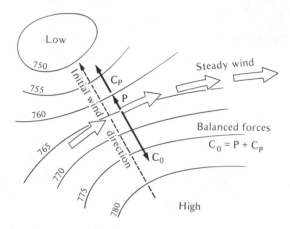

Figure 4-9. Wind Above a High-Pressure Area, Northern Hemisphere

we know that the Coriolis force and pressure gradient force are then
equal but act in opposite directions and hence balance.

Winds at an altitude of several thousand feet are nearly tangent to
the isobars and at right angles to the pressure gradient force. This is
the so-called gradient wind. The surface wind, weakened and deflected
by friction, is more nearly in line with the pressure gradient force.

From the sine of the latitude and the observed wind velocity one
may calculate the Coriolis force, hence may infer the pressure gradient
force. Then, if the barometric pressure is known for a few points in a
region, one may plot isobars (lines connecting points of equal pressure) with fair accuracy for the whole region.

In what has just been said we have disregarded another force, which
for fast winds is more important than either of the others. This is centrifugal force, C_f, which is felt whenever air or anything else is whirling
with even moderate speed.

Figure 4-9 shows what happens when air is descending in a high-
pressure area in the Northern Hemisphere. The pressure gradient force,
P, acts from high pressure toward lower pressure and sets the air to
moving toward the low pressure center. As the air moves, the Coriolis
force deflects it steadily toward the right (in the Northern Hemisphere). Presently, centrifugal force begins to be felt. It is always
directed outward, away from the center of rotation, and builds up rapidly as the wind gathers speed. Finally, when the wind is approximately
tangent to the isobars, $C_o = P + C_f$, that is, the Coriolis force is bal-

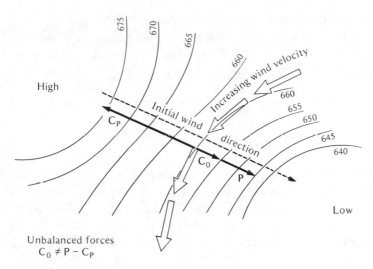

Figure 4-10. Wind Above a Low-Pressure Area, Northern Hemisphere

anced by the sum of the other two forces, and the wind becomes steady in direction and speed.

Figure 4-10 shows the contrary case, in which air is ascending in a low pressure area in the Northern Hemisphere. The pressure gradient force is still directed from high pressure toward lower pressure, but that is now toward the center of rotation. This reversal in direction still tends to deflect the motion toward the right, but it is the direction of the pressure gradient force that results (except for very low wind velocities) in a reversal in the direction of rotation. The Coriolis force may then be balanced by the difference between the other two forces, that is, $C_o = P - C_f$.

It is important to note that centrifugal force is proportional to the square of the wind velocity, whereas the pressure gradient force is proportional to the wind velocity itself. Thus with a moderate windspeed, $P - C_f$ becomes zero. At wind speeds just a trifle higher, $C_o = P - C_f$ becomes negative, hence the direction of rotation is reversed, becoming counter-clockwise in the Northern Hemisphere. As the wind velocity continues to increase, the counter-clockwise rotation becomes more and more violent, and equilibrium is never again regained. We now see why ascending air, in a cyclone or hurricane, is so destructive and dangerous. The isobars shown in Figures 4-9 and 4-10 are labeled with representative pressures in millibars (thousands of an atmosphere).

In short, the wind does blow, as one might expect, from high-pressure toward low-pressure areas. It begins to move in that direction, but soon "hauls around" to blow approximately tangent to the isobars. Its intensity and direction constantly change as it responds to accidental factors, such as changes in the intensity of incoming or outgoing radiant energy, or changes in temperature induced by precipitation.

Weather Forecasting

Our ideas about climate come from averaging temperature, rainfall or snowfall, humidity, wind velocity, days of sunshine or fog, etc., over many years. Because climate comes from averaging it appears to be stable. Weather, on the contrary, refers to the momentary state of a particular spot on the earth's surface together with the overlying atmosphere. It fluctuates erratically. Weather balloons, satellites, and weather observation stations on the ground gather weather data, simultaneously and automatically, over wide areas. Satellites also photograph cloud formations from as much as 2700 miles above the earth's surface and send back coded data on cloud formations, temperatures, humidity, and pressure. Radar permits rainfall to be observed at distances of up to about 200 miles.

Satellites also gather information about the amount and kind of radiation arriving at the earth from different directions in space, and about the chemical changes induced by radiation in the upper part of the atmosphere. All of these factors affect the weather. Radar stations, satellites, and airplanes track the movement of hurricanes, detect the approach of tornadoes, and determine the atmospheric conditions at various distances from the center of a disturbance.

Weather prediction must take into account the size and character of the dominant air mass and of others in contact with it. It is unlikely that any flood, prolonged drought, or large snowfall or rainfall will be duplicated in any given locality within a human lifetime. Yet computers, scanning current weather data in comparison with the experience of former years, may presently venture predictions two weeks in advance.

Conditions for Rainfall

Plenty of clouds but no rain is one of nature's most frustrating phenomena. Before the clouds formed, the air may have been very dry.

Even though the temperature may have been sufficiently reduced for the formation of a cloud, there may not be enough moisture in the cloud for water droplets to reach the size needed to descend as rain. The day is then destined to remain rainless, in spite of incantations. Cloudy months are often very dry ones.

When moisture condenses from supersaturated air into liquid droplets, each droplet forms about a dust particle or ion that serves as a nucleus for further condensation. Occasionally, air is so full of nuclei that the available moisture, divided among all of them, does not permit them to grow to sufficient size to descend as rain. This is one of the conditions for the formation of persistent smog in the neighborhood of great cities; and it is certainly a good reason for not expecting forest fires to be extinguished by rain.

At this point, alert readers might wonder why microscopic water droplets in a persistent haze or mist do not often combine to form drops that are large enough to fall as rain. There are two chief reasons: First, drops of liquid always become coated with a tightly adhering coating of absorbed air. Its presence is made evident whenever small droplets, falling into a basin of water, momentarily make little depressions in the liquid surface, instead of being immediately swallowed up. Second, the electrically charged dust particles or ions about which liquid has condensed to form a cloud of droplets are normally all of the same sign (all positively or all negatively charged). Particles of the same sign repel one another; thus the electrically charged particles less frequently collide and combine than they would if electrically neutral.

The electric charge on a cloud always attracts a charge of the opposite sign on the earth beneath it. Eventually, the difference in potential becomes so great that the electrical resistance of the atmosphere is overcome, and a bolt of lightning strikes through. Everyone has noticed how often a lightning flash is followed by a downpour of rain. The bolt decreases the charge in the individual droplets, so that their mutual repulsion is decreased, and they coalesce into drops that are large enough to fall to earth.

Figure 4-11 displays the chief factors that determine the behavior and fate of a raindrop. It is drifting sidewise with a velocity $\overline{a}$ (the horizontal component of the wind). Meanwhile, it is falling with a velocity $\underline{b}$, through an updraft that has the velocity $\overline{c}$. Thus its net rate of descent is $\underline{b} - c$.

If the air surrounding the droplet is supersaturated, the droplet steadily absorbs moisture from its surroundings, steadily gains weight

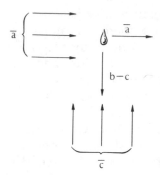

Figure 4-11. Fate of a Raindrop

and falls faster and faster. (In a vacuum, light and heavy droplets would fall at the same speed; but the friction of the atmosphere causes light drops to fall less rapidly than heavy ones.) As the rate of descent, $\overline{b}$, increases, the updraft, $\overline{c}$, may increase, too, because the droplet may reach an altitude at which the pressure gradient (the rate of change of pressure with changing altitude) is different. Finally, a steady state may be reached, in which $\overline{b} - \overline{c}$ remains constant. If $\overline{c}$ then exceeds $\overline{b}$, the droplet will never reach the earth. Many rains remain cloudborne.

There is one other point to be made, and one that is probably more important than that just mentioned. At temperatures below 32°F (0°C), some of the floating particles may be crystals of ice, rather than droplets of liquid water. At −20°F a good many of them and at −40°F nearly all of them are ice. Ice has a lower vapor pressure than liquid water at the same temperature. So, if ice particles are present, they gather in moisture, not only from surrounding supersaturated air, but also from neighboring droplets of liquid water. So we have evaporation of liquid water into water vapor, which is then condensed into ice. The ice particles, if they are not too numerous, grow enormously at the expense of their liquid neighbors. Finally, they are heavy enough to descend as hail through any ordinary updraft but as they do they may melt and become rain.

High-flying clouds are cold clouds. The best rain-makers are the towering cumulostratus clouds. Their upper strata (50,000 to 60,000 feet) are well below −40°C, hence precipitation from them always begins as ice spicules. These giants are the typical clouds of thunderstorms. Their interior is so turbulent that pilots of aircraft do their best to avoid them.

As rain pours from the base of one of these clouds, the cloud assumes an anvil shape. This is evidence that the ice particles or snowflakes that compose its upper strata are so very small that their rate of descent is very slow. Farmers, sailors, aviators, and amateur weather observers, by close observation of cloud forms, are able to learn a great deal about atmospheric conditions at different heights above the earth's surface. This is of great help in predicting the weather of the next few days.

Rain-making

Time was when rain-making, as practiced by the Indians, entailed a pow-wow, colorful paint, and the tribe's official rain-maker engaged in a violent and spectacular dance. Today we realize that rain-making is really just precipitation control—a purposeful alteration of a rain cloud.

Silver iodide "smoke," generated on the ground, may be carried into the clouds by updrafts, particularly in highland valleys, or may be scattered into clouds by small rockets. Precipitation as ice may thus be induced from supersaturated air at temperatures of 5° to 15°F.

Dry ice (solid carbon dioxide) induces precipitation only at a much lower temperature, beginning about −40°F (the temperature at which the precipitation of snow begins from very cold droplets of water in clouds). If a cloud is already near that temperature, the addition of a little powdered dry ice may have a spectacular effect.

Liquid water, sprayed into a cloud that is suspended in supersaturated air, furnishes droplets that are large enough to descend through moderate updrafts. On the way down, the descending droplets grow larger by incorporating into themselves some of the much smaller droplets that form the cloud. Dry ice and liquid water are expensive to use, since they must be introduced into the clouds by airplanes.

Rain-making has been attempted since about 1946 in many different parts of the world by national governments, private individuals, and corporations developing electric energy from impounded water. There may be some incidental benefits, since artificially induced precipitation, by decreasing the burden of water in the clouds, might decrease damage to crops by hail or, in forested areas, might lessen the risk of forest fires being kindled by lightning.

As experiments continue, the conditions (temperature, updraft velocity, relative humidity, abundance, scarcity of nuclei) that need to be considered in inducing precipitation will be better known and more easily measured. The mere general appearance of a cloud is, of course, some indication of its character.

Induced precipitation may some day be regularly practiced in regions in which the appropriate cloud conditions frequently occur. In too many cases, clouds dissipate or pass out to sea, where there is water enough already. It might seem to be no great triumph to induce precipitation where there might be precipitation without any aid, nevertheless, there are regions in which just a little more rain or snow would permit crops to be grown without irrigation.

Does artificially induced precipitation deprive downwind neighbors of rain that they would otherwise have received? That seems very unlikely. Only rarely does a rainstorm deposit much more than about 1 per cent of the moisture in a cloud. A rain usually stops, not because there is too little water in the cloud, but because the temperature of the cloud has increased, because the cloud is running out of nuclei, or because the updraft is too strong for raindrops of that size to reach the earth.

Rain Forests, Deserts, and Swamps

We now raise a question which from the beginning to this chapter has been our secret, deep concern: Why are certain areas of the earth made uninhabitable by too much water and others by too little?

The problem of too much water is the easier to answer. Because the temperature of the tropical zone is the highest on earth and because most of the water there is liquid, evaporation is rapid. About 80 per cent of the water vapor lifted by the sun's energy enters into the atmosphere of the tropical zone, which is only 40 per cent of the earth's surface.

As this moisture is carried over the Amazon Basin or over the highlands of Indonesia or Southeast Asia it reaches elevations at which precipitation is abundant during the two rainy seasons. The rainy region of equatorial Africa gets its heavy rainfall from a marine tropical air mass that moves in from the Indian Ocean and, in being lifted over the high mountains and plateaus of eastern Africa, is cooled to the dew point.

An annual precipitation of 200 inches or more is blessing ruined by abundance. Mineral nutrients needed by plants are leached from the soil by such a nearly continuous downpour. Over level areas, the soil becomes so waterlogged that the roots of plants are deprived of oxygen and few crops can be grown. Over hillsides, uncurbed precipitation sweeps away most of the soil and leaves what remains with such poor water-holding capacity that plants die of thirst during brief dry seasons.

Deserts are a little harder to account for. The Arctic and Antarctic zones are actually "cold deserts," because the air over them has such a low temperature that it can hold very little moisture. Precipitation from cold Arctic air is always sparse, although it may appear to be plentiful because the little that does come down does not rapidly evaporate or sink into the earth. Appearances, too, are deceptive, since it takes 10 inches of snowfall to produce an inch of liquid water.

The largest and best known deserts of the earth are all within about 25° of the equator. They are the places of origin of stable, continental tropical air masses. These air masses come down from great heights, carrying very little moisture with them. In descending, they are warmed, so that they are far from the dew point. In spreading out over a level plain they create deserts that may reach to the edge of the sea. Prevailing winds provide no remedy, for they blow from the wrong direction. Thus the Sahara, the Arabian Desert, and the Gobi Desert are pretty well explained.

Although the air mass over a desert sometimes contains considerable moisture, it brings no rain unless it can be made to drop its burden and move on. This is as if a tank truck full of water were parked on your lawn during a drought but a truck whose outlet valve no one knows how to open.

The Sahara air mass slowly moves out over the Mediterranean, picking up moisture as it goes, and brings moderate precipitation to southern Europe. Some other deserts, such as our own American Southwest and the border between Chile and Bolivia, have somewhat different causes, such as intervening mountain ranges or cold ocean currents.

Semidesert regions dominated by scrub trees and a "trash growth" (chemise, manzanita, etc.) often occur on the lee side of the low mountain ranges, where rainfall is scarce. In the hill country of central Florida, a barren zone exists because the soil is pure white sand, nearly devoid of humus, hence of low water-holding capacity. Rainfall is abundant, but it quickly drains away into deeper-lying, porous deposits of limestone.

Deserts, once formed, tend to be self-perpetuating for several distinct reasons: (1) Cold, dry air, descending from the heights, is very *stable*. It prevents a more effective barrier to the penetration of moisture into the Sahara Desert than do the Atlas Mountains. (2) Since there is no vegetation to add moisture to the air, nor any permanent lakes or rivers, the air over a desert remains permanently dry and cloudless. Every night there is excessive loss of heat by radiation, and the desert air remains quiet, cool, and dry all night long. After dawn, the rapid heating of the desert surface produces temporary instability and violent updrafts. Sand from Sahara sandstorms has often fallen in Sicily and Spain. Because so much energy is expended in lifting sand, updrafts in the Sahara rarely lift moisture to the heights at which clouds are formed or precipitation induced. (3) When precipitation does occur in desert areas, it is in violent "cloudbursts," which sweep away the scanty soil, and in sandy deserts are soon swallowed up in sand and rubble. Although deserts may be traversed by rivers like the Nile, the Tigris, and the Euphrates, which originate elsewhere, no perennial streams that originate in deserts reach the ocean.

So there is a vicious circle: Deserts create sandy or stony wastes in which the sparse rain seeps underground and there is but little vegetation. The air thus remains permanently dry. In Chapter 10 we shall discover another reason why arid regions are often uninhabitable: the sources of water supply and the soil itself may have been ruined by salt.

Rain forests and deserts are true opposites, representing opposite extremes of precipitation over regions of extended area. Swamps, by contrast, arise from poor drainage in an area that may be very limited. Thus South Africa has a swamp in the midst of a desert—the famous Okobongo Swamp, an important game refuge.

Barren lands do not always result from a scarcity of water. A region's soil may lack one or more micronutrients, sometimes called trace elements. These are elements that are needed in only minor amounts to support the life of plants and animals. The chief micronutrients, with the ion or ions that usually supplies them are: iron (Fe^{++} or Fe^{+++}), manganese (Mn^{++}), zinc (Zn^{++}), copper (Cu^+ or Cu^{++}), molybdenum (MoO_4^-), chlorine (Cl^-), boron (BO_3^{---}), and perhaps cobalt (Co^{++}) and vanadium (VO_4^{---}). Some plants need silicon (as SiO_2) to stiffen their stems and harden surfaces; and vertebrate animals need fluorine (as F^-), which hardens the surfaces of the bones and teeth, and iodine (as I^-) for thyroxin, which is secreted by the thyroid gland.

Sometimes the micronutrients, instead of being absent from a region's soil, are merely so closely bound to other elements that they are unavailable to plants and animals. In either case, a whole landscape may appear to be blighted by what previous centuries would have regarded as a mysterious and baleful "curse of Satan." Not a crop can be grown in spite of abundant rainfall or irrigation. Not an animal grows to maturity without the daily intervention of man. Examples of such "micronutrient deserts" are regions in Australia in which copper, molybdenum, and vanadium are either absent from the soil or unavailable to plants. To lift the curse calls for other than incantations. The remedy must come from biochemistry.

Fresh Water and the World's Food Supply

The inhabitants of desert regions are constantly on the verge of starvation. Only in oases is there enough fresh water to assure a steady supply to a scanty human population. A few crop failures may cause every community to perish or migrate. Nevertheless, many deserts have underground water supplies which await discovery and development. The present population may then be multiplied several fold before the food supply once more becomes inadequate.

At the other extreme are the rain-drenched areas of the Andes, Central and Eastern Africa, and Southeast Asia. Here, a superabundance of fresh water makes the food supply inadequate, not only by limiting food production but by hindering food transportation and distribution. Water-borne diseases help to decrease the imbalance between food supply and a population's need for food; yet malnutrition rather than infection is the cause of a considerable part of the high infant mortality.

Fresh water is not the only factor determining food supply. In India and its neighbors and in parts of Indonesia, Australia, and South America are areas in which the soil has been ruined by salt. There are others in which the soil from the beginning was of such a poor character that centuries of intelligent cultivation, with good irrigation practices and discreet use of fertilizers, would have been needed to fit it to grow significant crops. Yet the human population may be almost the densest in the world in places in which cultivation is by bullocks, turning over infertile clay soils with iron-shod crooked sticks, or in which grain is still transplanted and harvested by hand. In most of these hungry lands, improved crop varieties are unknown, and artificial fertilizers have never yet been introduced.

Europe and North America are the breadbaskets of the world. North America alone might feed the present population of the world, if food could be transported a little more cheaply or without too great loss by spoilage during transportation and distribution. This is the result of the

Figure 4-12. Food Supplies of the World

development of labor-saving devices and *scientific farming*. In the America of a century ago, and still today in India and its nearest neighbors, about half the population had to live upon the land, working with crude tools to support themselves and the other half of the population. Today, in the United States, an agricultural laborer, using modern methods for planting, cultivation, and harvesting and applying fertilizers in an effective way, may feed himself and about 45 others.

A map showing the regions of adequate, marginal, and deficient food supply (Figure 4-12) seems destined to be greatly altered as population comes under control in the most overpopulated parts of the earth and as scientific methods penetrate new areas. Any attempt just to feed the world from our abundance would waste not only labor but our mineral

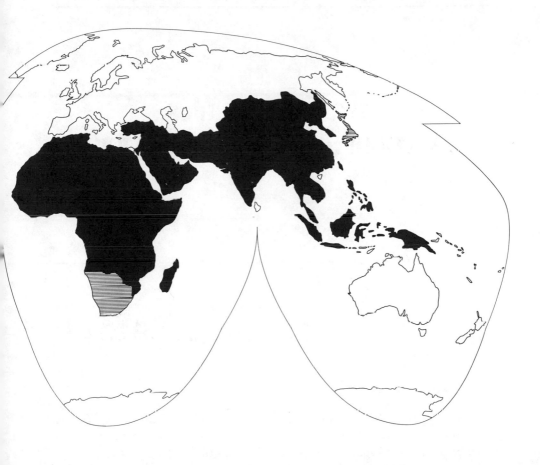

nutrients since all the nutrient elements except nitrogen come from the soil.

Until the hungry parts of the world have learned to restrain their population increase, America and Europe can do little more than instruct. What end is served if generous hearts give to permit overpopulated lands to perpetuate misery? Even instruction is nearly impossible until illiteracy has been conquered. The desperate need of the world is not for food but for self-discipline and, first of all, for teachers.

5

Water Molecules
Account for Water's Behavior

Because water is familiar, most people think of it as a typical liquid. Actually, it is a very unusual one, because its molecules fit it to be the vehicle for something quite special—life. The present chapter explains this in some detail.

Chemical Changes

The most amazing of familiar events are chemical changes. Examples are the seemingly magical way in which a black solid, carbon, when heated in air or oxygen, is converted into a colorless gas, carbon dioxide; or the way in which common salt, by the passage of an electric current, is converted into a white metal, sodium, and a greenish gas, chlorine. In a more complex but still familiar way, living plants and animals accomplish a multitude of chemical changes in their special and unique activities of growth, reproduction, motion, reaction to stimuli, or even meditative thought.

None of the philosophers of ancient times had any idea of how chemical changes are accomplished. Chemistry was one of the astonishing blind spots of the ancient world. Nevertheless, the Greeks, over 2400 years ago, passed on to modern time an idea that proved fruitful: they presumed that all material things—gaseous, liquid, or solid—are composed of invisibly small, indivisible particles called atoms and that the properties distinguishing characteristics of visible samples of matter are in some way determined by the kinds of atoms in them. That was as far as the Greeks could go because they did not know how many different kinds of atoms exist.

Elements and Compounds

The first step in accounting for chemical changes—now called chemical reactions or simply reactions—was to perceive that the numberless mixtures in nature may be separated into materials of invariable properties. These are called substances. Thus salt water may be separated by evaporation into fresh water and salts. It is variable in its properties because there are different kinds of salts, which may be present in salt water in variable proportions; but the substances separated from salt water have definite and invariable properties, unwavering as virtue.

Among the thousands of substances that chemists have identified were about ninety that until the twentieth century resisted all efforts to decompose them or convert them into one another. Water may be decomposed into hydrogen and oxygen, and common salt into sodium and chlorine. With these four simple substances, called elements, decomposition by chemical methods (heating, contact with other substances, or passage of an electric current) is at an end. The elements stand firm, undecomposed and invariable, in the midst of chemical efforts of every sort.

John Dalton, an English schoolmaster, in 1808 perceived the answer to the question which had baffled philosophers, alchemists, and practical experimenters during more than two thousand years: how many different kinds of atoms are there? Dalton's answer: There are as many chemically different[1] kinds of atoms as there are elements. The present-day count is just over a hundred.

An element (or especially a single atom of the element) is often represented by its chemical symbol. This is the first letter or a pair of letters of the Latin name of the element. Thus sodium (natrium) is represented by Na, potassium (kalium) by K, and iron (ferrum) by Fe. Fortunately there are many elements for which the adopted symbol is also suggested by the name of the element in English.

More than a century ago it was observed that the elements then known might be classified into groups of elements, with elements in each group forming a "family" of elements of similar chemical behav-

1. The words "chemically different" mean behaving differently in chemical changes. Atoms that do behave in this way are regarded as atoms of different elements.

Table 5-1.
The Periodic Table (Condensed)

NONMETALS

Alkali Metals	Alkaline Earth Metals	Heavy Metals	Boron Family	Carbon Family	Nitrogen Family	Oxygen Family	Halogen Family	Noble Gases
^{1}H								^{2}He
^{3}Li	^{4}Be		^{5}B	^{6}C	^{7}N	^{8}O	^{9}F	^{10}Ne
^{11}Na	^{12}Mg		^{13}Al	^{14}Si	^{15}P	^{16}S	^{17}Cl	^{18}A
^{19}K	^{20}Ca	^{21}Sc^{30}Zn	^{31}Ga	^{32}Ge	^{33}As	^{34}Se	^{35}Br	^{36}Kr
^{37}Rb	^{38}Sr	^{39}Y^{48}Cd	^{49}In	^{50}Sn	^{51}Sb	^{52}Te	^{53}I	^{54}Xe
^{55}Cs	^{56}Ba *	^{72}Hf^{80}Hg	^{81}Tl	^{82}Pb	^{83}Bi	^{84}Po	^{85}At	^{86}Rn
^{87}Fr	^{88}Ra **							

* Lanthanide Elements: ^{57}La——^{71}Lu
** Actinide Elements: ^{89}Ac——^{103}Lw

Note: The numbers given are atomic numbers.

ior. Then it was found that when the elements of each family were listed in a single column, the columns might be arranged in a logical order to form a periodic table, shown in abbreviated form in Table 5-1. In this table, observe eight groups of families or elements that have received special names.

Before the symbol of each element in the table is given its atomic number. This is its sequence number in the table. Counting forward, in passing through the table, the atomic number increases steadily, one unit at a time, from hydrogen (atomic number 1) to lawrencium (atomic number 103), the last element in the table, and the latest to be discovered (1961). The eleven elements of highest atomic number and several others near the end of the table are "synthetic elements," prepared from other elements by nuclear scientists. They are all unstable, hence probably do not occur in nature.

The Formula of Water Vapor

Dalton assumed that chemical changes are brought about by combining whole numbers of atoms into "compound atoms," now called molecules, or by disconnecting atoms from one another within molecules, rearranging them into new groupings, then recombining them to form a molecule of a different sort. Producing a different sort of molecule completely alters the properties of the substance concerned. Water vapor, for example, produced by the chemical union of hydrogen and oxygen, has entirely different properties from either of these gases: it can easily be condensed to a liquid, and it is neither combustible, like hydrogen, nor does it support combustion and respiration, like oxygen.

A molecule of an element contains one or several atoms of the element. A molecule of a compound contains at least one atom of every element contained in the compound. A molecule of a very complex compound may contain dozens, hundreds, or even an unlimited number of atoms—occasionally, of as many as a dozen different elements.

Dalton assumed that every molecule contains a definite and unvarying number of atoms of each of the elements present in it. In this way he tried to explain the definite and unvarying properties of substances, whether elements or compounds, as compared with the variable properties of mixtures. These are always mixtures of different kinds of molecules.

The simplest way in which two elements can combine to form a compound is for one atom of each to combine to form a molecule of the compound. Dalton assumed that this is true of water, hence he represented water by what would today be written HO. Half a century later, evidence convinced everyone that a molecule of water—or at least one of water vapor—contains two atoms of hydrogen, in chemical union with one atom of oxygen. Thus the formula for water vapor became H_2O. If we represent atoms by small circles a molecule of water vapor might be represented as ₒOₒ . The relative sizes of atoms of hydrogen and oxygen are about as here shown, and a molecule of water vapor is actually "kinked in the middle," at an angle of about 104½°. The cause of the kinking and the way in which it causes water to have unique properties can be considered after we have explained how it happens that atoms combine at all. That leads us to consider electrons and the part they play in linking atoms together.

Electron Pairing

Since the early years of our own century it has been suspected that every atom has a massive central core or nucleus, which carries a positive electrical charge. Yet, matter in general is electrically neutral. So it was thought that very small, indivisible, equal negative charges of electricity (now called electrons) make up the outer part of an atom, and that a sufficient number of electrons are present in every atom to cancel or offset the positive charge on the nucleus. Since opposite electrical charges attract, it was necessary to assume that the electrons revolve in orbits about the nucleus with sufficient velocity to prevent them from being drawn into the nucleus.

At about the time of World War I, the picture became clearer. The number of electrons in the outer part of every atom and the number of units of positive charge on the nucleus are both given by the atomic number of the element. Thus an atom of hydrogen (the first element in the table) has a nucleus with a charge of +1, and 1 electron, revolving in an orbit about the nucleus. Oxygen, the eighth element, has a nuclear charge of +8, and 8 electrons revolving in pairs in four separate orbits about the nucleus.

Why do electrons tend to pair off? Anyone who has driven or closely observed a team of horses will know the answer. Each horse instinctively avoids stumbling against the other—as if mutual repulsion existed between the two members of the team. Yet, their harness prevents their indefinite separation and compels them to move as a pair. In a similar way, electrons, always negative, repel one another; yet, complete separation is prevented by a force of attraction, a magnetic force that is produced whenever electrons (or electrical charges of any sort) spin on their axes, like a top. Electrons not only revolve about the nucleus of an atom but also spin.

When two adjacent electrons spin in the same direction, the resultant force is repulsive; and when they spin in opposite directions, the system's energy is minimal and the resultant magnetic force is sufficiently attractive to keep them close; that is, paired. It was first proposed on empirical grounds that the bond holding two atoms together in a molecule consisted of an electron pair; and advanced chemical theory (the Pauli exclusion principle) later demonstrated that this is indeed the case, and further that the electron spins must be opposed.

Assembling a Molecule of Water Vapor

We are now ready to assemble a molecule of water vapor, and thus discover how its famous kink came to be, and some of the surprising consequences of that peculiarity. We start (Figure 5-1) with the nucleus of an oxygen atom, with its 8 positive charges. It is represented by a circled 8+ in the figure. Ten electrons in five pairs are available in the atoms (O, H, and H) that are to be joined. One pair (as at a) is drawn in close to the oxygen nucleus. Yet only one pair can get into that space, because it repels any other electrons that approach it.

The other four pairs of electrons, because of their mutual repulsion, take positions as far apart as possible, while remaining within the range of attraction of the oxygen nucleus. If they were restricted to a plane, their positions would be at the four corners of a square. In space, however, the four electron pairs can get a little farther apart. They retreat from one another, with the result shown. Observe that they are then at the four corners of an equal-sided triangular pyramid, which chemists and geometers call a regular tetrahedron.

Now bring in the rest of the water molecule—namely, two hydrogen nuclei, which are called protons. Each proton is represented in the figure by a circled +. Since the two protons are positively charged, they are attracted and held fast by any two of the four electron pairs. The molecule H_2O is now complete.

The angle between any two vertices of a regular tetrahedron is 109° 28'; but the addition of the two protons in the final step weakens the repulsion between the two electron pairs to which the two protons became attached. The angle through which the two hydrogen atoms are linked to oxygen is therefore only 104° 38'. This angle has been inferred from measurements of the scattering of a beam of electrons in passing through water vapor.

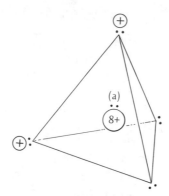

Figure 5-1. Model of a Water Molecule

We must do some violence to the actual structure of most molecules whenever we represent them in a plane. With water vapor, about the best that we can do is H:Ö: Observe two unused, "inert" pairs of electrons in this formula. They are available for linking a water molecule to other molecules or ions. In brief, the two unused electron pairs are responsible for the very striking chemical activity of water. If we represent each of the used electron pairs in a molecule of water vapor by a straight stroke and ignore the unused pairs, the result is H-O. This is also common representation of a molecule of water vapor.   H.

The evaporation of liquid water, producing water vapor, demands nearly half the energy that reaches us from the sun. In transforming and retransforming energy on a stupendous scale, it determines climate in every part of the earth, from the equator to the poles. Nor does water do this by its mere abundance, though it is about a billion billion times as abundant as petroleum, the only other liquid compound found in nature in million-ton quantities. Molecules of water, by their very structure, determine that the earth shall be surrounded by liquid oceans, that these shall gradually accumulate salt, that the earth shall have polar ice caps, and that life can exist upon the earth.

Polar Molecules

In any molecule consisting of atoms of different elements bound together by electron pairs, like water, the electrons are always closer to one kind of atom. A simple example is shown in Figure 5-2a, a model

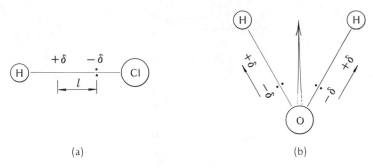

Figure 5-2. Polarity

of the hydrogen chloride molecule. The electron pair is closer to the Cl, so that the situation is as if there were a fractional negative charge, $-\delta$, placed as shown. But the molecule as a whole must be electrically neutral, there must be an equal and positive charge on the line of center as shown. This gives rise to a dipole moment, of magnitude $\delta \times l$.

Water may be represented as in Figure 5-2b, showing only the bonding pairs closer to the O. Each O-H will thus have a dipole moment, and the resultant vector shows the polarity of the H-O-H molecule.

One can see that relatively nonpolar substances are those whose molecules are electrically symmetrical. Examples are CCl_4, SIF_4, CO_2 (a carbon atom on a straight line between two oxygen atoms), Cl_2 (chlorine gas). Highly polar substances (H_2O, NH_3, NF, HCN) have electrically unsymmetrical molecules.

Polar molecules (dipoles) tend to orient themselves (i.e. take up definite directions) in an electric field, such as the space between two oppositely charged plates. The positively charged end of each is turned toward the negatively charged plate, and conversely. However, since molecules cannot be directly observed, the best test for polar character is to determine a substance's dielectric constant—a measure of its ability (in being oriented) to weaken the force with which oppositely charged plates attract each other. The dielectric constant for water at 20°C is 80.4, as compared with about 1.6 to 2.6 for the nonpolar liquids listed in the preceding paragraph. (For liquid ammonia, NH_3, at the same temperature, the dielectric constant is 17 and for liquid hydrogen cyanide, HCN, it is 117.)

We have emphasized (Section E, Appendix) that ionic substances exist as electrically charged ions, even in crystals. Crystals of common salt, for

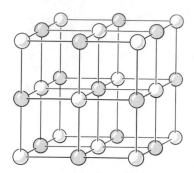

Figure 5-3. NaCl Lattice

example, are constructed of sodium ions, Na^+, alternating with chloride ions, Cl^-, in a space lattice—a three-dimensional checkerboard pattern (Figure 5-3). One does not need to dissolve an ionic crystal to obtain ions. The relative sizes of the ions Na^+ and Cl^- are about as shown in the figure.

The polar character of water comes into action in dissolving ionic crystals. Water molecules at the surface of such a crystal become oriented, as if approaching miniature charged plates. Where cations (+) occur in the crystal surface an unused electron pair (−) of an adjoining water molecule is turned in that direction and may bind the cation fast. Where anions (−) occur, a proton (+) of a water molecule may be turned in that direction and loosely held. In either case, energy is released at the expense of potential energy represented by forces that bind the ions to the crystal. In brief, these forces are weakened. Thus ions that have thus become hydrated (combined with water) separate from the crystal and wander away into the solution. Thus the crystal is slowly nibbled away.

Once detached, the hydrated ions sometimes become reattached to the crystal surface; but the high dielectric constant of water weakens the force with which the hydrated ions are attracted by ions of the crystal surface of opposite charge to themselves. In other words, the high dielectric constant of water makes all ionic substances more soluble in water than they otherwise would be. If water molecules were not dipoles the ocean might not be very salty; but then there might not be very much life on the land, because water in soils might not carry enough dissolved mineral nutrients to make plant growth vigorous.

Different kinds of salts differ greatly in their solubility in water. Yet the solubility of each may be foretold in a rough general way with the help of some rules that seem logical and reasonable:

1. When the charges carried by ions are small or when the center-to-center distance between the ions in a crystal is large, the forces that bind the ions to one another within the crystal cannot be strong. The crystal is then soft and weak. Water easily strips away ions from the surface of such a crystal, forming hydrated ions. Thus we account for the ready solubility of potassium nitrate (the ions K^+ and NO_3^-), which has singly charged ions, in comparison with the slight solubility of calcium carbonate (the ions Ca^{++} and CO_3^{--}), which has doubly charged ions (the ion Ca^{++}, moreover, being smaller than K^+; the radius of K^+ is $\frac{1}{3}$ longer). The only classes of salts invariably readily soluble in water are those composed of singly charged ions of rather large size.

2. By contrast, the only classes of salts that are invariably only slightly soluble are those in which both ions are doubly or triply charged and of rather small size. (The ready solubility of MgS and CaS is accounted for by the ease with which S^{--} reacts with water, thus being converted into HS^-, which is singly charged.)

3. Maximum solubility occurs when minimum energy is needed to transfer the molecules or ions of a substance from the surface of a liquid or crystal into the interior of a solvent. This happens whenever the molecules of the two substances are similar. In brief, "like dissolves like." The substances most readily soluble in water are those which, like water itself, are highly polar. Examples are some highly soluble bases: ammonia, hydrogen cyanide, and the hydrogen halides (HF, HCl, HBr, HI).

Water Is an Associated Liquid

In constructing a molecule of water we found that when an electron pair intervenes between two positively charged nuclei it may link them together. Can atoms also be linked in just the opposite way, that is, by a positively charged nucleus intervening between two electron pairs? If we examine that idea closely we find a difficulty: the nuclei of atoms are so large that electron pairs between which they intervene usually cannot approach them closely enough to be strongly attracted.

However, a hydrogen nucleus (a proton) is of negligible size in comparison with the nuclei of other elements. So, whenever a proton intervenes between two electron pairs that are carried by very small

atoms (those of N, O, or F) the electrical force is strong enough to produce a fairly stable linking. This is hydrogen bonding. It enables molecules of water to join with one another to form doubled-up or tripled-up
or even still more complex molecules, thus:

$$H-O_{\downarrow}H-O \qquad\qquad H-O_{\downarrow}H-O_{\downarrow}H-O$$
$$\;\;\;|\quad\;\; | \qquad\qquad\qquad\;\; |\quad\;\; |\quad\;\; |$$
$$\;\;\;H\quad H \qquad\qquad\qquad H\quad H\quad H$$

The small arrows, in these examples, point out protons that have become trapped between electron pairs carried by oxygen atoms, thus
becoming hydrogen bonds. A hydrogen bond is only about 4 per cent
as strong as a bond formed by an electron pair.

The linking of identical simple molecules through hydrogen bonds is
called association. Water is an associated liquid. Nevertheless, for simplicity, it is often represented by the simple formula H_2O, which actually represents water vapor.

Not all the molecules of liquid water are associated and not all of
them to the same degree. Hydrogen bonds, within liquid water, are
continually being formed and broken down. At any given moment
there may be a few molecules of considerable complexity. The average
degree of association of liquid water gradually decreases as the temperature is increased.

The Conductivity of Water

The formula of water indicates that it is viewed as being composed of
electrically neutral molecules, rather than ions. In other words, water
is a molecular rather than an ionic substance. The evidence for its nonionic character is very interesting. We need, first, to note that when an
electric current passes through a solution, electricity is actually carried
across, little charge by little charge, by the movement of ions through
the solution. The ions act like miniature ferry boats—two fleets of ferry
boats, in fact, moving in opposite directions (Figure 5-4) and ferrying
electricity across from one electrode to the other.

Ordinary tap water is a fair conductor of electricity, hence is judged
to contain ionic impurities (salts). A preliminary distillation in the presence of a little potassium permanganate frees it from dissolved ionic
impurities and traces of silica and oxidizable organic matter. Redistillation of this partially purified water, from vessels of quartz or platinum, with precautions to exclude ion-producing impurities (such as
traces of carbon dioxide and ammonia, present in the air) still leaves a
slight conductivity, which further redistillation does not diminish.

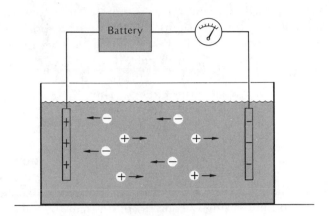

Figure 5-4. Conductance of Salt Solutions

To account for the slight residual conductivity of the purest water, chemists have concluded that it contains a few ions, derived from the water itself. It is assumed that an occasional pair of water molecules is changed into a pair of ions by the transfer of a proton, H^+, from one molecule to the other. Representing a molecule of liquid water, for simplicity, by H_2O, the formula of water vapor, the transfer of a proton might be represented:

The double arrow indicates that this chemical change is reversible. The arrow pointing toward the right is dotted to indicate that only a few ions are produced before this reaction is exactly offset by the opposite reaction, printed as a heavy arrow. The extremely slight conductivity of water at room temperature is accounted for by the transfer of only one proton for every 500 million pairs of water molecules. Section H of the Appendix shows that this assumption leads to an important idea—the pH scale of acidity and alkalinity.

Physical Properties of Liquid Water

The physical properties of liquid water are very unusual, yet they are readily accounted for by what we have learned about water molecules:

1. Water, heated through a temperature range just above its freezing point, contracts during the first small temperature interval and there-after expands. At its temperature of maximum density (about 4°C) the density of water (by the definition of a gram) is exactly 1 gram per mil-

liliter. This is only 0.013 per cent greater than the density of water at its freezing point (0°C). Yet this slight difference has important consequences in Arctic regions, detailed in Chapter 15. Obviously, heating water just above its freezing point breaks down a few of the doubled and tripled molecules of liquid water and produces simple molecules, H_2O, which pack somewhat more closely. Thus the slight increase in density is accounted for above 4°C. This effect, though it doubtless still persists, is more than offset by the expansion that is the normal result of increased temperature.

2. The surface tension (a measure of the cohesive strength of the surface film of liquids) is much higher for water than for any other liquid of similar volatility. This suggests that the surface molecules of water attract one another strongly. They do more than that: they become linked to form an invisible net, which permits water-spiders and a few insects to glide over the surface of water. Without such aid, these adventurers would soon drown, for spiders and insects (except occasionally in the larval stage) are land-based creatures, seldom venturing into water. The high surface tension of water, as noted in Chapter 2, is of importance in aiding water to penetrate every slight crack and fissure in the soil or underground; but since the degree of association of water decreases very rapidly with increasing temperature, surface tension does, too.

3. The boiling point of water (100°C) is much higher than that of hydrogen sulfide, H_2S, which is water's nearest relative. Sulfur atoms are apparently too large to become linked by hydrogen bonds. Thus hydrogen sulfide is a gas at or near room temperatures.

The high boiling point of water is a handicap in certain applications but an advantage in others. It makes water less suitable than more readily condensible vapors, such as ammonia or the fluorinated hydrocarbons (Freons) in refrigeration and the manufacture of ice; but water is less efficient than liquids of still higher boiling points (mercury or diphenyl) in the high temperature (hence high efficiency) conversion of heat into work.

4. The heat expended in vaporizing water is greater than that needed to vaporize an equal weight of any other liquid. This is evidently because a good deal of energy needs to be expended in breaking the hydrogen bonds that link molecule to molecule within liquid water—as a preliminary to the escape of simple molecules, H_2O, into vapor. In consequence, water vapor is a good carrier of energy in determining or modifying climates. It dominates the earth.

Table 5-2.
Properties of Water Compared with Those of Benzene (C_6H_6)

	Water (polar)	Benzene (nonpolar)
Freezing point (°C)	0	5.5
Boiling point (°C)	100	80.1
Surface tension (20°C) (dynes/cm)	73.5	28.9
Heat of vaporization (cal/g)	585 (20°C)	94.3 (80.1°C)
Specific heat (cal/g-°C)	1.0	0.4
Dielectric constant (20°C)	80.4	2.28

5. Water has the highest specific heat of any liquid. In other words, it takes more heat to heat water through a range of 1°C (for example, from 20°C to 21°C) than is needed for an equal weight of any other liquid. Water consequently does not need to be vaporized to be a good carrier of energy and a good moderator of climate. It can still do amazing things in transporting heat when it is in the liquid state, whenever there is enough of it. We have already had something to say (Chapter 3) about the effect of ocean currents on climate. In heating our homes in winter, liquid water radiators are used about as often as steam radiators.

The association of water molecules also accounts for the unusually high viscosity (resistance to flow) of liquid water. This results in slower runoff of rainfall into rivers. High viscosity, jointly with high surface tension, results in fields being less frequently in need of irrigation than they otherwise would be.

6. The high dielectric constant of water is a consequence of the fact that its molecules are highly polar. We have already noted that this helps to make water a good solvent for salt.

The Transparency of Water

A trip in a glass-bottomed boat will convince anyone that liquid water is remarkably transparent. Maximum transmission of light through liquid water is at a wavelength of about 4700 Ångstrom units (Å), which is in the blue part of the visible spectrum (Figure 5-5) and which is one reason water in deep layers appears blue. In the red end of the visible spectrum, a considerable fraction of the light entering liquid water is absorbed (converted into heat). Green algae and higher plants that use red light in photosynthesis are consequently restricted to moderate depths, and sometimes to within a few inches of the surface.

In the infrared part of the spectrum (wavelengths greater than about

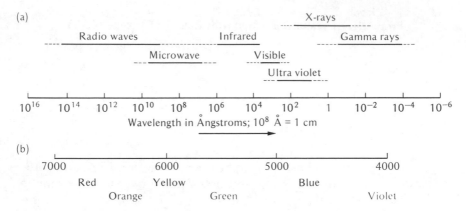

Figure 5-5. Electromagnetic Spectrum and Visible Spectrum

7500 Å) the absorption of light by liquid water is almost complete: only about 10 per cent of the infrared of sunlight penetrates through 1 meter, 1 per cent through 2 meters, and so forth. A trip in a glass-bottom boat proves that liquid water, if free from turbidity, is transparent to the wavelengths of light to which our own eyes are most sensitive.

The chief reasons for the impressive transparency of the water of certain springs are lack of turbulence in the water, and the fact that the character of water and sediment often favors prompt settling; furthermore, high mineral content and sometimes marked acidity and low content of oxygen to inhibit the growth of microorganisms that may make the water turbid.

Water vapor, unlike liquid water, absorbs radiant energy strongly in the near ultraviolet (about 2600 Å). In this way the surface of the earth is in some measure screened from the high-energy ultraviolet rays of the sun. Were this not true, one might hardly venture into direct sunlight, even in winter, without risk of sunburn.

Water vapor is transparent to visible radiant energy and that in the adjacent "near infrared." In consequence, as we have seen in Chapter 3, a good part of the energy of sunlight goes through to the surface of the earth, and the atmosphere is heated from below. The resulting turbulence is the chief means by which moisture is brought from evaporation sites, over the oceans, to distant sites of precipitation.

In the far infrared (wavelengths over 13,000 Å), both liquid water and water vapor are nontransparent. Thus air that contains even a small amount of moisture prevents reradiation of heat as long-wave radiant energy. A cloud covering prevents the temperature of the earth beneath from falling abruptly as soon as the sun goes down. The liquid droplets in a cloud permit the cloud to carry more moisture and give better insulation than would otherwise be possible. Yet, heat from a morning sun may soon dissipate the cloud and permit the earth beneath to be reheated.

This detailed description of the transparency of water might make it appear that water vapor has been endowed with the very properties needed to make life possible on this planet. Another possible conclusion would be that life is so adaptable and persistent that, even in unfavorable surroundings, it will somehow lay hold, make adjustment, and survive.

Dissolved Oxygen in Water

Although about 79 per cent of the weight of water is oxygen, this is combined with hydrogen and is quite unavailable to plants and animals. Creatures that spend their lives submerged in water must depend on the trifling additional amount of oxygen that can be dissolved in water—molecules of oxygen penetrating between the molecules of water.

The quantity of oxygen (or any other gas) that can be dissolved in water decreases rapidly with increasing temperature. When oxygen is under a pressure of 1 atm, 4.89 volumes of the gas will dissolve in 100 volumes of water at 0°C, but only 3.16 volumes in 100 at 25°C. In the presence of dissolved salts, oxygen is less soluble than when salts are absent. In sea water, the solubility of oxygen is about 4 per cent less than in fresh water at the same temperature.

The weight of any slightly soluble gas that can be dissolved in a liquid is proportional to the pressure applied to the gas. That is why lakes at high elevations have a lower content of oxygen than those nearer sea level. In the atmosphere, the pressures exerted by oxygen and nitrogen are in the ratio 21 : 78. Their molecules would dissolve in water in the same ratio were it not that under the same pressure oxygen is about twice as soluble as nitrogen. Water that is saturated with air therefore contains the two gases in the weight ratio $(21 \times 2):(78 \times 1)$. This is about 35 per cent oxygen, instead of the 21 per cent found in the atmosphere.

Water at the surface of a reservoir, pond, or lake is saturated with air that contains the percentage of oxygen just mentioned. From the surface, oxygen moves downward by diffusion, at a rate that increases very slightly with increasing temperature. In addition, oxygen may be carried downward because of convection (bodily movement of the water because of differences in density), or because the water is stirred by surface waves or moves through a rough channel.

As one might expect, molecules of water, in combining with one another to form associated molecules, tend to squeeze out and exclude gas molecules that otherwise might penetrate between them. Consequently, gases that do not react with water are much less soluble in water than in nonpolar liquids. For example, the solubility of oxygen in carbon tetrachloride (volume percentage dissolved) is about nine times, and in petroleum ether is about fourteen times its solubility in water.

What Happens When Water Freezes

Water is almost unique in still another characteristic. When most liquids freeze they contract, but a few (antimony alloys) expand a trifle in freezing, hence produce sharply outlined castings, as in casting type. The expansion of water in freezing is greater yet—about 9 per cent. In consequence, ice remains at the surface of freezing water and (since it is a poor conductor of heat) retards further freezing. Otherwise ponds and lakes would freeze solid almost every winter, in latitudes in which such an event is actually very rare.

It is not hard to explain the unusual expansion of water in freezing—the linking of molecule with molecule goes farther than in liquid water and leads to a regular pattern in space, as shown at the left in Figure 5-6. One may think of the oxygen atoms of ice as belonging to two groups. Each atom (M) of either group is in contact with four of the other group, at the four corners of a tetrahedron, but does not touch others of its own group.

This is actually the cubic symmetry of the diamond, for which a unit cube is shown at the right in the same figure. The striking difference in properties between ice and the diamond is in part due to the fact that the carbon atoms that compose the diamond are smaller than oxygen atoms, hence approach their neighbors more closely and bind them more firmly. Moreover, all of the bonds that link atom to atom within a diamond are of the covalent type (electron pairs), whereas half of those within ice are relatively weak hydrogen bonds.

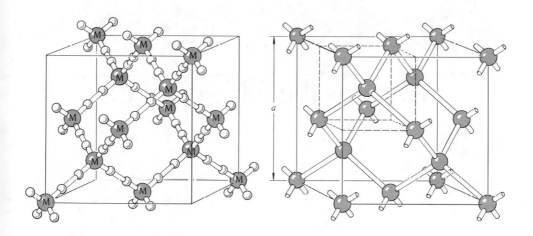

Figure 5-6. Structures of Ice and Diamond
(Wiley-Interscience, 1972), Figure 1. Figure 5-6, right, is from *Introduction to Solid State Physics*, 2nd ed., by C. Kittel (John Wiley & Sons, 1956), Figure 1-28. Used by permission.

Diamonds are formed under pressure. One might guess that by freezing water under pressure one might suppress its pores and make it denser. Just the contrary is usually true, perhaps because pressure tends to prevent good orientation. Under a pressure of 2045 atmospheres, the freezing of water into ordinary ice is at −22°C, and there is a 15 per cent expansion in volume, instead of the 9 per cent observed at 0°C.

As the pressure is still further increased, a denser form of ice is produced, with a nearly 5 per cent decrease of volume, when water freezes into ice. Under still higher pressures, three other, still denser forms of ice have been discovered. One of them has been observed under pressures up to 21,000 atm. Its melting point is 80°C.

6

Water as the Vehicle of Life

Water and Protoplasm

Water is a good solvent for most salts. The nutrient elements that plants need are brought to roots in solution in water, from mineral particles in the soil. Water is not a good solvent for proteins and other organic materials with complicated molecules. This is fortunate, for living plants and animals are built of such materials. If water dissolved them in the least degree it would sear like fire. This important limitation to the solvent capacity of water is doubtlessly owing to water molecules being linked together to form associated molecules of considerable size. These prevent other molecules of similar complexity from penetrating between them.

Yet water does diffuse into living tissues and swell them. There it interacts with protoplasm—an indefinite, turbid, sometimes colored, living semi-fluid mixture, which is chiefly composed of proteins and related nitrogenous substances. Water penetrates protoplasm almost without limit, yet does not dissolve it. Instead, the protoplasm is swollen into a jelly that becomes more and more fluid as more and more water is incorporated into it. Very young plant tissues or a jellyfish may contain 95 per cent water. The fluid in their cells may have only four or five times the viscosity of water, yet it is not only living but very active chemically.

As the water content of a group of living cells decreases, so does its chemical activity. Resting seeds, which contain only 3 to 5 per cent of water, are so completely at rest that their only discernible chemical activity is their very slow respiration. Are they alive? To find out, just moisten them!

The Plant Cell—a Bag Within a Bag Within a Box

Every plant or animal is subdivided into cells. More important, every plant or animal was produced by multiplication, subdivision, and differentiation of cells. Small cells may be less than one micron (1 μ) in diameter. (A micron is a millionth of a meter or a thousandth of a millimeter. A leaf of this book is about 50 microns thick.) Even a small cell contains more than a million million (10^{12}) molecules. An elongated plant cell may be up to 50 millimeters (3000 to 5000 μ) in length.

A single cell, suspended in a solution, may be nearly spherical, but a group of cells has a tendency to grow or expand and as it does each cell is compressed into a body with plane surfaces. A cell from the elongating part of a root or stem may measure 10 x 20 x 50 = 10,000 μ. A hundred million such cells would have a total volume of only one cubic centimeter.

In young plant tissues, cells have a fairly simple general structure, best described as a bag within a bag within a box (Figure 6-1). The innermost bag, the vacuolar membrane or tonoplast, contains one or several vacuoles (so called because they may appear to be empty). Actually, every vacuole contains a clear, transparent liquid, under considerable pressure. The cell is swollen by this pressure and its walls are forcibly pressed against those of neighboring cells, thus stiffening all of that part of the plant. A young cell may contain a single vacuole or several, each surrounded by its own membrane. Gradually, the vacuoles enlarge and coalesce into a single vacuole, which may finally occupy most of the volume of the cell. The vacuole continues to enlarge as long as the cell lives.

Not much goes on in the vacuole. It seems to be a place where waste products accumulate. The plant has no good way of getting rid of them, so it just walls them off within the tonoplast. Yet the pressure that is created within the vacuole by osmotic flow is important.

The outermost part of a plant cell—the cell wall—is the box that encloses the cell. It is almost as inert as the contents of the vacuole. It is absent in very young cells, but is gradually secreted by the contents of the cell as it matures. The cell wall is actually a double wall of cellulose. Its two layers are cemented together by a middle lamella of pectic material—the gelatinous stuff that stiffens fruit jellies.

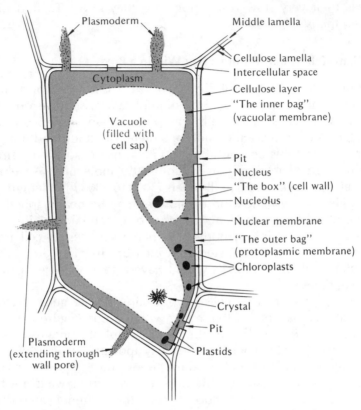

Figure 6-1. The Plant Cell—a bag Within a Bag Within a Box

The wall of a plant cell can be permeated by water, even after the wall has been stiffened into wood by the deposition of lignin (a modified cellulose). Yet it is probably just as dead as a sheet of cellophane. It displays osmotic flow and other manifestations of diffusion, but not much else.

The cell wall, because of its layered structure, has considerable stiffness, just as layered plywood does. Further stiffness is gained as cells absorb water, or as other materials are deposited in the cell walls of fibers, converting cellulose into wood, bark, cork, or the silica-rich coverings of maize or bamboo. Such are the devices that prevent tall shrubs or trees from being blown flat by the slightest breeze.

In the structures just described, plants have far excelled structural engineers in creating two-phase structural materials (strong fibers, embedded in a plastic matrix), which are both strong and flexible. Strong glass fibers, embedded in synthetic resins, became familiar in recent years in boat hulls, airplane wings, fishing rods, and the wonderfully strong and resilient poles that are responsible for new Olympic records in the pole vault.

Contrasting Dead with Living Membranes

The activities of life first come to view in what the cell wall encloses—the bag that surrounds another bag. The walls of both bags are so thin that they are also invisible under the best optical microscopes. A thousandth of the thickness of a leaf of this book would be an unheard-of thickness. Yet their presence is easily demonstrated. Just inject a dye solution into the space between the two bags. It will spread throughout that space (the cytoplast), but will not enter the inner bag.

The cytoplasmic membrane, next to the cell wall, is the more important of the two membranes, because nutrient molecules and ions must pass through it, in entering the cell, and the products of the cell's life activities must pass out through it, in being moved to other cells. The vacuole and its enclosing membrane, in most activities, are simply bypassed.

Although both membranes are very thin, they conceal a multitude of mysteries. They have the capacity for growth, self-repair, and sometimes mobility. These capacities (plus the ability to produce duplicates of cells by cell division) are the characteristics of life. They go far beyond mere diffusion and osmosis, which are displayed by both living and non-living membranes.

In carrying out the processes of life, cell membranes must discriminate and select—almost as if they had chemical intelligence. They must admit materials into the cell that the cell needs or tolerates and must exclude or reject all the rest. For example, the roots of plants must admit mineral nutrients that the plant needs, but must block soluble plant products that the plant needs, which would otherwise diffuse outward into the soil. Roots must admit traces of such elements as manganese, boron, or copper, while excluding larger quantities of the same elements, which would be toxic.

Just how the living membranes of plants and animals discriminate and select is still very much their own secret. A membrane invisible under the best optical microscopes may nevertheless be 200,000 atoms thick. These, linked into molecules of complicated structure, may bring into action yet effectively conceal a multitude of devices.

Membranes that seem to be simple may actually be many-layered. It is now thought, for example, that the outermost (cytoplasmic) membrane may be 4-layered, with two layers of lipids (compounds related to fats), sandwiched between two layers of protein. The outermost protein layer may reach out and engulf a molecule or ion that the cell needs; then turning inward, may push the engulfed particle through the lipid layer, which flows together again, closing the hole. This might appear to be a mechanical action were it not performed by a mechanism that can pick and choose. If we could penetrate the secrets of living membranes we should have better methods than any yet discovered for freeing water from dissolved ionic impurities.

Organelles: Nucleus and Ribosomes

Within the relatively small and constantly diminishing space between the two bags is turbid, living protoplasm. Under sufficient magnification, there may be seen in this a number of roughly spherical bodies and a net-like structure.

The largest and most important of these organelles is the cell nucleus, usually 5 to 10 μ in diameter. Except when it is about to divide, the nucleus is surrounded by a nuclear membrane. A nucleolus is a smaller body, one or several of which are present in every nucleus.

The nucleus has often been described as being like a center of government or a military command post, since it determines the sort of activities in which the cell is to engage—whether, for example, in unison with its neighbors, it is to serve in capturing the energy of sunlight in a green leaf, or in flexing the muscle of an animal, or in carrying a signal in a nerve. The nucleus also transmits the pattern of inheritance from each generation to the next.

Some other organelles deserve mention. The reticulum is shown by the electron microscope to be more than the mere net that its name implies. It is a labyrinth of interlacing tubes and interconnecting pockets or swellings. It is a sort of factory complex, in which a multitude of different substances are synthesized. It throbs with life and activity and is repeatedly ruptured, then mended, for it has the capacity for self-repair.

Ribosomes are the swellings in the multiply branched reticulum. Here and elsewhere within the cytoplasm the proteins are synthesized.

Among them are the enzymes, which are responsible for all but the very simplest of the chemical reactions accomplished by living cells.

Each kind of enzyme controls a single reaction or a related group of reactions. There are swarms of enzymes—dozens or hundreds of different kinds—in every living cell. They tend to congregate on the outer surface of the outermost cell membrane. Most of them come from distant cells and act as coordinators, in seeing to it that a group of cells shall act in unison—in brief, shall function as an organ.

Enzymes can be extracted from living tissue, then deactivated, reactivated, purified, and sometimes crystallized. Some of them consist of a larger protein part, the apoenzyme, to which a small part, the coenzyme, becomes attached. The coenzyme may be an atom or group of atoms of magnesium or one of the heavy metals (Fe, Mn, Cu, Zn, Mo); or it may be a vitamin, such as thiamine or riboflavin.

We still have to mention the plastids, which are bodies located in specialized cells in plants, but not in animals, for performing special tasks. Most famous of the plastids are the chloroplasts, which capture the energy of sunlight in the leaves of green plants.

The mitochondria are specialized bodies, concerned with the transformation and storage of energy. They bring about oxidation, but instead of releasing energy as heat they store it in the energy-rich bonds of adenosine triphosphate (ATP). This stored energy is afterward available as free energy in driving processes that otherwise would not take place. Plasmodermata are living protoplasmic threads that pass through openings in the cell wall and enable each cell to extend its influence into neighboring cells or into the watery fluid between cells.

DNA and the Pattern of Heredity

The nucleus is chiefly composed of a material called chromatin, because it is readily dyed. Usually the chromatin appears as a confused net; but when a cell is about to divide, its chromatin is readily perceived to consist of rodlike bodies called chromosomes, which can be counted. The number of chromosomes is definite for each species (46 for man).

Nearly every cell normally contains an even number ($2n$) of chromosomes, half derived from the father and half from the mother. Yet in many plants there are regions in which some multiple ($4n$, $6n$, $8n$, etc.) of the fundamental diploid number of chromosomes is present. On the other hand, mature sex cells (pollen grains and ovules, in plants) have only the haploid number (n) of chromosomes. It is by joining sex cells

that the diploid number is restored and the possibility created of combining the characteristics of two individuals in a single individual
among their descendants.

Several generations of research by many different scientists have
shown that the chromosomes are composed of deoxyribonucleic acid
(DNA). Its molecules are double helices—long ribbonlike structures, in-
tertwined and cross-linked. Each helix is composed of sugar molecules,
alternating with phosphate residues. The cross-links are of four different
amino acid sequences called nucleotides, which connect the sugar
molecules or one helix through a hydrogen bond with the sugar molecules of the other.

The sequence of the nucleotides in DNA determines the characteristics of the species and thus the pattern of inheritance. The external
shape of the cross-links in DNA in some way determines the sequence
of amino acids in another compound, ribonucleic acid (RNA) which in
turn controls the formation of proteins in neighboring cells. The chemical pattern, DNA, is confined to its own cell. The RNA seems to be a
sort of chemical messenger, which transfers the pattern of the DNA
into neighboring cells, where particular enzymes and proteins are being created.

It is believed that every physical characteristic or chemical capacity
that can be transferred from one generation to the next by mere re-

Figure 6-2. Stages in Cell Development

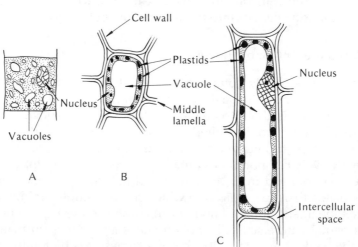

duplication of mechanical features must be brought about by the DNA molecule, in transferring its code or pattern to RNA. The RNA is the chief component of the nucleolus.·

So many wonders are assembled within the space of a single cell that one might wonder whether any more are possible. Yet wonder joins wonder in creating organs for every imaginable purpose, and in assembling organs to produce not only a single plant or animal but innumerable species. We are fearfully and wonderfully made, and in infinite variety. Perhaps the crowning wonder is that man—a creature who is mechanically so like his humbler counterparts—should have the urge and capacity to penetrate so many of these mysteries and speculate on the origin and meaning of the universe of living things. Water, in serving as the vehicle of life, permits many major and minor inventions to be joined in a single individual—amoeba or giant redwood, mosquito, mouse, or man.

Figure 6-3. Cell Differentiation

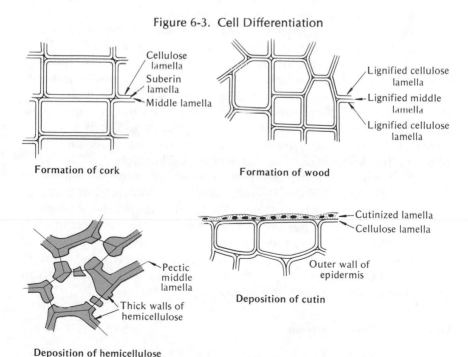

Stages in the Development of a Plant Cell

Some of the early stages in the development of cells that are to stiffen a plant or conduct water are shown in lettered sequence in Figure 6-2. Newly formed cells, Figure 6-2A, at first merely divide, without changing their shape. In this earliest stage of development they have no cell wall; but this is gradually secreted by the contents of the chloroplast, as the cell grows and presently begins to elongate. The middle lamella is the first layer of the cell wall to be deposited. It must remain extensible and pliable enough to continue to surround the cell as this expands into its final size and shape.

After that, Figure 6-2C, the cell wall gradually stiffens and hardens by the deposition of cellulose, then of cutin or lignin. The final cell may be a woody fiber, designed to lend strength to a growing stalk; or it may be a tracheid cell or conducting vessel, for carrying water (Figure 6-3). Fibers, tracheids, and vessels may all completely lack living material after they have become fully mature. They are then all greatly thickened by lignification—the formation of wood.

The central part of all three types of cells is an open lumen (channel or canal), but this is much smaller in fiber cells than in either tracheids or vessels. Cells of many other types exist in different parts of the same plant. Yet they all begin as simple cells of meristematic tissue, and only later become differentiated. Up to a certain stage of development many distinct routes of differentiation are probably open to developing new tissue. Yet when differentiation has once begun and a cell has commenced to show a given type of differentiation, it usually remains committed to that type and does not go over to another type.

It seems remarkable that all these different types of differentiation probably arise from the same genetic elements, contained in chromosomes and transmitted from DNA to RNA. It is fairly late in a plant's development that a higher command seems to step in, to confer on certain cells the ability to produce replicas of themselves, capable of their own chemical activities. The plant as a whole is more than an aggregate of cells. It is a living organism in which each individual organ has its own duties and ways of working.

More About Photosynthesis

Most of the chemical changes accomplished by living cells take place between substances dissolved in water. Yet water is more than a mere solvent in such reactions. In some of them it acts as a reactant, hence, disappears; but in others it is a reaction product—in other words, is created. In photosynthesis, water and carbon dioxide, with the aid of energy of sunlight, are converted into organic matter and oxygen is set free. Yet both water and carbon dioxide contain oxygen. From which does the liberated oxygen come? This question was settled with the aid of a radioactive tracer (heavy oxygen, O^{18}). The oxygen set free comes from the water.

So it is plain that photosynthesis takes place in at least two steps. If there are only two steps, these may be written:

$$2H_2O \quad + \quad h\nu \quad \longrightarrow \quad [4H] \quad + \quad O_2$$
$$\text{Radiant}$$
$$\text{energy}$$

then,

$$[4H] \quad + \quad CO_2 \quad \longrightarrow \quad CH_2O \quad + \quad H_2O$$

Here, [4H] represents an intermediate product, not necessarily hydrogen gas, which has absorbed sufficient energy to be capable of reducing carbon dioxide.

We need not be surprised that such a simple reaction proceeds in stages. What could appear simpler than the direct union of hydrogen and oxygen gases to produce water? This reaction nevertheless takes place in a number of successive steps, which depend on the temperature and the presence or absence of catalysts.

From the mystery product, CH_2O, which may or may not be formaldehyde, all the other products of the life of green plants appear to be made, without the further intervention of sunlight. The other reactants needed are water, ammonia or nitrate (absorbed through the roots of plants), nutrient ions, and atmospheric oxygen. The first compounds in the sequence that leads to insoluble products (carbohydrates, fats, and proteins, for example) must be soluble, since they must all be carried in solution in water from the places of their origin to distant parts of the plant, where they are incorporated into the plant's framework, or stored until needed.

The simple sugars, which chemists call monoses, are particularly rich in hydroxyl groups, —OH, for they have one of these for each carbon atom. Hydroxyl groups favor solubility by becoming attached to water molecules through hydrogen bonds. Thus they tend to drag the hydroxyl-containing compound into solution. It is therefore not surprising that monoses are prominent among the early products of photosynthesis.

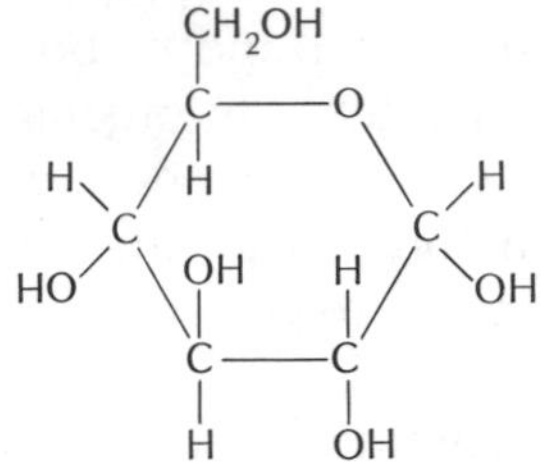

Figure 6-4. A Molecule of Glucose, $C_6H_{12}O_6$

The Formation of Insoluble Carbohydrates

We shall now consider how plants link simple molecules together to form complex molecules of insoluble carbohydrates, such as starch or cellulose, and how they similarly produce soluble or insoluble proteins. Glucose shares with 23 other monoses the formula $C_6H_{12}O_6$. These correspond to 24 different ways for arranging the atoms and hydroxyl groups of glucose in space. Actually, a molecule of glucose, the most important monose, contains five carbon atoms and an oxygen atom, linked to form a ring. Attached to the five carbon atoms of the ring are five hydrogen atoms, four hydroxyl groups, $-OH$, and a $-CH_2OH$ group, as shown in Figure 6-4. If we include the oxygen atom of the ring, this corresponds to a total of $C_6H_{12}O_6$.

Glucose can be converted by plants into insoluble carbohydrates, such as starch and cellulose, both of which have the formula $(C_6H_{10}O_5)n$, in which n stands for a large, indefinite, variable whole number. To produce either of these products, n glucose molecules must be linked together according to definite plans or patterns, one of which results in cellulose and several others in different forms of starch. To accomplish this, the plant needs the aid of enzymes: reaction-inducing and reaction-directing substances produced by the plant itself. The special secret of enzymes is one that they share with counterfeiters. They have full-scale patterns or models of whatever they are to make. The first step in producing cellulose is to link two glucose rings together to form a molecule of a "biose" sugar, cellobiose. The two glucose rings do not quite fit the pattern for cellobiose unless a molecule of water is squeezed out. Two hydroxyl groups furnish this water, leaving an atom of oxygen, marked by a short arrow in Figure 6-5, to link the two glucose rings together.

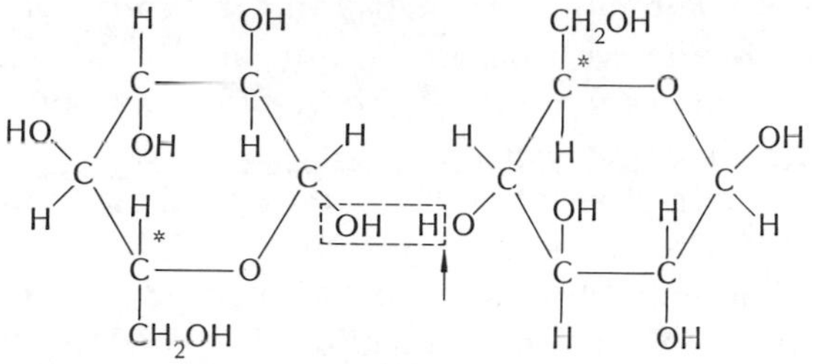

Figure 6-5. Formation of Cellobiose

It is cellobiose, not glucose, which is the repeating unit in creating the long chain that is a molecule of cellulose. With each new link spliced into the chain a molecule of water is set free, precisely as occurs on creating a molecule of cellobiose. The reason cellobiose is the repeating unit is clearly shown in Figure 6-5. The order of the atoms (C*, O, C,C,C,C) is counter-clockwise around one ring but clockwise around the other. (Here, C* represents an atom of carbon that is attached to a CH_2OH group). This repeated reversal of the order of the atoms around the glucose ring prevents the cellulose chain from twisting continually, either to the right or left, as new cellobiose links are added. Instead, the chain remains untwisted, unkinked, and unsnarled.

A cellulose fiber produced by a cotton or flax plant consists of two "cables," twisted in opposite directions about each other. Each cable may contain several hundred cellulose chains (molecules), laid down side by side, roughly parallel, and crosslinked by hydrogen bonds.

Other enzymes may bring about the linking of glucose with other monose sugars, to form other bioses. In sucrose (cane or beet sugar), for example, a molecule of glucose is linked with one of fructose. In maltose, two molecules of glucose are linked with a molecule of water split out, just as in forming cellobiose; but the order of the atoms, in maltose, is the same around both rings. If maltose is linked with itself, creating a molecule of water for each new link formed, the product is not cellulose but one of the forms of starch.

Amino Acids and Proteins

Amino acids are compounds containing one or several amino groups, NH_2 and one or several carboxyl groups, $—COOH$, in every molecule. These two groups are of opposite character, the amino group being basic (capable of combining with acids) and the carboxyl group acidic (capable of combining with bases). Amino acids that have the same number of groups in every molecule are therefore amphoteric (capable of combining with either acids or bases). If the number of amino groups exceeds the number of carboxyl groups, the amino acid is predominantly basic. The converse is also true.

Over thirty different amino acids have been formed from plant or animal proteins by hydrolysis—a reaction in which water enters to break linkages and so converts complicated molecules into simpler ones. This is just the opposite of the type of reaction in which insoluble carbohydrates are produced from the simple monoses or bioses, with the aid of enzymes. The hydrolysis of proteins is brought about by the use of enzymes or by boiling the proteins with dilute acids.

The fact that amino acids may be prepared by the hydrolysis of proteins suggests that protein molecules are formed by linking amino acid residues together, with a molecule of water set free for each new link formed. The first step might be:

$$RNH_2C - OH + H NHR' - COH \rightarrow RHN_2 - CONH - R' COH + H_2O$$

$$\underset{O}{\overset{\|}{}} \qquad \underset{O}{\overset{\|}{}} \qquad \underset{O}{\overset{\|}{}}$$

Two amino acid molecules   A molecule of dipeptide

Here, R and R' represent atom groups, which may or may not be identical. Dotted lines surround a water molecule that is to be created from two groups of atoms. In creating a polypeptide the groups are —COOH and —NH$_2$. Splitting out water leaves —CONH—, which connects what remains of the two groups.

From the dipeptide we may next prepare a tripeptide, then a tetrapeptide, and so on. Research chemists have prepared a 19-peptide. The later members of this sequence of products were colloidal in character and showed some of the reactions of proteins. Yet over 500 links would have been needed to attain the molecular weight of the simplest natural proteins (about 32,000). Moreover, the synthetic polypeptides contain only rather simple amino acids, and several of those necessary to the growth of young animals were not included.

What proved to be a better approach to the problem of protein structure was from the opposite direction—namely, by tearing down protein molecules, instead of trying to construct them. Chemists learned how to begin with a protein found in nature and strip away amino acid residues, one at a time, identifying each in turn. Thus the order in which amino acids are linked in some well-known proteins was at length determined. This was very necessary because order of linkage is just as important as amino acid identity in determining protein character. There are seventeen different amino acids that may be incorporated into a protein in almost any order, and some of them may be used repeatedly. That gives almost limitless possibilities. We perhaps differ just as definitely in our body proteins as in our fingerprints. It is not any structural sense that all men are created equal.

How Root Tips Penetrate the Soil

Since ordinary plants absorb practically all of the water that they need through their roots, it is very necessary for roots to be able to penetrate the soil. The growing root tip is actually a flexible probe—the meristem —a region of small, rapidly dividing cells of very small size. Each cell, on attaining this size, divides into two cells, which increase to the prescribed size, then divide again.

The meristem has a total length of only about 400 microns—about eight times the thickness of a leaf of this book. Its tip is usually protected by a root cap. As this is worn away it is repaired or replaced. The descending root tip is swollen sufficiently to be reasonably stiff, yet it absorbs very little water. Most of the water that a plant needs enters its roots a little higher up, through "root hairs."

Each root tip, capped or uncapped, is driven steadily downward, as one might drive a spike. The driving force is chiefly applied by the elongation of cells that are a little higher up. There is a simple way to show that newly formed cells do not immediately elongate. Let equal distances be laid off along a day old root by spotting it with a colored lacquer. A day later the spots will be distributed, as shown at the right of Figure 6-6. It is evident that most of the elongation comes in sections of the root that are immediately above the growing tip. Those farther up elongate less and less rapidly, until a region is reached above which cells do not elongate at all. The parts of the root that are still higher up are so thick, mature, and branched that they are not driven upward by the elongation of cells beneath them.

The root tip takes the path of least resistance between soil particles, and is guided in its descent by the force of gravity, the concentration of mineral nutrients in the soil solution, and the presence or absence of toxic substances in the soil. The descent of the root tip is scarcely ever more than about a millimeter before cells that were formed at the tip

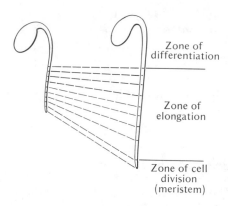

Figure 6-6. How To Locate the Region of Most Rapid Elongation in a Growing
Rootlet

find themselves so far above it that cells at still higher levels are no
longer elongating. They therefore remain at that level, indefinitely.

The meristematic cells at the growing tip absorb a good concentration of mineral nutrients, but there is no way to get water into them
except by diffusion downward through dozens or hundreds of cell
walls. A growing plant, as soon as it has arranged for penetration of the
soil by a root tip, must provide good ways for absorbing and transporting water. Most higher plants do this by sprouting numerous root hairs,
just above the point at which cells cease to be elongated (Figure 6-7).
Thus the surface through which water can be absorbed is multiplied
several fold. Next, plants must provide special channels through which
water is rapidly pulled up, chiefly by evaporation through the leaves.
The elongation of cells just above the root tip is the beginning of a
process that presently results in vascular bundles—channels that carry
water and mineral nutrients to the growing shoots of the plant above-
ground.

Root Systems

A germinating seed may begin its growth by sending down a single root
tip. Within a few hours, branch roots begin to be formed. Ultimately, a
root system comes into existence with hundreds or tens of thousands of
multiple root branches. A rapidly growing tip moves downward into
the soil as much as 40 microns a minute, which is a millimeter (1/25

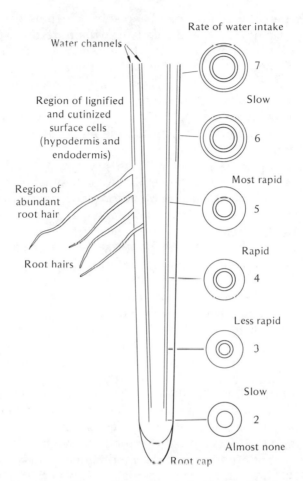

Figure 6-7. Rate of Water Intake at Various Levels

inch) in less than half an hour. The rapidly dividing small cells of the meristem may number 100,000. A single plant of winter rye, at the end of four months, may have over 40 miles of roots with an area of about 3000 square feet and over 14 billion root hairs! The dry matter in the roots of an acre of grassland may amount to 1 to 7 tons.

Roots are obviously important as anchors, but their chief service is as organs for absorption and transport of water and mineral nutrients, and for the storage of such synthetic products as sugar and starch. Some roots also serve, as with the potato and some creeping grasses, for the propagation of a new generation of plants without resort to seeds.

The rate of growth of every crop, hence the profit in growing it, is largely determined by the rate of growth of the root system. This is influenced, more than most people realize, by the temperature of the soil. The most favorable temperature, for many or most of our useful species, is between 25° and 30°C (77° to 86°F). The season of planting and the shading of young seedlings during hot weather is therefore of great importance.

Roots do not penetrate the soil "in search of water and food."[1] The simple fact is that when a root tip is able to take moisture from the soil, the tip will grow; but when the soil is too dry for growth the tip will stop growing at that very point, without any searching. If the soil is too wet, root growth is retarded and roots die. The importance of aeration is readily demonstrated with plants grown in water culture. A slow stream of air, bubbled through the water, will often double or more than double the rate of root growth for many common vegetables and grains. Most rapid growth of crops in the field is when the soil contains about half the "field capacity" for moisture.

The rate of growth of roots is also greatly influenced by the nature and concentration of the mineral nutrients in the moisture film of the soil. It is incorrect to speak of different mineral nutrients as serving different purposes in the plant. Such functions as root growth, fruiting, development of shoots, and the production of leaves require the joint presence of several different mineral elements. Magnesium, for example, is needed in the production of leaves, since chlorophyll is a magnesium compound; yet chlorophyll cannot be synthesized without the aid of nitrogen, phosphorus, and several other elements.

Most plants are surprisingly tolerant to acids and alkalies. Some of them will grow in soils that are moderately acid (pH 4) or distinctly alkaline (pH 9) (see section H, Appendix). However, the growth of many crops is improved when acidity or alkalinity of the soil is controlled, perhaps by such a simple expedient as replacing sodium nitrate by ammonium sulfate, when nitrogen is to be applied in a fertilizer.

Root competition, particularly competition with the roots of another species, should be avoided, as even amateur gardeners soon discover. Root boring roundworms (nematodes) and the bacteria and fungi re-

1. The term *plant food* is here reserved for organic compounds, derived from the seed or produced by the plant itself, and destined to be used by the plant in its life activities. The inorganic ions that plants absorb through their roots are called *plant nutrients*.

sponsible for root rot need to be controlled in many regions; otherwise crops may be destroyed, with a loss of millions of dollars, and whole agricultural industries may depart for other areas.

Contest for Water Between Plant and Soil

The lower the percentage of moisture in the soil the more strongly the soil holds this moisture. With pure sand, a decrease in water content does not very greatly increase the tension with which the remaining moisture is held. With a silty loam, a decrease in moisture content from 20 per cent to 15 per cent may cause the soil to resist further loss of water with a moisture tension of several hundred atmospheres. With a further decrease of water content to 10 per cent, the loss of more water is resisted by tension of perhaps 1000 atmospheres. The water-retaining capacity of the colloids of the soil is supplemented by the osmotic pressure of the soil solution. This is less important, but may amount to several atmospheres, in soils that have been irrigated with somewhat brackish water.

When a plant takes water from the soil it must overcome the combined pulls just mentioned. The osmotic pressure of the solution within a root cell may be sufficient. Yet, this is always supplemented by imbibition pressure—the pull of the colloids of the plant in being swollen by water. Dry seeds, because of their considerable content of water-swellable proteins, compete for water even more vigorously than roots do. Some of them will take water from a soil that is so dry that the further loss of moisture from it is resisted by a moisture tension of 1000 atmospheres.

A plant must win its contest with the soil for water, and by more than a small margin if it is to survive. The surplus pull by the plant serves, first of all, to keep the plant tissues turgid (swollen with water). Figure 6-8 shows that as the contents of a cell are diluted during swelling, diffusion pressure (the sum of osmotic pressure and imbibition pressure) decreases, whereas wall pressure (the resistance of the cell walls to being stretched) increases, at first slowly, then more and more rapidly. When the cell is fully swollen the diffusion pressure deficit (diffusion pressure minus wall pressure) is zero. Further entrance of water into the cell ceases. Diffusion pressure deficit obviously means net pressure, effective in swelling a cell that is in contact with pure water.

It sometimes aids clear thinking to speak of water as being moved

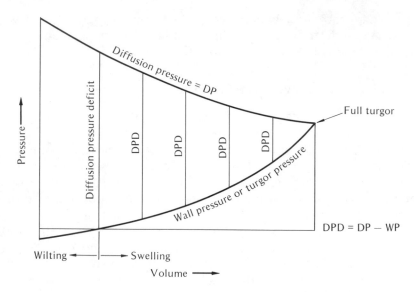

Figure 6-8. Diffusion Pressure Opposed by Wall Pressure
The excess of the former over the latter is called the diffusion pressure difference (actually a surplus).

into or through a plant under the combined pull of osmosis and imbibition, the two chief creators of unbalanced diffusion. At any point, the
pull is measured by the pressure that the inflowing water sets up. The
spontaneous movement of water by diffusion is always from points at
which the pull is weak to those at which it is stronger. By contrast,
when water is forced through a tube or channel by an applied pressure,
flow is always from points at which the pressure is great to those at
which it is less.

Water Channels in Higher Plants

About 400 to 1000 microns (0.4 to 1.0 mm) above a growing root tip, a
few cells may still be slowly elongating, but cell division, the chief characteristic of meristematic tissue, has ceased. Modification of cells then
begins to produce special kinds of tissue, such as appear in root hairs
and water channels. Then certain cells are hardened by the deposition
of suberin (cork) or lignocellulose (woody material), while others produce the waxy covering called cutin, which reduces unwanted evaporation. These are all examples of cell differentiation.

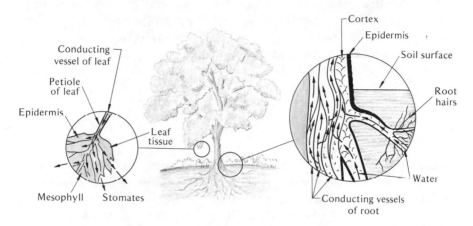

Figure 6-9. The Path of Water Through a Plant from Roots to Leaves

Cell division, cell elongation and enlargement, and cell differentiation create all the infinite variations of the world of living things. A small group of actively dividing cells, according to the possibilities of the pattern of heredity that it carries with it, may end up as an organ of any species. Nature seems never content with solving a problem, such as the problem of providing a growing plant with a sufficient supply of mineral nutrients and organic food. Nor does she seem interested in finding the "best" solution. She may seem to behave more like a computer, with a magnetic memory supplied with all the fundamental laws of physics and chemistry, and capable of all the combining and interpolating expedients of mathematics. By reviewing them, she comes up with what to us may appear to be all possible solutions to the problem at hand. From this habit comes the bewildering complexity of the universe of living things.

Accordingly, in describing the manner of ascent of water in plants, there is nothing that we might describe as typical. There are humble members of the plant kingdom fungi, for example, in which cell differentiation does not go very far beyond that which we have described for growing root tips. Among what we call the higher plants, differentiation is accomplished in such innumerably different ways that there is no such thing as a typical root system, stem, or leaf. So the best we can do is describe a reasonably common path for the ascent of water through the interconnected and ramified channels of a vacuolar bundle. This is attempted in Figure 6-9.

Observe that water absorbed by the roots and especially, in most species, by temporary root hairs, ascends through the vacuolar bundles, but evaporates en route as it goes through the walls of the conducting vessels, and passes as water vapor into open spaces, usually filled with air, that are called intercellular space. These end in stomata, little openings in the leaves, which plants have the ability to open or close, according to their momentary need for water.

Transpiration

Water is moved upward through a plant by being pulled up by transpiration—evaporation through the walls of water channels into air-filled intercellular spaces. This is a little like pulling up a rope from a cellar into an attic. To be lifted in this way, liquid water must have considerable cohesive strength.

The cohesive strength of a liquid is also called its internal pressure. Relative values for different liquids may be roughly deduced from heat of vaporization or from surface tension: the liquids that require the most energy in being vaporized, and those that ascend highest in a wick or capillary tube, are the ones whose molecules attract each other the most strongly and which therefore have the highest cohesive strength. The cohesive strength of water is about five times as great as for a typical non-polar liquid, benzene. This is evidence of the ability of water molecules to combine with one another through fairly strong hydrogen bonds.

Actual measurements of the cohesive strength of water are made difficult by the fact that it is very hard to apply a tension evenly across a measured cross-section. Moreover, the least trace of dissolved air or oily impurities on the surfaces between which a film of water is interposed will always decrease the measured strength. A cohesive strength of 33.5 atm has been observed on water. This would be sufficient to lift water to a height of over 1100 ft; whereas the tallest trees (Douglas fir, eucalyptus, two species of redwood) are rarely much more than 300 ft high. The tallest known tree (a redwood, 367.8 ft high) is probably 400 ft from root tips to the topmost leaves.

There is a little evaporation from every part of a plant's outer surface. Yet evaporation through the roots or bark is of no help in elevating water. Thus it is not surprising that plants conserve water by a deposit of cork or corklike material on these surfaces. Most of the ineffective leaf surfaces are covered with cutin, which is thickest when a plant grows in bright sunlight.

Although transpiration is a very effective way of getting water through a plant, it is very wasteful of water. Hardly 1 per cent of the water that enters the plant is used by the plant in chemical synthesis. The plant, nevertheless, has one very important way to conserve water: at night or on cloudy days, when the supply of solar energy fails, the plant shuts down a large part of its synthetic activity—one might almost say, it sleeps. There is then no need for lifting water, hence, little openings in the leaves slowly close; but with the rising of the sun or the dissipation of clouds the plant resumes its synthetic work, needs more nutrients and therefore more water, and the little gates swing open.

These adjustable openings (stomates or stomata) in the leaves of plants, in most species of the higher plants, are found in both the upper and lower surfaces of the leaves. In many trees, they are found only on the lower surface, where they are less likely to be clogged by fine dust particles or particles of smoke. In the floating leaves of water lilies they occur only on the upper surface. When stomates are small they are usually numerous and spaced close together, hence the fraction of the total leaf surface that is occupied by them varies less than their number or distance apart.

The size of the stomates is adjusted by kidney-shaped or bean-shaped *guard cells,* occurring in pairs. In at least some instances, the adjustment appears to be made by changes in the turgor (swelling) of the guard cells. When this increases, each pair of guard cells is swollen to a cylindrical shape. The thick walls that separate the two cells are compressed into a shorter length, and spring apart, like a compressed pair of bows. When turgor decreases, the bows regain their former length and the opening between them is decreased. The changes in turgor that control the stomatal openings appear to be brought about by changes in osmotic pressure, as insoluble starch granules are converted into soluble carbohydrates.

Because light usually makes the stomates open, most plants wilt more rapidly during the day, but recover from wilting at night. However, there are numerous exceptions. The more light that has been absorbed during daylight, the slower the closing at night. The size of the stomatal openings varies from about $3\mu \times 7\mu$ in the bean to $8\mu \times 38\mu$ in the oat. The number of stomates in one square centimeter may range from about 1400 to 6000 in wheat to over 100,000 in different varieties of oak. However, these sizes and numbers vary widely, not only with the species but also with the season and the conditions under which plants are grown.

The stomates serve not only for the escape of water vapor into the air but also for the entrance of oxygen and carbon dioxide from the atmosphere into the plant. The molecules of all three substances are so small in comparison with stomates that their passage is no more impeded than is that of insects through a railroad tunnel.

Since gas or vapor molecules move through the stomates by diffusion, the rate of their passage is determined by the difference of their concentrations within the intercellular spaces as compared with the outside air. Yet the rate of diffusion seems not always proportional to the total stomatal area. Perhaps this is because molecules of water vapor, diffusing into the atmosphere near the outer rim of a stomata, have some advantage in not needing to offset the diffusion of moisture inward from air that has already gained considerable moisture. It is easy to see that the fluttering of leaves in the wind or fluctuations in the wind velocity may create a pumping action that aids the removal of water vapor through the stomates.

The stomatal openings also respond the changes in temperatures, since they open at temperatures at which synthetic activity is most pronounced, and close at neighboring temperatures. They also often respond to changes in the humidity of the surrounding air, by opening wider as the humidity increases and by forming new leaves in which stomates are rather numerous and of a different size. The water channels of plants form an interconnected system; hence cutting off the roots on one side of a plant usually wilts all the branches equally.

Fungus disease (leaf blights) sometimes fill the intercellular spaces of the host plant with fungus growth. Transpiration fails, the crop dies, and famine may ensue. Leaf-destroying insects, such as locusts, grasshoppers, mites, and red spiders, by limiting transpiration, have caused numerous crop failures and brought thousands of farmers to bankruptcy.

Transpiration Rates

Different species have very different transpiration rates because of variations in the total leaf surface, the size and spacing of the stomates, the pattern and extent of the root system, the thickness of the cutin layer, and the structure and length of the conducting water channels. Measurements have brought constant surprises, since many species have much higher transpiration rates than one would expect from their structure.

For broad-leaved plants in temperate regions the transpiration rate is usually between 0.5 and 2.5 g/dcm^2 (0.85 and 4.25 lb/100 ft^2 per hour), based on measurements of the total leaf surface. Very unfavorable conditions may decrease the rate during sunlight hours to half the smaller figure here given, and very favorable conditions may double the larger figure. Transpiration from a field of corn during the growing season may be equivalent to 15 inches of water over 24 hours in the entire field. The linear flow of water through the conducting vessels of a plant varies from a rate that is barely detectible to as much as 75 cm (2½ ft) per minute.

The transpiration rate in trees is very difficult to estimate because it is hard to determine the total number of leaves and their total area. An oak forest in the southern Appalachian district has been calculated to transpire, each year, moisture equivalent to 17 to 22 inches of rainfall. Does an oak tree "drink like an elephant"? Estimating 80 trees on an acre and 20 inches of rainfall, there would be 6790 gallons of water for each tree. The water drunk by a herd of 80 elephants depends on the weather as much as on their size. The quantity just stated would give each elephant 18.6 gallons a day, the year around. That is about half of what an elephant drinks during an average day in Georgia, and it provides nothing extra for mud in which to wallow.

Transpiration in most plants follows a daily cycle that has been studied in detail for some important crops. With alfalfa, for example, the transpiration rate near midday is over 10 or 12 times that after dark. Increasing rate of illumination during the early morning hours rapidly opens the stomates. More gradual is the warming of the leaves, which brings about considerable increases in vapor pressure of water in the nearly saturated air that fills the intercellular spaces. Consider, for example, a temperature increase in the leaves from 20° to 30°C. This increases the vapor pressure of water from 17.5 to 31.8 mm. The surrounding air, at 30°, may be only 40 per cent saturated. This corresponds to vapor pressure of 40 per cent $\times$ 31.8 = 12.7 mm. Since the absolute humidity of the atmosphere, at locations far from the sea, does not change very much during the day, we may assume that at daybreak the vapor pressure of water in the atmosphere was about the same as at noon—namely, 12.7 mm. The "diffusion pressure difference" at daybreak was therefore 17.5 − 12.7 = 4.8 mm as compared with 31.8 − 12.7 = 19.1 mm at noon. Thus the rate of transpiration at noon would be expected to be 4 times that at daybreak. Several slight corrections might make this a five-fold increase. In brief, as the day advances, about half of the increases in transpiration rate may be caused by increased temperature and about half by the wider opening of the stomates.

During the afternoon the changes just described are reversed. Transpiration may then withdraw water from the plant more rapidly than water is being absorbed through the root system. There is then a loss of turgor, with temporary wilting. The reader will find it interesting to decide whether wilting will tend to be corrected or will be made worse by the change in the opening of the stomates that a decrease in turgor produces.

In trying to estimate the needs of a growing crop for water it is neither easy nor very useful to separate transpiration by plants from evaporation from the surface of the soil. Their sum is often called evapotranspiration. Add to this unavoidable losses, such as evaporation from the surface of ponds and ditches, seepage through the banks of watercourses, and penetration into underground aquifers, and one gets agricultural consumptive use of water by any crop. From this, by comparison with rainfall, one gets the water demand in irrigation.

Forest species and harvested crops are limited in their distribution by climatic factors; but their rate of growth and hence their capacity for being grown profitably are often determined by the availability of water. A growing crop usually has one dominant need: water in the right amounts and at the right times.

What Goes on in Lakes and Ponds

In every permanent lake or pond are plant and animal populations that are never menaced by drought: they pass all their lives in water. A limiting factor for most of them is not water quantity but water quality —the temperature, salinity, content of dissolved oxygen and carbon dioxide, the pH, and especially the depth to which the water is penetrated by sunlight.

The shores of most lakes and ponds are bordered by a littoral zone (Figure 6-10), in which rooted plants find anchorage in mud and reach upward toward sunlight and air. Farther from the shore, in all but the shallowest lakes and ponds, is a limnetic zone—a region of deep water, in which limnologists (students of fresh waters) have recognized two different types of plant and animal communities, living in different depths of water, with behavior as distinct as East and West.

Most of the small plant denizens of the sunlit, upper layer of the limnetic zone get their energy from sunlight, just as higher plants do.

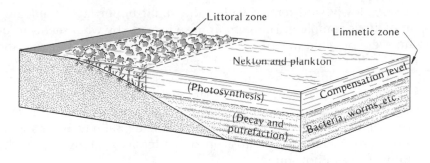

Figure 6-10. Zones in a Lake or Pond

They have green chlorophyll granules and often various other colored substances; hence, their color ranges from green through blue-green, brown, russet, yellow, and red. They include such species as green and blue-green algae, diatoms, and flagellates. Since they live submerged in water they have no need for the elaborate structures that higher plants have for absorbing and transporting water. That leaves them free to develop an amazing variety of forms, which fill artists with delight. One meets desmides (green algae) in the form of single cells, clusters of cells, chains, spoked wheels, ribbons, plumed cockades, twisted cables, feathery or leafy branches—nearly all of them on a microscopic scale. The very numerous types called diatoms display their own special artistry. They are usually single-celled organisms of many shapes, covered with a siliceous pill-box shell (one part fitting over the other). This covering usually bears an intricate design of ridges, furrows, pits, and points.

These inhabitants of the illuminated stratum of a lake or pond are often referred to as plankton (wanderers). They lack the capacity for self-directed movement that is possessed by the nekton (swimmers), which are chiefly insects and fish. The plankton of every lake or pond encounter an interesting problem in specific gravity (relative heaviness in comparison with water). If lighter than water they would rise to the surface and promptly be killed by exposure to too much sunlight. If heavier than water they would sink to the bottom, out of the reach of sunlight, and so would presently die because photosynthesis would fail to support them.

Accordingly, plankton must compromise. Their protoplasm is a little heavier than fresh water, but their size and shape are such that they sink very slowly, and remain within the sunlit upper layer until their span of life is complete. This compromise is made by what seems to us to be every possible way. Objects that are heavier than water sink the more slowly the smaller they are. Thus we account for predominance of microscopic forms. The rate of descent is greatest for sphered and less for rods or plates or objects that because of branching have an exaggerated surface. Diversity of form is thus accounted for. This may serve to maintain flotation in spite of changing salinity or changing temperature. Some algae flourish in or under ice; others live in the scalding water of hot springs.

In the sunlit photosynthetic layer, plankton use the energy of sunlight to reduce carbon dioxide to organic matter, setting free oxygen gas. Beneath this layer, bacteria and other organisms, large or small, carry on the reverse process: they use oxygen to break down dead or living organic matter and set free carbon dioxide, releasing energy as heat.

$$\underset{\substack{\text{Radiant energy} \\ h\nu \\ \text{Heat energy}}}{CO_2 +} \quad \underset{\substack{\text{Respiration} \\ \text{and decay}}}{\overset{\substack{\text{Photosyn-} \\ \text{thesis} \\ \longrightarrow}}{\longleftarrow}} \quad \text{Organic matter} + O_2$$

At the compensation level—a sort of biological Iron Curtain—these two opposite ways of life come into contact. Oxygen is there set free in photosynthesis and arrives from above by diffusion at the same total rate as oxygen is removed in the two opposing processes (respiration and decay). The concentration of dissolved oxygen and carbon dioxide at that level therefore remains nearly constant. The compensation level, in very turbid or highly colored water, may be only a foot or two beneath the surface; but in unusually clear or color-free water, it may be many yards beneath it.

Left to themselves, these two opposite ways of life coexist very well. Bacteria, fungi, and worms, waiting as scavengers in the murky depths or buried in bottom slime, consume dead organic material that descends in a steady rain from the photosynthetic region above. Oxygen or carbon dioxide, set free or consumed in one stratum, is all withdrawn or set free in the other. So the lake's population of bacteria, plankton, insects, fish, and weeds remains fairly stable.

However, algae are subject to pulses, surges, or "blooms" caused by slight fluctuations in the concentration of nutrients or by other factors not yet identified. Water that has been found to have ten thousand algae in a gallon at one moment may have two hundred million a few weeks later!

Even a very large lake may not be contaminated with sewage without risk. Chlorine used for disinfecting sewage effluents becomes ineffective after a few days of exposure to sunlight. Mineral nutrients contained in the effluents may then cause an incredible increase in the short-lived algal population of the lake. The rate of arrival of dead organic matter, settling from the surface layers into the depth of the lake, may then suddenly become too great for the scavengers of the lake bottom to handle. The water below the compensation level becomes so depleted in oxygen that fish perish. The annual catch of Lake Erie blue pike has decreased almost to zero since 1936. In the Green Bay area of Lake Michigan and in the southern third of that lake, similar results are beginning to appear from long continued contamination. It is plain that an increase in human population everywhere creates problems which human science and ingenuity can hardly overcome.

Comparing Plants with Animals

The most important difference between plants and animals is in the way in which they obtain energy. The energy needed by green algae and green-leaved plants is won from the sunlight in photosynthesis. It is stored as chemical potential energy in the molecules of chemical compounds that these plants synthesize.

Animals and many simple organisms, such as aerobic bacteria and molds, win energy in just the opposite way, by oxidizing the organic compounds that are produced by plants. This is respiration and decay. Animals have important synthetic duties, too, but these begin where plants leave off.

Since the early stages of synthesis are performed for animals by plants, animals are free to launch out in new directions. Relieved of photosynthesis, they need not expose maximum surface to sunlight. Instead of being multiply branched, like an annual plant or a tree, animals are more compactly built.

Because all but the very simplest animals have chemical tasks that are very different from those of plants, animals are very differently organized. Those at the top of the scale of development have a respiratory system (lungs or gills) to take in oxygen and get rid of carbon dioxide. They also have a digestive system, to resolve complex molecules, present in their food, into simpler ones. A circulatory system (heart, arteries, and veins) carries the products of digestion, together with oxygen, to all parts of the body, where they serve as raw material in the animal's own synthetic tasks or are oxidized, releasing energy.

In addition, an excretory system permits animals to get rid of waste products. An important service of the digestive and circulatory systems, working together, is to conserve water and salt. Finally, animals have a nervous system, which brings in signals from the animal's environment—signals that we recognize as being of different kinds, corresponding to different senses. Plants respond to stimuli, too, but in a very different way. Do they experience a kind of pain? No one knows.

By the circulation of the blood and by the evaporation of water from the lungs and the surface of the skin, an animal's body is maintained at about the right temperature, in spite of the release of heat set free by the oxidation of organic matter in every part of the animal's body. The smaller the animal the more surface it has in proportion to its weight, and the more rapidly it cools by radiation and evaporation from the body's surface. The extra heat lost must be made good by extra food. Thus the most rapacious carnivore is not the lion or tiger, nor the much smaller hyena or wolverine, but the insect—eating shrew, half the size of a mouse. It tears into its prey in a frenzy, and hardly ever stops eating.

The blood of animals presents many problems to physiologists. What volume must it have, in comparison with the total volume of the body fluids, to conserve water in dry climates and support oxidation at the rate needed to maintain the body temperature? What fraction of the proteins of the circulating blood may be walled off in the little sacs called blood corpuscles, without the blood becoming too viscous to circulate? Are these corpuscles in osmotic equilibrium with their watery environment, or will they plasmolyze (section I, Appendix)? What is the best concentration for each of the different mineral ions in the blood, to maintain osmotic equilibrium and at the same time ensure that each of the mineral nutrients shall be present in sufficient supply in every part of the body in which it is needed? Fortunately the animals themselves live out their lives in peace, quite unconscious that they or their blood are a problem to anyone.

The chemical composition of sea water is tabulated in our final chapter. If sea water is diluted with about four times its own volume of fresh water, the ionic composition of the diluted liquid is approximately that of mammalian blood. From this fact it has been argued that our ancestors came up out of the sea, bringing samples of it with them enclosed in their own bodies. The sea may well have been our ancestral home. Yet the comparison just made is only weak evidence in support of this idea, since the composition of sea water today may be very different from its composition at the time of the "great migration." We ought not to underestimate the ability of living things to discriminate and select. If it suits their needs to select and use K^+, Ca^{++}, Mg^{++}, and HPO_4^- in certain proportions, they will do so whatever the composition of the surrounding medium.

Water Balance and Water Economy

Animals use water more economically than plants do. When water is drawn up in a plant and discarded as water vapor through the stomates, that is the end of the plant's use of it. By contrast, the blood and watery fluids of animals are purified in the lungs, kidneys, and intestines, then recirculated.

There are just four ways in which an animal—one-celled or billion-celled—may satisfy its need for water. It may ingest or drink water, absorb water through its outer surface, get ready-made water from its food, or produce water in synthesis or by oxidation of hydrogen compounds in its food. The oxidation of a pound of starch, protein, or fat produces 0.56, 0.40, and 1.07 pounds of water, respectively. Only a very small part (about 12 per cent) of the water requirements of most animals can be supplied by oxidation of the organic matter of their food. Yet this source of water may be vital for a few desert animals.

A part of the water that an animal gains in any of the four ways just mentioned is used in building new tissue for itself or, in females, is incorporated into milk for its offspring. Much of the rest serves as the medium in which food is digested and in which the products of digestion are absorbed into the animal's body and assimilated. Water, in the form of blood, transports oxygen to every part of the animal's body. Throughout the body, blood picks up carbon dioxide, which is carried to the lungs and expelled in the act of breathing. Water swells the colloidal components of the animal's body, just as it does those of plants, and plays a part in most of the chemical processes of the body.

Except for very simple aquatic animals, which spend their lives submerged in water, there is always some danger that an animal's loss of water by evaporation or secretion may exceed its water intake. Water economy is their important problem. The simplest means for economy is to cover a good part of the animal's surface with a water-impermeable coating, as in a crab, a turtle, and many insects.

Nature, however, has found a much more ingenious and sophisticated way to conserve water than merely to waterproof an animal's surface. Beginning with such simple animals as roundworms (Nematodes), different animal classes have come to possess primitive or well developed kidneys, which concentrate the watery fluid in which waste nitrogenous products are discarded from the animal's body. First, by a kind of ultra-filtration, a clear solution is obtained, while colloids are held back. From this solution, the kidneys reabsorb water and salt, while soluble, waste nitrogenous products are passed to discard in the concentrated solution (urine) that remains. It will surprise many readers to learn that mollusks (clams, oysters, snails), crustaceans (crabs, lobsters, shrimp), and even insects have kidneys with much the same capabilities as our own.

Animals that live in brackish water or in the sea have the opposite sort of difficulty in maintaining water and salt balance. They must get rid of salt—or, more precisely stated—must get rid of sodium, magnesium, sulfate, and chloride, while retaining potassium, phosphate, some calcium and small amounts or traces of such heavy metals as iron, manganese, and copper.

Since marine mammals (seals and whales) may lack this capacity for discarding salt, they may have difficulty maintaining water balance, in the presence of the ocean's salt. Water economy for the mother whale, rather than special needs of her nursing offspring, may be the reason why a whale's milk is of about the consistency of rich cream—about 50 per cent solids instead of the 13 per cent normal to cow's milk.

Water Content at Different Ages and for Different Species

As an animal matures, its water content decreases. This may be 90 per cent for an egg or developing embryo, 75 to 80 per cent for a newborn calf, and 40 to 60 per cent for an adult animal (the less, the fatter the animal). Most of the non-fat soft tissues of an adult animals contain 70 to 90 per cent water.

Of the 60 per cent water in the body of a mature mammal, a little over half is intracellular water (that found within cells). Most of the extracellular remainder is in the liquid part of the blood and interstices between cells; but there is a little transcellular water, in hollow organs.

This not only carries on such obvious functions as digestion, but lubricates joints and areas in which organs rub against or slide past one another. It also acts to distribute pressure. Water diffuses so freely across cell walls and other membranes that no water molecule can be viewed as being included more than momentarily in any one of the classes of water just mentioned.

Our own bodies maintain their water balance rather precisely. An adult person in average weather may drink about 1650 cc of water, may eat food containing about 750 cc more, and may produce by oxidation of food about 350 cc. If this total, about 1700 cc is ultimately lost as urine, about 500 cc as perspiration, about 400 cc by evaporation through the lungs, and about 150 cc is discarded with the feces.

A man usually becomes thirsty when he has lost about 1 per cent of his normal water content. If water is unavailable, thirst is quickly transformed from mere discomfort into an agony that may end in death. The opposite condition, excess water, tends to be corrected by increased production of urine; otherwise it results in a lowering of the salt concentration of the body and in symptoms (nausea, dizziness, and sometimes muscular cramps), which at first may be allayed by salt tablets, but which may end fatally if prolonged.

Figure 6-11. Water Requirements of Man and Some Non-desert Animals

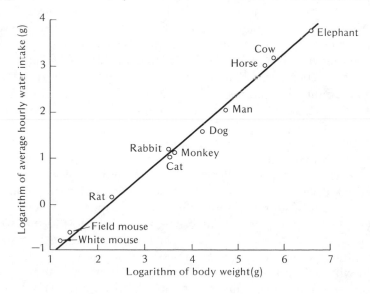

The water requirement of an animal is by no means proportional to its weight. Even for many mammals of very different species it is, however, roughly proportional to the 0.88 power of the weight. This is the same as saying that the logarithm of the normal water requirement of a mammal plots as a straight line against the logarithm of its weight, as shown in Figure 6-11. One may calculate that an elephant weighing 3 million grams (something over 3 tons) may have a water intake of 8 liters an hour, which is about 50 gallons a day. Zoologists have reported 20 to 50 gallons a day, according to the weather. Some other important physiologic variables of mammals such as heart rate, urine flow, blood volume, and nitrogen excretion follow a similar law, even in very different species, although the exponent is no longer 0.88.

Osmotic Equilibrium

The outer covering of the simplest animals is so completely and reversibly permeable to water that one may alter the volume of the animal just by removing it from a given saline solution into another that is a little more or less concentrated. Water always flows by osmosis from the more dilute into the more concentrated solutions—tending to bring them ultimately to the same concentration (section I, Appendix).

Osmotic flow stops when the solutions on opposite sides of a membrane or cell wall have the same concentration. We then have osmotic equilibrium. In a living plant or animal, equilibrium is reached when ions in a given volume, outside a cell are just as numerous as ions plus organic molecules, inside the cell. (A molecule of any soluble compound has practically the same effect as an inorganic ion in creating an "osmotic pull" that tends to take water from a more dilute solution on one side into a more concentrated one on the other side of a cell wall.)

Osmotic flow is actually the diffusion of water molecules from a region in which they are numerous into one in which they are less numerous. Each molecule is self-propelled. Movement by osmosis consequently does not call for an outlay of energy. It is often accompanied by the diffusion of ions and molecules in the opposite direction. This is dialysis. It, too is a spontaneous process, needing no external source of energy.

By contrast, when molecules or ions of any sort are moved from regions in which they are present in low into regions of higher concentration, energy must be obtained from an outside source. When eels or sea birds concentrate and reject salt, or when animals of any sort snatch back water and salt from dilute urine, energy is needed to accomplish the feat. Presumably, it is electrical energy. But how is it generated and brought into action? That famous life-saving invention, the artificial kidney removes urea from the blood by dialysis, while holding back body proteins (colloids) by ultrafiltration; but two other kidney functions, the recovery of water and common salt, are beyond its capabilities.

Water for Livestock

An animal on a starvation diet may lose most of its fat and half of its protein, yet still survive if it gets plenty of water to drink. A loss of about a tenth of its water is very apt to bring death. Water consumption by different kinds of livestock depends on the species, the age of the animals, its rate of growth, the kind and amount of food intake, and especially the body temperature. For most farm animals, fed on dry foods, the weight of water drunk is 2 to 4 times the intake of food.

The water content of forage is very important. Sheep, grazing on succulent forage, drink very little water; those grazing on salty grasslands drink more than the average amount.

Most animals drink about 50 per cent more water when the surrounding air is at 80°F than they do at 50°F; and raising the air temperature to 100°F may increase the water intake 50 per cent or even double it, as compared with 80°F. Yet different species differ very greatly in their ability to compensate for hot weather by drinking more water. It may be significant that the great livestock regions of the world are all in temperate latitudes, where plenty of succulent forage is at hand, and where prolonged high temperatures are infrequent.

Experiments in many parts of the world have established the importance of abundant drinking water, if livestock is to grow rapidly and yield a profit. Sheep, watered daily on dry ranges, may gain weight four times as fast as those watered every second day; whereas those watered every third day may steadily lose weight. Dairy calves, watered adequately gain weight about 50 per cent faster than those receiving too little water. Plenty of water for cows increases milk production, especially with cows rated as high producers. Several pounds of extra water are needed for each extra pound of milk produced. Steers on a fattening ration drink twice as much water as those on a maintenance ration.

Adequate water for poultry increases food intake, hence increases egg production and rate of growth. Details for different kinds of live-stock, at different stages of growth, under different weather conditions, are available at your local agricultural experiment station.

Desert Animals

Desert creatures have the double problem of warding off heat and conserving water. The "plated decks" of the turtle were perceived by Ogden Nash to be a handicap to survival. Yet they do act as protective armor, conserve water, and (in the brightly colored turtles of the tropics) reflect away radiation. These advantages are won by denying the turtle the cooling effect of evaporation from body surface. Nature, ever resourceful, has solved that problem by providing the Florida tortoise ("gopher") with a "water tank" which absorbs enough heat during the daylight hours to keep the creature warm through chilly night hours that are spent in the depths of its burrow. It is only within the past few years that some Florida and Arizona residents have used rooftop water tanks to accomplish the same result.

The clothes moth survives without liquid water, and the kangaroo rat of the Arizona desert gets no water after it is weaned. The wild ass of the Gobi desert, and the desert antelope appear not to drink water.

Camels can go without water for at least ten days, and during the first few days of this time can travel 60 to 100 miles a day. Such legendary feats of the camel are in part explained by the fact that travels by camel train are practical only in winter, when the heat is less intense. The camel is able to get water in the same way that sheep and even rhinoceros do—namely, by browsing on succulent herbage, such as shallow-rooted grasses, which spring up wherever there is the least dew or even a trace of rain.

A camel does, however, have several easily discerned ways for conserving water:

1. He can lose about a fourth of his body water before his blood volume is decreased by 10 per cent. With a similar loss of body water, a man's blood decreases in volume by one-third and so greatly increases in viscosity that it no longer circulates freely, in getting rid of the body's surplus heat through the lungs and skin. The man's body temperature therefore rises, and he collapses in a "heat stroke."

2. The camel and some other ruminants, including sheep and dairy cattle, do not need to excrete much urea into their urine. They inter-

cept it on its way to excretion and return it, by way of the blood stream, to the animal's chain of four stomachs. There it is rebuilt into proteins. This remarkable feat is accomplished with the aid of bacteria that work in the ruminant's stomachs, digesting cellulose. It greatly lessens the animal's waste of water in getting rid of waste nitrogen.

3. The camel has a more flexible body temperature than most other mammals. This may rise to 105°F, during a hot day, before the animal begins to sweat very freely. At night it falls as low as 93°F, in preparation for the heat of the next day.

The camel has long been credited with a sac or fifth stomach, for the storage of water. Anatomists have found none. His fatty hump has sometimes been assumed to be a source of water, since oxidation of a fat produces somewhat more than its own weight of water. But oxidation calls the lungs into action, and the water produced by more rapid oxidation might easily be offset by increased evaporation from the surface of the lungs.

The camel's hump is a reserve of energy, rather than of water. Instead of being layered under the skin or interlayered between muscular fibers, as in most other mammals, it is gathered into a hump, where it is less of an obstacle in getting rid of heat. There it provides the camel's rider with an elevated although not very comfortable seat and benefits them both by providing a reserve of energy while they are enroute to the next oasis, more than a hundred miles away.

A Look at Ourselves

The rate of oxygen consumption (a common measure of vitality) is nearly proportional to the human body's content of water, regardless of age. This fact, too, makes water appear as the vehicle of life. We age because we become dehydrated. An average man, between the ages of 30 and 80, loses about 18 per cent of his body water. This loss is intimately related to a loss of about 12 per cent in body weight. Nearly every organ, from the heart and other muscles to the kidneys and brain, suffers the loss of a considerable number of cells. There is a consequent loss of function, which is very roughly in proportion to the number of cells lost. The filtration rate through the kidneys may decrease 43 per cent, and plasma flow through the kidneys almost as much.

Yet these are all average figures. There are men of 80 whose rate of oxygen consumption and kidney function are those of a man of 50. One of the most earnest problems of this century is that of determining why a few persons continue to function well into very advanced years. If we could confer this ability to everyone, we all might continue to be taxable at 80, instead of retiring on Social Security and relapsing into Medicare at 65. This hope is surely as worthy of governmental attention as rocket shots to the moon.

The Conveyance and Storage of Water

Water Supplies in Ancient Times

In the earliest historical times, as often today in arid lands that have remained undeveloped, each village or town had its own well, which perhaps began as a natural spring. Here the women of the community fell into line in the cool of each evening, to bring home water in earthen jars, gracefully poised on heads or slung across the backs of donkeys. Long before the Christian era, small towns grew into cities, which sometimes had a million inhabitants. More generous sources of water had to be developed. To divert a stream to flow through the city was recognized as dangerous, so the stream was dammed or intercepted and its water brought to the city through an aqueduct.

In Egypt, canals and reservoirs for the conveyance and storage of water were in use at the time of the Hebrew exodus (about 1500 B.C.). At this time there were extensive irrigation systems in Babylonia and Assyria and in the drier parts of China and what is now called the Middle East. The Phoenicians, in Syria and Cyprus, drove tunnels for the conveyance of water through solid rock, and siphoned water across valleys and over hills, instead of lifting it on tiers or arches, as was later the custom of the Romans.

Of the two aqueducts that supplied Jerusalem in the time of the kings, that built by King Hezekiah (Kings II 20:20) is still in use today. Grecian aqueducts were famous, too. One of square cross-section (8′ × 8′) drove nearly a mile through a rocky hill to bring fresh water to the city of Samos. Hadrian's aqueduct, supplying Athens, remained in service until 1929.

The first aqueduct for the city of Rome was built in 312 B.C. Others followed until, more than 500 years later, there were eleven in all, varying from 10 to 48 miles in length and from 7 to 50 square feet in cross-section. The first nine of these aqueducts had a capacity of about 130 million gallons a day, of which perhaps 90 million were actually delivered to the city.

Of the Roman aqueducts, several are still in use today, after extensive repairs. A part of the water brought in by them was sold to wholesalers, who retailed it to customers coming to the dispensing places with bullock carts and small or large containers. Some of the water was distributed through lead pipes to fountains and public buildings. Part of this distribution system still exists.

Today, however, everyone is aware of the danger of lead poisoning when water is conveyed through lead pipes, and especially when drinks are stored in lead containers. One may wonder whether the short average length of life of some of the patrician families of Rome did not come from the unfortunate observation that wine kept better when stored in lead containers. Of course it did: bacteria were killed by the lead. Even today, children have died after drinking orange juice that was stored in bright-hued, lead-glazed jugs.

Outside of Italy, the Romans built many aqueducts, both north and south of the Mediterranean. At Segovia in Spain, an old Roman aqueduct, crossing the valley on two tiers of arches, still delivers water to the city. At Pont du Gard in southern France, another aqueduct, on three tiers of arches, is still in good repair. No longer bringing in water, it serves as an automobile road.

It was fortunate for the builders of early aqueducts that the labor of slaves or prisoners of war could be had for almost nothing. One of Rome's early aqueducts was built by the surrendered remnants of the army of Pyrrhus, a famous Grecian invader of southern Italy.

The water supply systems of ancient times win our admiration when we consider that their builders did not have modern materials of construction or labor-saving devices. Lacking dynamite, tunnels were dug by slaves who broke out brittle rocks with sledges or swung suspended logs shod with iron beaks. They split stones by slow and tedious methods. Where the modern stonecutter uses power-driven saws, his counterpart of ancient times often used emery dust and crude drills to drill holes in the rock. Wooden pegs, driven into lined-up holes, were so strongly swollen by being wet with water that even granite was split into neat slabs or squared blocks.

The aqueducts of Roman times usually crossed valleys on walls or tiers of arches, instead of being siphoned under pressure through water-tight conveyors. The water simply flowed down a nearly uniform slope, from source to outlet, through a stone-lined canal, roofed with stone slabs to prevent pollution. Siphons were avoided in building the Roman aqueducts, not because siphons were then unknown, but doubtless because they often become inoperative by trapping air, which needs to be continuously removed by ejectors or air pumps. The Romans seem never to have possessed such devices.

The Roman engineers must also have realized how great is the pressure created when water descends even moderate slopes in closed conduits and how inadequate their engineering materials were to deal with such pressures. In the time of Julius Caesar, the Romans had cement whose enduring quality is evidenced by roads and aqueducts that still exist. Roman cement was prepared from a naturally occurring mixture of clay and volcanic ash, without the benefits now furnished by chemical control. It would set and harden under water. Its chief defect was that the Romans never learned how to make cement as impervious to water as that made today. Water would seep through it and gradually weaken it. It is thus not surprising that a good part of the water carried by the Roman aqueducts was lost by leakage on the way to its destination or was stolen by men through whose lands it passed.

Not only did the Romans never have cement pipe, today an important means for conveying water under pressure; they had not yet learned how to convert brittle cast iron into the much stronger and more corrosion-resistant product called wrought iron. Nor had steel been invented. Furthermore, the art of producing iron or steel castings of considerable dimensions was still to be developed. Lacking good pipe, conveyance of water under pressure was impossible. One way remained: the Roman aqueducts strode across the countryside on stilts.

The world awaited portland cement, modern explosives, diesel-powered earth-moving machinery, and a better knowledge of hydraulics (the science of storing and conveying liquids), before it could have watertight conveyors, water moved under pressure or through siphons, and quick construction.

Victims of Warfare, Sand, and Silt

Prehistoric or early historic waterworks have nearly all been abandoned. They often fell victim to the hazards of war. A conqueror would just strike and pass on, quite unconcerned that in destroying an irrigation system he was destroying the ability of the land to support a human population.

When Carthage fell to the Romans (146 B.C.), the city was razed and its site sown with salt. (Even then, salt was symbolic of the destruction of the soil's fertility.) Within a generation, better judgment prevailed and the Romans rebuilt the city. The true death of the surrounding countryside came with its conquest by the Moors, more than 800 years later (A.D. 698). Its irrigation canals were abandoned and its 50-mile aqueduct destroyed. Since vegetation perished, there was nothing left to prevent rippling coastal sand dunes from taking over the whole area. The man-made desert thus created has persisted until our own century, although just beneath the carpet of wind-blown sand is an abundant supply of fresh water; in what is now northern Tunisia.

In other desert and semi-desert areas, from the western Sahara through Arabia, Asiatic Russia, Mongolia, and the Gobi Desert in China, irrigation systems often perished through neglect. There have been century-long epochs in which there was not enough authority in all the land to protect the land's most precious heritage—its aqueducts and irrigation systems. These gradually filled with sand, were abandoned, and after a few generations were often forgotten. In other instances it was the slow accumulation of salt in the soil that destroyed the soil's fertility and led to the whole area being surrendered to the desert. This important cause of human migrations will be discussed in a later chapter.

Sources of Water for Modern Cities

At present, about two-thirds of the largest cities in the United States depend, at least in part, on surface water, as most large cities did in ancient times. This is in spite of the fact that surface water is used and re-used, over and over again. Each city in a great river basin pollutes the water of those that lie downstream, in spite of every precaution or regulation. Other large cities depend on ground water, furnished by wells or infiltration galleries (nearly horizontal tunnels that tap underground supplies of water in a hilly or mountainous terrain).

If both sources of water are available to a city, the more expensive one may be used only in seasons of greatest demand. Ground water is often so hard that it must be softened, as described in a later chapter, before it is fit either for household or industrial use; whereas surface water always needs to be chlorinated or otherwise disinfected before it is safe for household use.

The concentration of dissolved solids in surface streams varies with the season. As one would expect, it is least in the season of floods and greatest when the stream is at low ebb, since practically all of the water then comes from underground sources, through hidden springs. The nature and concentration of the dissolved solids in a river depends on the character of the watershed. A forest may contribute color, due to decaying vegetation. Farmland may add nitrates, calcium and magnesium salts, and water-soluble pesticides. Ammonium salts and urea do not leach appreciably from soils until bacteria have converted them into nitrates. Water-soluble phosphate fertilizers revert to the insoluble condition soon after being applied to the soil, and so do not pass into the rivers.

The farther downstream the water in a river goes, the larger, usually, is the concentration of dissolved salts. The Mississippi River at New Orleans has about twice the concentration of dissolved solids that it has at Minneapolis. The concentration of solids is the more nearly constant the larger a lake or reservoir. Lake Erie showed an increase in dissolved solids of only about 6 per cent between 1940 and 1960, in spite of gross pollution by the cities of its densely populated southern shore. However, its content of dissolved oxygen, on which the life of fish depends, was disastrously diminished.

Most of the water supplies of the large cities of today are municipally owned, but a few are owned by private corporations. Metropolitan New York has what at first might seem a strange mixture of municipal and corporation ownership. Yet in areas in which population is rapidly increasing, there is often a good reason for a county-wide or multi-county water development to sell water at a wholesale price to corporations who already have distribution systems. These retail water to individual householders. This practice is the modern equivalent of the old Roman method of distributing water with the help of wholesalers, who bore a part of the cost of distribution in return for a chance to win a profit.

Cities in Competition with Agriculture

Thirsty cities, with their never-satisfied demands for water and energy, may end by competing with agriculture. A nation like Israel, intent on quick industrialization, must have rapidly growing cities, to supply its

need for labor. Yet it must also develop agriculture, not only to provide agricultural exports but also to provide the cities with food. The
two needs come into conflict in Israel or any other nation with limited
water supplies but a need to win a place for itself in the modern world.

The water available in Israel in an average year is only about 1.4 million acre-feet. Its cities will presently demand about 23 per cent of this,
and several per cent more will be needed for a reserve. This leaves for
agriculture only about 40 per cent of the water that would be needed to
bring its irrigable land to full production. Irrigation with saline water,
as described in a later chapter, may be one means of alleviating the
problem.

The modern state of Israel is about 60 per cent desert. It has the
heavy geographical handicap that much of its irrigable areas are in the
southern part of the country whereas most of the available water is in
the Jordan River and other watersheds, in the north. To provide the
water to the south, Israel recently completed the first stage of a great
north-to-south water carrier. This began by taking about 130,000 acre-
feet each year from the Sea of Galilee. Two later stages will increase
the yearly transport to about 430,000 acre-feet.

The quality of the water delivered by the carrier is not very high, for
it contains about 1000 ppm tds of which chloride ions account for
about 365 ppm. This is in spite of the fact that the primary purpose of
the development was water for irrigation, and salt risks damaging most
crops grown in ordinary soils. By diluting this slightly saline water with
water of better quality, desalinated water or water pumped from wells,
Israel hopes to get water that is fit for irrigation.

Water of better quality is available in some neighboring Arab countries, but instead the Israelis use the slightly saline water of the Sea of
Galilee. When ancient hatreds collide with present-day needs, there is
little hope that the hatreds will be buried for the sake of such mutual
advantages as the joint development of a water resource. Old animosi-
ties are likely to win control, in spite of all the teachings of all the prophets that these arid sandscapes have produced.

The Penalty of Size

There are in the United States about 150 cities with a population of
over 100,000. The total urban population (in communities of over 2500)
is about 170 million.

The demand of cities for water has grown much more rapidly than their growth in population, because cities use water in ever more lavish ways and constantly in new ways, in the creation of new industries. The demand of American and Canadian cities for water, indeed the demand of cities throughout the modern industrial world, has risen steadily, from about 18 or 20 gallons per person per day in 1790, to about 160 gallons in 1972. A fair estimate is that American cities now withdraw 300 times as much water from surface and underground sources as the whole nation needed in 1790.

As cities have grown larger they have had to go ever farther afield for their water supplies—5 or 10 miles, at first, for New York, then 30 miles, then over 100 miles to sources in the Catskill Mountains. Metropolitan Los Angeles, with its satellite cities (population more than 7½ million) long ago turned from neighboring well fields to the Colorado River, about 150 miles away. It will presently share with smaller cities and agricultural districts the great California aqueduct project, described in a later chapter.

Millions of people, tiring of blizzards and snowdrifts, have found in Southern California a home in an equable climate. Most of them probably never stopped to think that an equable climate is usually a dry climate, in which rainfall will not support an abundant agriculture and is even less able to support the growing demands of a great city. Thus with continuing growth Los Angeles must continue to get its water from farther and farther away, and ever more expensively.

Growing cities often find that the quality of the available water gets worse and worse, the farther away they have to go for water. The problems of adequate water supply and waste disposal are now critical in many a city that (just because of its large size) had too many problems already: problems in education, transport, air and water pollution, civil government, employment opportunities, taxation, cultural development, racial tensions. The multiplicity of problems tends to obscure the central problem, which creates all the rest: too many people. The nation looks with apprehension toward the end of the century, hardly more than a generation away.

Early in the next century the United States will probably have 350 million people—about two-thirds as many as there are in India today. Unless the trend toward living in cities can be halted, most of this human swarm will live in super-giant cities, each sprawling through 100 to 300 square miles of land already marred by congestion. An average city may then have 250,000 inhabitants. American and Canadian citizens will then view their national parks as nature's most precious gift to man. Few may recall having read that the whole continent was gracious and unspoiled in the days of La Salle, Daniel Boone, Lewis and Clark, and the Hudson's Bay Company.

Quick Construction by Earth-Moving Machinery

Projects in which water is moved long distances often call for complicated engineering structures, which cost considerable sums in the mere planning. Yet small cities, wherever rainfall is as abundant as in the states east of the Mississippi, often get a satisfactory water supply by retaining a small stream behind a compacted earth dam (Figure 7-1). The special machinery that has been developed for such tasks is usually powered by diesel motors—the smoking monsters that move diesel trucks over our highways.

A hundred cubic yards of bank soil may expand to 130 when dug out and ready for transport. At the dam site this may need to be compacted to 75 cubic yards. Modern earth-moving machinery can accomplish such tasks in a hurry. A large power shovel can excavate and load 5000 cubic yards of bank earth in a single day. A fleet of trailer vehicles, each carrying 45 to 50 cubic yards, and aided by a few rollers capable of compacting the hauled earth, can transform a landscape in a few days. A motor grader, with eight sweeps up and down a gully a mile long, may convert it into a grassed waterway, highly resistant to erosion.

Earth-moving machinery has rescued many cities that faced economic disaster on account of repeated water shortages. Lake Sara, at Effingham, Illinois, brought into existence by an earth dam, has a ca-

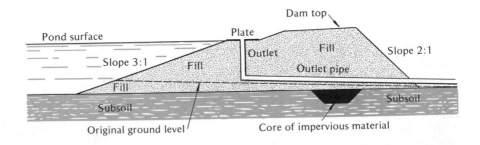

Figure 7-1. Dam Structure for a Small Water Supply System

Figure 7-2. A Dam

pacity of 4,500,000 gallons. It will carry the city's homes and industries through five years of drought. Bloomington, Indiana, in a similar way, has provided itself with a water supply believed to be sufficient for the next hundred years. These two communities may serve as models for others of similar size.

8

Water as a Carrier of Energy

Water Wheels and Hydraulic Turbines

In early Grecian times, slaves were used to drive a tunnel through a mountain's heart, to provide the city of Corinth with a protected and nearly secret supply of water. Yet this and other tunnels never transported anything but water. Since its builders knew nothing of energy, they could not guess that the controlled descent of water might be made to light their city at night, heat its homes in winter, cook food, power every loom, and make slaves and slavery unprofitable.

For centuries the weight of descending water has been made to perform such simple tasks as grinding grain, compressing air, and throwing the shuttles of a loom. The earliest white settlers in North America put water to such uses. The water-driven wheel moved westward with them during the continent's pioneer stage of development. While the steamboat was still on the Mississippi and the bison and wandering Indian tribes were still on the plains, every small stream had its dripping, dropping, rolling wheel, which powered a roaring mill, howling saw, or snorting furnace. In California, where water was already growing scarce in 1849, cautious men harnessed small streams to grind wheat into flour, which was sold at a dollar a pound to venturesome men who panned the same streams for gold.

After the Civil War the winning of energy from water gradually changed. Men learned how to extract electrical energy from water. The water-driven wheels of a legendary past disappeared, one by one, and were replaced by electric motors, often powered by diesel engines.

The mill ponds of the old wheels gradually filled with silt and were at length incorporated into farmland.

Many people think of the water wheel as having been superseded by the electric motor. On the contrary, the motor compelled the improvement of the wheel and looks to it still for a considerable part of the electrical energy that the motor needs to carry out its tasks. Water wheels still exist, but they are giants. They are the hydraulic turbines that drive the electric generators at Niagara Falls, Hoover Dam, Grand Coulee, and dozens of other centers of hydroelectric development, wherever falling water is abundant, the world over.

Pressure Within Water at Various Depths

Every diver knows that the pressure on anything or anyone submerged in water increases in proportion to increasing depth. The rate of increase in fresh water is 1 atmosphere (about 14.7 lb/in^2) for each 33.9 feet in depth. In sea water, on account of its greater density, the rate of increase is 1 atmosphere for every 32.5 feet. The greatest known depth of the ocean is nearly seven miles. At that depth the pressure is about 110 atmospheres.

Gases are so readily compressible that about half of the atmosphere lies below a height of 3 miles. Water is nearly incompressible. Yet the fantastic pressure in the depths of the ocean lowers the ocean's surface about 200 feet.

The pressure within a liquid is called hydrostatic pressure. It exerts a uniform force against equal areas, submerged to the same depth, regardless of their inclination to the surface or to each other. The best way to deflate an air mattress or air raft is consequently to submerge it with the air valve open, because pressure applied uniformly over the entire surface drives out the air quickly.

The upward thrust against the bottom of a submerged body is equal to the weight of the body's own volume of water. The submerged body appears to weigh that much less than it would if it were submerged. Archimedes (about 250 B.C.) was the first to show how this principle may be used to find the specific gravity (relative heaviness) of bodies that are heavy enough to sink in water. Engineers use it to this day to find the density of bodies of irregular shape (gravel, broken rock, and concrete, for example) whenever these are heavy enough to sink in a liquid of known density.

An object that weighs less than an equal volume of water will sink until it displaces its own weight of water. Upward and downward thrusts then balance and the body floats. The weight of a ship is thus often called its displacement.

Observe that the hydrostatic pressure at any point within a body of water depends on its depth beneath the surface, and not on the volume of the water. The pressure (pounds per square inch) against a dam that retains a lake a hundred miles long is no greater than that within a narrow crack, filled with water to the same depth. The total force (pressure times unit area) against the dam is the sum of the forces found by multiplying the total area of the dam at each depth by the pressure at that depth.

Pressure as a Measure of Energy

Hydrostatic pressure, produced by the weight of the water itself, is nearly always in addition to atmospheric pressure. There may also be some extra pressure, applied by a pump or due to trapped air or gas. The total pressure is called static pressure whenever the water is at rest.

Static pressure is a measure of practical energy in a unit volume of the water (conveniently, 1 cu ft). For example, if the static pressure is 500 pounds per square foot, the corresponding energy is 500 foot-pounds per cubic foot ($lb/ft^2 = ft\ lb/ft^3$).

Figure 8-1. Constant Hydrostatic Pressure Along a Pipe

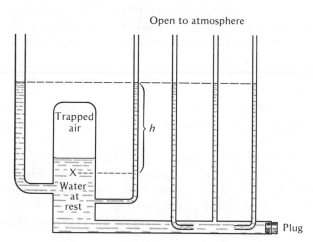

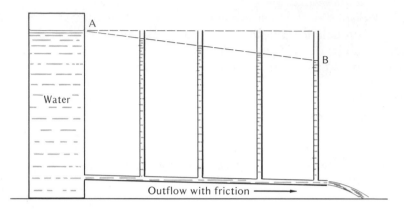

Figure 8-2. Frictional Loss of Head During Flow

A diver may carry a pressure gage that indicates depth or the pressure at any depth. To an observer outside the water, static pressure at any depth is shown by the height above that depth to which water ascends in a vertical tube or riser, let into the wall of the container or conveyor at any point. For fresh water, each 33.9 feet of rise above a given level represents 1 atmosphere of pressure, applied to the water at that level, and carried by the water to anything submerged in it or to any wall that retains it. If the water in the riser ascends higher than the surface of the water at some nearby point, we know that an extra pressure is being applied at some intervening point by a pump or a trapped gas.

If the water is at rest in a pipe or tube it will rise to the same height (Figure 8-1) in all of a set of risers along the way. If it did not, differences in height would indicate differences in pressure, and the water would not remain at rest.

If water, instead of being at rest, is moving through a pipe, successive risers along the way always show (Figure 8-2) that the pressure from point to point is steadily decreasing. Water escaping through small holes or nozzles in spray irrigation (Figure 8-3) shows a similar decrease in pressure along the way.

This steady decrease in pressure as water flows through a tube or pipe under pressure is called frictional loss of head. It represents kinetic or potential energy that is converted into heat overcoming friction. It is responsible for most of the cost of distributing water through the mains of any city built on reasonably level ground. If a pipe of smaller diam-

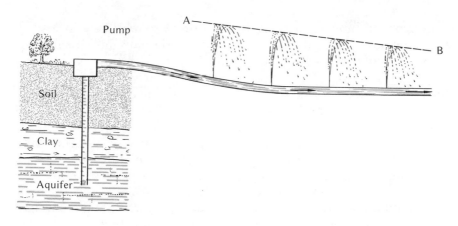

Figure 8-3. Loss of Head in Spray Irrigation.

eter is substituted for that shown in Figure 8-2 or a pipe with rougher walls, or if water is replaced by a more viscous liquid, or if the water is made to flow faster by increasing the pressure, the slope of the line AB in the figure is steeper.

Streamline vs. Turbulent Flow

The energy wasted in overcoming friction when water is moved through a pipe or open canal is least when the water moves smoothly. This is streamline or laminar flow. The water then moves in vanishingly thin films or shells, which slip smoothly past one another. The most rapidly moving film is always farthest from the walls or banks of the conveying pipe or canal. In contact with every wall is a film that does not move at all.

In streamline flow a cylinder of water moving through a cylindrical pipe is soon changed into a tapering, hollow cone. Similarly, a cube of water, moving through a canal may become a rhombus.

Streamline flow is most likely when water moves under low or moderate pressure, and when the walls of the conveyor are parallel or convergent. A smooth canal is a little better than a smooth pipe of the same cross-section, because the canal has less surface in contact with the flowing water. The only friction that needs to be overcome in perfectly streamline flow is that which is owing to the viscosity (internal friction) of the water itself. This is only moderate for water and decreases gradually with increasing temperature.

Rough walls, divergent walls, or high pressure are likely to lead to turbulent flow. In this there are no smoothly slipping shells or films of water but only confused swirls or eddies. Turbulent flow is apt to be fluctuating and unpredictable. It is greatly influenced by accidental factors, such as silt, dissolved air, and roughness of the conveyor walls.

Motion, in turbulent flow, is so very haphazard and disorderly that it easily becomes the disorderly motion of individual molecules that we call heat (section A, Appendix). Yet heat is not effectively reconverted into other forms of energy except at high temperatures (in a steam boiler, for example). That is why we speak of energy that is converted into heat in overcoming friction as having been dissipated.

When turbulent waves in a storm break over cliffs, boulders weighing many tons may be rocked and tumbled in their beds. Yet the dissipation of energy is so rapid that a few yards beneath the growling and hissing surf there is quiet water, in which cuttlefish and minnows swim unperturbed.

By contrast, waves in sufficiently deep water in the open sea show motion that is largely streamline. Each particle of water, as the wave passes, moves in a circle, just behind or just ahead of a neighboring particle, traversing a neighboring circle. Thus there is minimum friction. Tidal waves created by Alaskan earthquakes have often reached the shores of Hawaii or South America, still carrying enough energy to do great damage.

The Potential and Kinetic Energy of Flowing Water

The elevation of water above any convenient reference plane is a measure of gravitational potential energy (section A, Appendix). This and the energy represented by static pressure are both examples of potential energy, since they both depend on a force (the force of gravity or a force exerted by a pump or trapped gas). But water in motion has kinetic energy. This may easily be measured at any point in the cross-section of the flowing stream. Just insert into the stream a right-angled riser called a Pitot tube (Figure 8-4), with its horizontal arm pointing upstream. The extra height to which the water then rises in the tube, beyond the height to which it rises when the horizontal arm points sidewise, is called the velocity head. The velocity head is proportional to the square of the velocity at that point in the stream's cross-section, and hence is a measure of kinetic energy ($KE = \frac{1}{2}\ mv^2$).

Whatever the shape of the cross-section of the stream, the ratio of

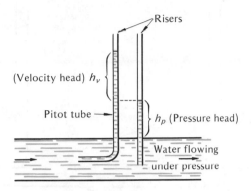

Figure 8-4. Measuring Velocity Head

the velocity at any point to the average velocity is usually known. For example, the velocity at the center of a tube of circular cross-section is between 1.16 and 1.27 times the average velocity. (The larger the pipe the smaller this number.)

The Pitot tube is not the only method for determining the velocity of a flowing stream, nor is it always the best one. A modified Pitot tube on the leading edge of an airplane's wing has one arm open forward and one toward the side. The difference in pressure between the two arms, carried mechanically to the cockpit, indicates the plane's velocity with respect to the surrounding air. Comparing this with the observed ground speed, over terrain where distances are known, one may deduce the direction and velocity of the wind at that height.

Mathematics Provides a Key

The three kinds of energy just mentioned (gravitational, static, and kinetic) vary from point to point within water at rest or in motion. Their sum gradually decreases in streamline flow and more rapidly in turbulent flow, as one passes from a point A to another point B, farther downstream. The decrease represents energy that has been dissipated as heat, between A and B.

This simple key to the behavior of flowing liquids is probably the most important advance since Archimedes, in re the principles that govern hydraulic engineering. It is most simply expressed in terms of energy. Yet its discoverer, the Swiss mathematician Daniel Bernoulli, derived it in 1738 from the general properties of fluids, without any

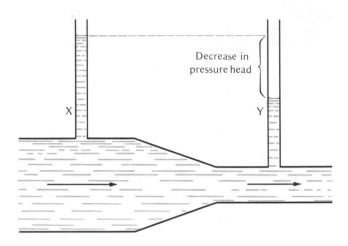

Figure 8-5. Bernoulli's Principle: Flow Past a Constriction

reference to energy, which entered scientific thinking about a hundred years later.

As an example of Bernoulli's principle, consider water flowing through a pipe that is narrowed or constricted between the points X and Y (Figure 8-5). The velocity, hence the kinetic energy, of the water must increase between X and Y, because the pipe is there constricted. One might guess that to make the water move faster the pressure upon it might need to be increased. Just the opposite is true. The increase in kinetic energy must come from potential energy. The pressure head must, therefore, decrease between X and Y. If the pressure becomes negative, air will enter the pipe at Y, whenever there is an opening in the pipe at that point. This is one way in which water flowing through a pipe may be continuously aerated.

The hydraulic engineer is interested in knowing more about water than its energy content. He must know something about the rate at which it is transferred under various conditions. For streamline motion, the volume rate of flow is often easily calculated. Practical experience, however, is always with transfer of liquids under conditions that involve some turbulence. Engineers have patiently compiled in hydraulic handbooks data regarding the loss of head and velocity of flow through conduits of different materials, having walls of different degrees of roughness, with different depths of water in a canal, or water flowing under different pressures through a closed conduit.

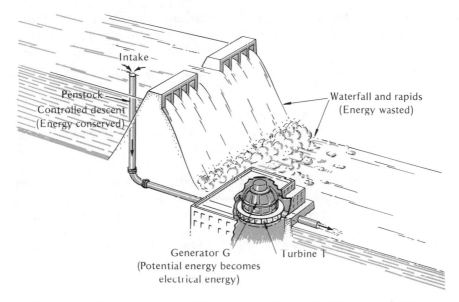

Figure 8-6. Electrical Energy Won from the Controlled Descent of Water

Energy from the Controlled Descent of Water

Popular writers have often said that hydroelectric energy is "won from falling water." The exact opposite is true. Nothing is won from the freely falling water at Niagara Falls except the pleasure that tourists get from seeing it fall. The water that tumbles over the falls dissipates its energy in turbulence at the base of the falls. The heat thus set free would warm the water about 0.25° C were this effect not masked or reversed by heat that disappears in evaporating part of the water. In any case, the heat set free is at such a low temperature that it is valueless.

But water in controlled descent may yield energy—mechanical energy in turning the rumbling old water wheels of pioneer days, or hydroelectric energy in modern power plants. A part or all of the water at the top of a cliff is diverted into a penstock—a non-leaking, nearly vertical strong steel pipe that the water completely fills. Water descending through a penstock steadily gains pressure energy as it descends, and loses gravitational energy. At the end of its descent it is under very high pressure, hence is able to exert an enormous pressure against the vanes of a hydraulic turbine, which it sets to spinning (Figure 8-6).

Mounted on the same shaft with the turbine is an electric generator, often called a dynamo. As its coils spin in a magnetic field an electric current is set up, which is carried away, cross-country, over high-tension lines, as alternating current. Very little energy is dissipated in friction during the descent of the water, and the conversion of pressure energy into electric energy is accomplished with a loss (conversion into heat) that is often not more than 3 per cent.

Water under pressure is not only a source of electrical energy but, still today, of mechanical energy in the hydraulic press and hydraulic jack or elevator. Water has an advantage over compressed air in having considerable mass and in being very slightly compressible. It is best suited for tasks in which a considerable force is suddenly applied and abruptly cut off: baling fibrous products, lifting heavy weights, stamping and riveting metals. Compressed air holds its own in competition with water under pressure for such lighter tasks as spraying liquids, pushing packages through delivery tubes, lifting small quantities of water, drilling, inflating tires. Water under pressure is less dangerous than

Table 8-1.
Some of the World's Largest Reservoirs

Rank	Location	Completed	Capacity (Cu Miles)	Millions of Acre-feet
1	Owen Falls (Uganda)*	1954	49.1	166.0
2	Bratsk (USSR)	1961	42.9	145.0
3	Kariba (Northern Rhodesia)	1959	38.5	130.0
4	High Aswan Dam (Egypt)	U.C.	27.6	127.0
5	Akosombo (Ghana)	1964	35.5	120.0
6	Manicouagan No. 5 (Canada)	U.C.	34.0	115.0
7	Portage Mtn. (Canada)	U.C.	18.6	63.0
8	Krasnoyarsk (USSR)	U.C.	17.6	59.4
9	Kuibyshev (USSR)	1955	13.9	47.0
10	Mangai (Pakistan)	U.C.	13.3	45.0
11	Bukhtarma (USSR)*	1960	12.7	43.0
12	Irkutsk (USSR)*	1936	10.9	37.0
13	Lake Mead (Hoover Dam- Ariz., Nev.)	1936	9.6	32.5
14	Volgograd (USSR)	1958	8.0	27.2
15	Glen Canyon (Ariz.)	1963	8.0	27.0
16	Oahe Lake (S. Dak.)	1960	7.0	23.6
17	Roosevelt Lake (Mont.)	1942	2.7	9.0

Note: U.C. Under Construction, 1966
Source: World Almanac, 1966
* Natural Lake with raised level, 1 cu mile = 3,379,000 acre-feet

compressed air, since the high compressibility of air enables it to store more energy. If anything gives way, the fragments hurled into space by compressed air may well be lethal.

Artificial Reservoirs and High Dams

Since prehistoric times, the lakes and ponds of the world have been supplemented by artificial reservoirs. In the United States alone, over 2300 such reservoirs have been listed (Thomas and Harbeck, 1956) with a total capacity of about 80 cubic miles. The total capacity of the world's 20 largest reservoirs, completed and under construction, is about 360 cubic miles (see Table 8-1).

Some of the earth's largest reservoirs are primarily designed to store water for irrigation (Figure 8-7). Others have as their main purpose the development of hydroelectric energy. In either case, the dam may serve such secondary purposes as flood control, navigation improvement, debris removal, recreation, or the creation of a water supply for a great industry or a metropolitan area. A reservoir of large capacity permits a steadier and more dependable rate of withdrawal, during drought years as in times of flood. It also yields better water, whenever

Figure 8-7. Reservoir Storage for Irrigation

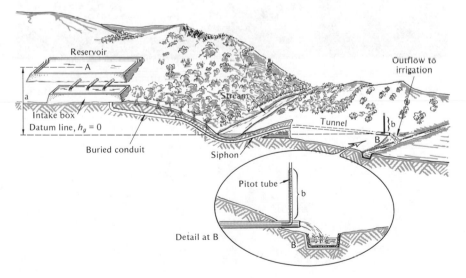

Figure 8-8. Grand Coulee Dam
Photo by F. B. Pomeroy. Bureau of Reclamation, Department of the Interior.

Table 8-2.
Some of the Largest American Hydroelectric Developments

Name	Location	First Operation	Constructed by	Capacity (kw)
Hoover Dam	Ariz., Nev.	1936	Bu. Rec.	1,355,000
Grand Coulee	Wash.	1941	Bu. Rec.	1,974,000
Glen Canyon	Ariz.	1964	Bu. Rec.	450,000*
Niagara	N.Y.	1966	NYPA	2,190,000
St. Lawrence	N.Y.	1966	NYPA	1,829,000
Chief Joseph	Wash.	1955	CE, USA	1,024,000*
John Day Dam	Ore., Wash.	1968	CE, USA	1,300,000
Dalles Dam	Ore.	1957	CE, USA	1,100,000*

* Capacity to be doubled or greatly increased in later years.

Figure 8-9. Grand Coulee Dam and Lake Roosevelt
Photo by F. B. Pomeroy. Bureau of Reclamation, Department of the Interior.

turbidity is a problem, since a large reservoir gives the water more time to be clarified by settling before being withdrawn.

Hoover Dam (height 726 feet) was until recently the highest dam in the United States. It is now slightly surpassed in height by the Oroville Dam on California's Feather River; and there are about a dozen others, mainly in Switzerland and the Soviet Union, that are higher than Hoover Dam by as much as 260 feet. A very high dam permits proportionately more hydroelectric energy to be extracted from each cubic foot of water passing through the turbines. (A thousand cubic feet of water needs 42.6 feet of frictionless, controlled descent to generate a kilowatt-hour of electrical energy; conversely, an electric pump, operated with perfect efficiency, needs 1 kilowatt-hour of energy to lift 1000 cubic feet of water 42.6 feet.)

Energy for the Future

The hydroelectric projects just indicated and many others have been built and are operated by the Bureau of Reclamation (Bu. Rec.) or by the Corps of Engineers, U.S. Army (CE, USA). But many projects have been developed by private enterprise, without the aid of tax money or government supported bonds. A noteworthy example is the New York Power Authority (NYPA).

It is interesting to note that a considerable part of the world's hydroelectric energy is devoted to the production of metallic aluminum. A good-sized aluminum plant demands as much electrical energy as a city of several hundred thousand. Alcan, in eastern Canada, and Intal, in the state of Washington, are centers of aluminum production that have caused the development of substantial new sources of hydroelectric energy. Yet aluminum still reaches out for new supplies of energy, as new uses for this metal are developed; cross-country electric transmission lines, skyscrapers, trains, automobile engines, airplanes, aluminum nets for landing fields, cans, kitchen foil.

Less than a fifth of the electrical energy used in the United States is derived from the energy of falling water. Over three-fourths is from steam, produced by burning coal and petroleum. Gas-burning internal combustion engines account for less than one per cent, and nuclear energy, although supplementing other sources of electrical energy in several metropolitan areas, is still very small. The relative contributions of these different sources of electrical energy change very slowly. In addition, railroads are now powered by diesel-electric locomotives, which generate their electric current by burning oil.

The world's supply of descending water is, after all, quite limited. If it were fully developed in every part of the world by the construction of new dams, costing many billions of dollars, it would supply only a small part of the world's anticipated need for energy at the end of the present century. The world will then be still more dependent than to-day on energy set free by burning coal, natural gas, and petroleum, and on energy from atoms.

Energy from atomic fission is often called atomic energy. Yet the name nuclear energy is more precise, since the energy is usually re-leased by splitting the heavy, positively charged nucleus of one of the elements near the end of the Periodic Table (Chapter 5). Actually, ura-nium is the only element from which energy has thus far been derived for other than military purposes, although thorium is an approaching possibility. Uranium atoms are either split or are converted (in two steps) into atoms of plutonium, in an instrument called a nuclear reactor.

The first nuclear reactor was set up at the University of Chicago's Stagg Field in 1942. Its sole purpose was to demonstrate that a nuclear reaction converting uranium into other elements can be self-initiating, controllable, and capable of being stopped and restarted at will. For that reason the first reactor was operated at such a low rate that its tem-perature did not rise perceptibly above that of its surroundings.

Immediately afterward, reactors were set up at Hanford, Washing-ton, to produce plutonium for the atomic bombs that destroyed Hiro-shima and Nagasaki and brought about the surrender of Japan at the end of World War II. These reactors were cooled by water from the Columbia River, which was then stored in basins until it had returned to nearly its former temperature, then was returned to the river.

From that day to this, the development of new uses for nuclear en-ergy has exceeded all expectations. Heat energy drawn from a high temperature source is more completely convertible into mechanical and electrical energy than heat from a source of lower temperature. (The remaining part of the heat escapes conversion and is transferred as heat to some body of lower temperature.) For this reason the reactors being built were made to operate at higher and higher temperatures.

At first, interest in nuclear energy was limited to its possible military applications. The first nuclear-powered submarine, the *Nautilus,* was launched nine years after the close of the war. It used hot water, continuously circulated under pressure, to transfer heat from the ship's reactor to its boilers.

Somewhat later, the government relinquished the monopoly it previously held in the ownership of "nuclear fuel" (enriched uranium). The Atomic Energy Commission, which had been created to lead the way in the development of nuclear energy for military purposes, then became the leader in the creation of civilian uses. Reactors of improved design, much greater power, and operable at higher temperatures were rapidly forthcoming.

One of the important advantages of nuclear power plants is in their compactness. One hears such statements as "a chunk of uranium the size of a man's head will yield as much energy as a trainload of coal." Such a vague comparison is about the best that can be done, since the efficiency of reactors as a means of releasing energy varies greatly with their design. A breeder reactor, which converts thorium into a uranium isotope (U-233) as an incident to the release of energy, is theoretically possible. Such a reactor would create its own fuel as it went along.

The development of nuclear energy has been helped in recent years by plans for its use in "dual-purpose" plants, which use heat set free at high temperatures to raise steam under boilers that drive electrical generators; and waste heat at lower temperatures to desalt ocean water.

Recent developments (as of February 1974) have pointed up the vital need for energy in this nation and the world. In a very real sense, this may be looked on as a preview of the time when no conceivable agreement among nations, no conceivable exercise of force, or no conceivable new technology will make available adequate supplies of coal, oil or natural gas. There does not seem to be general agreement as to when this time will come, but come it will; and although much research should and will be done on new sources such as solar energy, geothermal energy, fuel cells, and fusion, it would in our opinion be short-sighted to slacken research on development of nuclear energy.

Most people think of nuclear energy as something mysterious and magically powerful, differing in kind from anything else in our culture and background. The dangers of radiation have been recognized since the work of Mme. Curie, and it is thought by quite a few that nuclear power plants represent much greater risks than any other peacetime activity.

The U.S. Atomic Energy Commission and the International Atomic Energy Agency are greatly concerned with ensuring safety in the development of nuclear energy. Extensive and thorough studies, by Government and non-Government scientists, including consideration of the most remote possibility of danger, have provided no basis for alarm. Multiple levels of fail-safe protection are built into each installation, far in excess of those provided in any other industrial operation. Much research is continuing and will continue so as to even further raise the already high level of safety.

Also of concern to some informed observers (for example, P. P. Micklin, *Science and Public Affairs,* April 1974; *Chemical And Engineering News, 52* 34, 1974) is the task of safely managing long-lived radioactive wastes. For years, there has been a search for long-term storage modes for permanent disposal ensuring isolation of wastes from the biosphere for hundreds of millennia. Although bedded salt deposits are preferred, and investigations to locate favorable sites are under way, difficulties encountered in establishing a permanent repository in salt has caused AEC to turn attention to retrievable surface storage.

Fifteen years of research on high-level waste immobilization has resulted in a viable fixation program, involving drying the waste, melting it after adding glass-forming chemicals and casting the molten glass into stainless steel canisters. Such solidified waste will be encapsulated in heavy-walled steel vaults, and it is maintained by AEC that such storage will be totally safe and reliable. The amount of radioactive waste generated by a typical 1000 megawatt reactor is about 65 cubic feet per year when solidified, and based on current growth estimates this would by the year 2000 require between 100 and 1500 acres, depending on type of storage. Eventually, storage will be far underground, presenting no threat to future generations.

9

Remaking a Continent

Hydraulic Engineering

When prehistoric man first turned from hunting to tending flocks and herds and cultivating crops he began to divert small streams to bring water to his animals or to irrigate fields. In areas in which the land was too wet for important crops it was sometimes drained by ditching. Draining often brought an unexpected benefit, since the scourge of malaria vanished from drained lands.

Yet, the improvement in public health thus won was almost always soon lost, since the drained areas reverted to swamps which bred mosquitoes. It was only in the present century that the connection between mosquitoes and malaria became evident. The silting of the estuary of the river Tiber put an end to effective drainage of that region. The low-lying land became a salty marsh, the habitat of salt-loving aquatic weeds, shell fish, minnows, frogs, and mosquitoes. Malaria became a constant threat to public health, and finally the ancient city of Ostia, down the river from Rome, had to be abandoned.

The applied science of hydraulic engineering came into existence as the result of practical experience in the control and distribution of water, long before there was any hydraulic science (orderly thinking about water, based on general principles). Hydraulic engineering developed slowly during many centuries. Then, in our own day, it sought out and began to use data from all the modern applied sciences: the stability of different geologic formations, the resistance of earth and concrete structures to shocks and stresses, the strength of quick-setting or prestressed concrete, the immunity of certain materials to destruction by corrosion, abrasion, electrolysis, alternate freezing or thawing, or penetration by water under pressure.

This new knowledge makes possible the control and distribution of water on a scale never attempted in ancient times: improving inland waterways, controlling floods and erosion, linking rivers by navigable canals, creating new harbors along seacoasts or beside meandering rivers, diverting or reversing the direction of flow of rivers, irrigating vast new acreages, providing dozens of rapidly growing cities with water that is safe to drink and with water and energy from the cities' manifold industries. Thus every continent that is under the control of nations with adequate resources and technical skill is steadily being remade.

Scale Models

The problems of hydraulics are made difficult by the many variables that need to be considered, and especially by the fact that variations in one factor affect all the rest in unpredictable ways. When mathematics fails, experiment must take over. Consequently, small-scale models of hydraulic projects came into use to predict the behavior of their large-scale counterparts; dams, spillways, and other flood-control measures, coastal harbors exposed to the action of waves and tides, projects for the improvement of larger or small river basins. In Europe, scale models have been widely used since the beginning of this century. In the United States, at Vicksburg, Mississippi, the hydraulic Division of the Corps of Engineers, U.S. Army, operates the largest hydraulics laboratory in the world. It has about 70 models of river estuaries, coastal harbors, and other engineering structures. It has means for studying and automatically recording the effect of proposed small improvements on the behavior of water in rivers and harbors and on the flood plain of the lower Mississippi.

Near Jackson, Mississippi, about 40 miles east of the Vicksburg station, the Corps of Engineers operates a 200-acre model of the entire Mississippi system, from its outlet into the Gulf of Mexico upstream to Sioux City, Iowa, a distance of about 1700 miles. The scale of reduction in horizontal distance, in both models, is 1 : 2000, and in vertical distance is 1 : 100. The rough preliminary work of grading and drainage was done by several hundred prisoners of war (Rommel's Afrika Korps), August 1943 to May 1946. Thus, the twentieth century temporarily resorted to a source of labor which in ancient times might have ended in permanent enslavement.

More recently, advances in computer technology have made feasible (in many cases) the devising of mathematically based analytical models of river basins, comprehending economic, industrial, agricultural, recreational, and environmental factors along with the basic geohydrological considerations. Such models are often complementary to the physical setups referred to earlier and will no doubt have increasing importance.

The Mississippi River has an area of about 1,250,000 square miles. Running from the Gulf of Mexico into Canada and having branches that extend into the Appalachians and the Rockies, it flows through 31 states and a small part of 2 Canadian provinces. It presents flood-control problems, large and small, on many different tributaries as well as on the main river, below the point where it is joined by the Ohio, flowing in from the east.

The problem of coordinating the multitude of flood-control projects, existing, authorized, or proposed on all of these rivers is not only immensely important but very difficult. Within the whole Mississippi Basin are more than 200 great reservoirs, several thousand miles of dikes and levees, with gates and spillways to provide shortcuts to the ocean, whenever the great river, in times of flood, threatens to overtop its levees. All these details are reproduced in miniature in the model at Jackson. Its most important service is to coordinate the work of improvement by local groups and the Corps of Engineers, to obtain maximum basinwide and statewide benefits. Control of floods in small and uncomplicated river systems can be based on simple calculations; but control of the great Mississippi River System as a whole needs the help of the scale model.

The surface of the completed model is permanently molded in concrete. Centrally located instruments, especially designed for the model, provide automatic control and measurement on all the major streams. So mighty is the Mississippi that even though its volume rate of flow in the model is 1,500,000 times less than the river, the pumps must supply about 1000 gallons of water a minute when the whole model is operating as a unit.

The completed model had to be "verified," river by river, by making sure that specified amounts of water in specified locations produced the depths of flood and times of flood arrival downstream that history had recorded. Obstacles of different kinds, simulating the roughness of river banks, were introduced at various points to adjust flow rates in the model to those actually recorded in the past in the rivers themselves. That accomplished, the model had the ability to predict. In the record snow-melt flood of 1952 the model correctly predicted the height of the flood and its time of cresting in the upper reaches of the Missouri. This allowed time for measures to be taken that prevented millions of dollars of flood damage downstream.

Flood Control on the Lower Mississippi

The floodplain of the Mississippi extends from the river's mouth upstream well beyond St. Louis where the main stream is joined by the Missouri. When De Soto first came upon it in the summer of 1541, the great river was in flood. For four hundred years afterward frequent floods brought heavy damage to many parts of the river's alluvial plain. The area subject to flooding was at first 35,000 square miles—about the area of Indiana.

Local efforts to control flooding began with levees at New Orleans. These were gradually extended downstream and upstream, until they had a total length of hundreds of miles. As successive floods overtopped or broke through the levees, these were raised ever higher and became more and more costly. Local efforts seemed quite inadequate to the control of the river, hence the Mississippi River Commission was established in 1873 to combine local efforts with basinwide river planning and control.

Nevertheless, flooding continued. A great flood in 1927 did so much damage that the flood control responsibility for the Mississippi Basin was assigned to the Corps of Engineers. The engineers build flood-control and river improvement projects; but local groups secure rights-of-way, maintain levees and recruit and train a force of experienced engineers and workmen, to be summoned in emergencies.

Flood control and navigation improvement have been sustained with determination, year after year. The total cumulative cost amounted to $1.5 billion by the end of 1967, and is still mounting. Levees have been lengthened and lifted ever higher. They link hilltops into massive walls on both sides of the river. Dams on distant tributary streams delay the discharge of the dammed streams into the Mississippi; impound water for irrigation or navigation improvement, and municipal water supplies; make recreation areas and good fishing possible; and sometimes develop hydroelectric energy.

Most rivers that are old from a geological point of view have so low-ered their valley that they no longer flow very rapidly. In consequence, they deposit silt, which further impedes flow. The rivers then begin to meander. The flood plain of the Mississippi shows dozens of places where the river has changed its course within the last century or two, leaving crescent-shaped or oxbow-shaped lakes. These are important to local fishermen and sportsmen but maintain the water table at so near the level of the surrounding fields that a considerable part of the region may be denied to most cultivated crops.

A part of the work of the Corps of Engineers in this region is to get rid of some of the crooks and bends in the river's channel. About 170 miles have been eliminated from its last thousand miles. This was not merely to save distance but to make overtopping of the levees less fre-quent. A worker on a levee was heard to remark: "When river run straight he run fast; when he run fast he run low; when bend slow him down we spill over." Had this man ever heard of Daniel Bernoulli, who never saw the Mississippi, but who used mathematical symbols over two hundred years ago, to express the same idea? Flood crests along the Mississippi have been lowered as much as 15 feet, just by straight-ening the channel.

The lower Mississippi is now well protected against floods. Land that was nearly worthless immediately after the great flood of 1927 has re-cently sold for as much as $600 an acre. Yet flood control has done more than make river valleys safe for agriculture. It has opened great new areas to industry. More than a billion dollars have been invested in lower Louisiana, along the banks of the Mississippi, in oil refineries, petrochemical plants, and the manufacture of paper and paperboard and metal products, electronic equipment, and even carpets. The area has vast resources in sulfur, salt, lime, natural gas, and forests. It has abundant labor and a mild climate. All that was still needed to ensure rapid industrial development was abundant fresh water and access to domestic and foreign markets. The river itself could furnish them if it were only protected from pollution.

In the early 1950's this new industrial area was threatened with ruin in an unanticipated way. The great river seemed bent on finding a new outlet into the Gulf of Mexico through the Atchafalaya River, a few miles to the west. The industrial area between New Orleans and Baton Rouge would then have become a salt water estuary, and industry would have had to move elsewhere. This new threat to the river's in-dustry has fortunately been parried, though at considerable cost.

With flood control and channel stabilization both presumably achieved, the efforts of the Corps of Engineers may turn, more and more, to such tasks as keeping the main stream within its banks, free from snags and sandbars, and wide and deep enough to carry the river's enormous and rapidly increasing commerce. New levees and embankments, floodgates and spillways, bank and channel stabilization, cutoffs and secondary channels—all these are in evidence everywhere as the Corps of Engineers continues its work of improving and developing the great river's capabilities.

River Traffic Then and Now

Our great inland waterway has always played an important part in the settlement of this continent. This began thousands of years ago, as Indian canoes crept from village to village, along the banks of the principal rivers. The first white settlers used the rivers themselves and trails along the river banks to transport their goods and families. Commerce followed, as the new settlers began to remember things left behind, along the country's Atlantic seaboard and in Europe. As soon as the forests could be cleared away, agriculture and manufacturing moved in, too.

Big rafts were used at first, then barges and flatboats. Emigrant families, domestic animals, household goods, provisions, and lumber were all crowded into narrow quarters, drifting downstream together. On arriving at the end of a trip to St. Louis or New Orleans, the barges or flatboats had to be broken up and sold for lumber, since until the invention of the steamboat there was no way to re-ascend the river. Railroads came considerably later. The first railroad train penetrated beyond the Mississippi in 1856. By that time all the states except Minnesota, on both sides of the Ohio, Mississippi, and Missouri rivers, as far west as Nebraska, had been settled and admitted to the Union.

The Civil War and competition with ever-lengthening railroads nearly ended the steamboat traffic, made famous by Mark Twain. Then, suddenly, in spite of competition from diesel-driven trains and trucks, pipelines, and cargo planes, freighting by river-borne barges expanded enormously. Its rebirth came in part from improved channel maintenance of the nation's inland waterways, which are now navigable for over 25,000 miles. A part of this improvement has been the development of marvelous fresh water harbors, such as those at Green-

Figure 9-1. River Navigation
Photo by A. G. D'Alessandro. Bureau of Reclamation, Department of the
Interior.

ville, Mississippi, created from loops of the meandering Mississippi River, and at Memphis, Tennessee.

Improved channels and harbors have led to the development of more powerful diesel-driven towboats. The largest of these are now of 6000 to 9000 horsepower, and can shove 60,000 tons of freight upstream in a fleet of broad barges, linked to form a unit. Dozens of barges, with a total area of perhaps 5 acres, may compose such a unit. By 1965, diesel-driven river-barges accounted for 10 per cent of the nation's ton-miles of inland freight. It has been estimated that traffic on inland waterways will reach 900 million tons overall by the year 2000. At least three-fourths of the total water-borne burden is ordinary "bulk freight" such as coal and grain. Chemical shipments are expected to rise to 128 million tons, compared with 21 million in 1969.

To handle certain chemicals there are special barges for liquids, such as petroleum, gasoline, liquefied petroleum gases (propane and butane), and liquid chlorine. Giant vacuum-jacketed "Thermos bottles," each holding many tons, permit molten sulfur to be maintained at a temperature just above the boiling point of water, and liquid hydrogen or oxygen, under slight pressure, at about $-180°C$. The inland waterways handled 35 per cent of the chemicals that potentially they could have carried in 1969. By 2000 they are expected to have won a 45 per cent share or more.

The cost of moving freight long distances by barge is only about a fifth of that incurred by shipping it by rail, and only about 4 or 5 per cent of that of shipping by diesel truck. Liquids can often be shipped in large quantities by barge at only about a tenth of the cost of pumping them through a pipeline.

This increase in the capacity of the nation's inland rivers for transporting freight cheaply has brought about great changes in the industrialization of the area involved. Not all of the recent developments are on the Mississippi and its tributaries. New industries, ranging from the production of ammonia in Virginia to a pulp and paper plant on the Columbia River in Oregon, have been springing up everywhere. The Trinity River, which empties into the Gulf of Mexico near Galveston, Texas, is being widened and straightened at a total cost of about a billion dollars, to convert it into a barge-carrying waterway. It will ultimately transport ocean freight 370 miles inland, to Dallas and Fort Worth. Texas cattle, which in frontier days were driven overland to railroads in Kansas, will presently float comfortably downstream, and at the Gulf be transshipped to the Mississippi or to the Atlantic seaboard.

The Improvement of Northern Rivers

Although the problems created by Mississippi floods were most serious in the river's southernmost thousand miles, the northern reaches of that river were subject to destructive flooding, too, from spring rains or the sudden melting of winter snows. Thousands of acres of farmland and a great dairy industry have been flooded or endangered every winter. Here, several hundred little streams, instead of a single great river, have had to be controlled and made to do useful work instead of spreading destruction. The great detail involved in this work is evident to anyone passing through the area. The northern part of the Mississippi basin has now received about two-thirds of the expenditure that it will need to be fully protected from flooding.

The Missouri River presents vexing problems of a very different sort. The area that it drains is about a sixth of that of the 48 coterminous states. Its channel, when first observed by Lewis and Clark and other early explorers, was shifting and unstable. Its flow was very irregular, and its flood-plain often miles in width. Its improvement has called for six great reservoirs in the middle reaches of the river, and for stabilizing its channel in its lower basin, as far as its junction with the Mississippi, just north of St. Louis.

These reservoirs have a combined power-generating capacity of over 2,000,000 kilowatts. Their total waterstoring capacity is sufficient to keep the Missouri flowing at a steady rate for over three years, thus stabilizing the flow of the river through wet and dry seasons alike, in spite of all the caprices of weather.

Because of controlled flow and stabilized channel, the Missouri is now navigable from its confluence with the Mississippi as far upstream as Yankton, South Dakota, a distance of about 750 miles. In the years to come, more storage for water will be provided by damming the river's tributary streams. New irrigation systems will be created, erosion will be lessened, and new areas will be opened for fish and wildlife conservation. About half of the work planned for the improvement of the Missouri Basin had been completed in 1965.

The problems presented by the Ohio River are in striking contrast to those of the Missouri. Its valley is so narrow and its banks are so crowded with factories, cities, and highways that there is no possibility for important new storage of water except on a few tributary streams. Each of these is being independently developed. The chief problems are the creation of new municipal and industrial water supplies and the prevention of pollution. These call for much the same measures as channel improvement.

The Civil Works Program of the Corps of Engineers

The Civil Works Program of the Corps of Engineers is in addition to the military duties of the Corps and at present calls for three principal activities: (1) improvement of navigation on the Great Lakes and control of lake levels; (2) channel stabilization, flood control, power generation, and navigational improvements on the nation's principal rivers; (3) stabilizing coast lines, improving harbors, and conducting experiments intended to provide better ways of doing all these things.

Figure 9-2. River Traffic
U. S. Army photo, Army Engineers, St. Louis, Missouri, Engineer District.

The Corps provides groups of specialists in the different departments of hydraulic engineering. These men carry on the work of the
Waterways Experiment Station on the Mississippi, undertake the construction work incidental to the many hydrologic tasks that are in progress at the same time, carry on research in the three chief departments
of hydrology in which the engineers are involved, and operate a hydrologic training center. The total annual cost for their civil works is approximately $1.6 billion.

By a so-called Rivers and Harbors Act, enacted every two years,
Congress authorizes programs that the engineers have recommended
and appropriates money for them and for projects already begun. Public hearings concerning these projects are apt to be prolonged and de-
bate often acrimonious, since there are always differences of opinion
when the benefits and damage done by expenditure of such vast sums
are discussed.

For a long time in the future the development of new projects and
the upkeep of old ones on the nation's waterways are bound to call for

somewhat the same outlays as in the recent past. Yet they must constantly compete with other public needs: the improvement of airports
and rail transport, slum clearance, control of air and water pollution,
the problem of getting distinct races to live together in harmony, the
control of crime, public education. The nation has too many people
already. Thus, even if we have the good sense or good fortune to avoid
war, the long-term trend in hydraulic engineering outlays is probably
no more strongly upward than the gross national product—a rough
measure of the nation's total spending for goods and services.

Beyond all this are differences of opinion that are usually viewed as
merely political, but which are more important than this word suggests, because they actually involve moral considerations. Is not the
eviction of citizens from their homes to make way for public improvements a serious loss of liberty, even though every effort is made to
compensate the dispossessed persons fairly? Is it fair and just for the
government to develop hydroelectric power at dam sites, then sell this
in competition with privately produced power, which is moreover
taxed to create this competition?

10

Water and Energy
from the Pacific States

California's Central Valley Project

The state of California is shaped like a great arm, 200 miles wide and about 850 miles long. It hangs straight down from a shoulder in Oregon, then bends toward the southeast, as if the arm had to support the weight of Nevada. The wrist and hand, which are extended toward the east, are hidden within Arizona.

Along the eastern border of the arm are the ranges of the Sierra Nevada with many peaks over 10,000 feet high. This is high enough to induce precipitation, as moist air masses, coming in from the Pacific, rise to cross the mountains. Thus the eastern border of the state gets rain, which is abundant in the north but more and more sparse as one goes southward.

The water descending from the Sierra is carried away by two rivers, the Sacramento and San Joaquin, which flow in opposite directions toward the middle of the state and pour their combined waters into San Francisco Bay, just below the elbow of the great arm. This is the famous Delta region, which is a rich and varied agricultural area, described in an earlier chapter.

The state's surplus water has always been in the north, whereas new immigrants, especially since 1900, have chiefly settled in the south. By 1950 it was evident to everyone that a great aqueduct was needed to carry surplus water from the rain-drenched, flood-ridden north to the semi-arid (but nevertheless often flood-ridden) south. The anticipated cost was staggering—about half a billion dollars, enough to launch a

Figure 10-1. Oroville Dam
Department of Water Resources, State of California

few rockets to the moon or support a minor war for perhaps two weeks. Many years were needed for the project to take form in the minds of engineers and from thence to come before the public. Then, in 1960, the state's voters gave permission to their Department of Water Resources to complete plans, let contracts, and provide for the sale of bonds that would eventually pay for the construction of the aqueduct and supplementary projects and leave them free from debt.

The great round-up of the waters is on the Feather River, in the heart of the northern Sierra. There, America's highest dam, 747 feet high and a mile along its crest, was begun in 1962 and completed in 1969. It is a few miles upstream from Oroville and about 65 miles due north of the state's capital at Sacramento. This is the very district overrun by the stampede for gold in 1849.

The great dam contains about 78 million cubic yards of compacted

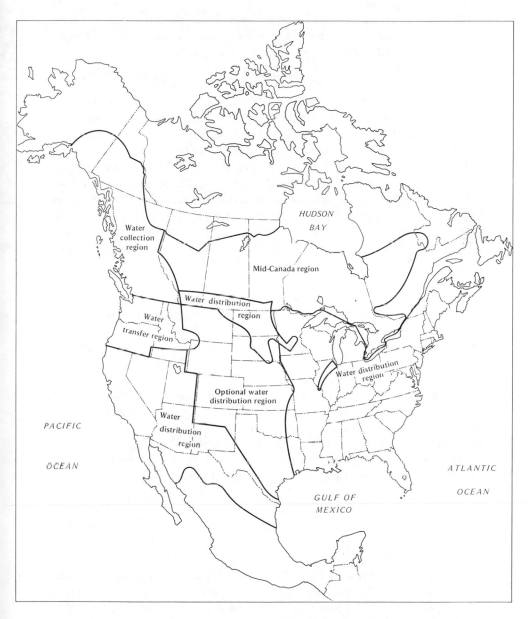

Figure 10-2. NAWAPA Regions
From *North American Water and Power Alliance* (December 1964) (The Ralph
M. Parsons Co., Los Angeles, Calif.), Drawing 8. Used by permission.

earth and gravel, which had to be hauled about eleven miles in being brought to the dam site. There are several smaller dams on the Upper Feather River, but the Oroville Dam itself will retain about 3.5 million acre-feet of water in a reservoir that will cover about 25 square miles.

Two power plants' combined capacity is 710,000 kilowatts. This is enough to supply the needs of a city of about a million persons for electrical energy. The total cost of the Oroville facility is about $508 million. Of that amount approximately 14 per cent or $69.6 million was expended on flood control by the U.S. Corps of Engineers.

The impounded water, after passing through the turbines of the power plants or after being released through spillways in time of flood, will be parcelled out to various users according to a plan which seeks to anticipate the chief ways in which water will be used in 1990 (the year of the State Water Plan's completion). This allows for water that will be supplied by existing or planned federal or local water supply projects.

Thirty public agencies, large or small, have contracted to buy the water and electric power that the project will produce, from the present moment until all is completed and in full operation. Two-thirds of the people of California live in the area that this development of water and energy will serve. Some of the most important features of the development are shown in Figure 10-2.

The total length of the great aqueduct that will convey water from the pumping station at sea level in the Delta to the Perris reservoir, near the southern border of the state, will be 444 miles. From the Oroville Dam the water flows down the Feather and Sacramento rivers to the Delta, a few miles northeast of San Francisco. Flowing southward, a branch canal supplies cities and agriculture to the east and south of San Francisco Bay. The rest continues southward in a great canal down the west side of the San Joaquin Valley.

At the southern end of the San Joaquin Valley are the Tehachapi Mountains, over which the southbound water must be lifted by pumps. In 1990, when the aqueduct will be completed and running at full capacity, about 108 million gallons of water an hour will need to be lifted. The lift will need to be over 1900 feet. With pumps working at 100 per cent efficiency, 3.14 kilowatt-hours of electrical energy are needed to lift 1000 gallons 1000 feet. Thus anyone may calculate a demand of about 650,000 kilowatts for the Tehachapi pumps alone.

There are several other lifts that will demand further quantities of electrical energy, and every pumping station must provide standby capacity for emergencies and must look to possible extra demands as the original facility is expanded. Thus the state of California is seeking to provide a generating capacity of 2 million kilowatts.

Several hundred thousand kilowatts of hydroelectric energy will probably be brought in over high-tension lines from distant power sources. Yet the chief reliance for power for pumping will probably be locally generated steam power.

Nuclear energy, without government subsidy, is now barely competitive with coal and oil. As improvements are made in the reactors by which nuclear energy is produced, its competitive position will improve and its use will be expanded. Nevertheless, the demand for electrical energy from all sources is expanding so rapidly that coal and petroleum have a bright future, too.

The chief cost of delivering water to the southern end of the great aqueduct is not the cost of building and maintaining the aqueduct itself, including interest charges, but the cost of pumping. It is estimated that water can be sold at the southernmost end of the aqueduct for about $45 to $65 an acre-foot, which is about 14 to 20 cents a thousand gallons. This is expensive as irrigation water, but is much cheaper than anything that has thus far been developed for winning fresh water from brackish water or the ocean.

The Earthquake Threat

Modern hydroelectric plants, if designed by well-trained engineers, have a surprising resistance to destruction by earthquake shocks. A great Alaskan earthquake in the spring of 1964 had its epicenter within 35 miles of a power plant at Eklutna, and the hydraulic head under which the generators were running at the moment of the shock was about 850 feet. The concrete intake pipe was cracked and some rocks and mud got into it; yet the powerhouse itself was not badly damaged, and was soon repaired and restored to normal operation.

California has more to fear from earthquakes than damage to hydroelectric plants. Big earthquakes rupture water distribution lines and lead to fierce fires that get out of control—as happened after the San Francisco earthquake of 1906. Water distribution mains in earthquake country must therefore always be placed where damage by earthquake shocks may be quickly repaired.

Within the next century there will almost certainly be one or more large earthquake shocks along the great San Andreas fault. This slices from the Salton Sea near the Mexican border, through the Tehachapi Range from south to north, trending a bit toward the west, then passes out into the Pacific Ocean about 100 miles north of San Francisco. In many great California earthquakes of recent times the land along one side of the great fault has shifted northward a few feet. Where the great aqueduct must cross the fault it should obviously cross as an open canal, not as a buried conduit, in order that sidewise displacement at the fault may quickly be repaired.

Any attempt to prevent the displacement will of course be thwarted by the tremendous stresses in the earth's crust. For millions of years, these have created a rent that extends for several hundred miles along the surface and downward to unknown depths. Where a mountain range has been torn asunder, what chance have any of the man's puny works of standing up to the shocks?

Of course, as mentioned in an earlier chapter, water that has been expensively lifted to a high elevation may be used to generate electric power as it descends on the other side of the mountain through the turbines of a hydroelectric plant. In the same way, electric trains descending one side of a mountain range generate electricity that helps to haul other trains up the other side of the range. The descent of water through the underground tunnels and penstocks of the Devil's Canyon power plants, near the aqueduct's southern end, will recover a good part of the energy needed by the Tehachapi pumps. Perhaps the earthquake threat was one reason why no attempt was made to tunnel directly through the mountains.

A Continental Idea: NAWAPA

The North American Water and Power Alliance (NAWAPA) distributed no water, generated no power, and was not an alliance. Neither was it North American, although it could have been developed as to be worthy of that name. It was just an attempt to estimate the fresh water resources and fresh water needs of the continent and to redistribute the resources to satisfy the needs better. Otherwise expressed, NAWAPA was a plan for intercepting fresh water that is on its way to be wasted by flowing away to the ocean, and for bringing it to parts of the continent where water is scarce. If the needs of the continent for water are ever to be met, the less populous parts of the continent must contribute from their surplus.

In comparison with the solid accomplishments of the Corps of Engineers, NAWAPA may seem to be of the substance of dreams. Yet even the smallest engineering venture must begin by comparing needs with possibilities. There is no reason why a grander one, which plans to remake a continent, should not begin in the same way. It is by passing through the brains of competent men of good will that dreams become realities.

Details of this far-ranging plan for redistributing the fresh water resources of North America were first published in 1964. The plan suffered from the handicap of needing international agreement for the pooling of water resources, land capabilities, capital, hydroelectric energy, and engineering skills, yet the continent's record of more than a century of peace should incline everyone to believe that agreement will be easier than on continents that are deeply divided by senseless religious intolerance and venomous political rivalries. Most lands have too much history that must be forgiven and forgotten before they can work together for mutual benefit. It is not engineering difficulties that prevent the remaking of continents and a more even distribution of the earth's fresh water resources. The obstacle is in the hearts and minds of stubborn and unforgiving men.

International agreement for redistributing the fresh water resources of North America would demonstrate to the rest of the world that tolerance and good will are themselves valuable resources, whose market value ranks with that of fresh water because it makes fresh water available that would otherwise be wasted. Agreement in advance should ensure that each of the three nations concerned shall get a fair share of the benefits to be parceled out among them. Only the wildlife of the continent may not have their rights sufficiently protected. They need their own special advocates.

Water from the Far North

The Pacific Coast of Canada, as far north as the turn of the coast near Skagway, Alaska, is blessed by abundant rainfall. There is some precipitation almost every month, although it tends to be heaviest in the fall and winter. In the Rocky Mountain Region of Canada and in Canadian provinces still farther to the east, precipitation is lighter and tends to be seasonal; yet the total area over which it takes place is so vast that the total volume of fresh water that falls from the skies is enormous. A good part of it goes to waste in the Arctic and North Pacific oceans. Only the fresh water that flows through the St. Lawrence into the North Atlantic is in a region far enough south, hence climatically mild enough, to support a dense population.

The 17 continental states west of Iowa are less fortunate. Washington, Oregon, and northern California receive on their Pacific slopes what is regarded as abundant rainfall; farther to the south, rainfall decreases rapidly because the maritime polar air masses, which bring in moisture from the North Pacific, usually come in farther north than San Francisco Bay. Southern California averages only about a fourteenth as much rainfall as the northern counties of the state, and mountains prevent the little moisture that then remains from passing very far to the east.

In consequence, the Mojave and Arizona deserts exist, on the western border of the Great American Desert, which leads from eastern Oregon southward into Northern Mexico. Altogether, the desert country includes most of the 17 arid continental states that lie west of Iowa and 3 of the northern-most Mexican states. It has been estimated that Canada dumps enough fresh water, unused, into the ocean, to supply the present needs of the United States, twice over. Topographically, the NAWAPA concept may be separated into four regions, as shown in Figure 10-2:

1. Water Collection Region, comprising mountains and plateaus of Alaska, Yukon Territory, and British Columbia,
2. Water Transfer Region, comprising the northwestern United States,
3. Water Distribution Region, comprising the Canadian and American plains, the southwestern United States, and northern Mexico, and
4. Mid-Canada Region, a vast region of adequate but poorly distributed water supply, wherein rivers now washing into Hudson Bay and James Bay will be redirected to areas of need.

Canada was asked to estimate her own future needs, then sell a part of her surplus to her neighbors to the south or let them have it in exchange for hydroelectric energy. This seemed a good way for Canadians to secure the funds that are needed for the development of their own land's resources and industries. The alternative was to raise the billions of dollars needed by direct taxation or to sell bonds that will call for interest payments over many years, perhaps chiefly to foreigners. Nature, by providing Canada with abundant water, has given her something that might well bring in a continuous flow of capital.

Thirty-three of the Western states of the United States would have received fresh water from NAWAPA. So would have seven provinces of Canada, the Yukon Territory, and three large and very arid states of

Northern Mexico. About 56 million new acres could have been opened to irrigation. Mexico's share of these could have been about eight times what Egypt hopes to irrigate from the Aswan High Dam.

Water and Power from the Great Trench

The heart of NAWAPA's Western project was the Rocky Mountain Trench, a scenic gorge 500 miles long, which extends from near Jasper National Park, in Canada, southeastward to Flathead Lake in Montana. Within this gorge the Columbia, Fraser, Kootenay, and Peace rivers all arise and flow away in different directions. The plan was to dam the northern end of this gorge, thus reversing the flow of the headwaters of these rivers and creating a 500-mile storage lake. The initial flow into this lake could have been ultimately increased by water pumped from storage lakes created by damming the upper Yukon and Tanana rivers, and perhaps even by diverting rivers that now flow into Hudson Bay.

From the great storage lake water would be drawn to stabilize the flow of the Columbia and Fraser rivers and to irrigate the arid southwest. Both the Columbia and the Fraser have a tremendous long-term and seasonal fluctuation. The highest annual flow of the Columbia (1884) was about 30 times the least flow (1937). During a single year the greatest rate of flow may be 5 times the least.

High water in the Columbia and Fraser rivers comes in summer, when snow and ice are melting in the mountains of British Columbia. This is the season when the demand for hydroelectric power, on account of the long period of daylight, is very low; hence a good part of the water of both rivers, during the summer months, flows away into the ocean unused. In winter, when the headwaters of both rivers are frozen, the demand for energy is greatest. Under NAWAPA, the flow of water through the Columbia at McNary Dam would be increased by about 8700 cubic feet per second (cfs) during the winter months, and the flood crests of summer would be lowered by 60,000 cfs.

Closely related to the power-generating project just mentioned were plans for the lower reaches of the Clearwater and Salmon rivers, in central Idaho. Dams could accumulate water and generate power in both rivers, which flow into the Snake River, near the southeast corner of the state of Washington. Hydraulic engineers here would have a choice. They may develop hydroelectric energy, again and again, as the water plunges through the turbines of a series of power plants, along the Snake River and the lower Columbia. Or they may direct the flow along a more nearly level course, with just enough slope to keep the water moving at the needed rate. All the potential energy of the water is then gradually dissipated as heat in overcoming friction, but most of the water then arrives at some very distant destination, for example, the three northernmost provinces of Mexico.

NAWAPA proposed that water from the great storage trench shall be used in both these ways. Most of the power development, perhaps better termed energy recovery, would be in the swift-running rivers of Idaho and in Columbia. Most of the water distribution would be through tunnels and canals that carry the water southward through Idaho, Utah, and southeastern Nevada, into California, Arizona, New Mexico, and then into the arid northern provinces of Mexico itself. Thus modern engineers could begin to lift the blight that desiccation, alkali, and salt have lain upon the Great American Desert for millions of years, ever since a great fresh water lake (Lake Bonneville), with an area of nearly 20,000 square miles, squarely in the midst of this land, was cut off from outflow into the sea, and began to dry up.

Tragedy on the Yukon

One of the more distant future projects of NAWAPA aroused early opposition. The upper Yukon River and its tributary, the Tanana, would have the direction of flow in the headwaters reversed. A dam at Rampart, Alaska, 530 feet high and 4700 feet long, would create a lake that would take about 20 years to fill. This lake would finally have about the same area as Lake Erie. The chief purpose of the dam would be the development of hydroelectric power—more than 5 million kilowatts of power, or about two and a half times the total power—producing capacity of Niagara, under international agreements now in force.

The Corps of Engineers, in a 1965 appropriation, was allotted over a million dollars for a preliminary study of this project. Meanwhile, the U.S. Fish and Wildlife Service, in reviewing the project, anticipates an "overwhelming" destruction of fish and wildlife if the dam is built. The broad, marshy Yukon Flat, with its estimated 36,000 little lakes and ponds, would be drowned under 400 to 500 feet of water. Nesting places that annually contribute 1,500,000 ducks, 12,500 geese, and thousands of little brown cranes to America's wildfowl resources would disappear.

In addition, over 270,000 salmon, which now pass this point each year, on their way upstream to spawn, would be stopped at the dam, in spite of possible help from "fish ladders." The present "moose range," perhaps the most important one in North America, would be overwhelmed, and most fur-bearing animals would be blotted from this part of Alaska.

We here see two different branches of government in disagreement —as has often happened in the past when industrial interests have come into conflict with those interested in preserving a part of our continent in its original, unspoiled state. Fortunately, another source of hydro-electric energy, sufficient for the Alaska of today, may soon be made available by damming Devil's Canyon, on the upper Susitna River, which flows into the North Pacific Ocean a few miles west of Anchorage, Alaska. Moreover, there are substitutes for hydroelectric energy, even for the rapidly expanding aluminum industry. Steam-generated electric energy, unlike most other commodities tends toward lower costs; and atomic energy, too, is now nearly competitive.

11

A Horrid Word for a Horrid Deed: Pollution

Blow the horrid deed in every eye.
Shakespeare, Macbeth

Contamination vs. Pollution

Water is such a good solvent that it dissolves a part of nearly everything it meets: gases from the atmosphere, salts of many different kinds from rocks and minerals of the soil, organic coloring matter from decaying vegetation, even traces of silica, the nearly insoluble substance that is the chief component of ordinary white sand. From the chemical composition of the solid residue obtained by evaporating a sample of water that has spent some time underground, a chemist or hydrologist can usually determine the nature of the strata with which the water came in contact during its underground journey. Sometimes he may even estimate the relative times that the water remained in contact with strata of different sorts.

Even rain water, although rated pure by most housewives, contains dissolved oxygen and nitrogen, with a much smaller quantity of carbon dioxide, all three derived from the atmosphere. It also contains minute amounts of every accidental impurity that the air itself contains: solid particles of dust, ash, and soot, together with traces of common salt, ammonium salts, sulfuric acid, and perhaps as many as a dozen identifiable organic impurities (impurities that are compounds of carbon), some of them malodorous. Distilled water is never much better than rain water unless special precautions have been taken to destroy organic matter and other oxidizable impurities and to exclude impurities that might otherwise be contributed by a glass still or glass containers, or by contact with the atmosphere.

The accidental impurities in water are sometimes even beneficial. For example, dissolved oxygen relieves deaerated water of its flat taste, and is needed to support the life of aquatic organisms, from microscopic plants or animals upward to fish. Water that is even slightly warm dissolves far less oxygen, hence will not permit certain species of fish to live. Any impurity that makes water unfit to drink or less fit for any other use is said to *contaminate* the water. *Pollution* is a stronger word, implying complete befoulment.

Contamination often comes from natural sources, as when salt from an underground deposit enters an underground stream, or when an aquifer (the conveyor of an underground stream) comes into contact with a mineralized vein that contaminates the water with salts of copper, iron, lead, or other heavy metals. Contamination on a grand scale results when the Colorado, the muddy Missouri, and the great Mississippi dump hundreds of tons of mud every day over farms or into smaller streams along their banks. This was occurring long before the first white settlers took over the continent and began to cultivate its prairies and uplands.

Sanitation Zero

Nomadic tribes, in prehistoric times as today, had little need for sanitation. The dunes of the surrounding great outdoors quickly hid and desiccated human wastes of every sort. If pestilence appeared or if wells went dry or if accumulating salt destroyed the soil's fertility, the tribe just moved on, hoping to leave disease, thirst, and famine behind.

Whenever rainfall was abundant, sanitation was still disregarded, not because it was needless but because of universal ignorance. The great rivers of the tropical rainbelts provided water not only for drinking and cooking but also for laundering. That they, in addition, served as sewers was perhaps never noted except near seacoasts, where the tides of the ocean brought yesterday's sewage once more into view.

As the human burden on the rivers continued slowly to increase, century after century, pollution became fantastic. In rainy Southeast Asia, thousands of homes, palm-thatched or roofed with tinned or zinc-coated iron, rise on stilts from the murky waters. Thousands of houseboats are moored in other places, where the water is more sluggish. Water everywhere finds every sort of use, though it is rarely boiled. Nearly every small stream serves as a laundry, although bleaches and detergents tend to be shunned because they spoil the taste of the drinking water of downstream neighbors.

Even in lands in which abundant water does not invite lack of sanitation, there has often been no sanitary progress since the invention of chopsticks. In lack of sewers, the clop-clop of the night soil specialist, carrying his fetid burden to distant fields in the dead of night, is a familiar sound to all who are awake at "morn's most unsavory hour." Sanitation zero is almost world-wide, near the end of the twentieth century.

Water-Borne Disease

Polluted water and tainted food join with malnutrition to account for the high infant mortality of the lands of sanitation zero. Half the children born in Vietnam die before they reach the age of five. The average age attained there by peasants is about thirty-five years—just half of what may be expected for anyone born in the United States.

Throughout history, water-borne diseases must have been an important restraint on population growth. It is nevertheless probable that the great cities of the ancient Mediterranean world, with their admirable aqueducts, had safer water than most rural areas of their own or later times. The ancients, although they knew nothing of bacterial disease, were well aware that polluted water supplies are dangerous, and they had strict laws to protect water against pollution.

The chief water-borne diseases are cholera, dysentery, and typhoid. Sudden and widespread epidemics usually come from infected water supplies, although these diseases are not exclusively water-borne. Personal contact plays a part, and so does transmission through soiled clothing and lack of personal cleanliness.

The cholera of recent times (Asiatic cholera) is a different disease from that of the sixteenth century. There were six or more great epidemics of Asiatic cholera in Europe and America during the nineteenth century. There were tens of thousands of cases of illness in every Western country, with mortality sometimes as high as 60 per cent. These great pestilences were all traced back to India, and especially to Bengal, where lack of sanitation was universal, the rivers were all polluted, and poorly drained soil near the river mouths remained polluted from year to year.

The drinking of tea, which originated in the Orient, compels water to be boiled and no doubt has often saved the countries of its origin from decimating pestilences. Yet how can anyone escape infection if the water in which he bathes is swarming with disease-producing organisms?

Cholera shows very clear evidence of being water-borne. An outbreak in Hamburg in 1895 caused more than 8600 deaths in the part of the city supplied with unfiltered river water, but was stopped at streets bounding a suburb in which the water was filtered through sand. Nevertheless, it is now realized that filtration through sand is not at all reliable and should always be followed by chemical disinfection.

The medical treatment of cholera has been greatly improved and the death rate greatly reduced since the beginning of this century. International inspections at airports decrease the risk of cholera being spread by travelers, and means for inoculating against it have been developed. There were at least a half-million deaths from cholera in India in 1918 and 1919, but it has only seldom been a threat to Western Europe or America during the twentieth century.

Dysentery includes at least five distinct diseases, caused by different microorganisms, differing in the frequency with which they are met in different parts of the world. Amoebic dysentery is of greater incidence in the tropics, whereas bacillary dysentery, which is more contagious, is encountered everywhere.

In both diseases the organisms multiply in the bowels, and in bacillary dysentery produce toxins (poisons) that may affect the heart. Both diseases are cured by the proper intestinal medicines; but those who have had amoebic dysentery may have permanent bowel damage, and convalescents are likely to act as carriers. There are some countries in which the natives seem to have a degree of immunity, so that those who become ill are chiefly tourists. Travelers in these lands may carry pills that give some protection against infected food or drinking water. Fortunately, a good many fruits, bought in native markets, are thick-skinned enough to be edible after being sterilized by being submerged for a few hours in a weak formaldehyde solution.

Typhoid, although a water-borne disease, is often transmitted by milk, shellfish, flies, and typhoid carriers, persons who have had the disease and who for many years thereafter harbor and excrete typhoid germs and may transmit the disease to others in handling food or milk. The onset of the disease is less sudden and terrifying than that of the other water-borne diseases just discussed, but the mortality may be considerable.

Typhoid, in some wars, has produced more casualties than enemy bullets have. Beginning with the Russo-Japanese War of 1904–5, it was subdued in the Japanese army by sanitary measures: drinking water was boiled, privies were disinfected with "chloride of lime," flies were controlled, wells were inspected and marked "safe" or "unsafe," and pills were provided that gave some protection if a soldier had to fill his canteen with water of unknown quality. Anti-typhoid inoculation has since become an important means of control.

In absence of modern sewage disposal, typhoid passes from typhoid carriers into septic tanks and from these through gravel beds into the soil. There it lingers, to be picked up on the feet of those who walk on the soil and it is thus carried into the home. There are doubtless areas in many great cities where the soil has been polluted for centuries.

Although most germs are killed by drying and exposure to sunlight, many kinds form thick-walled spores that may slumber indefinitely and awaken to life when conditions become favorable. The vacuum cleaner is a more important sanitary agent than the toothbrush.

This by no means completes the list of water-borne diseases. Among those that rarely appear outside the tropics is bilharzia, which is endemic (continuously present) in Africa, the West Indies, tropical South America, the Near East, and tropical Asia (China, Japan, the Philippines, and elsewhere). It is transmitted from fresh-water snails to man by the larvae of the snails—free-swimming "flatworms." Penetrating through the skin of persons who wade or swim in infected mud or river water, it enters the bloodstream, burrows into the liver, and infects the whole abdominal area. Damage done to any of these organs may cause death. The extension of irrigation systems in many tropical and subtropical lands has led to a great increase in this disease. It is now a major health problem in all the tropical countries we have mentioned.

The disease may be controlled in individuals by administering antimony tartrate; but it is controlled on a larger scale by exterminating the snails. A concentration of only 1 g of copper sulfate in 1 million liters (1 part by weight in 1 billion) will result in the snail's complete eradication. Several organic compounds are also effective in very small concentrations. The problem is then to prevent reinfection of the river from small tributary streams. The moral for troops or tourists (or for natives) is simple: Don't swim or wade in water not known to be free from these parasites. They are dangerous as crocodiles but less apt to be noticed. Mere contact with the water may be fatal.

Modern Sewage Disposal

The great cities of the modern world could not exist without provision for sewage disposal. Industry, even in the most progressive countries

Figure 11-1. Sewage Effluent Plant—City of Phoenix
Photo by E. Hertzog. Bureau of Reclamation, Department of the Interior.

of the world, would otherwise be located in small towns and villages, as in the America of a century ago, and in most parts of populous China and India today. The invention of bacterial oxidation and reduction for the treatment of sewage and the use of chlorine in disinfecting water supplies are among the most important scientific achievements of modern times.

The essential features of a modern sewage disposal plant are shown in the photographs. The outflow from the sewer must pass through a coarse screen to remove roots, rags, and other solid trash, from which iron and steel cans and scraps are removed by magnets. The solids that get through the screen are finely ground, and they pass with the liquid into settling basins. From the bottom of these, solid particles are continuously removed by scrapers and are carried to a "digester," in which aerobic bacteria (those that are active in the presence of a good supply of air) oxidize and destroy organic matter.

In the most modern installations, oxidation is accomplished by "activated sludge." This consists of floating flocs of sludge, laden with bacteria and kept in suspension by a vigorous current of air, which bubbles up through holes in the bottom of the digester.

Better circulation and aeration are thus obtained than was possible with an older process, which involved trickling filtration from shallow ponds through sand. Therefore oxidation is now much more rapid than with the older process and a smaller area is needed for the sewage disposal of a city.

Regardless of how the biological treatment just described is carried out, the solids that resist being oxidized are subjected in a closed digester to the opposite treatment, reduction. This is carried out by anaerobic bacteria (those active in the nearly complete absence of air). A considerable part of the solids that have resisted oxidation are thus reduced, forming methane gas, CH_4. What still remains is nearly free from odor and may be dried and sold as organic fertilizer.

The sewage disposal system of a great city may cost several million dollars and may cover many acres, at a point rather distant from the city itself. Small communities may be served by shallow settling ponds, in which aerobic bacteria are active near the surface, and anaerobic bacteria at greater depths. The liquid effluent is further purified by filtration through sand, before being chlorinated and discarded. This method of disposing of the sewage of a few dozen or a few hundred people is simple and practical. Under competent supervision, it rarely creates a nuisance.

Septic Tanks

Rapidly growing cities are often surrounded by suburban areas in which the disposal of human wastes is by septic tanks. These carry on aerobic and anaerobic fermentation in deep closed containers that overflow through one or more drainlines of open-jointed tile, which are buried in crushed stone or coarse gravel, and are often covered with sod.

It is important that septic tank drainlines shall not be underlain by compacted clay or hardpan and that during rainy seasons they shall be above any possible level reached by flood water. Otherwise, in rainy seasons, the householder may need to reach his front door in a boat, rowed through a lake of sewage.

Septic tanks are generally a temporary expedient, to be replaced by a connection with sewers when available. They need to be pumped out every two or three years. Householders need to remember that bacteria are rendered inactive by heavy metal salts, borax, and many detergents. For this reason, the kitchen and laundry should have a separate drain-line from the septic tank. Special types of yeast, sometimes sold as aids to fermentation in the tanks, are actually of little value.

People should be more aware than they usually are of the dangers incurred by the use of septic tanks. In times of flood, septic tanks may infect a public water supply. Or tidal lands along a coast may be polluted, so that the oysters there must not be eaten. Or public beaches may become so polluted that they are closed by the public health authorities.

The public is not often well aware that when any of the evils just mentioned occur, the cure may need years, for a sewage system is not created overnight and disinfection of polluted mud may be impossible. Developers of housing areas, unless compelled by law, are not likely to anticipate the disasters that may follow long after a new area is opened. By that time the developers will have sold out and gone to new hunting grounds. Let the buyers of lots in new developments do all the worrying. Wherever septic tanks exist, a local ordinance should demand that every lot be large enough to accommodate a home, garage, and septic tank, with drainlines and an extra area for drainline replacement. In lack of sufficient space, the householder may find that home is anything but sweet.

The Problem of Liquid Effluents

The disposal methods just described are actually very primitive. They get rid of solids and the soluble organic part of human wastes, but they leave a solution rich in soluble salts, including common salts that furnish plant nutrients that are needed for the growth of plants and that most plants get from the soil solution that wets their roots. In addition to nitrogen, the most important plant nutrients are the non-metals phosphorus and sulfur and the metals calcium, magnesium, and potassium, with smaller amounts of iron and manganese. The liquid effluents from sewage treatment have usually been discarded into the nearest stream, with or without chlorination. Thence, they have found their way into ponds and lakes, which have often been dangerously polluted.

The simplest and most logical way to get rid of the liquid effluents might seem to be to redistribute them through special mains for the irrigation of parks, orchards, and farms (but of course not garden crops). Thus plant nutrients might remain near their places of origin, circulating endlessly through a cycle that leads from harvested crops through human beings, back to the land, and so again into crops. In such a cycle there might nevertheless be a slow accumulation of nutrient elements, owing to the use of fertilizers and the fact that great cities get their food from all over the world. After a time, this accumulation might decrease the need for fertilizers that supply nutrients other than nitrogen.

Yet local industries often pollute the sewage effluents with substances injurious to plants and household laundries may add excessive concentrations of boron. However, the most serious objection to the use of sewage effluents in irrigation is that they may find their way into a deep-lying aquifer, whence it may be impossible to remove them. In parts of Missouri that are underlain by limestone, rifts in the limestone and the collapse of caves have permitted the drainage from old barnyards to penetrate into aquifers. Distant springs and wells then sometimes contain such a high concentration of nitrate that livestock and people are affected adversely. (The nitrate is formed by the bacterial oxidation of nitrogen compounds in the drainage from the barnyards.)

A promising method for dealing with the problem of the liquid effluents containing nutrients may be to use them for the cultivation of algae in shallow basins exposed to sunlight. The algae might be harvested by draglines, dried, compressed, and sold as stock feed. This possibility deserves more study. There are also areas in which salt water underlies the fresh water aquifers. A cased well sunk to this zone would provide a means for disposal of the liquid effluents. Unfortunately such wells are expensive and not feasible at many locations.

Pollution from Long Ago Claims Victims Today

In the early nineteenth century the tide of immigrants and settlers passed beyond the Mississippi and began to penetrate the West. Moving ever upstream and westward, first by riverboat and trail, then by oxcart and wagon, they reached the prairies of Kansas in the days of old John Brown. Each little farm had its barnyard, manure pile, pigsty, and privy within a whiff of the farmer's front door. Sometimes it rained for days on end, and one could hear the roaring of swollen Coon Creek, more than a mile away. Yet farmers who went outside to do their chores and came back wet to the skin scarcely noted that their yards were strangely free from cascading water, in spite of all the downpour.

Where was all that water going? Much of it was penetrating the filth in the farmer's front yard and porous soil beneath, then was trickling through fractured limestone, deep underground, and was dripping from the ceiling of a limestone cave. Organic matter carried by that water had been long ago destroyed by bacteria. Its carbon went to increase the store of dissolved carbon dioxide in the water. Its sulfur was almost all precipitated as gypsum. But its nitrogen, derived from proteins and the simpler organic compounds of the barnyard wastes, was first converted into ammonium salts (the ion NH_4^+) then, by oxidation, into nitrates (the ion NO_3^-).

Then farmers in Missouri, proud of their new deep wells, began to pump water from the hidden limestone caves. The result: death of mules from nitrate poisoning. In far away New Mexico a similar thing was happening: children sickened mysteriously from what soon was diagnosed as poisoning by nitrate, "blue baby disease."

The Results of the Pollution of Lakes and Ponds

Microscopic and near-microscopic plants and animals, which spend their life floating or drifting in water, are called plankton (drifters). They are found not only in fresh and saline water but in the ocean, beneath glacial ice and in hot springs, in every climatic zone. There are hundreds of different species, among which algae are prominent and important.

The algal population of lakes and ponds often fluctuates violently with slight changes in the concentration of dissolved nutrients, changes in temperatures, and other factors not yet identified. Plant nutrients contained in sewage effluents or in the runoff from cultivated fields may cause an incredible increase in the short-lived algal population. Water that contains 10,000 algae in a gallon at a given moment may be found to have 200,000,000 in a gallon a few weeks later. They may clog the screens of a city's water intake. As the algae die, they sink to the bottom and decay. Decay consumes oxygen. Finally the dissolved oxygen in the water is so far depleted that fish begin to die. Their decay still further decreases the supply of dissolved oxygen. Finally, there is putrefaction—decay in nearly complete absence of air. It is brought about by anaerobic bacteria, worms, and other scavengers that live in the mud at the bottom of the pond or lake.

Figure 11-2. Clarifying Tank: Denver Sanitation Plant
Photo by A. G. Turner. Bureau of Reclamation, Department of the Interior.

The enrichment of water by nutrients, which risks the sad results just related, is called eutrophication. The danger that it offers depends on the size, shape and depth of the lake, the climate, human activities (agriculture, mining, or manufacture), the density of the human population, and many other factors. The elements derived in largest amount from fertilizers are calcium, magnesium, and nitrogen (nitrate). Most of the phosphorus comes from sewage rather than from the runoff from fields, unless the fields are being eroded. The reason seems to be that phosphorus present in the soil as phosphates is quickly altered to a form that is adsorbed (held fast on the surface) by clay particles in the soil.

Dead and Dying Great Lakes

Even the largest lakes may not be polluted indefinitely. The chlorine used for disinfecting effluents disappears after a few days of exposure to sunlight. Dissolved nutrients may then rouse algae into a fatal up-surge. Fish perish by the million, litter all the beaches, and fill the air with putrefaction.

Lake Erie has an area of 3500 square miles. It took little more than a century from the time of the first white settlers for its pollution to become so great that many of its edible fish species perished. The annual catch of blue pike in Erie has been reduced almost to zero since 1936, and many of Cleveland's beaches have been condemned.

Lake Michigan faces a similar problem. It is larger and much deeper than Erie, but is nearly a closed basin, since most of the outflow from Lake Superior is through Lake Huron and eastward through the St. Lawrence. Several hundred communities of every size in the four adjacent states discard sewage or sewage effluents into Lake Michigan and many of those fail to treat their sewage in any way. Here in civilized America, near the end of the twentieth century, are areas as neglectful of sanitary practices as communities of savages. In addition, there are also various industries dumping pollution of every sort into the Lake.

People still swim on the Chicago beaches, in spite of everything, yet continued pollution will compel the beaches to be closed. The Chicago River, with its flow reversed, diverts Chicago's sewage effluents into the Mississippi drainage, but this is only a small part of the region's sewage. Someone has suggested that an "interceptor," swinging in a great arc along the lake front, from Milwaukee to Michigan City, could be built to round up the region's effluents and divert them into the Mississippi. Can anyone foresee what damage that will do in the far-off Louisiana region or the Gulf of Mexico? Moreover, the problem of agricultural runoff into Lake Michigan would still remain. Around Green Bay and farther north the population is less dense, hence pollution by sewage is less but that from agricultural runoff is intense.

Lake Michigan occupies a great trough, scooped out by glaciers in very recent geological times—about 11,000 years ago. Properly managed, it can remain vital for millions of years.

Correcting the damage is costly and slow. Well-organized and prolonged investigation is needed to determine: (1) the sources of the nutrient elements; (2) which nutrients must be reduced, to what level, and at what cost; (3) the best way to reduce the nutrient content of the liquid effluents; (4) to what extent good farming practices, such as strip cropping and terracing, will reduce contamination by agricultural runoff; (5) what may be done to remove the nutrients that the lakes have already accumulated in slime and bottom sediments, or dissolved, and (6) the effect of climate, variations in rate of inflow or outflow, aeration, sunlight, turbidity, temperature, and other factors on the damage done by individual nutrients.

A small army of specialists will be needed and several generations will have to exert effort to find relief from eutrophication. It is not alone the Great Lakes whose fate is being determined. Wisconsin has about 5000 smaller lakes similarly threatened. As so often before, it is being shown that the inordinate increase of the human species creates problems that human ingenuity, backed by all the resources of science, can hardly solve. Can the cities of the Great Lakes become seaports as well as manufacturing centers, yet remain pleasant places in which to live?

Chemistry Intervenes To Control the Sea Lamprey

The dismal prospects of pollution of the Great Lakes are partly offset by an important triumph—the control of the sea lamprey, followed by stocking the lakes with new kinds of game fish. The Great Lakes contain four species of small, non-parasitic lampreys, which do no harm to fish. The sea lamprey, by contrast, is very destructive. It is found on both sides of the Atlantic, from Iceland as far south as Morocco, and from Newfoundland to Florida.

The sea lamprey spawns in early spring in nests of pebbles and small stones in shallow streams. The fertilized eggs hatch in a few weeks into blind worm-like larvae, which spend the next five years growing to a length of 5 to 7 inches, in little tunnels that they excavate in the river mud. Meanwhile, they subsist on barely visible or microscopic creatures.

Then comes a startling event: the larvae are suddenly changed into eel-like adult predators—horrendous creatures, pitiless as vampires. A jawless, round mouth, rimmed by several rows of teeth and always open, acts as a suction disc, which enables the lamprey to inch its way several feet up the slimy wall of a concrete dam or to attach itself to a fish. Its tongue is a twisting rasp, tipped with horny teeth. As if that were not enough to ensure its being well fed without effort, the saliva of the sea lamprey contains enzymes that break down torn flesh and prevent blood from clotting. In less than a minute, the lamprey bores through scales, skin, and flesh; then it just hangs on, in spite of the victim's writhing, until the fish dies or the surfeited lamprey slips away into the mud. There it lies until its meal has been digested. Then it may latch onto another fish, then yet another.

Soon after becoming an adult predator the sea lamprey may return to the ocean, although those established in the Great Lakes remain there. In either case it feeds greedily and grows amazingly. After several years, perhaps already two feet long and weighing half a pound or a little more, it returns to a fresh water stream to spawn, then promptly dies. By this time a single lamprey may have destroyed 20 pounds of fish.

All the work of survival and even a part of the chemical work of assimilating food is done for the lamprey by its victim. No wonder that it has not progressed very far along the path of evolution: You become what you work to become. You lose what you never use. The sea lamprey is not even self-propelled. Biologists rate it as the most primitive of the fishes, indeed the most primitive of all the backboned animals.

Sea lampreys have always been common in the St. Lawrence and its tributary streams and in Lake Ontario. With the opening of the first canals, during the early years of the American republic, they became established in the Finger Lakes of central New York. The first Welland canal (1829) opened a way for them around Niagara Falls. Yet they did not appear in Lake Erie for nearly a century afterward (1912), perhaps because that lake was a trifle too warm for them or because the lake's tributary streams do not have good spawning grounds. Nevertheless, this barrier was finally passed, and in the mid-1950's sea lampreys appeared in Huron-Michigan, passed through the Soo Locks, and became established in Superior. Quickly, the catch of lake trout, whitefish, and chubb fell off to about 5 per cent of its former value, and nearly all commercial fisheries were abandoned. Sea lampreys have even become established in several inland lakes of the lower peninsula of Michigan.

Efforts to cope with migrating adult lampreys have all been failures, although lampreys, like other fish, can be deflected in their migration by an alternating electric current or lured into traps by a pulsed direct current. Yet, fortunately, the larvae are killed by very small concentrations of certain synthetic chemicals (halogenated nitro-phenols), which are harmless to fish. Systematic testing of about 6000 different substances by a research group during six years resulted in the discovery that treatment of larvae-infested streams with minute concentrations of 3-trifluoromethyl—4-nitro-phenol reduced the infestation by more than 90 per cent without injuring fish. Repeated treatment brought the parasite under complete and permanent control.

Restocking the Lakes

The control of the sea lamprey was just the first step in the restoration of Great Lakes fishing. Fortunately, the destruction of lake trout in Lake Superior was not so complete as to prevent the self-restoration of trout fishing when the threat from the lamprey had been removed. In other lakes, trout were reintroduced as fingerlings, raised in the fish hatcheries of Michigan and neighboring states.

By the end of 1966 over 15 million young lake trout had been released in Superior alone. Yet the most spectacular success was with varieties of salmon, well known on the Pacific Coast though new to the Great Lakes.

The most promising of the new fish at first appeared to be the kokanee—red or landlocked salmon—native to the streams of the Pacific Coast from Oregon to Japan. The average size of the adult fish is about 14 inches, with a weight of one pound. Kokanee fingerlings are being released in deep, cold lakes that have a plentiful supply of zooplankton (nearly microscopic animals), the favorite food of this fish. Its average life span is 4 years, and ranges from 2 to 7. The eggs for the first plantings of kokanee came from Washington and Colorado. Fingerlings produced from them were released in 1965 and spawned in the fall of 1968. Thus another species was added to the permanent fish population of the Great Lakes.

The coho or silver salmon, also known as the hooknose salmon, is a much larger fish than the kokanee and grows rapidly to a weight of 30 pounds or more. A million eggs, taken from Columbia River coho salmon in 1964, produced about 850,000 fingerlings, which were released into Michigan streams in 1966, with millions more in subsequent years. Since Coho salmon spend most of their lives in the Pacific Ocean, there was some doubt at first that they would be able to spend all their lives in the fresh water in the Great Lakes. Yet the first fingerlings reached adulthood and spawned in a normal way in the Great Lakes tributary streams. So another great gamefish was added to the region's fish resources.

The chinook salmon is a still larger game fish, which often attains a weight of more than 30 pounds. The first million eggs came as a gift from the state of Washington to the state of Michigan. Chinooks are strong swimmers, which easily ascend the rapids and "fish ladders" at Bonneville Dam and other hydroelectric sites on the turbulent Columbia River. The chief food of the young chinook is insect larvae, small worms, shrimp, crawfish, and the like. Later, the same fish, grown larger, feeds chiefly on smaller fish, such as minnows, herring, and alewives. The chinook salmon matures in 2 to 3 or 3 to 7 years, according to the temperature and other factors. During 1967, about 850,000 chinook fingerlings were hatched in Michigan and introduced into near-by rivers and small lakes. The good fishing that this produced, less than a year later, was astounding.

After commercial fishing on the upper Great Lakes had been almost completely extinguished by the sea lamprey, an interesting secondary effect of the lamprey infestation appeared. The big fish fed chiefly on alewives—silvery minnows, only four or five inches long. With the big fish gone, the alewives took over the lakes, swarming everywhere by the million, and so overloading the lakes that the already decreased supply of dissolved oxygen was everywhere seriously depleted. Their dead bodies littered widely scattered beaches, from Buffalo to Chicago. The lamprey itself then faced extinction, for it seems not to regard the diminutive alewife as worth the effort of latching on to. Yet as soon as the lakes had been successfully stocked with lake trout and big chinook salmon, both feeding on alewives, the supply of alewives was decreased to what had formerly seemed normal.

What has just been said about the restoration of good fishing on the Great Lakes is an indication of the benefits that may be obtained elsewhere. The improvement of smaller lakes and streams will often have to await study to develop better methods for controlling pollution by human wastes and for disposing of polluted mud. Yet once the streams have been restored to something like their original purity, good fishing will often return without further effort. Once more, the Hudson River may become a fisherman's paradise where sturgeon and other game-fish may be pulled in by anyone having the necessary gear and a boat.

The Menace of Aquatic Weeds

In the southern states, nutrient-rich solutions of any sort often rouse aquatic weeds to such a furious growth that slow-moving streams are clogged, navigation becomes difficult, and the flow of water through canals or aqueducts is seriously decreased.

Plankton is limited to the depth to which sunlight penetrates water. Higher plants, whether rooted in the bottom mud or just floating, overcome this handicap by growing taller. Reeds, cattails, and grasses are stiff enough to reach up to where sunlight is plentiful. The water hyacinth of Florida rests on floats or pontoons, filled with air. These lift it high above the surface of the water. It is also aided by being able to migrate with the wind, without waiting for birds or insects to scatter its seeds, or for passing motorboats to entangle it in propellers. Its stiff leaves, often cupped to catch each little puff of a light breeze, are spread like the sails of a square-rigger, one above the other, to a considerable height. Each little breath of air may propel these blue-flowered pests against a fair current, trailing roots through the water. A year from the time of escape from someone's garden, they may be found a mile upstream, clinging together in a dense colony that thickens every day.

Control by mechanical harvesting, pushing the cut weeds over a dam, is useful in small reservoirs, but is impractical for extended waterways. It calls for a little special treatment—a simple dragline. Manatees or "sea cows" (500 pound, torpedo-shaped marine mammals) have been encouraged as a means of controlling aquatic weeds in the Florida Everglades. They are natives of Florida and similar climates, on both sides of the Atlantic. They greedily devour sea weeds, cattails, water hyacinths, and almost every other kind of aquatic vegetation except water lilies. A handicap is that they do not always survive the brief cold spells that occur in Florida winters. Worse yet, manatees are "reluctant breeders." Until manatees become less or human beings more reluctant, the pollution of Southern waterways by human wastes and the menace of aquatic weeds are both very likely to increase, and the manatees will provide no solution to the problem.

Ordinary weed killers will not serve for the control of aquatic weeds, since they would pollute water intended for drinking. The most promising remedy seems to be "plant harmones," which rouse plants to a frantic growth in which they fail to form blossoms or set fruit and so presently may become extinct in that particular watercourse where the hormones are used.

12

Industrial Pollution

This chapter deals with a form of pollution that is dangerous, but susceptible to control—the pollution of water by industry.

The iniquities that man inflicts on nature's two most precious material gifts—fresh air and water—are almost unbelievable. The Potomac is polluted with sewage at the very doorstep of the nation's capital. Pesticides are washed into the great Mississippi in such quantities that fish are killed. Detergents pass from household laundries into sewers and thence into rivers, until small streams are covered with a yard-thick blanket of foam, and aquatic life perishes for lack of oxygen.

Pulp mill chemicals, by-products of the paper industry, pollute both water and atmosphere, miles from the source of pollution, until the whole countryside reeks with the nauseous, sulfury discard. The manufacture of dyestuffs and the dyeing industry have sometimes dyed the rivers themselves. The manufacture of rayon and mercerized cotton has often made a neighboring stream too alkaline to support any form of aquatic life; or the descaling of sheet steel has made a river corrosively acid. Fruit canning and animal slaughtering have often laden both air and water with foul odors and have set putrefying solids adrift. The strip mining of coal in West Virginia and neighboring states exposes sulfide minerals to oxidation. Sulfuric acid is produced and it pollutes small streams in sylvan regions.

Such evils cure themselves whenever an industry finds that a waste product is sufficiently valuable to pay for its own salvaging. It then be-

comes a recovered by-product, instead of being discarded into atmosphere or running water. Ledger entries that speak of short-range
profits seem more persuasive than the Golden Rule. Yet still another
force is beginning to be felt—the realization that, without fresh water,
industry itself would soon cease to exist.

Contamination or Pollution by Salt

Many of the present land areas of the earth were formerly submerged
beneath the ocean, sometimes repeatedly. Thus the least soluble of the
ocean's salts were often laid down in deep layers on almost every continent; deposits of gypsum, limestone, and dolomite, often thousands
of feet thick. Even the more soluble salts (chlorides and sulfates of sodium, potassium, and magnesium) were accumulated in past deposits
in many places in which shallow arms of the sea, cut off from the main
body of the ocean, were repeatedly flooded at high tide, then evaporated by the heat of the sun as the tide receded.

In the settlement of the 17 irrigated Western states a century ago,
the fresh water supply was sufficient for the sparse population of that
time, but salt was needed for livestock. Herds of cattle sometimes
perished if denied salt. Thus salt springs, in pioneer days, instead of
being the threat to fresh water that they are today, often were a source
of salt for cattle or for prairie schooners bound for the Far West.

Among primitive tribes, down to this very hour, salt springs are regarded as a natural resource, to be contended for in ceaseless wars
with their neighbors. In civilized lands, however, our needs have been
reversed. There is salt enough for everyone, but fresh water is growing
scarce. Salt springs are worse than useless and need to be controlled.
Sometimes control is easy, by capping, impounding behind dikes, or
draining into abandoned mines. In the past, wells drilled for fresh
water or petroleum sometimes struck salt water, then were simply
abandoned instead of being sealed off.

Worse yet, industries based on salt formerly discarded salty residues
into the nearest stream, and thus polluted rivers and wellfields far
downstream. Now and then a giant among natural salt springs defies
every effort to control it. The Clifton Hot Springs in Arizona contaminates the Gila River with 20 to 70 tons of salt every day. This is unfortunate, since expensive dams destine most of the river's water for irrigation, and too much salt in irrigation water is ruinous.

Pollution by the Iron and Steel Industries

One of the oldest and most needless sources of pollution of our great rivers has come from the iron and steel industries. In rolling red-hot steel into sheets or in shaping hot steel by stamping, the surface of the metal exposed to the air quickly becomes covered with a tightly adhering black coating of magnetic iron oxide, Fe_3O_4. This is usually removed by "pickling" the sheets—passing them quickly through dilute sulfuric or hydrochloric acid. The acid dissolves enough of the metal to free the magnetic oxide, which separates in heavy flakes. The resultant, highly acid "waste pickle liquor" was often just dumped into a neighboring river.

When protests and lawsuits put an end to this source of pollution, the liquors were neutralized with limestone and the resulting sludge discarded into ponds on neighboring waste lands. Settling was then so slow that after 25 years the contents of the ponds were often still liquid. The slow settling was owing to the fact that the dissolved iron in the solution was precipitated as ferrous oxide, FeO, which is so hydrous (swollen with water) that its density is nearly that of water. By contrast, the more highly oxidized magnetic oxide holds little water, hence settles quickly.

The problems of the waste pickle liquor was so easily solved that any high school student of chemistry might have found the answer had he known that the problem existed. The key is in the two concluding sentences of the preceding paragraph. The waste liquor was neutralized with limestone, heated nearly to boiling, and air blown through it until all the ferrous oxide was oxidized to magnetic oxide. The resultant mixture of gypsum (calcium sulfate) and magnetic oxide could be drained free of water and used as landfill in reclaiming waste land. Thus a steel mill may create a public park instead of a public nuisance. Or the two components of the mixture may be separated magnetically, thus producing two marketable products.

During recent years, hydrochloric acid has largely replaced sulfuric acid in the pickling of steel. Distillation of the waste liquor recovers most of the acid, which may be used over again. The residue then yields ferric oxide. It has also been proposed to use the neutralized ferric wastes to precipitate phosphates from polluted water. There are also some steel plants at which it is possible to discard neutralized liquor through cased deep wells, extending below all the fresh water aquifers.

How Streams Are Endangered by the Paper Industry

For more than a century, paper has chiefly been made from wood. Examination of wood with the unaided eye or with a small lens shows that it consists of bundles of fibers, cemented together with a darker material. The fibers, after being purified, turn out to be cellulose, a substance that is seen, nearly pure, in cotton and linen. The dark cementing material is a mixture called lignin. Since about half of most woods is lignin, which is discarded in paper-making, one would think that the mere existence of the giant paper industry would be a threat to all our streams. To explain how this threat has been escaped, we must begin by describing what must be done to wood in converting it into paper pulp, which is then incorporated into paper.

The first paper was made in China, at about the end of the first century. The raw material, then and long afterward, was short vegetable fibers, derived from cotton and linen rags or the soft, inner bark of certain trees, such as the mulberry. From its place of origin, paper-making soon spread to Japan and India, then (after many centuries) to Arabia, and finally, about A.D. 1160, into Europe, in Spain and Sicily. Since other sheeted materials were then available for manuscripts and records, and since printing from fixed blocks was not then widely practiced, paper long remained just a curiosity, almost without use.

Several centuries later, after a good part of the people of the Western world had learned to read and write, paper became everywhere more familiar. In the nineteenth century, two events lifted the art of paper-making into a great industry. The first of these was the development of the paper-making machine (the earliest one in France, then another form in Pennsylvania, in the United States). For the first time, this made it possible for paper to be produced in continuous rolls of indefinite length, instead of in separate sheets. The second was the development of several methods for converting wood into paper pulp.

The manufacture of paper pulp and paper is now the leading Canadian manufacturing industry, when industries are ranked in the order of the money value of their annual product. In the United States, paper manufacturing ranks fifth (after automobiles, meat products, steel, and petroleum). It is probably the world's most rapidly growing industry, because paper and paper products are constantly finding new uses. In industrially developed countries, from Canada to Sweden, and around the world to Japan and Australia, the annual consumption of paper and paper products is from 100 to 400 pounds per person. In industrially

Table 12-1.
The Production and Uses of Paper Pulp

Name of Product	Treatment Used	Kind of Wood	Characteristics of Pulp	Uses
Groundwood (mechanical wood pulp)	Grinding	Spruce and other coniferous woods	Short-lived	Newsprint
Sulfite pulp	Digestion with solution of an acid sulfite	Spruce, hemlock, fir, and other conifers	Easily bleached	Writing paper
Soda pulp	Digestion with solution of NaOH	Poplar, cottonwood, etc.	Soft, glossy	Book paper
Sulfate pulp (kraft pulp)	Digestion with solution of NaOH and Na_2S	Long-fibered conifers (Southern pine)	Strong, hard to bleach	Bags, wrapping paper

backward countries it is 10 pounds or less. Thus the per capita consumption of paper is a measure of what we are tempted to call civilization, though it may actually be only the degree of conforming with the manner of living toward which the world is now moving.

The four chief ways in which paper pulp is produced from wood are determined for each kind of wood by the use to which the paper is put, as Table 12-1 shows.

Groundwood is made from debarked spruce of hemlock logs. These are pressed against the rough surface of a rotating stone while being wetted by a stream of water. The wood fibers thus torn away are screened to remove coarse material and are sometimes bleached with hydrogen peroxide, but ordinarily receive no other treatment before being mixed with about one-fourth their own weight of sulfite pulp. The mixture is newsprint, the stock on which most newspapers are printed. The non-cellulosic impurities in groundwood are gradually oxidized on exposure to air and sunlight, becoming yellow and brittle. Newspapers consequently crumble and fall to pieces. Thus the most temporary and ephemeral part of literature is consigned to paper that is equally short-lived. Newspapers intended to be preserved in libraries for perusal by readers in future generations are usually printed on special paper stock derived from linen rags.

Sulfite pulp is made by heating wood chips, under pressure, for 8 to

12 hours, with a highly acid solution of calcium or magnesium acid sulfite ($CaHSO_3$ or $MgHSO_3$). A good part of the lignin, amounting to about half of the weight of the wood chips, dissolves in the acid solution to form a brown liquor. There is often a preliminary digestion with a 12 per cent sodium sulfite solution, followed by a briefer treatment with sulfurous acid, under pressure, as a means for obtaining cellulose of better quality.

The bundles of cellulose fibers, released by the acid digestion, need to be washed free of the acid reagent, then separated and frayed by "beating"—a process in which they are "mechanically mauled" in the presence of water. The fibers are thus somewhat shortened, and become frayed and split lengthwise. This causes them to absorb water and become swollen. A web formed from such material is much stronger than one made from unbeaten fibers.

Efforts to recover sulfite from the waste brown liquor have not been very successful, hence the waste liquor has often been discarded into the stream that supplied the mill with water. The discard is not only highly acid but greedy for oxygen (sulfite being oxidized to sulfate). In consequence, it may wipe out every form of life in the stream, as completely as if the stream itself had been heated to boiling.

It is fortunate that two other paper-making processes have come into use, in both of which the reagent used in dissolving the lignin is easily recovered and used over again. In the recovery, the dissolved lignin is burned, so that the danger of great pollution of streams is to that extent decreased. In both these methods the reagent is alkaline, hence the digestive chamber may be of steel instead of acid-proof brick, set in acid-proof cement. Digestion at about 170°C, during 4 to 6 hours results in a black liquor, containing an excess of the reagent, together with dissolved lignin, including the sodium salts of the complex lignic acids.

In either process the black liquor is evaporated to dryness, and the solid residue is burned to ash in a gas-fired furnace; or the black liquor may be ashed directly by being sprayed into the combustion zone of the furnace. The costs of the recovery are considerably decreased by the fact that combustion of organic matter (lignin) in the waste liquor yields a good part of the heat that is needed for evaporating water.

The "black ash" thus obtained is impure sodium carbonate mixed with considerable carbon. This mixture in the soda process, is extracted with hot water and converted into sodium hydroxide, NaOH, by the addition of quicklime, $Ca(OH)_2$. In the sulfate or kraft processes enough sodium sulfate is also added to replace any sodium oxide that has been lost. The black ash must then be fused, at a higher temperature than is attained in the formation of the ash. During fusion, sodium sulfate is reduced to sulfide by the carbon in the ash. Thus the active reagent in the sulfate or kraft process is sodium hydroxide, supplemented by sodium sulfide, which moderates the destructive effect of alkali on cellulose.

The Threat to Dissolved Oxygen

The recovery of the reagents in the soda and kraft processes is profitable enough to ensure that it shall be practiced. Fortunately, waste lignin is meanwhile disposed of by burning. Thus there is no tendency to gross pollution of streams by mills using either the soda or kraft processes. Yet a considerable threat remains, because fibrous material always escapes the screens that are supposed to remove it, and soluble organic material results from washing and beating the fibrous product dumped from the digesters. Slow oxidation of either suspended or dissolved organic material, carried out by microorganisms, may so remove dissolved oxygen from a stream that fish and other aquatic life perish.

The concentration of oxygen that water will dissolve from the atmosphere is proportional to the barometric pressure—hence, is distinctly less at high elevations than at sea level. It decreases rapidly with increasing temperature and at "room temperature" (about 25°C) is only about two-thirds as much as at the freezing point of water. Salt water dissolves less oxygen than is dissolved by fresh water at the same temperature, and the decrease is almost proportional to the concentration of the salt.

Water that contains all the dissolved oxygen that it can retain in contact with normal air of its own temperature is said to be saturated with atmospheric oxygen; but in contact with pure oxygen it will dissolve and retain about five times that amount. If the temperature of water that is saturated with oxygen or any other gas is increased a trifle, the water will usually not immediately lose part of the dissolved gas, but will for a short time remain supersaturated with the gas. Then it will gradually lose the surplus of gas, most rapidly when it contains suspended particles on which bubbles of gas gradually form and escape.

Fresh water at 20°C will dissolve 9.17 parts oxygen per million of water (ppm or mg/kg) from air under atmosphere of pressure; but sea water at the same temperature will dissolve only 7.43 ppm. Water in which green algae are growing vigorously is often supersaturated with oxygen during daylight hours, since photosynthesis sets free oxygen. Although it is easy to determine the amount of dissolved oxygen in water that is nearly free from color, there are many sources of error which only a well-trained chemist will know how to avoid.

Dissolved oxygen (DO) is of great importance in judging whether water that has been contaminated with oxidizable impurities of water that has been warmed still contains enough oxygen to support the life of organisms that depend on oxygen for survival. A determination of DO is most useful when there has also been a determination of biochemical oxygen demand (BOD). This is a measure of the quantity of oxygen (ppm or mg/kg) that disappears from polluted water when a sample of the water is suitably diluted with pure water that has been saturated with atmospheric oxygen, then incubated for a standard period of time (usually five days) at suitable temperature (usually $20°C$), in the presence of bacteria of the type usually present in sewage.

Several months of incubation at $20°C$ might be needed to oxidize all of the oxidizable organic matter present in a polluted sample. Such a delay in knowing the condition of a sample suspected to be polluted would of course be intolerable. Fortunately, a five-day period of incubation at a definite temperature gives results that permit the relative degree of pollution of different samples to be judged.

In some waters, a determination of BOD is made difficult or impossible by the presence of ions of the heavy metals or other impurities that decrease or inhibit bacterial activity. An approximation to the BOD is then found in the chemical oxygen demand (COD). This is inferred from the quantity of dichromate ion ($Cr_2O_7^{--}$) needed for the complete oxidation of dissolved organic matter in a contaminated sample.

The DO is a measure of the suitability of water momentarily to support forms of life that depend on oxygen for survival. The BOD (or the COD), by contrast, is an indication of unsuitability for such life, because it measures the oxygen needed to destroy organic or other oxidizable impurities by bacterial action. No wonder that states that have become conscious of the dangers of pollution have set very strict standards for both DO and BOD in all waters in which the survival of aquatic life seems important.

There is plenty of opportunity for every pulp mill adversely to effect the DO and BOD of any stream within its own watershed. So the mill must spend a considerable sum as an incident to ordinary operation, just to meet standards that have been set to safeguard against pollution. In one instance (the Coosa River plant, near Childersburg, Alabama) about $2.5 million was spent in providing better facilities to prevent pollution, and about 5 per cent of that sum has been spent every year since their completion, just to keep them in operation.

In 1966, the addition of a 274-foot clarifier and a 370-acre lagoon to already existing facilities permitted both the DO and BOD to be more rigidly controlled. The waste waters, after passing through the mill, were compelled to spend an average of several weeks in the lagoon, exposed to the action of bacteria, well supplied with atmospheric oxygen. This gave time for suspended solids, fibrous or nonfibrous, to settle out, and for a good part of the dissolved organic impurities to be oxidized by bacterial action, using oxygen dissolved from the air. Thus the content of suspended solids was decreased by 97 per cent, and the BOD by 35 per cent during the winter and by as much as 78 per cent during the warmer summer months. Thus, if the proportion of discarded water to unpolluted river water was kept within attainable limits, there was no difficulty in meeting the standards that Alabama had set for DO and BOD.

To the surprise of everyone, the construction of a dam, a short distance above the mill, for supplying the penstocks of a new hydroelectric plant, resulted in a serious diminution of the DO in water reaching the mill. Better oxygenation of the incoming water was secured when the power company voluntarily installed submerged weirs (underwater obstacles that promoted turbulence).

The sludge of swollen fibers removed from the water by the clarifier was thickened by centrifuging, its content of dry matter being thus raised from about 5 per cent to about 18 per cent. This was not a very successful operation, and the thickened sludge has found no better use than as landfill.

Rebirth of the Sacramento

In California's early days the Sacramento River was an important means of access to the goldfields (1849) and later to inland towns in the northern part of the state. For a long time, steamers plied regularly scheduled passages between San Francisco and the river towns of Antioch, Sacramento, and Yuba City. This river traffic was doomed to disappear after railroads penetrated into northern California. Yet long before that happened navigation on the Sacramento and its tributaries was gravely injured by hydraulic mining—the exposure of gold-bearing gravel by washing away whole landscapes by jets of water delivered under high pressure. As the eternal hills were washed away into the rivers, fabulous riches in precious metals were brought to light; yet the damage done to the Sacramento and its tributaries has never since been repaired, in spite of millions that have been spent in dredging.

About a century after steamboat transportation almost disappeared from the Sacramento, this stream once more became an important spawning ground for salmon. Yet the fishing industry in its turn was threatened by lumbering, which burns a good part of its wastes yet contaminates streams with scrap lumber, bark, small branches, and other trash. The Kimberly-Clark Corporation, which operates the paper mill in Alabama that we have described, was a leader in bringing a new industry to the Sacramento Valley. If its mill, based on waste wood, could have been located below the spawning grounds of salmon (the gravelly part of the river), there would have been little danger of damage to fish. Unfortunately, the lumber industry was well upstream, and to haul waste wood any great distance would have been unprofitable. There was no choice but to erect the paper mill above the spawning ground, then take precautions to avoid damage to fish or their eggs.

The conditions to be met by the mill were strict and difficult, yet had to be, since the effluent from the mill entered the river less than a mile above the important spawning grounds. Normal prohibitions related to health hazard, pH limits, creation of nuisance and unsightly landscapes. For the protection of salmon eggs, no discernible bottom deposits would be permitted, however long the plant might operate. The temperature of the river was not permitted to rise to a point unfavorable to the development of salmon or steelhead trout. Dissolved oxygen was not to fall below 7 ppm within the spawning gravel of the river. The plant was not permitted to deplete the dissolved oxygen in the river more than halfway to the point at which normal aquatic life would be effected. Limits were set for specific contaminants likely to enter the river from kraft or groundwood operations.

To establish the tolerated limits, a great deal of biochemical research had to be performed. As this work progressed over years, restrictions tended to become ever tighter. Yet the mill had some advantages that late-comers to every industry have over their predecessors: they have more guiding principles, better developed techniques, and better-trained personnel. So they make fewer mistakes. They find the costs of doing business, including the cost of pollution abatement, to be higher than ever before. Yet they benefit by the experience of others, which is a matter of record in the literature of engineering and costs nothing.

The plant included a continuous digester, with a capacity of 150 tons of kraft pulp a day. All the pulp was bleached by improved methods: chlorine dioxide, followed by hypochlorite and optional hydrogen peroxide, replacing hypochlorite bleach, which is better for other kinds of paper pulp than for kraft. The primary clarifier produced sludge with about 15 per cent to 35 per cent dry matter content. This was used as landfill in want of any better method of disposal.

The liquid effluent from the primary clarifier passed through holding basins to an aeration basin, where air was blown through it until it was nearly saturated with oxygen. Here, at a slightly elevated temperature (38°C), most of the oxidation occurs that gets rid of dissolved organic matter and lowers the BOD. The aeration basin replaced the much larger lagoon already described, where oxidation is carried on at room temperature. Some experiments are being made on the effect of adding limited quantities of nutrients (ammonia and phosphoric acid) to the liquid in which microorganisms are at work, oxidizing dissolved organic matter and lowering the BOD. The dissolved oxygen needed was 1.14 pounds for each pound of BOD removed.

The average removal of BOD was 85 per cent, when the aeration basin was treating over 11 million gallons of liquid a day. Thus it was possible to operate a large sulfate (kraft) pulp and paper plant, within a mile of important spawning grounds of fish, without damage to the fish.

Pollution by Detergents

Hard water precipitates ordinary soap as a slimy curd that adheres to fabrics washed in it and often stains them. For this reason, in most industrially developed countries, soap has been almost completely replaced by newly developed synthetic detergents ("syndets"). An unpleasant result has been the sudden appearance of a new form of pollution.

The longest known and most widely used of the new detergents are sodium salts of strong organic acids, derived from sulfuric acid. Otherwise expressed, the new detergents consist of sodium ions, Na^+, in association with an equal number of detergent anions, which we may represent by $R \cdot C_6H_4 \cdot SO_3^-$. In this, the R represents a "branched" or "unbranched" hydrocarbon chain—actually, a tight little coil of carbon

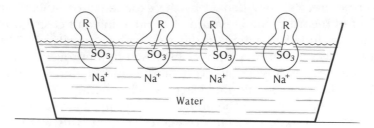

Figure 12-1. Detergency

atoms, linked to one another and to atoms of hydrogen; whereas C_6H_4 is the core or central part of the famous "benzene ring" of six carbon atoms.

The negative charge on each anion is limited to the sulfonate group, which is derived from sulfuric acid and is as readily soluble in water as is this acid itself. In the presence of water this "active," negatively charged end of each anion dissolves, together with an equal number of Na^+ ions, to form an electrically neutral solution. But the hydrocarbon chain, R, of each anion is derived from petroleum, which is itself a hydrocarbon, insoluble in water. This end of each anion resists being dissolved.

The result is a compromise: the active end of each anion dissolves, but the hydrocarbon end does not. The detergent dissolves in and spreads out over the surface of water, like a supply of Indian clubs, each weighted at one end. The weighted end of each club is submerged, but the unweighted end protrudes into the air, as shown in Figure 12-1.

The two-ended nature of detergent anions enables detergents to serve as wetting agents and foam stabilizers. The surface of each bubble in a froth or foam is covered with a double layer of dissolved detergent anions.

The active, negatively charged end of each anion is turned toward and dissolved in the liquid film; but the hydrocarbon end is turned toward and protrudes into the air in the interior of a bubble. The Na^+ ions all congregate in the water film, since they are attracted by the negative charge on the active end of the detergent anions. The foam is stabilized by the presence of closely packed, strongly oriented detergent anions.

Most household detergents are mixtures of substances of the type just described or similar "surface active" substances with inexpensive water softeners, such as Borax or Calgon. Some of them are effective in detergent concentrations as little as 0.1 per cent.

Although there is no very close connection between foam stability and the effectiveness of a substance as a detergent, some of the most widely used detergents produce foams that may persist for days or weeks. When heavy foamers are in use, bubbles may suddenly appear in startling numbers in streets and homes, far from their origin in sewers. Small streams, previously uncontaminated, may become blanketed with several feet of foam. The penetration of atmospheric oxygen into the water is then so greatly retarded that aquatic life of every sort, from algae to fish and oysters, may be suffocated and destroyed.

The hydrocarbon groups of a detergent may be either branched or unbranched, and several different groups may be attached at different positions around the benzene ring. Different hydrocarbon groups differ greatly in the readiness with which they are biodegraded (broken down by the action of bacteria). The most readily degraded hydrocarbon groups are those with unbranched chains. Bacteria, attacking a detergent anion, seem to nibble away at the branches, only later severing the chain at its attachment to the benzene ring. Thus the remedy for pollution by detergents seems to be in the hands of their manufacturers. They are making an organized effort to limit production to detergents known to be readily degraded.

Pollution by Pesticides

Compounds designed to kill insects, rodents, and other pests are called pesticides. In pioneer days there was much more danger from their use than today, since most of those then used were toxic to man or his domestic animals. Today, the pollution of streams by pesticides is largely needless, for many better methods are known for getting rid of either insects or rodents than by the use of substances that are dangerous to us.

Fossil insects bear witness that their race has swarmed over the earth about 250 million years before humanity appeared, and about 50 million years before the first birds flew. Their long tenancy of this planet has given insects time to evolve into numberless physical forms, corresponding to about 800,000 known species, which entomologists classify into about 30 different orders. It has been estimated that there are about 2,000,000 species of insects still to be discovered. Known insect species amount to about three-fourths of those of the whole animal kingdom.

Some insect species came into existence quite recently, as geology counts time; whereas others are scarcely distinguishable from their fossil ancestors of a hundred million years ago! Only about 20 of the hundreds of thousands of known insect species have been thoroughly studied. As one might guess, these include the honey bee, famous for being useful to man, the mosquito, famous for its ability to transmit disease, and the grasshopper, famous for its appetite and fertility.

Insects that transmit disease to man sometimes threaten domestic animals as well; and different species of flies, in different parts of the world, decrease milk production, ruin hides intended for the leather industry, and kill thousands of sheep and cattle every year. Practically no important crop in all the world is immune to the attack of insects.

Some of the many kinds of damage that insects do to the leaves, shoots, stems, bark, roots, fruit, or seeds of plants are familiar to everyone. It is not so generally realized that a large part of the damage done to crops by insects is in spreading plant diseases. Sometimes this is by the mechanical transport of bacteria, fungi, or viruses from plant to plant, on the legs, mandibles, or other body parts of insects. At other times an insect may become infected by the infectious agent, then serving as a host in a phase of a disease that otherwise might scarcely injure plants at all. In other words, an insect sometimes transforms an infectious agent into something more dangerous than its original form, because its character has been altered in passing through the insect.

In our war against insects, anything goes: flyswatters, clubs, traps, "black light," and poisons; alteration of the environment to put the insect at a disadvantage in contending with its natural handicaps or enemies; taking advantage of turns of the weather to bring about death by desiccation, drowning, or starvation; importation of adversaries from the insect's original home in a distant part of the world; development of resistant plant varieties or resistant rootstocks for grafted varieties; and interference with the sex life of the insect.

Before the twentieth century a few simple inorganic poisons were developed to control chewing insects. They were applied to crops by dusting or spraying or were incorporated into "baits"—mixtures of bran and molasses for the control of grasshoppers. These controls were usually compounds of the elements arsenic, fluorine, mercury, zinc, and copper. These elements are all very toxic to man and domestic animals; for it seemed not to be recognized that insects are so very different from ourselves that there was a good chance of finding compounds that would destroy them and yet be harmless to us.

In addition to soluble or insoluble poisons for chewing insects, soluble poisons for sucking insects were discovered, including some that were produced by plants (examples: nicotine, rotenone, pyrethrins). These were very toxic to certain insect species, but nearly harmless to mammals. Fumigants (gases or volatile liquids) have long been used to control insects in flight and to destroy insect eggs, larvae, and pupae, underground or in stored grains or nuts.

During and immediately after the Second World War there was a sudden very great increase in the number of synthetic organic insecticides, extremely toxic to insects but nearly harmless to man and domestic animals. The first of these new insecticides was DDT (a chlorinated hydrocarbon). It was lethal in low concentrations for a wide range of insects. Moreover, it lasted a long time after being applied, for it was chemically stable and of low volatility. Other chlorinated hydrocarbons were created in great numbers, with similar capabilities or specialized applications.

The use of organophosphorous pesticides (malathion and parathion) was also rapidly expanded, in spite of their being extremely toxic to mammals. Systemic poisons were introduced to control aphids and other sap-feeders. Applied to roots or leaves, these poisons soon spread to every part of the plant, making every part toxic to insects for several weeks. They are fortunately soon destroyed within the plant and leave no toxic residue at harvest time.

An interesting and promising discovery is that the toxicity of certain insecticides toward insects is increased or their period of effectiveness is prolonged by the use of organic compounds called synergists (intensifiers). This possibility deserves continuous study. It is also important to remember that our purpose is usually not the complete extermination of an insect species, which is usually impossible anyway, but rather its control. We have succeeded in controlling it if its population is so reduced that accidents and natural enemies prevent an increase from one generation to the next. The damage that the insect does to crops and domestic animals may then be negligible.

The careless use of insecticides has resulted in a new form of pollution. It usually comes from their use near running streams or canals carrying drinking water, or from the spraying of large areas to prevent infestation of crops or weeds by insects. The damage done depends on the toxicity of the insecticide to mammals, fish, or birds, on the temperature, and on the rate at which the insecticide is destroyed by oxidation or reaction with water, with the aid of bacteria.

Parathion, for example, although extremely toxic to man and domestic animals, becomes harmless after a few days of exposure to air or water. Children and farm workers have often been killed by mere contact with incompletely emptied bags or boxes that were originally filled with parathion. Such containers should not be allowed to accumulate. They should not be burned. They should be buried in moist spots, far from the haunts of men or the pasturage of domestic animals.

Small concentrations of DDT appear to be harmless to mammals. Yet, since they accumulate in body fat, continued ingestion may cause death. Fish may accumulate so much DDT in their bodies that they are unfit for human consumption. DDT has been detected in coho salmon caught in the Great Lakes, in concentrations of 3.5 to 19 ppm. While awaiting further study a temporary limit of 7 ppm has been set (1969) on the tolerated concentration of DDT in commercial fish. Because not only men and birds but other fish eat fish, the danger of pollution of fish by DDT is far-reaching. It is now suspected that the osprey, a fish-eating hawk, faces extinction because in eating DDT-polluted fish, its eggs become too soft-shelled to be brooded.

Government regulation of pesticide use has become much more stringent. Safe tolerances for each pesticide are determined before legislation for control can be enacted. The registration and approval of all insecticides should be required in every state. All labels should carry directions for use, warning of possible toxicity, and an indication of antidotes. Approval by the United States Food and Drug Administration is a recommended precaution.

Neighboring farmers can collect damages for injuries to crops or livestock resulting from winddrift or stream pollution. Conservation departments of individual states have collected damages for the destruction of fish in streams under their supervision.

Sex Interference and Sex Attractants in the War Against Insects

Interference with the sex life of an insect sometimes offers a spectacular means of control. An example is the control of the screwfly. This is a large, noisy, metallic-blue fly which lays its eggs in the head cavities or in wounds of sheep and other domestic animals. Larvae hatched from the eggs tunnel into and clear out dead tissue; they also attack living tissue and may finally cause death. Control is by breeding the male flies in captivity. They are sterilized by X rays or gamma rays, then are released—thousands of them within a comparatively small area. They are as "eager and ardent" as normal lake flies but leave no offspring.

The method of control just described had been so successful that everyone would like to try it on other insects, such as the mosquito. Every detail of this creature's sex life has been studied. It is known that the female does not begin to lay eggs until she has gorged on good red blood. It has also been noted that male's two terminal body segments are physically altered in a fairly late stage of maturity. If biochemists learn how to inhibit this alteration, they can destroy the capacity for breeding.

Sex is a capacity possessed by all but a few of the simplest members of the plant and animal kingdom. Though deplored by ascetics, it is one of nature's most important inventions. Its presumed purpose is to see to it that improvements that appear by chance in separate individuals of a species shall finally be joined in a single individual among their descendants.

Another way of interfering with the sex life of an insect, in the hope of bringing the damage done by a species to an end, is through the use of sex attractants. The control of the destructive cotton boll weevil may presently be accomplished in this way. Chemists of the United States Department of Agriculture have identified four components of the male-generated sex attractant. They are present in the insect's body and feces in concentrations of 0.06 to 0.76 ppm. If three of these compounds are mingled in the right proportions, both sexes of the insect may be lured upwind as much as 400 feet, and collected in traps. At present, the chief use of the method is in revealing which parts of large cottonfield are infected, so that insecticides may be applied there, and the rest of the field may be skipped. Presently the traps themselves may receive both insecticide and lure, instead of spreading insecticide on the field. Thus the risk of harming useful insects or domestic animals will be diminished. In a typical year (1968) the weevil did an estimated $113 million damage to the American cotton corporation, in spite of $75 million spent in attempts at control.

About 30 different species of destructive butterflies and moths may be near control because we have learned to create effective sex attractants. Nor is it the male-generated attractant alone that is being used. A whole field may be made so fragrant with the female-generated attractant that most of the males are frustrated in their efforts to find a mate.

The United States Department of Agriculture has been using insect lures as a sort of early warning system. Airports at this end of the international air route are often ringed by traps containing lures for insects that might attack local crops. Insects inadvertently imported from abroad may thus be captured and destroyed before they have spread very far. A spectacular example of the success of such a program was the quick control of a new infestation of the Mediterranean fruit fly in Florida citrus groves in 1966. The effort cost about $11 million, but the destruction caused by the fly in a single year might have been double that amount had the attempt at control not succeeded.

We have described in some detail a few of the many ways (mechanical, chemical, biological) in which insects have been controlled. We have come a long way from the days in which poisonous baits set out for the destruction of grasshoppers killed dairy cattle instead. For when creatures as physiologically different from ourselves as insects compete with us they are at a disadvantage. They must have been on the earth for a longer time than we, but our chemists are smarter. No holds are barred. We will take advantage of all their weaknesses. The trend is away from the use of poisons that endanger mammals, birds, and fish or that are only slowly biodegradable, and their use may be forbidden altogether.

Specific lures and specific poisons exist for most insects, and we have reasonable control. We grant insects enough of the earth to perpetuate their race, but we do it grudgingly. To persist very long they must constantly develop immunity against new specifics which our chemists and entomologists are creating for their destruction.

Effects of the Thermal Alteration of Water by Industry

During cold winter months, some species of fish tend to congregate where streams are slightly warmed by industrial use. A mile below the point at which fish are congregating in slightly warmed water, however, the banks of the stream may be littered with dead fish, which have perished for lack of oxygen. In discussing pollution by the paper industry we emphasized that water which is slightly warmed dissolves far less oxygen than water just a few degrees colder. So, when heat has been passed into pond, lake, or stream, immediate aeration is often necessary. This is sometimes very difficult, especially when the warmed water has been contaminated with oxidizable material, so that its BOD is high. Yet in the absence of oxidizable pollutants, aeration is easy whenever the stream has even moderate velocity if underwater obstacles are placed where they will create turbulence and thus increase the rate at which oxygen dissolves from the air.

Should the addition of heat to a water supply be termed thermal pollution? That obviously depends on the kinds of aquatic life present, their individual demands for oxygen, and the ways in which an increase or decrease in the abundance of one species affects others.

The damage done to aquatic life in water that has passed through an industrial plant is often quite unanticipated. Oysters grown just below such a plant have sometimes been noted to have an abnormally green color because of traces of copper derived from copper tubes through which the water has passed. A very slight warming of the water of a canal may kill blue crabs by the thousand and greatly reduce the population of softshell clams, white catfish, and striped bass. Increasing the temperature of the Susquehanna River altered the type of plankton present, and so decreased the abundance of shad.

Since the chief use of water in industry is in cooling, the chief threat to aquatic life comes from that use. Part of the cooling water serves to cool an industrial product, such as steel or canned fruit. A more rapidly growing use is in condensing steam. Even when steam is expanded through many successive stages, in an effort to convert it as nearly completely as possible into mechanical energy, there comes a time when the heat that remains is discarded into the air or transferred to cooling water in a condenser. A plant producing electric energy from coal or petroleum usually has an over-all efficiency of 35 or 40 per cent. That means that 60 or 65 per cent of the heat energy released in burning the fuel must be transferred to cooling water or discarded into the atmosphere. It has been estimated that a million-kilowatt plant, burning coal, discards 45 trillion Btu into cooling water, in a single year.

The rapidly growing use of nuclear energy in producing electrical energy is the greatest threat of all. Our final chapter will give some details. A large nuclear reactor may set free so much heat that the water of a sizable stream may be warmed as much as 10°C, and may be perceptibly warm for as much as 20 miles downstream. Unless present trends are reversed, as much as a fifth of our surface runoff may be needed for cooling before the end of the century.

The most obvious cure for the threat to the aquatic environment that comes from thermal discard is the use of cooling towers to discard heat into the atmosphere instead of into running water. A tower to be completed in 1970 at a cost of $1.5 million will cool waste steam from the Yankee reactor on the Connecticut River to the river temperature. This will call for no engineering techniques not already known. Other suggestions are to erect industrial complexes in the neighborhood of power plants and supply them with waste steam from the plant (for the desalting of sea water, for example). Or the waste heat from a power plant might be used to propagate commercial fish and shellfish in fish ponds of controlled salinity temperature and plankton species. This is large-scale fish farming.

The Federal Water Pollution Control Administration, now the Environmental Protection Agency, has made grants for the development of a monitoring network on the Delaware River, above and below points of possible thermal alteration, and for determining the effects of thermal addition on aquatic life in Biscayne Bay, Florida. Other grants will be spent on pollution studies in collaboration with the Atomic Energy Commission, the Federal Power Commission, and the Tennessee Valley Authority.

Let's Save the Tidal Flats

An estuary is an area where a river empties into the ocean. Most estuaries present problems in the economy of wildlife in its competition with the demands of an expanding human population. The character of an estuary is always changing. The salt of the ocean brings about the flocculation of clay that is carried in suspension by the fresh water stream until it is intermingled with salt water. Yet the precipitated clay seldom forms a stable landscape. Tidal movements and differences in density that are caused by differences in salinity create currents that carve out channels. The water is often so shallow that new bottom areas are uncovered and covered every day. Nutrients that the river extracts from upland soil are mingled with nutrients from the ocean and spread out over a wide area of the estuary, which is thus enabled to support hundreds of different species of plants and animals.

Can anyone imagine a better environment than an estuary for the support of life of the most varied kinds? The river brings in nitrogen in the form of nitrates, traces of phosphate, and smaller amounts of other nutrients, including traces of the heavy metals zinc and copper (needed by many marine species). The ocean brings in calcium, magnesium, and sulfur (sulfates) in abundance, and traces of iodine. So plankton of a wide range of forms are able to flourish, using the energy of sunlight to begin a food chain that reaches right up to our own dinner table, whenever we serve shellfish, lobsters, mackerel, or tuna.

Every degree of salinity exists in the waters of an estuary, from almost zero, where the river is about to be mingled with an incoming tide, to that of the salt-laden ocean itself (or a little more, whenever there is evaporation in a bay with limited outlet into the ocean). In an estuary there is also every degree of oxygenation, from almost zero at the bottom of a deep channel, to full saturation at the surface (or a little supersaturation, where plankton are busy with photosynthesis in abundant sunlight). Creatures that demand different concentrations at different stages of their development may find that, too, just by swimming or drifting to a new part of the estuary as their needs are altered. Even shellfish, although they are prevented from moving around after they have passed their earliest phase, must be as happy and contented as we are assured that even prisoners may be, whenever a penitentiary is properly managed.

No wonder that estuaries, if undisturbed and unpolluted by man, are apt to be among the most fertile and biologically productive spots in all nature. The production of protein in a generous estuary may be ten times that in the same area of good garden land. Although an estuary is sometimes referred to as a "tidal flat," "mud flat," "grass flat," or "submerged land," it might better be called a "marine garden." Its advantages over a terrestrial garden should be evident to everyone except people who would like to exploit it. It never needs to be planted, cultivated, or irrigated. Nutrients in just the right concentration for each species are brought in, free, by the river or by salt-water currents. It is extended, far out of sight of land, by the migration of fish hatched within its waters. All that it needs to produce an abundance of many useful species is the energy of sunlight, and that, too, is free.

Practically all of the shellfish, crustaceans, and swimming foodfish have their spawning grounds and nurseries and spend a part of their early life in these "sweet sylvan glades beneath the sea." Their loss would be a great disaster to all mankind, in view of the problem presented by a human population explosion. Yet we are rapidly and needlessly turning over these precious marine resources to new land developments. During a period now extending over more than a hundred years, the Federal Government has turned over to the individual states over 65 million acres of tidal lands. These have passed to developers who often quickly ruin them, then move on to other hunting grounds, until only a pitiful fraction of our heritage remains.

Recent surveys show that about 90 per cent of the tidewaters, from Maine to Virginia, have already been affected by dredging and filling. Of the 4500 acres of salt march left in 1959 along the coast of Rhode

Island, all but a scanty 400 acres are now designated for development. Should we permit more of our marine gardens, nature's gift to all the people, to be destroyed forever? Should concrete retaining walls dedicate beaches to private ownership, in spite of the principle (confirmed by many seacoast states) that land between the water and mean high tide, is in the public domain? Once lost, free access to beaches·may never be regained. Are beaches and marine gardens in your own area threatened by proposed improvements? Let everyone be alert.

Pollution by Oil

It has long been realized that great quantities of petroleum (crude oil) and oily petroleum products are constantly finding their way into the ocean. Yet the ocean is so vast that the estimated 2 million tons of these contaminants that enter it each year usually seem just to disappear and be harmlessly dispersed. Chief sources of oil pollution are the flushing of ballast tanks of ships, the intentional dumping of oil that has become mixed with sea water, and natural seepage from underground deposits of oil, such as those along the coast of Southern California.

The spectacular wreck of the *Torrey Canyon* in the spring of 1967 made everyone realize how serious is the damage that may be done by oil pollution. This wreck dumped 60,000 tons of oil into the English Channel, killed thousands of sea birds at the peak of their nesting season, and destroyed millions of lobsters and oysters. It compelled a part of the fishing industry of the nearby French coast to migrate to the Mediterranean, more than 500 miles away. Tourists shunned the 150 miles of defiled beaches, on both sides of the Channel, for several seasons, in spite of all efforts to collect and dispose of the oil.

The efforts to get rid of the *Torrey Canyon*'s oil were not very well advised. Petroleum is a liquid, lighter than water, but insoluble in water. It therefore spreads over the surface of water until the downward pull of gravity, which tends to spread it farther, is balanced by the restraining pull of surface tension. The oil film may then be only a few hundred molecules thick. Although this is thick in comparison with a single molecule, it is so thin that the film is broken into innumerable little pools by the slightest wave or ripple. If the oil has been set afire, the fire then goes out.

Efforts were next made to scatter the oil with high explosives, burn it by setting it on fire with napalm, and disperse it by detergents. We have already explained how the remarkable double-ended character of the detergent anion accounts for detergents dissolving in water in an indecisive manner. The negatively charged, active end of the anion dissolves in water, together with Na^+, while the inactive hydrocarbon end remains undissolved and protrudes into the air (or into oil, if the surface of the water is covered by oil). The oil is thus spread into an ever thinner film, and ultimately into a film only one molecule thick. This is nevertheless thick enough to decrease very greatly the rate of penetration of oxygen into the depths where fish and oysters live. The visible menace of the oil is decreased, but the destruction of fish and oysters is very much increased, because more surface is covered by the oil. Moreover, some dispersants are toxic to marine life.

In recent years, research and development have produced increasingly effective means for dealing with oil spills. Technological approaches may be broadly categorized as containment, chemical treatment, surface treatment followed by mechanical pickup and/or disposal, and direct mechanical pickup. Following the obvious first line of defense—containment—mechanical and physical collection of spilled oil should be employed wherever possible. Mechanical devices include rotating cylinders, moving belts, centrifuges, and hydrocyclones, and their variants.

Among the variety of materials available to treat floating oil are floating absorbents (straw, sawdust, etc.), polymerics (e.g. polyurethane foam), and getting agents (to solidify the oil). Mechanical skimming devices, with or without absorbent pretreatment, are under development, and bid fair to surpass other procedures in situations where wave motion precludes simpler approaches.

Legal Measures To Control Pollution

The most nauseous and offensive forms of pollution are such an affront to sensibilities, such a threat to health, and do such damage to property that they should never have been tolerated for an instant. Yet control by legislation has often had to await studies to determine how much pollution of each kind may be endured. The harm done by a pollutant depends on many factors. Pollution of a swiftly flowing stream does less harm than pollution of a sluggish one, and pollution in winter may be more endurable than in a hot summer. If pollution is intermittent, one needs to consider how often it is likely to occur, and how quickly plants and animals are likely to recover from its effects.

Control of pollution is attempted at every political level. City or
county ordinances make it an offense to dump garbage on vacant lots
or to litter beaches or parks. State law sets standards of water quality.
North Carolina, for example, created a Stream Sanitation Commission,
which began by listing the water resources of the state and mapping
the limits of every watershed. It was then possible to classify the waters
of each region and indicate the best use for each. After completing
such preliminary technical studies, public hearings were held and the
best use of each water resource was decided. In the order of decreasing merit, the quality standards recognized were:

A-I. Water needing only effective disinfection to be suitable for
drinking, cooking, or food processing.

A-II. Water needing other treatment, in addition to disinfection, to
be suitable for the uses just stated.

B. Water suitable for bathing or any use other than drinking, cooking, or food processing.

C. Water suitable for fishing but not for any of the uses indicated
for classes A and B.

D. Water suitable for agriculture, industrial cooling, fish survival,
but not for any of the uses specified for A, B, or C.

E. Water suitable for navigation or sewage disposal but not for any
of the uses specified for the preceding classes.

SA, SB, SC, SE. Saline waters, suitable respectively for commercial
shellfishing, bathing (under sanitary control), fishing, and navigation.

For each of these classes, limits of contamination were set to prevent
the water resources of each group from passing into a lower one or
(when possible) to permit the upgrading of each group into a better
one. Quality standards for drinking water are discussed near the end
of the next chapter.

National Pollution Control

In the United States, national control of large rivers and their tributaries
and the control of lakes are necessary because some of the soluble contaminants and suspended industrial discards find their way into surface
water anywhere in a great river basin. They may be carried far beyond
state boundaries, on their way to the sea. A good part of the common
salt that is carried by the Mississippi at New Orleans must have been
leached from the soils of the upper Mississippi and Ohio valleys or
from the saline and alkali soils of the arid West, in far-away Montana,

Wyoming, and Colorado. Traces of arsenic, fluorine, and zinc may point to pollution by smelters in Missouri and in the Rocky Mountain States.

The Chicago drainage canal dumps industrial wastes and sewage effluents into the Mississippi. Pittsburgh's sewage effluents reach the Mississippi by way of the Allegheny and Ohio rivers. Cleveland's wastes are an international menace because they are discarded into Lake Erie and thence pass out through the St. Lawrence, which flows through Canada.

Until recently, there were no very effective Federal laws for the control of pollution. A broadly based pollution-control act was approved in 1956, amended in 1961 and 1965, and supplemented by the Clean Water Restoration Act of 1966. This legislation sets forth national goals and policies as follows: elimination of discharge of pollutants into navigable waters by 1985; water quality level providing for protection and propagation of fish, shellfish, and wildlife by 1983; prohibition of all toxic discharges; Federal assistance in construction of public waste treatment works; research, development, and planning to eliminate discharges of pollutants into navigable waters, waters of the contiguous zone, and the oceans. The Environmental Protection Agency is in charge of pollution control. It works in collaboration with other Federal agencies, state agencies, municipalities, and the different industries in development of programs for improving the sanitary condition of surface and underground waters, and for decreasing pollution. The Army also lends assistance to public and private agencies and individuals in studies relating to the causes, prevention, and control of pollution. Grants-in-aid to states and municipalities are provided in this Act for a period of years—$1 billion for fiscal 1969.

The Oil Pollution Act of 1964 prohibits the discharge of oil, sludge, and grease into navigable waters, including those along seacoasts, within the jurisdiction of the United States. These far-ranging regulations deserve to be rigidly enforced. The time for action is rapidly running out.

New forms of pollution, each clamoring for control, are constantly appearing. For example, the phosphate industry produces limitless quantities of slimy mud, which is retained behind dams, for lack of suitable methods for making it settle out. When dams break, adjoining rivers are polluted, fortunately often without permanent damage to fish. Fish are famous for being cannibals. The bursting of a dam in Florida dumped great quantities of phosphate sludge into the Peace

River. Nearly a million large fish were killed. Yet their removal gave the fingerlings a better chance for survival, and within a year fishing in the river seemed about as good as ever.

Along seacoasts, when fresh-water streams are diverted, grassy tidal flats may be so polluted by fresh water that marine life is injured or extinguished. It begins to look as if the mere presence of too many human beings on this planet threatens many forms of wildlife with extinction. A limit to human population on the earth will not be set by lack of standing room or lack of food, but by the tensions set up by overcrowding. If the human race should suffer a sudden eclipse, we wonder how many other species will already have vanished because we were not well enough informed to protect them.

The lack of laws to limit pollution is not chiefly owing to indifference or the opposition of industry. The interaction of the different species of plants and animals that inhabit fresh or saline water is a very complicated matter. Details are only slowly being disclosed by efforts of thousands of biologists and biochemists. In many instances, as in pollution by the paper industry, legislation has had to await the discovery of guiding facts and principles. So pollution control is very properly in a state of continuing development. Details of its current status are available in publications of the Environmental Protection Agency, Washington, D.C.

13

The Worldwide Menace of Salt

Sources of the Ocean's Salt

Water, in its relentless attack on the earth's mountains, uplands, and plains, is aided by oxygen and carbon dioxide, by living plants and bacteria, and by the activities of man. Every rock and mineral species finally yields to their combined efforts, is split into fragments, crumbles, disintegrates, dissolves, and is carried away toward the ocean. The ocean now contains about 3.5 per cent of dissolved ionic solids, collectively called salts. If these were removed from the ocean in the solid state, they would have a total bulk about a fifth of that of all the continents above sea level.

Yet water forever presses its attack on the land. The ocean now contains about 2.5 per cent of common salt, its chief dissolved component, yet is still far from saturated with this compound. Plenty of the ions of common salt and other salts of sodium, potassium, calcium, and magnesium (the ions Na^+, K^+, Ca^{++}, and Mg^{++}) remain to be extracted from the rocks, minerals, and soils of the earth's crust. However, it is not certain that the ocean is growing saltier, for the removal of salts into the ocean by running water is largely or completely offset by salt spray that is carried inland by the winds, along all the seacoasts of the world, and by fresh water poured into the ocean by the melting of polar icecaps. The ocean, at least in its surface layers, is already slightly supersaturated with calcium carbonate, and perhaps also with calcium sulfate.

The rocks, minerals, and soils of the earth as we know it are not the chief source of the ocean's salt. In the ocean the order of decreasing abundance of salts is chlorides, sulfates, carbonates. In rivers it is just the reverse. In salt-laden soils or salt lakes a much larger portion of the accumulated salts is calcium sulfate and magnesium sulfate, and a much smaller portion is magnesium chloride than in the ocean.

The two ions of common salt may have entered the ocean from different sources—Cl^- as hydrochloric acid, which is often plentiful in the gases emitted by volcanoes, and Na^+ as sodium sulfate and carbonate, extracted by running water from minerals of the earth's crust. The first oceans may have been of limited area and were perhaps slightly acidic. Life must have been impossible in them until enough carbonate had been extracted from the earth's crust to bring the ocean to approximate neutrality. All this must remain just speculation until we know more about the early history of the earth. We introduce it here merely to emphasize that the two principal ions of the ocean were probably not both derived from the same source.

Salt Accumulation in Soils

Sometime, during past geological ages, a great fault block has been uplifted and interposed between a flowing stream and its outlet into the sea. Then all the salt that the stream would otherwise have discarded into the ocean is left to accumulate in salt lakes and at length in low-lying spots in the soil. The soil becomes loaded with salts (chiefly sulfates and chlorides) and with alkali—a name that in agriculture usually means the carbonate or bicarbonate of sodium (the ions Na^+ and CO_3^{--} or HCO_3^-). On our arid Western plains there have thus come into existence the Great Salt Lake, Death Valley, Searles Lake, and hundreds of little ponds, all loaded with salts, alkali, and sometimes borax, in association with limestone and gypsum.

Almost every part of the world has such regions, where human life and agriculture are both limited, not only by scanty rainfall but also by the accumulation of salts and alkali in the soil. Many different types of soil have been recognized, including three different kinds rich in salt:

1. *Saline soils.* In soils of this type the accumulated salts are either chemically neutral (the ions Na^+, Cl^-, and SO_4^{--}) or slightly acid (the ion Mg^{++}). Carbonates (the ion CO_3^{--}) or bicarbonates (the ion HCO_3^-) are absent. The redemption of such a soil usually depends on the possibility of leaching its sodium (Na^+) away to lower depths, below the reach of the roots of crops.

2. *Saline-alkali soils.* In the soils of this type, salinity is due to a mixture of neutral salts with sodium bicarbonate (the ions Na^+ and HCO_3^-). The pH (section B, Appendix) of such salts is usually below 8.5. If neutral salts are leached away in an effort to improve the soil, the toxicity of Na^+ toward plants is increased and the soil itself may actually be damaged.

3. *Alkali soils.* These soils contain sodium carbonate (the ions Na^+ and CO_3^{--}) as their principal source of alkali. Their pH is above 8.5 and is sometimes as high as 10. This is about the degree of alkalinity shown by a solution of sodium carbonate of the same concentration. Such soils are entirely unsatisfactory, since their clay is greatly swollen and impermeable to water, in the presence of that much sodium.

Alkalinity in a soil is often past remedy, since it has its origin in poor drainage. If drainage can be improved alkalinity may be gradually leached away. A top dressing of gypsum (calcium sulfate) will gradually decrease alkalinity by precipitating it as calcium carbonate. Yet this leaves the soil with as much Na^+ as before, and for some crops may overload the soil with sulfate.

Plant Growth in the Presence of Salt

Too much salt in irrigation water or soil may cause plants to be misshapen and to have foliage that is a greenish blue in color, instead of the bright green of normal vegetation. These effects are observable even with plants grown in water culture in the presence of dissolved nutrients in too high a concentration. Though the crop may not be killed, the yield is always decreased if enough salt is present in the soil or irrigation water to produce the effects just described.

The damage done by salt depends on the kind of salt present—whether it is common salt or something else—and on the concentration of salt in the film of liquid that wets soil particles and comes in contact with the roots of the crop. This film concentration is usually unknown, and may be two or three times or even ten times the concentration of salt in the irrigation water.

The distribution of salt that has accumulated in a field is often very irregular. Places where the drainage is poor (perhaps because of an impervious layer of "hardpan"), may accumulate enough alkali to be marked by the characteristic white or black film. Before this happens, the crop tends to die out in spots, and salt-loving weeds make their appearance. From the species of plants that invade such salt areas, ecologists can often infer the nature of the salt accumulated in the soil and its approximate concentration.

Damage Done by Toxic Elements

When an element damages plants or animals in a way that is readily recognized as being caused by that element, it is said to be toxic. Both the ions of common salt are toxic when present in more than a minimum concentration in the soil solution. If leaves, after being dried in an oven at 105°C, are found by chemical analysis to contain more than 0.5 per cent of either Na^+ or Cl^-, the toxic effect of either ion may produce a brown or tan-colored border of dead leaf tissue, surrounding a central area of normal green. This marginal leaf burn is the larger the higher the concentration of either ion.

Nuts, berries, grapes, and stone fruits of any kind are subject to toxic injury of the kind just described, caused by either Na^+ or Cl^-. Citrus and some shrubs show a browning of the entire leaf surface, followed by premature leaf fall. Certain varieties of a species are more resistant than others to the ions of common salt. Certain rootstocks for grafted trees are better than others, not only for resisting the attacks of root borers but also in resisting damage by salt. If a crop is sensitive to damage by either of the ions of common salt, the electrical conductivity of the irrigation water (explained in section D of the appendix) is not a good measure of possible damage to the crop by irrigation with this water.

Boron in soils and irrigation water is toxic to many crops, especially to citrus and walnuts. Leaf burn is a common symptom. For boron-sensitive crops, boron should not be present in a concentration exceeding 0.67 ppm. For other crops, the concentration of this element should not usually exceed 2 or 3 ppm.

Most plants get the nitrogen they need from nitrates (the ion NO_3^-), present in the soil solution that wets their roots. Yet a few plants (paddy rice, for example) which grow in waterlogged locations, where aeration is poor, do not need to await the oxidation of ammonia to nitrate by bacteria of the soil, but absorb and use ammonium salts as their source of nitrogen. A concentration of nitrate of a few parts per million in the soil solution may stimulate plants to luscious growth in which they display a bright green color. In a higher concentration, nitrates may be toxic to plants, just as salts in the general area. Higher concentrations still of nitrate may be toxic to animals, as noted in Chapter 1.

Plants need at least traces of five or six heavy metals (iron, copper, manganese, zinc, molybdenum, and perhaps vanadium). These elements are probably all needed in building enzymes (substances that bring about chemical reactions that otherwise would not take place). Molybdenum, for example, is needed for the reduction of nitrate to ammonia, which is then built into protein. This may be the only role of molybdenum in plant life, for plants that get their nitrogen from ammonium salts appear not to need molybdenum.

If much more than the needed amount of these heavy metals is present in the soil solution, they may be toxic. Even lower concentrations of unessential heavy metals (lead, cadmium, silver, etc.) may be toxic to crops. It might take a chemical analysis of soil extract to discover what element is at fault, if toxicity appears.

Alkali is the most harmful of the toxic agents likely to be present in the soil solution. "Black alkali" is mostly sodium carbonate, Na_2CO_3. It is actually white when pure but may contain enough dissolved organic matter to be colored black. Thus it may appear as either a white or a black film on poorly drained soils. The damage done by black alkali to a crop is sometimes owing so sodium ion Na^+, associated with CO_3^{--} in the alkali. This not only injures the soil, as presently explained but tends to prevent crops from assimilating calcium, Ca^{++}, which is less toxic because its alkalinity is less pronounced.

The Sensitivity of Different Crops to Salt

If soils were all reasonably free from salt, and irrigation water pure as rain, irrigation would never need to be coupled with drainage. One would irrigate whenever the moisture content of the soil fell beneath a certain figure, and that would be the end of it. In the presence of salt, drainage is needed, and a little calculation will indicate how much.

For most crops, reference to books or a government bulletin will show what concentration of salt (expressed either in parts per million or the conductivity, section D, Appendix, of a saturated soil extract) will probably result in a 50 per cent decrease in the crop, hence will probably make the crop profitless. (We shall presently present such data for a few important crops.)

Let us assume, for example, that the crops in field corn, for which the "no profit concentration" is that corresponding to conductivity of 7 millimhos per centimeter (7 mmho/cm). If the irrigation water has a conductivity of 1 mmho/cm, it may evidently be concentrated seven-fold before its salt content becomes intolerable. In other words, if the salt removed from the soil by the crop is negligible, the crop and evaporation from the soil may jointly remove all but a seventh of the water applied in irrigation before the accumulation of salt becomes critical. The seventh that still remains (or better, much more) must be discarded by drainage.

Irrigated field corn commonly gets 16 to 25 inches of irrigation during the growing season, with an average of about 21 inches for the actual consumption (evaporation from the soil plus transpiration through the leaves of plants). If this is to be six-sevenths of the total irrigation water applied, the remaining seventh is $1/6 \times 21 = 3.5$ inches, which is $3.5/12 = 0.29$ feet of water. In other words, for each acre irrigated, at least 0.29 acre-foot (12,500 cubic feet) of water must be drained away and discarded to lower depths before the end of the growing season. If there is rainfall, irrigation is suspended until there is again need for water and drainage is kept as low as possible unless the soil already needs leaching or is getting water-logged.

Vegetables and root crops are less subject to varietal differences in resistance to damage by salt than are fruits and forage crops. Table 13-1 gives an idea of how great is the difference in salt-sensitivity among a few common crops. The upper figure in each case is the conductivity (mmho/cm at 25°) of the saturated soil extract at which the crop reduction is 10 per cent; and the lower figure the conductivity at which the

Table 13-1.
Sensitivity of Vegetable and Field Crops to Salt

Vegetable Crops

Beet	Broccoli Tomato	Cabbage	Potato	Sweet Corn	Lettuce	Carrot	Beans
8	4	2.5	2.5	2.5	2.0	2.0	1.5
12	8	7.5	6.0	6.0	5.0	4.5	3.5

Field Crops

Barley	Cotton Sugarbeet	Sorghum	Wheat Safflower	Soybean	Corn	Broadbean
12	10	6	7.5	5.5	5.0	3.6
18	16	12	14.5	9.5	7.0	6.5

Source: *Agricultural Information Bulletin* No. 28a, U.S.D.A.

crop reduction is 50 per cent and the crop probably profitless. Separately, for vegetable crops and field crops, the table lists crops in approximately their order of increasing sensitivity to salt.

These statistics may be of interest to readers with small home gardens in a saline region, but commercial farmers need more detailed information.

Plants in their earliest stages of growth are much more sensitive to salt than those that have become well established. Seeds for transplants should be germinated and sustained in the best water available, even at extra cost. If the seeds are to be germinated and irrigated in rows in a field, a little observation and thought will show where water evaporating from the soil is leaving a deposit of salt. Seeds should be planted downhill from this location, not on the ridge between rows.

Salt Tolerance

The opposite to the crop characteristic just discussed is salt tolerance. Salt-tolerant crops are important in arid regions because they permit some financial return from soils that otherwise would yield none. The United Nations program for arid zone research seeks to discover what crop varieties are least affected by accumulated salt or by an excess of micronutrient elements that plants can use only in trace. Yet the program is more than an attempt to identify the crop varieties that can profitably be grown in the presence of salt: in particular geographic locations, climates, or types of soil. It seeks above all to discover the factors that lead to salt tolerance, and the best ways to create tolerant new varieties.

The intake of water from the soil solution that wets a plant's roots into the interior of the plant is accomplished by the spontaneous movement of water molecules that we term *diffusion* (section E, Appendix). Water molecules diffuse in both directions through the cell walls of plants; but if the plant is to thrive, the net rate of diffusion of water must always be from the soil solution inward into the plant (Figure 6-10).

There is actually a contest for water between soil solution and cell solution. The outcome of the contest is determined by the particle concentration—the number of dissolved particles (ions and molecules) in equal volumes of the two solutions. The greater the number of dissolved particles in any given volume of a solution, the greater the tendency of the solution to retain water, or to pull in water from an adjoining solution through a membrane or cell wall. Since water must flow inward from soil solution into cell solution if the plant is to thrive, we conclude that the cell solution must contain more dissolved particles than an equal volume of soil solution. That limits the concentration of salt that a plant can tolerate in the soil solution that wets its roots. If the soil solution is too strong, the direction of flow is reversed. Water then flows outward from the plant into the soil. The highly hydrous (water-swollen) protoplasmic lining of the plant's cell pulls away from the cell wall and presently dies. This is *plasmolysis*.

Salt-tolerant plants, often termed *halophytes,* differ from less tolerant ones either in being able to admit into their tissues an unusual concentration of salt ions or in creating and retaining within their tissues an unusual concentration of neutral molecules and ions, such as those of simple sugars. In exerting a pull on water, one dissolved particle (ion or molecule) is as good as another. It is the particle concentration that counts.

The tendency of a solution to retain water or to pull in water from a less concentrated solution (by evaporation or by passage through a membrane) is called its *osmotic pressure* (section E, Appendix). The flow of water is always from a less concentrated solution (or pure water) into the one whose osmotic pressure is stated. For this reason one might wish that it had been named "osmotic pull."

The excess pull that the solution within a plant's tissue has, in comparison with that of the solution that wets the plant's roots, is called the plant's "osmotic surplus." For alfalfa, a moderately salt-resistant crop, grown in soils of various degrees of salinity, the osmotic surplus has been found to be 10 to 12 atmospheres.

Since salt-tolerant crops admit salt into their tissues, their growth and harvesting gradually rid the soil of salt. The rate of removal is nevertheless so slight that soil improvement by such means is hardly worth considering. The real importance of salt-tolerant plants is in giving the farmer some return from his land while the best means for dealing with salt is being sought.

Salt tolerance is somewhat dependent on climate, since salt does more damage when the weather is hot. A farmer who has endured weeks of drought, gazing skyward every morning in hopes of some token of rain, is faced with an agonizing decision. Shall he continue to hope for rain and risk losing his crop for lack of water? Or shall he risk damaging the crop and perhaps the soil itself with one or more irrigations with water containing a little salt?

How the Soil Itself May Be Ruined by Salt

Common salt, when accumulated to a moderate concentration in a clay soil, ruins the soil by displacing calcium. The sodium part (Na^+) of common salt moves into the clay and calcium (Ca^{++}) moves out and is leached away.

Soils ruined by sodium are slimy and sticky when wet and dry to almost stony hardness. A dry clay soil with too much sodium may shed most of the next downpour of rain; in consequence, soils most in need of leaching may refuse to be leached. In such nearly impenetrable soils, plants die both for lack of moisture and because of poor root development in lack of air (that is to say, oxygen) about their roots.

Damage by sodium may appear with avocado, stone fruits, and citrus when only 5 per cent of the exchangeable calcium and magnesium has been replaced by sodium. For beans, the damage may appear at about 10 per cent replacement, and for most other crops at about 15 per cent. Even though considerable calcium may still remain in a sodium-laden soil, sodium predominates, and crops may fail because of difficulty in obtaining calcium.

Since the change by which sodium displaces calcium from clay is reversible, clay soils overburdened with sodium may sometimes be benefited by the application of a calcium compound, such as gypsum, limestone, or even calcium chloride. Organic matter or powdered sulfur often benefit such soils—organic matter by increasing the acidity of the soil and adding humus to it and sulfur by slow oxidation, producing sulfuric acid. In either case, the acid reacts with the precipitated limestone in the soil, bringing calcium (Ca^{++}) into the solution. This may then displace sodium (Na^+) from the clay.

Thus the soil is gradually improved, though expensively. One must remember, however, that there may be no way of leaching away the displaced sodium. The consequent ruination of the soil is then as irreversible as death.

Irrigation with Saline Water

We have warned very earnestly against irrigation with water that contains more than a trace of salt. Yet experiments have revealed one condition under which saline water or perhaps even sea water may be used in irrigation. The requirement is that the soil shall be pure sand or gravel, unmixed with clay, and that there shall be good drainage, downward to great depths. Then a wide variety of crops, including grasses, grains, legumes, and such vegetables as melons, squash, and tomatoes, show an amazing tolerance for salt, under conditions that kill plants grown in soils containing even moderate amounts of clay.

The explanation seems in part to be that sodium, Na^+, is adsorbed (strongly held on the surface) by clay particles, causing them to swell, and seriously decreasing the rate at which water drains away to lower depths. In gravel or pure sand, by contrast, the downward flow of water through the soil is very rapid. The root hairs through which the plant absorbs water and mineral nutrients may be submerged in saline irrigation water only a few moments; then the water drains away and is replaced by air, leaving only a discontinuous film of liquid water, adhering to individual sand particles. Thus the root hairs are well aerated and may gain from aeration an increased vitality that may make the crop more tolerant to salt.

The tolerance of plants for saline irrigation water is probably also increased because naturally saline water always contains one or more of the chief mineral nutrients (calcium, potassium, phosphorus, sulfur, etc.) that plants demand. That is one reason for thinking that diluted sea water or brackish water of low salinity might sometimes be useful in irrigation. Brackish water that is alkaline might be almost neutralized by sulfuric acid, mixed with a little phosphoric acid to increase its nutrient value.

In the use of saline water in irrigation, the most feared consequence is that the salts in the soil solution may be concentrated by evaporation. By good fortune, the most harmful salts (those of sodium and magnesium) are sufficiently soluble to remain dissolved until they are carried away to deeper depths in the absence of very much clay. Salts may even be deposited as crystals in the surface soil when saline water containing them moves upward by capillarity and evaporates from the surface. Even then, the roots of a crop are usually well below the level at which damage may occur.

Experiments in the use of saline water in irrigation have been under way in Israel, Italy, Tunisia, the United States, the Soviet Union, and other lands having the problem of arid or semiarid areas. The fountain of destiny distributes rainfall or snowfall so irregularly that about a fifth of the land areas of the earth are either arid or semiarid.

Within these dry and desolate regions are vast expanses of rippling sand dunes, whose total area is about twice that of the 48 coterminous states. The very ocean, along a part of the coastline of every inhabited continent, is bordered by dry areas, with drifting coastal sand dunes; and within the great deserts of the Sahara, Arabia, Central Asia, Mongolia, and Central Australia are some regions as large as California or Texas, which irrigation with salt water may conceivably make important producers of human food.

Salt-Laden Zones of the United States and Canada

There are over 70 million acres of irrigable land in the 17 arid Western states, and about two-thirds of these are actually irrigated. Although some of these soils are non-saline, in much of the West the accumulation of salt is a constant threat to crops. The threat is acute in the interior valleys of California, the great basin of Utah and Nevada, the Colorado River basin (from Wyoming and Colorado to California and Arizona), the Rio Grande basin of Texas and New Mexico, and parts of the Columbia River basin in Idaho and Washington.

The detailed attention that has been given these Western soils, during nearly a century, has begun to give a much better understanding of how the threat from salt should be met. For example, soils containing as much as 2 per cent salt in the topmost foot of soil may often be improved by application of irrigation water that is sufficient to provide for some root zone leaching, in addition to water for the growth of the crops. More strongly saline soils may sometimes be effectively leached by 1 to 4 ft of good quality irrigation water, applied during winter. Saline water with 1000 to 3000 ppm of dissolved salt can usually be used for irrigation if the soil is well drained. Year by year, the testing of new crops and new varieties should constantly reveal which of them are most resistant to salt.

The problem of salt accumulation in soils is also important in the Great Plains section of Alberta and Saskatchewan, in Canada, and in semiarid interior regions of British Columbia. Salinity is one of the important features used in rating such soils. Soils with over 1 per cent of soluble salts, exclusive of $CaSO_4$, in the upper 2 ft are considered unsuitable for irrigation. In Saskatchewan the soluble salts are mainly sulfates of Ca^{++}, Mg^{++}, and Na^+, with much less chloride and carbonate.

About 900,000 acres of soils have been classed as alkaline (pH above 8.8, section G, Appendix). Most of this land is in the arid brown soil regions of southwest Saskatchewan. The unusually pure irrigation water of this district, chiefly runoff from melting snow, is practically free from chlorides and carbonate, but may contain considerable bicarbonate (HCO_3^-). Since sodium is low in these waters, continuous irrigation over many years has often done no harm to soils rich in calcium.

A Glance at Mexico

In nearly all of Mexico the problem of saline water and saline soils is very serious. Along the western coast, irrigation water is abundant and soils reasonably free from salt; yet, even in these favored localities, bad irrigation practices have sometimes ruined good soils. Throughout the rest of Mexico, the accumulation of salt in the soil has resulted in the same problems as in the western part of the United States.

The damage by salt has been particularly bad in the valley east of Mexico City, where the drainage of Lake Texcoco has exposed soil so laden with common salt and nitrates that no vegetation will grow without expensive preliminary soil treatment. The valley in which the city lies is surrounded by a ring of mountains, in which rainfall creates an abundant water supply. Springs bring this water to the surface, primarily to the west and north of the modern lake, at only a slight elevation above its surface. Thus the land has been well enough drained to support abundant crops during almost 2000 years. Thousands of fertile and well-tended vegetable and flower gardens (*chinampas*), each nearly surrounded by fresh water canals, have had manure and vegetable remains regularly applied and have produced crops that were the foundation of Aztec prosperity and power.

Today, relics of the former luxuriance of these gardens can be seen in the tourist center of Xochimilco. However, during centuries of intense cultivation, salt was steadily concentrated at the lowest level of the valley. Even in Aztec times, the lower part of the great lake had to be cut off from the rest of the valley by a long dike of earth and stone, held together by stakes interlaced with branches. Through the centuries, too, nitrogeneous compounds in the fertilizer and compost were being oxidized to nitrate, which accumulated with other salts in the salt-laden modern lake. But the great city is inexorable in its demands for water. Beginning in Aztec times, but especially in recent years, it has brought in water in covered aqueducts from the mountains to the west. It now takes an eighth of all the water available in the valley, the rest being largely lost in evaporation. Now that the old lake is being drained, the fact that soils can be ruined by salt is plain for all to see.

The soils of Mexico have the handicap of being less studied than those of the United States and Canada. Nevertheless, good progress has been made in identifying crops that are somewhat tolerant of salt.

India and Pakistan

These two countries together have nearly a sixth of the world's population, in spite of extensive salt-ruined soils. The problems posed by saline water and especially by saline soils are desperate in many regions. There are salt-ruined upland plateaus, saline marches along the coast, salt-flats, often flooded by the ocean, and deltas of great rivers where the soil, although constantly leached, is nonetheless laden with salt.

The great Sakkur Barrage, built in 1932, under British rule, irrigates 25 million acres; yet at least 100,000 acres of the reclaimed land have had to be abandoned each year, because of the accumulation of salt in unskillful irrigation. Once abandoned, such land is often lost past reclaiming by being eroded or blown away.

In this broad subcontinent, many different kinds of problems are posed by salt-laden soils. The causes of salt accumulation and the best remedies for it have been actively studied for nearly a century, beginning under British rule in 1876. In the regions southeast of Delhi the difficulty is with sodium salts that are brought to the surface by capillary action and surface evaporation. Canal irrigation makes this salinity worse. Contributing factors are: alternating wet and dry seasons, low water gradients (slopes less than 5 feet per mile), high water table, rocks rich in sodium minerals, poor quality of ground and canal water, and cation-exchange reactions in the soil. The most evident remedy seems to be to lower the water table and irrigate sparingly.

Over a million acres in India and Pakistan are classified as alkali soils, soils laden with sodium chloride, sulfate, and carbonate. These salts probably originate with the weathering of soil particles rather than by being brought in by irrigation. When common salt and limestone are present together, a hardpan may form that seriously limits drainage. The remedy is not in attempts to break up the hard layer, but to understand how it came to be formed, then to reverse the conditions that led to its formation, and patiently to await gradual improvement.

Studies of the salt tolerance of different crops are an important part of the soil-improvement program of India. As in western North America and in many other parts of the world, the character of the native vegetation serves almost as well as chemical analysis to indicate the type of soil and the kind of salts that have accumulated in it.

Salt Balance and the Fate of Nations

Salts come into the soil from three different sources: (1) from a neighboring ocean, salt lake, or salt deposit; (2) always, in some degree, from irrigation water; (3) from the weathering of minerals in the soil.

Since the last of these processes is very slow, a sudden increase in the salt content of a soil is usually accounted for by either of the first two processes; but when a soil newly opened to cultivation is saline or alkaline, there may be doubt about the source of the contaminant.

Salts are removed from the soil in three different ways: (1) removal by harvested crops; (2) drainage or leaching; (3) removal of particular ions by ion-exchange or by precipitation reactions in the soil.

When gain and loss of salts by a soil are equal there is salt balance. Soils that are laden with salt and alkali are gradually improved if the removal of salts from the soil in the three ways just mentioned can be made to exceed the input of salt into the soil by the three opposing processes. Salt-tolerant crops, which are fortunately also salt-removing crops, can be cultivated persistently. In years in which there happens to be abundant rainfall there may be opportunity for leaching. On a small scale and at considerable expense, the soil may be improved by chemical treatment. Thus, with patient management the soil may gradually be improved.

The fate of nations was nevertheless often determined before the first human settlers entered a national territory. In many lands, including some that are densely populated today, the problems of saline soils are desperate and may take centuries to solve. While awaiting their solution, the peasant is patiently at work with bullock and iron-shod crooked stick, turning over salt-ruined soils. Untouched by the modern world, burdened by poverty, and chained by superstition, he is caught in a pitiless treadmill: he dribbles his life away in heroic devotion to his family, rearing another generation of undernourished people to go on doing the same.

It has sometimes been said that the lack of modern agricultural methods in the Far East is not to be deplored, since there is plenty of manpower available. Yet all these ineffective laborers must themselves be fed. The truth seems to be that whatever economics, science and inventiveness achieve are soon canceled by the increase in the human burden on the land. Must everyone be forever burdened by drudgery, so that no one has time to think? This may be an inner meaning of the complaint that "man is born unto trouble as the sparks fly upward."

14

Making Water Fit To Use

Chlorine and Hypochlorites in Water Purification

The nearly complete safety of the drinking water supplied by most cities in the industrialized modern world is largely owing to the nearly universal use of chlorine as a disinfecting agent. Chlorine gas (elementary chlorine, Cl_2) is a greenish yellow gas with a sharp, choking odor. It is painful and dangerous to inhale chlorine even in slight concentrations. The maximum concentration that may be breathed for about half an hour is about four volumes of chlorine in a million of air. Breathing chlorine, even briefly, in a concentration of one volume in a thousand is fatal.

Although elementary chlorine was first prepared in 1774, its use in disinfecting water had to await its first commercial liquefaction, more than a century later (1910), since it could then be readily shipped to the place at which it was to be used. Previous to that time, chlorinated lime, a mixture containing calcium hypochlorite, was sometimes used in disinfecting water and sewage.

Today, nearly pure calcium hypochlorite, $Ca(ClO)_2 4H_2O$, a soluble dry powder, is often used instead of chlorine itself in disinfecting limited quantities of water—for example, in the sanitary control of swimming pools. This chlorine substitute, often termed "high-test chlorine," calls for the preliminary adjustment of the water to definite but very slight alkalinity (pH 7.2 to 7.4) (section G, Appendix).

Chlorine for the disinfection of water supplies is usually drawn from a cylinder of liquid chlorine. Gas drawn from the cylinder is metered into a small stream of water, which is then mingled with a larger stream. Pretreatment with chlorine is usually just after submerged or floating trash has been removed from the incoming stream of water by coarse screens and just before the water is stored in lakes and ponds to permit suspended solids (mud) to settle out. One purpose of the pre-chlorination is to prevent the growth of algae or weeds in settling basins. It also serves to oxidize readily oxidizable organic matter, hydrogen sulfide, and ferrous and manganous salts (the ions Fe^{++} and Mn^{++}). The latter are oxidized to their higher valence states (Fe^{+++} and Mn^{4+}).

Coagulation and Filtration

After the preliminary chlorination, surface water usually needs to spend a few days or several weeks in a natural or artificial settling basin to give the chlorine time to complete the oxidation of all readily oxidizable impurities, and time for mud to settle out. Sand will settle out in a few hours, and clay may require days or weeks. Filtration through sand will then completely clarify many waters.

Nevertheless, most cities remove the last traces of turbidity by a simple treatment (coagulation and filtration) which greatly shortens filtration time, prevents the sand of the filter bed from becoming clogged, and aids in the removal of objectionable taste and odor. A small amount of aluminum sulfate, usually (but somewhat incorrectly) termed *alum,* is dissolved in the water, then a calculated amount of slaked lime (calcium hydroxide) is added. A slowly settling, sticky precipitate (sludge) is formed:

$$Al^{+++} + 3(OH)^- \rightarrow Al(OH)_3$$
Aluminum
hydroxide

The sticky aluminum hydroxide is actually much more hydrous than the formula here given indicates. In settling out it carries with it most of the clay particles that are still suspended in the water and a good part of the remaining bacteria. The overlying liquid is then filtered through sand to remove practically all of the remaining turbidity. It then needs further chlorination, to make sure that disease-producing organisms have actually all been destroyed.

In repairing a city's water mains or in laying new ones, or sometimes as a result of flood, mud and iron rust suddenly enter water that previously seemed free from turbidity. It is usually possible to get rid of these impurities by installing a simple filter in the water tap. Filtering alone will not rid water of dangerous bacteria, however. Water must be boiled as well.

Final Disinfection by Chlorine or Chlorine Dioxide

After the water has been completely freed from turbidity it must be chlorinated again. The amount of chlorine needed at this stage depends on the length of time that the water will spend in the mains before being used in the home. A concentration of several parts by weight of chlorine to ten million of water is usually sufficient. A million gallons of water then calls for 2.5 to 4 pounds of chlorine.

Water that is to be used outdoors (as in outdoor swimming pools) needs much more chlorine than is needed indoors. This is because when chlorine is dissolved in water it is partially converted into hypochlorous acid (reaction a), which is then gradually decomposed in sunlight, losing oxygen, as shown in reaction c:

$$
\begin{array}{ccccc}
 & & \text{(hydrochloric)} & & \text{(Hypochlorous)} \\
 & a & \text{acid} & & \text{acid} \\
Cl_2 + H_2O & \rightleftarrows & HCl & + & HClO \\
 & b & & & \\
 & & & c & \downarrow \\
 & & & & \rightarrow HCl + \tfrac{1}{2}O_2
\end{array}
$$

Only a part of the chlorine that is dissolved in water at any given moment is present as HCl and HClO, since reaction a is reversible. Yet as hypochlorous acid, HClO, is gradually decomposed in the sunlight (reaction c), more of it is formed. The water thus loses all of its dissolved chlorine if the exposure to sunlight is prolonged. For this reason, sewage effluents containing an excess of chlorine soon lose this protection against being reinfected. If they then encounter typhoid bacteria they are as dangerous as ever.

Water contaminated with industrial wastes and water in which algae flourish sometimes contain phenols. Chlorination then produces chlorophenols, which have a disagreeable, tarry taste or odor. The remedy is to follow chlorination with treatment by chlorine dioxide (ClO_2) in a concentration of about 0.5 parts per million (ppm). The ill-tasting compounds are thus oxidized and destroyed.

Chlorine dioxide has recently displaced other oxidants in bleaching flour, linen, paper pulp, and other organic fibrous or powdered industrial raw materials. It is produced where it is to be used by the reaction of sodium chlorite with chlorine:

$$2NaClO_2 + Cl_2 \rightarrow 2NaCl + 2ClO_2$$

When water that has been disinfected with chlorine is about to enter the distribution mains of a city, the residual (surplus) chlorine may be 0.1 to 0.2 ppm to gain some protection against reinfection by bacteria on the way to the consumer. The residual chlorine is sometimes removed by spraying the water into the air, just before its final distribution. Yet aerated water, having picked up additional oxygen, corrodes iron pipes. For this reason, some cities prefer to finish their purification of water by adding a little ammonia gas. This converts the residual chlorine into chloramines, which have some germicidal value but a less evident taste than chlorine.

A simple filter, charged with activated charcoal and attached to the kitchen faucet, may be the best way for the housekeeper to deal with the nuisance of water that too frequently tastes of surplus chlorine.

Disinfection by Ozone or Ultraviolet Light

On a small scale, water is occasionally treated with ozone. This may readily be prepared, in admixture with a considerably larger volume of air, by passing air through a narrow space in which it is subjected to a rapidly alternating electrical stress. (Actual sparks do not pass.)

Ozone (O_3) differs from ordinary oxygen in having three atoms in a molecule instead of the usual two. It is such a vigorous oxidizing agent that mere traces of it, when present in the atmosphere, soon reveal their presence by coating silver or mercury with a dark-colored film of oxide. A little ozone in the air makes rubber collapse to a sticky mass, destroys odors, and kills bacteria. A commercial ozonizer needs expert design and competent supervision, else the ozone that it produces may be contaminated with poisonous oxides of nitrogen.

Ultraviolet light for the sterilization of water, air, biological preparations, or milk is more expensive than the oxidants just mentioned but has the advantage of introducing no foreign substance, not even oxygen, into the material to be sterilized. In using it, one needs to remember that ordinary glass is not transparent to ultraviolet light. Vessels with quartz windows are used.

Water Discolored by Plant Residues

Water draining from swampy or forested lands may be of about the color of tea, from prolonged contact with decaying plant residues. The presence of tannin in such water (or in tea) may be demonstrated by the black color that tannin produces when a drop of ferric chloride solution is added. Rivers are sometimes black as ink when they emerge from swamps in which the vegetation is rich in tannin and the soil rich in iron.

The chief objection to water discolored by plant residues is in the putrid, fishy, garlicky, grassy, moldy, or otherwise objectionable odor or taste, which ruins coffee for all except persons inured to this sort of contamination. To remove or even greatly reduce color and odor is sometimes very difficult. A little exploration may reveal that a good part of the nuisance comes from a small tributary stream, draining only a limited area. Some ditching, slashing, and burning during the dryest season may be helpful.

Flocculation to remove mud from a city's water supply may get rid of a good part of the color and odor as well. Municipal plants sometimes add activated charcoal to materials that remove turbidity by flocculation. If the difficulty with bad taste is too frequent one may try a simple filter attached to a household tap and charged with activated charcoal. If color and odor are traced to algae, killed by prechlorination and later decaying in the settling pond, then oxidation by chlorine dioxide may be needed.

Fluoridation

The human body contains a trace of fluoride (the ion F^-) which hardens the surface of the bones and teeth with a coating of the mineral apatite ($Ca_5(PO_4)_3F$). If drinking water contains less than about 1 ppm of fluoride, the hydroxyl ion (OH^-) replaces the fluoride ion in the enamel of the teeth and dental decay is more frequent. Many extended tests have been made in which the water of one city received a measured addition of fluoride while that of a neighboring city received none. The tests have shown very definitely that dental caries are less frequent if the fluoride content of drinking water is in the range of 0.6 to 1.7 ppm.

Since everyone drinks more water in hot weather, the concentration of fluoride in drinking water may be less during the summer months. Weather records of recent years permit the average maximum temperature in any locality to be estimated in advance with fair accuracy. At 50°F 1.2 ppm of fluoride (F^-) is prescribed. At 90°F the prescribed concentration is only 0.7 ppm. Many natural water supplies, before being softened, contain fluoride within this range of concentration.

There are of course instances in which the drinking water of a community naturally contains too much fluoride when it is impounded for treatment and distribution. As much as 16 ppm results in brown spots on the teeth (mottling) but without other apparent injury to health. Higher concentrations than this may be a health hazard.

When fluoride is to be added to water, this is usually done after any softening that might be necessary and just after the softened water has been stabilized by the addition of acid. In 1967, over 3100 communities in the United States added fluoride to water, for the most part in the form of sodium fluoride, sodium fluosilicate, or fluosilicic acid. Their total population was about a third of that of the whole country. Currently more than a third of America's largest cities supply fluoridated water to the cities. In addition, several million people live in communities in which the water contains enough natural fluoride to protect the teeth. There is of course nothing in the idea that fluoride added to water is any more dangerous than fluoride derived from the minerals of the soil. Fluoride is fluoride, and that is the end of it.

Simple Ways To Get Rid of Hardness

Industry tends to shun regions in which the water is corrosive, ill smelling, of nauseating taste, or very hard. Yet the hard-water country of the arid Southwest is famous for its pleasant climate.

Hard water contains the salts of calcium and magnesium (the ions Ca^{++} and Mg^{++}). Not only will it not form a lather with soap, but it deposits a sticky sludge (a calcium or magnesium soap) on fabrics washed in it unless the soap is replaced by a synthetic detergent, described in the preceding chapter, whose calcium or magnesium "soap" is soluble in water. If ferrous or manganous salts (the ions Fe^{++} or Mn^{++}) make up part of the hardness, their precipitation by soap will produce rust spots on fabrics washed in such water, and bleaches will only intensify the stains.

In the boilers of stationary or steam locomotive engines hard water gradually coats the walls of the boiler tubes with "hard scale" of calcium sulfate or silica (SiO_2) or a "soft scale" of calcium carbonate. Unless this deposit is frequently removed, during expensive shutdown of the boilers, the boiler tubes may overheat, buckle, and tear loose from their anchorage in the end-plates of the boiler. The result, a boiler explosion, wrecks the building and is often heard for miles.

Magnesium hardness in drinking water makes the water corrosive and distinctly acid, and gives it a harsh metallic taste. Magnesium salts are also laxative. Otherwise, the magnesium ion (Mg^{++}) is just a nuisance, not a menace to health. The real threat is to boilers, not to human anatomy.

In hard water country, some municipalities soften all the water that they distribute to their residents. Unless hardness is extreme, the householder elsewhere is usually left to deal with the nuisance as best he can. Some water can be softened by boiling. This is bicarbonate hardness, formerly called "temporary hardness." It is caused by calcium acid carbonate, $Ca(HCO_3)_2$. This is decomposed by heating, releasing carbon dioxide gas, and depositing calcium carbonate.

Photos token in hard water country in early railroad days often show twin water tanks beside the tracks, wherever the puffing old wood- or coal-burning locomotives needed to replenish the water. The two tanks were for softening the water. To the water in either tank, enough slaked lime (calcium hydroxide) was added to precipitate all the magnesium in the tank as magnesium hydroxide. Then, in the same tank, enough soda ash (impure sodium carbonate) was added to precipitate all the calcium as calcium carbonate (including calcium just added as slaked lime). Each precipitate was formed by the incorporation into it of the two ions that compose it:

$$Mg^{++} + 2OH^- \rightarrow Mg(OH)_2 \qquad Ca^{++} + CO_3^{--} \rightarrow CaCO_3$$

In water	In the slaked lime	Precipi- tated ↓	In water	In the soda ash	Precipi- tated ↓

The mixed precipitates slowly settled into the tapering lower part of the tank, leaving clear, softened water above. Twin tanks permitted each locomotive to find a supply of completely settled, clear water, while the contents of the other tank were just beginning to subside.

The process just described is still the cheapest one, and is still in use for softening water for the boilers of stationary engines, now that the steam locomotive has been replaced by the diesel-driven electric motor. Observe that the sodium (Na^+) of the soda ash remains in the softened water as sodium chloride or a mixture of sodium salts. In other words, the lime and soda process does not actually purify water, but merely exchanges hardness (Mg^{++} and Ca^{++}) for sodium (Na^+). After being softened in this way the clear water is usually stabilized by the addition of sufficient dilute sulfuric acid to bring it to faint acidity (pH, 5 to 6.5).

Standards of Water Quality

The American Public Health Association has indicated (1962) the maximum concentrations of a few ionic impurities, in ppm, that should ever be tolerated in household water supplies. In addition, the American Water Works Association has indicated (1962) the maximum concentration that is to be regarded as ideal for domestic use:

	Al^{+++}	Fe^{++}	Mn^{++}	Pb^{++}	Ba^{++}	Cu^{++}	Ag^+	Zn^{++}	Cl^-	SO_4^{--}	NO_3^-	Dissolved Solids
A.P.H.A.		0.3			0.5	0.2	0.02	1.0	250	250	45	500
A.W.W.A.	0.05	0.05	0.01	0.03	0.5	0.2	0.02	1.0			22	

The recommended range of concentration for F^- (A.W.W.A.) ranges from 1.2 in winter down to 0.7 ppm in summer, as already discussed.

Hardness, with water for household use, is ordinarily no more than a nuisance—but one that is taken so seriously that it has created a new industry, synthetic household detergents. Industrial waters, with hardness reckoned as all due to $CaCO_3$, are rated as soft when they contain less than 60 ppm; moderately hard, 60-120; hard, 121-180; very hard, over 180.

With increasing boiler pressure, in pounds per square inch (psi), permissible hardness (ppm $CaCO_3$), alkalinity, and suspended solids, stated in parentheses in that order are: 0-300 psi (3500, 700, 300); 451-600 psi (2500, 500, 150); 751-900 psi (1500, 300, 60); 1001-1500 psi (1000, 200, 20); 2000 psi or higher (500, 100, 5).

For industrial water ($Fe^{++} + Mn^{++}$) should be less than 0.5 ppm and tendency to corrosion should be negligible. This last requirement is usually met if the pH is between 6 and 10, when the water is free from dissolved air and the dissolved solids are less than 500 ppm.

The maximum permitted concentration of poisonous elements or ion (Se, CN^-, Cd^{++}, Cr^{6+}, and As) is, in each case, 0.01 ppm. Such extremely slight concentrations of metallic and non-metallic elements in water are usually determined with a mass spectograph.

Bacteriological Examination

Different varieties of bacteria are distinguished not only by differences in appearance under the microscope but by the conditions under which they grow and multiply and by the chemical substances that they consume or produce. For example, bacteria of the coliform group ferment lactose (milk sugar), producing gas within 48 hours, at 35°C. Names formerly used for these bacteria were *B. coli,* and the *Coli-aerogens* group.

The United States Public Health has indicated the precautions to be taken in collecting samples of water for sanitary tests. It states how often the tests shall be made and the way in which they shall be carried out and interpreted. Contrary to a widespread impression, it is impossible actually to count bacteria. The investigator has to be content with stating what fraction of tests made on subsamples of a sample of water were positive, and the most probable number of coliform bacteria in a sample of the stated size. If probable contamination is indicated, immediate efforts must be made to find and eliminate the source, then to prove by further tests that the water has been made safe.

The preceding part of this chapter tells what is probably being done to make the water of your community safe to drink and better suited to industry, if you are living in any of the more sanitary-conscious parts of the world. The methods used in the hundred largest cities of the country (1962) are described in *U.S. Geological Survey Water Supply Paper, 1812.* The rest of the chapter deals with problems that you may need to face if you own your own well, or if you live in a small community or rural area that gets its water from a source that seems not to be well supervised. Begin by seeing that the well is properly cased, as shown in Figure 1-10.

Victims of the Old Oaken Bucket

Water is nearly always safe to drink when it has been freed from disease-producing organisms, past all doubt, by any of the methods just described. Only rarely does it contain poisonous substances such as heavy metal salts, insecticides, algacides, or radioactive wastes. Still more rarely does a city get pure water from a snowfield, then permit it to become contaminated during distribution.

Is the danger of water-borne disease then totally banished? Unfortunately, no. Some of these diseases, particularly typhoid, are also spread by contaminated food and milk, by flies, and by human carriers. Infant mortality is still much higher than it should be, even in sanitation-conscious America.

Moreover, many farms and small rural communities are still supplied by wells that have never been properly lined, sealed, or cased to prevent their water from being polluted by drainage from neighboring privies, cesspools, and barnyards, sometimes only a few yards away from the well. The continuous danger is made evident by the prevalence of dysentery, diarrhea, and jaundice in many neighborhoods that never had a typhoid epidemic.

A well must never be judged safe just because its water is sparkling, clear, and cool. The old oaken bucket seemed to be dripping with enticing coolness as it rose from the well. Yet children who turned its creaking windlass and drank from its iron-bound, moss-covered brim often failed to grow up to enjoy in fond recollection the scenes of their childhood.

Water Testing

Water-purifying equipment for the household or small business is often sold by a man who offers a free water analysis. Water testing has been so simplified that even persons without chemical training may carry through tests to recognize and to estimate roughly turbility, hardness, iron, manganese, and hydrogen sulfide. A water-testing laboratory, with every operation simplified, may be contained in a suitcase and costs only a few dollars.

Results obtained in this way, even by untrained observers, may indicate the general nature of the trouble to be overcome. Yet the best way to overcome it is not always easy to discern, and one should not be too quick to adopt the recommendations of persons who are agents to promote the sale of equipment of a particular kind. Water softeners, for example, may fail by clogging, may have insufficient capacity, may soon rust out, may be too expensive to operate, or may be serviced by unreliable people. Before buying expensive equipment one should interview persons who have found it satisfactory with water of the same type, in one's own neighborhood, during several years of use.

Tests to demonstrate the presence or absence of disease-producing bacteria are beyond the capacity of amateurs, and are rarely attempted by experts. The isolation and identification of particular organisms are difficult for the specialist, who will at first concern himself with establishing the presence or absence of the coliform group. Its presence indicates contamination from the intestinal tract of human beings or animals. Such contamination shows that disease-producing organisms could have been introduced with the coliform group at the time of their entry into the water supply.

Iron and Manganese in Water

When underground waters are poor in oxygen and rich in carbon dioxide, they sometimes dissolve objectionable amounts of iron and manganese (the ions Fe^{++} and Mn^{++}). These ions give water a harsh, metallic taste, so much so that it may be rendered unfit to drink. When such water is exposed to the air, or when hypochlorite bleaches are used with it in laundering, the iron and manganese are oxidized and deposited as a brown stain. (This stain is a mixture of hydrous oxides, usually represented as $Fe(OH)_3$, a component of iron rust, and $MnO(OH)_2$.)

If hydrogen sulfide is also present, a black deposit of ferrous sulfide, (FeS) soon covers the surfaces of tubs and sinks. When water containing either Fe^{++} or Mn^{++} is softened by zeolites the same slimy brown or black precipitate may soon clog the pores of the exchanger bed and put an end to its operation.

Moderate amounts of Fe^{++} and Mn^{++} are precipitated in getting rid of Ca^{++} and Mg^{++} by the lime-soda process (page 263). Larger amounts make trouble by clogging the filter bed with a brown or black sludge. A good remedy is to chlorinate the water or aerate by spraying it into the air (thus oxidizing iron and manganese to their higher valence states (Fe^{+++} and Mn^{4+}). Trickling through shavings removes the precipitate.

The surface water of a storage lake or reservoir usually contains very little manganese or iron, since the oxygen of the atmosphere oxidizes these elements to their higher valence states in which they react with water and are precipitated as insoluble hydrous oxides just mentioned.

By contrast, the lower part of a deep body of fresh water usually contains organic matter that is putrefying (decaying in the presence of a very limited quantity of air). This process consumes oxygen. Under such conditions, manganese and iron remain in solution in their valence states (Mn^{++} and Fe^{++}) and fail to be precipitated. So, in early winter if the temperature of a lake or reservoir first falls below that at which water has maximum density (4°C or 39°F), the whole body of water "turns over," bringing Mn^{++} and Fe^{++} to the surface. This event presents a city's water supply system with an emergency, whenever the city obtains its water from a deep lake or reservoir containing manganese or iron.

Yet fishermen may notice that the cold, crystal clear water of a lake that is "turning over" provides the best fishing. The upheaval brings up minnows and other small creatures in abundance and the big fish follow them.

Getting Rid of Hydrogen Sulfide

In many parts of the world surface wells and springs yield water that is unfit to drink because of dissolved hydrogen sulfide gas, distinguishable by its odor, which is similar to that of a rotten egg. This round-the-world nuisance (H_2S) is the nearest relative of water (H_2O) and has often been credited with curative powers. Actually, in concentrations in the air of only 0.5 to 1000 ppm it can bring dizziness, unconsciousness, and death if breathed for more than a few minutes. Fatalities have occurred in poorly ventilated bathhouses supplied by sulfur springs.

Hydrogen sulfide is produced in the depths of the earth in almost every imaginable way except the simplest one of all—direct union of hydrogen and sulfur. An important source of H_2S is the decay of plant and animal residues in the nearly complete absence of air. Such residues almost always contain a certain amount of sulfur or sulfates (the ion SO_4^{--}) which may be reduced to sulfides by organic matter. (The sulfide ion is S^{--}.)

Hydrogen sulfide that has entered water sources is easily removed by simple aeration (or by bubbling carbon dioxide through it, if the solution is alkaline). Devices may be purchased for aerating household water supplies; or the water may simply be adjusted to a slight acidity (pH 5), then left overnight in shallow pans.

15

Fresh Water from the Ocean

Fresh Water for Mariners

It may have been fear of thirst rather than fear of storms that kept early men from venturing on long voyages. European voyagers, with limited water supplies, crept from island to island in the Mediterranean and made short excursions southward from the Mediterranean along the coast of Africa, or northward to the British Isles and Scandinavia. Before Columbus, apparently only the Norsemen, in short ventures from one fresh water supply to another, got as far as North America.

On the other side of the world, the Polynesians discovered and settled the islands of the vast Pacific Ocean. Some of their voyages were as long as two thousand miles, in frail outriggers having no great storage capacity for drinking water. These voyages were through regions in which rainfall is usually abundant and dependable in certain seasons of the year. Outriggers are famous for being difficult to capsize; and what better collector for rainwater could be imagined than a waxed fabric, stretched between outrigger and canoe? It little mattered if some sea water got caught up with the rain water. The Kon-Tiki expedition found that fresh water, mingled with two-thirds of its own volume of sea water, was still potable in hot weather. The salt content of this mixture is about 14,000 parts per million.

In the Western world, in the days of Drake and the Spanish Main, sailing vessels were often deliberately run aground at mid-tide, near the mouths of rivers that were entered by the tides. The diminished salt content killed the barnacles that had gathered on the ship's hull.

The hull could then be scraped clean, while the ship lay careened on her side at low tide. The rest of the crew, meanwhile, ventured far enough upstream to fill the ship's casks with fresh water. The best places to obtain fresh water were carefully noted in each ship's log, and were ultimately recorded in nautical almanacs.

From about the time of Drake, the water supplies of sailing ships were often supplemented by distillation of sea water in crude stills. Each still was set on a stove on the ship's galley, where the cook usually had a good fire burning. An ordinary iron pot was fitted with a wooden lid, sometimes made tight with a gradually hardening mixture of clay and boiled linseed oil. A wooden tube carried away the stream and delivered it into a condenser—a copper tube that passed through water in a cask. With this simple device many a crew was supplied with fresh water enough to survive a long calm in the doldrums. If the same crew later died of scurvy, that was because the preventive virtues of lime juice were still unknown. Vitamins that prevented scurvy and other nutritional diseases remained undiscovered until the twentieth century.

Steamships ended the need for a galley still, since voyages took less time, steamships were immune to becalming, and steam from the ship's boiler was available to heat a still. Moreover, water from the ship's condensers was often fit to drink if filtered through charcoal (to remove traces of oil), then aerated. Passenger ships now usually carry drinking water in tanks and have one or several stills for emergency use.

Dissolved Salts in the Ocean

The composition of the ocean is not everywhere the same. Where seas are nearly land-locked or where few rivers enter, evaporation from the surface may raise the total content of dissolved solids (chiefly salts) from 3.36 to 3.68 per cent to as much as 4 per cent (the Red Sea). On the contrary, where rainfall or inflow from melting snow is abundant, or where many rivers empty into a limited area (the Baltic Sea), dissolved solids may be less than 3.0 per cent.

Nevertheless, concentration and dilution never go very far, because ocean currents, deep running waves, and especially diffusion join in diminishing concentration differences. Thus it is possible to calculate an average concentration, sometimes called standard sea water, from which no part of the ocean ever deviates very much (see Table 15-1).

Because a salt solution is electrically neutral, the number of positive

Table 15-1.
Composition of Sea Water

Cations	Milligrams per liter	Equivalents per liter	Anions	Milligrams per liter	Equivalents per liter
Na^+	10,818	0.4703	Cl^-	19,441	0.5484
Mg^{++}	1,303	0.1072	SO_4^{--}	2,713	0.0565
Ca^{++}	410	0.0205	HCO_3^-	145	0.0024
K^+	389	0.0099	CO_3^{--}	7	0.0002
Others	12	0.0004	Br^-	67	0.0008
Total	12,932	0.6085	Total	22,373	0.6083

Density at 20°C = 1.0243 g/ml.

charges (equivalents of cations) is equal to the number of negative charges (equivalents of anions). Since a liter of sea water contains about 0.6 equivalents of either kind, we may say that it has a normality of roughly 0.6 (see Table 15-2).

Standard sea water at 20°C has a pH of about 7.5 to 8.5 and a density of 1.0245 g/ml at 20°C. Water in the mid-Atlantic had been reported to have at 30°C a pH of 7.37 and a density of 1.0197, corresponding to a density of 1.0223 g/ml at 20°C.

From the density and composition of standard sea water, it may be calculated to contain 35.88 g of dissolved salts in every liter. The density of solid sodium chloride is 2.163 g/ml. The other salts present have densities in the solid state that are known with equal accuracy. We may easily calculate that a cubic mile of sea water will yield enough well-drained solid salt to cover a square mile of land to a depth of nearly 90 feet. The Gulf of Mexico (560,000 cubic miles) would yield enough solid salt to cover Florida to a depth of about 500 feet. The total salt content of the oceans of the world is enough to cover the whole land

Table 15-2.
Some Minor Components in Part per Million (= mg/kg)

Boron	4.6	Barium	0.05
Silicon	0.02 to 4.0	Iodine	0.05
Fluorine	1.4	Arsenic	0.01 to 0.02
Nitrogen (com-		Iron	0.002 to 0.02
bined	0.01 to 0.70	Manganese	0.001 to 0.01
Aluminum	0.5	Copper	0.001 to 0.01
Lithium	0.1	Any other	Not over 0.005
Phosphorus	0.001 to 0.10		

area of the earth to a depth of about 300 feet. Its total mass is about 10 per cent of the mass of the moon.

The ions of common salt in standard sea water is about 70 per cent of the total weight of dissolved salts. It is 2.78 per cent of the total weight of the ocean. Yet this is only about a tenth of the weight of common salt that the ocean's water can dissolve at the average temperature of the ocean.

With respect to its least soluble constituent, calcium carbonate, the ocean, especially at the surface, is already slightly supersaturated. The ocean is probably not supersaturated with respect to two other slightly soluble salts, gypsum ($CaSO_4 \cdot 2H_2O$) and dolomite ($CaCO_3$ in association with $MgCO_3$). Nevertheless, great quantities of both these salts have accumulated on the floors of former oceans, when concentration of either of their component ions becomes locally high enough to induce precipitation.

Treasure from the Ocean

Nearly everyone has heard that by the examination of sufficiently large samples of sea water using sufficiently delicate tests, every stable element may be detected. Yet, the fact that we have italicized a few words should make every thoughtful reader wonder whether it is possible to extract any element from the ocean at a profit. Nevertheless, hundreds of amateur chemists have flocked to the seaside in the hope of acquiring, not merely a coat of tan, but a fortune, by extracting gold, platinum, rare earth metals, and other elements from ocean water.

The total of all the dissolved cations less abundant in ocean water than the four most abundant ones (Na^+, Mg^{++}, Ca^{++}, K^+) is only 0.7 milli-equivalents per liter (0.7 meq/l). The average equivalent weight of these elements is about 28, hence their combined total weight, roughly estimated, is 20 mg/l, which is 20 ppm. This is only about 2.5 oz. in 1000 gallons. An element making up a tenth of the total weight of these cations would yield only ¼ oz. in 1000 gallons, and would have to be pretty valuable, just to pay for pumping 1000 gallons, from the ocean to the plant, treating it, and letting the extracted residue spill back into the ocean.

Only two elements, magnesium and bromine, have ever been extracted profitably directly from the ocean. Magnesium, but not bromine (except as a by-product), can be more cheaply extracted from the ocean than from other sources. Yet the production of common salt by solar evaporation in tidal basins has been practiced for ages and is still in use in China, around the Mediterranean, in the Bahamas, in Southern California, and elsewhere along low-lying coasts around the world.

So far, the only possible chance of profitably recovering the ocean's scarcer components is to make the recovery an incident to the recovery of fresh water or salt. In the production of fresh water from the ocean by distillation, there is often a preliminary removal of scale-forming impurities (Ca^{++} and Mg^{++}). The former and any desired part of the latter may be precipitated by the lime-soda process, described in Chapter 9. Then the remaining Mg^{++} may be precipitated as $MgNH_4PO_4$ and Mg^{++} and K^+ jointly as $MgKPO_4$. The latter precipitate, serviceable as a fertilizer, has a market value greater than that of the reagent used, since it contains potassium, recovered from the ocean.

The most valuable mineral products recoverable from sea water as an incident to the production of fresh water are potassium salts. About 3 pounds of potassium chloride are in 1000 gallons of sea water. Its recovery might yield a profit of as much as 20 cents, thus significantly reducing the cost of producing 1000 gallons of fresh water.

Other elements that may presently be recovered from sea water as an incident to the production of fresh water are fluorine, lithium, and iodine. Fully to exploit this source might "swamp the market" for these elements. Yet a cheap new source of anything always results in new uses. Sea water, partially purified in any way, may be marketed as a source of common salt for the production of chlorine and caustic soda, in competition with mined salt, which must always be purified before being used for this purpose. A third competitor in the Atlantic Coast States is salt produced in the Bahamas by solar evaporation.

There are sulfur domes just beneath the earth's surface, in the Gulf of Mexico. Yet the future of mined sulfur is a bit uncertain, since there are several industrial processes that produce elementary sulfur as a by-product. Drilling for natural gas and petroleum on the continental shelves (land beneath shallow water, adjacent to the continents) is a well-established and profitable industry. On the continental shelves are also deposits of phosphate nodules. Other nodules contain iron, titanium, the rare earths, and precious metals. In deeper waters, copper, nickel, and cobalt ores occur, and ferromanganese nodules, ranging up to a meter in diameter. Nickel is already in short supply.

Altogether, about 50 heavy metal minerals have been identified on the ocean bottom. Yet most of them are low-grade ores and deposits are of limited extent. Furthermore, good methods have not yet been developed for locating these deposits or for mining ore from the few that happen to be rich. So, for the indefinite future, metals from the sea will not contribute to national stockpiles, just as gold coins recovered from sunken Spanish galleons along both coasts of Florida have not increased the store of gold in Fort Knox. For a long time to come, the only treasures recovered in significant amounts from beneath the sea are likely to be the two that are already recovered on a large scale: natural gas and petroleum.

Special Properties of Salt Water

Water, in dissolving salt, has its properties somewhat altered. For example, its vapor pressure is lowered—by a fraction or percentage that is roughly proportional to the concentration of dissolved salt, but is nearly independent of temperature. The vapor pressure of sea water is about 1.84 per cent less than that of fresh water at the same temperature. In consequence, only 70 to 90 per cent as much water evaporates from the ocean as from an equal area of fresh water at the same season of the year and in the same latitude. This is in spite of the ocean's turbulence.

Lowered vapor pressure results in a higher boiling point, as is clearly shown in Figure 15-1. The relationships among vapor pressure, boiling point and freezing point of water and its dilute solutions are shown on a graph of vapor pressure vs. temperature; this is not drawn to scale, but only to illustrate principles. AO is the vapor pressure curve for ice, and OB, that for pure water. The boiling point, T_B, is the point at which vapor pressure equals standard atmospheric pressure, 760 mm; represented by P. O^1B^1 is the curve for a dilute salt solution; the dissolved ions hinder the escape of water molecules, thus the curve must lie below OB. The vapor pressure of the solution does not reach 760 mm until P^1, so the boiling point is T_B^1.

The freezing point may be defined as the temperature where ice and liquid have the same vapor pressure (coexist). The freezing point, T_f, of pure water is at O; but here, the vapor pressure of the solution is less than that of ice. The solution therefore does not freeze until T lowers to T_f^1; at O^1, solid and liquid are at equilibrium (have the same vapor pressure).

The boiling point of sea water is about 0.46° higher than that of fresh water, when the pressure is so low that boiling is at 75°C. It is 0.55° higher than the boiling point of fresh water at 100°C and 0.60° higher at 125°C.

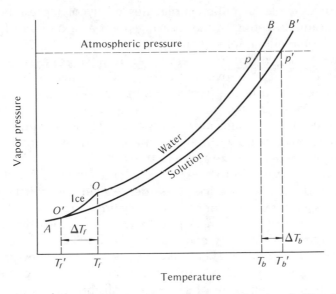

Figure 15-1. Relations Among Vapor Pressure Lowering, Boiling Point
Elevation and Freezing Point Depression
From *General Chemistry*, 2nd ed., by H. Sisler, C. A. Vanderwerf and A. W.
Davidson. (Macmillan Company, 1959), Figure 16-3. Used by permission.

At 100°C the heat of evaporation of sea water is about 539 calories
per gram, which is nearly the same as for fresh water at that temperature. The specific heat of sea water is about 3.5 per cent less than that
of fresh water. Otherwise expressed, it takes a trifle less heat to heat
sea water to any specified temperature than is needed for fresh water;
but the heat that disappears in evaporation is nearly the same for both.

Salt water, like fresh water, may be supercooled (Chapter 3); but
when freezing once begins, in either case, the heat liberated promptly
raises the temperature to the true freezing point. At this temperature
ice and liquid water may remain indefinitely in contact with each other,
in equilibrium; but if heat continues to be withdrawn from fresh water
in contact with ice at the freezing temperature, freezing continues at
that temperature until all the water is frozen.

The freezing point of water and of most other liquids is lowered by
dissolving anything in it. If the solution thus produced is very dilute,
the lowering of the freezing point is very nearly proportional to the
number of molecules or ions that are dissolved in any given weight of
water; but it is hardly affected at all by the nature of the dissolved sub-

stance. For example, a million molecules of glycol ("prestone") give about the same lowering of the freezing point as a million of alcohol or glycerol, or a million ions of any salt.

We have already noted (Chapter 3) that fresh water has its maximum density at 4°C, just 4° above its freezing point. Thus fresh water that has not quite cooled to the freezing point always underlies water that is freezing. Consequently, fresh water always begins to freeze at the surface. Water that contains more than about 2.5 per cent of salt (consequently, sea water), however, has its maximum density at the freezing point, hence begins to freeze at the bottom.

Fresh water may begin to freeze in winter as soon as a surface film has cooled to 0°C. Because ice is less dense than water, it floats; and because it is a poor conductor of heat, a coating of ice on a lake, pond, or river delays further cooling. Nevertheless, in regions that are very cold in winter, freezing may continue at 0°C until the whole body of fresh water is frozen solid. There may then be a delay of several weeks, while a neighboring gulf or arm of the ocean is being cooled to −1.91°C (the freezing point of sea water), all the way to the bottom. Then this water, too, begins to freeze, but freezes first at the bottom. A familiar sight to all who venture upon Arctic or Antarctic seas in winter is the little spicules or furry balls of ice that rise from the depths when the ocean has begun to freeze.

Most important of the special properties of salt water is perhaps osmotic pressure, explained in Section I of the Appendix. Osmotic flow (the spontaneous movement of water by diffusion through a membrane) is always from the more dilute into the more concentrated solution. It therefore always tends to equalize differences in concentration.

The osmotic pressure of ocean water is 23.1 atm. This means that when ocean water is separated from salt-free water by a water-permeable membrane, a pressure of 23.1 atmospheres must be applied to the ocean water to prevent fresh water from diffusing through the membrane and diluting ocean water.

Fractional vapor pressure lowering, freezing point lowering, boiling point elevation, and osmotic pressure are all related properties, since they are just different ways of measuring the same thing: the extra resistance of salt water as compared with fresh water in suffering loss of water (by evaporation, by incorporation into ice crystals, or by diffusing through a membrane into fresh water). From any one of these properties the others may be calculated. All depend on the temperature and the particle concentration (the number of dissolved particles, counting both molecules and ions, in unit volume of the solution). The kind of ion or molecule or the charge on an ion makes little difference!

The osmotic pressure of a solution used in experiments with living plants and animals is usually inferred from a measurement of the freezing point. Rarely is it determined directly, since direct measurements of osmotic pressure are tedious and difficult.

Desalination Methods

Desalination (the removal of salt from salt water) can be accomplished in at least five different general ways:[1]

1. *Distillation.* This is *evaporation,* combined with *recondensation,* In evaporation, the dissolved salt is left behind as a concentrated brine. Then, when the vapor is cooled, or is compressed and cooled, it recondenses to liquid fresh water. Distillation is still today the most important process for desalination of sea water, as it was in the days of the sailing ships.

2. *Freezing.* When salt water is incompletely frozen, it separates into ice crystals, almost free from salt, and a concentrated brine. The problem is to separate the ice from the brine and to recover and use the heat set free in the freezing.

3. *Reverse Osmosis.* This is not like ordinary filtration; instead of a porous filter one uses a nonporous membrane of special structure. If sufficient pressure is applied to salt water in contact with such a membrane, water passes through but the hydrated ions do not.

In the above three processes, *water is removed from salt.* In the two processes next mentioned, *salt is removed from water.*

4. *Ion Transport.* Common salt and most other salts, whether in crystalline form or dissolved, consist of oppositely charged ions (Na^+ and Cl^-, in the case of common salt). In dissolving a salt in water, these ions become *hydrated* (weakly combined with water). Thus the crystal structure is broken down and the ions become capable of moving in-

1. There is a color, 16 mm sound film on saline-water conversion available throughout the United States to schools, colleges, universities, scientific and industrial organizations, business and civic clubs, etc., and for public service broadcasting. It is entitled *New Water for a Thirsty World* and runs twenty-two minutes. The film should be requested by name from the Office of Saline Water, Department of the Interior, Washington, D.C. 20240. There is no charge for the film, but the user must pay postage. We also highly recommend the following volumes: *Principles of Desalination,* edited by K. S. Spiegler (Academic Press, 1966); *Salt Water Purification* by K. S. Spiegler (John Wiley & Sons, 1962); and *Water Production Using Nuclear Energy* (University of Arizona Press, 1966).

dependently. Since the two kinds of ions are oppositely charged, they move in opposite directions when they are placed between oppositely charged electrodes. To use this principle in desalting water, one usually needs electrically charged membranes, as utilized in the electrodialysis process, later described.

5. *Chemical Methods.* These include ion exchange and precipitation, both already described as means for softening water.

There is no one "best" method for desalting water. For a desalination plant to supplement the water supply of a coastal city, desalination at a low cost per thousand gallons is chiefly desired. For a lighthouse or Coast Guard station on a lonely coast, reliability and the ability to operate without supervision may be more important. Where fresh water is in demand, but where there is also a good market for electrical energy, a dual purpose plant, perhaps based on nuclear energy, may be a good way to meet both needs.

We shall concentrate on general principles. It is only by understanding these that the average reader will gain something more than a vague idea of how desalination is accomplished. The reader of more than average earnestness and better than average preparation may even, through an understanding of general principles, aspire to make some contributions of his own to this important technology. Our references to books for more advanced readers will permit them to fill in the gaps in our own very elementary discussion.

Why Desalination Is Expensive

Water is made expensive to purify by the very qualities that make it useful. It is useful because it is a liquid, rather than a gas; because it dissolves and brings to the roots of plants the mineral nutrients (chiefly ions) that plants need; and because it penetrates into, swells, and interacts with living tissue, without dissolving it. These properties fit water to serve as the vehicle of life.

All these properties depend on the fact that a molecule of water vapor is polar (contains positive and negative charges within the same molecule, centered on points that do not coincide), as shown in Figure 5-2. Polar molecules are chemically active. They combine with polar molecules of other kinds and with ions, and even with molecules of their own kind. Thus water molecules combine with ions to form hydrated ions and with other water molecules to form complex, "associated" molecules.

It is only in the vapor state that a molecule of water is properly represented by the formula H_2O. Liquid water or ice are both best represented as $H_{2n}O_n$, in which n is an indefinite number, varying from molecule to molecule, and whose average value decreases as the temperature is raised. Each aggregate in liquid water is multiply branched and continuously changes its structure, when protons (H^+) are transferred from one molecule to another, as they make contact in a sort of shuffling or jostling motion. A sample of liquid water is more like a stack of hedge clippings than a stack of billiard balls.

The confusedly branched structure of molecules of liquid water makes desalination expensive. If it is by distillation, the complex, multiply branched molecules of liquid water must all be broken down into the simple molecules, H_2O, of water vapor, in being vaporized. A great deal of energy is needed to do this, and energy costs money.

If desalination is to be by ion transport instead of by distillation, the multiply branched nature of the molecules of liquid water is still an impediment. The hydrated ions must be electrically propelled through a liquid whose molecules cling together in entangling networks, which require extra energy in overcoming the resistance. This is in much the same way that extra energy would be needed to drive a barnacle-encrusted ship through a mass of tangled and interlacing seaweed.

You may conclude that if water were less polar it would be less expensive to purify. But water would not then dissolve salt, so the problem of saline water would not exist. Life, if it then existed, would need to be based on some other, less polar liquid, such as ethyl alcohol—in which some persons, even today, seem to find promise as the vehicle of life and possible substitute for water.

Least Demand for Energy in Desalination

Vaporization of water causes heat to disappear. Recondensation of water vapor to liquid water releases heat. In distillation, these two processes are combined. If they could be accomplished at the same temperature the quantities of heat disappearing and set free would be equal. Then, except for accidental losses of heat, the net demand for heat in desalination by distillation would be zero.

Two difficulties prevent this hope from being realized. The simpler one and the one more easily understood is this: the vapor pressure of saline is a trifle less than that of fresh water. Accordingly, the vapor escaping from a still containing salt water cannot be recondensed to liquid fresh water at the still temperature unless it is first slightly compressed, to increase its density and the pressure that it exerts. If this is done, the heat that disappears in evaporation in the still is all set free again in the condenser, in recondensation of the vapors. If a way could be found to recover all of this heat, it might be used over again in evaporating a new quantity of salt water. The only energy that is spent, past any hope of recovery, in such a process is that needed to compress the vapor from salt water until it exerts the same pressure as vapor from fresh water at the still temperature. This is the least possible energy needed to desalt water by distillation (or indeed by any process).

For ocean water, the least energy requirement in desalination is about 2.9 kilowatt-hours for each thousand gallons of fresh water produced (2.9 kWh/1000 gal). As the concentration of the undistilled residue in the still increases, the vapor pressure of the escaping vapor steadily decreases. Thus the energy that must be spent in ensuring recondensation at the still temperature steadily increases. There is also difficulty in recovering the heat set free in the condenser and in transferring it to a new quantity of water. One may guess that actual demand for energy in desalting sea water by any process may be four times the least demand, just calculated, for desalting it by distillation. This would be about 11.6 kWh for each 1000 gal of fresh water produced. At the 1970 "big industry" rate of 0.7 cent per kWh, the cost of energy alone in producing 1000 gal of fresh water from the ocean would be about 8 cents.

To this must be added other costs, depending on the size of the plant and the equipment used. The total cost for each 1000 gal of fresh water produced usually decreases as the size of the plant increases. From the original cost of the plant and its expected life and production capacity in gallons per day it is possible to estimate the cost per thousand gallons that must be ascribed to supervision, labor, repairs, taxes, depreciation, and obsolescence. It presently takes very good design to produce potable water (less than 500 parts common salt in a million of water) at a total cost of less than 60 cents for each 1000 gal of water produced. This is about $200 per acre-foot, as compared with $1 to $14 per acre-foot for irrigation water in many important agricultural areas.

It is plain that desalination gives little current promise of making "deserts blossom as the rose." Its purpose is to supplement the water supplies of seacoast cities or those of communities in areas where the ground water is alkaline or saline. (If irrigation were with water with a higher salinity than 500 ppm, the cost of producing water for irrigation would be somewhat decreased, for it is almost proportional to the decrease in salinity that is secured by desalination.)

The realistic figure of 60 cents a thousand gallons is compared toward the end of this chapter with the costs actually incurred in important plants using different desalination methods.

Solar Stills

In Chapter 3 we remarked that incoming solar energy, during the summer months, is at a maximum at about the latitude of New York; but more southerly locations have an advantage in having fewer cloudy days. So most of the experiments with solar evaporation of salt water have been in the tropics and sub-tropics. Florida, Arizona, the Virgin Islands, North Africa, Israel, and Australia have all experimented with solar stills of different types.

Solar energy costs nothing, but in a typical location in Florida amounts to only about 1290 btu (325,000 calories) per square foot per day, during the summer months. This is sufficient to evaporate at 25°C about 0.148 U.S. gallons of water. The best yield in a plastic-covered unit near Daytona Beach, Florida, was about 0.13 U.S. gallons per square foot per day. This is almost 90 per cent of the predicted maximum yield. Attempts to supplement solar heat by electrical heating have not been very successful, since the destiny of the water vapor overlying the liquid is thus increased, with consequent interception of the sun's rays before they reach the surface of the water.

The fatal defect of solar evaporation is that the heat energy that disappears in evaporating water is used but once, and that is the end of it, whereas in multiple-effect evaporation (later described) a very large part of the heat energy that disappears in evaporation is recovered from the condenser and used over again, perhaps several times. Thus the yield of distilled water is multiplied by at least 2.5. In vapor compression distillation it may be multiplied by 10.

A good type of solar still (Figure 15-2) consists of a basin in which a black, porous plastic (polypropylene) wick floats. It has a sloping cover of lightweight glass or an air-supported one of transparent sheet plastic, sealed at the edges. The sun's rays (radiant energy) pass through this transparent cover with little reflection or absorption; but on striking the blackened surface they are converted into heat. Thus the surface of the water in the wick is maintained at a temperature a trifle higher than that of the under side of the transparent cover. Water

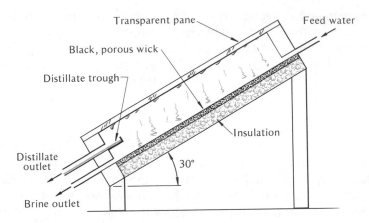

Figure 15-2. Tilted Wick Still

evaporates from the wick and the vapor diffuses to the cover, and is there condensed to liquid, that drains away into a stainless steel trough.

A plastic-covered still can be built for about $1.00 per square foot of surface. Heat insulation beneath the still greatly increases its efficiency. Such a still needs almost no supervision, and during an average summer day in Arizona or Florida may yield 8 to 12 gallons of fresh water for each 100 square feet of cover.

Sparse populations in nearly cloudless temperate or subtropical regions may depend on solar stills for drinking water, if the stills are not damaged by windstorms, hail, or sandstorms and are protected from vandals and marauding animals. To provide for domestic animals is not so easy. Yet many of them tolerate more salt in their drinking water than human beings do; hence, the product of a solar still may be used to dilute a saline source to an acceptable concentration for animals.

In a modification of a solar distillation called solar humidification water vapor that has been evaporated by the sun is swept by a current of air into a separate condenser, where it is cooled by the incoming saline stream until liquid water separates. This air current may be created by a windmill, or on an ascending mountain slope, which is sometimes self-maintaining.

Small solar stills have been made, in which floating, transparent plastic bags provide surface for the condensation of vapor that is evaporated from black wicks. These have been tried as a source of water for survivors of marine disasters, afloat in lifeboats or life rafts. Besides being unmanageable in rough weather, they are inoperative on cloudy days. The ancient Polynesians, with their simple rain collectors, had a better solution of the problem of drinking water for long voyages.

Multiple Effect Evaporation

The galley still of sailing-ship days would be intolerable today. It desalted sea water in small batches, one at a time, instead of continuously. The inner walls of the still became covered with scale, which decreased the rate at which heat passed through the still's walls, hence soon decreased the rate of distillation to a small fraction of what it was in the beginning. Worst of all, heat used in evaporation was never recovered in the condenser and used to evaporate more water.

The difficulty found in recovering heat from a condenser, then introducing it into another still, comes from the nature of heat itself; heat always flows downhill, from bodies of higher to those of lower temperature. So each still, in a succession of stills, in multiple-effect evaporation, must have a lower temperature, and if the temperature difference between each condenser and the following still is very small, the water distilled by a definite quantity of heat may be multiplied tenfold.

In principle, it is easy to do this, since water will boil at lower and lower temperatures as the pressure upon it is decreased. The steam in each still is automatically under a little lower pressure, hence is at a little lower temperature than that in the next preceding still if the escaping steam has to overcome the pressure created by an intervening column of water.

High-pressure steam from a steam boiler passes to the first of a series of stills (often called effects). Here a part of it condenses, yielding heat that passes through the walls of a set of vertical metallic tubes and evaporates a part of the incoming stream of saline water. The liquid condensate from the first effect is returned to the boiler; but that from later effects composes the salt-free distillate.

Steam from each effect passes into the next effect, where it evaporates a further quantity of water. The saline stream, which flows in a thin film down the inner walls of the bundle of metallic tubes, within each effect, passes on from each effect to the next, becoming increasingly concentrated. Both the hot distillate and hot concentrated brine that issue from the last effect yield heat to the incoming saline stream in a heat exchanger. The brine is then discarded or is used in the recovery of by-products, such as potassium salts.

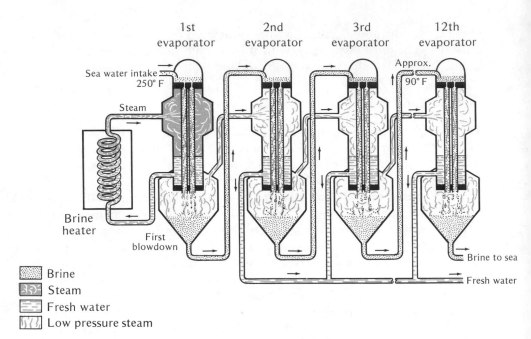

15-3. Vertical Tube Distillation

An example of multiple-effect evaporation is long-tube vertical evaporation, shown in Figure 15-3. Sea water enters the first chamber (effect) and is heated by jacketed steam as it flows as a thin film down the inside of thin-walled tubes. Condensed water from the first chamber is returned to the heated coils to generate more steam; the vaporized water enters the second chamber (at lower pressure and temperature), where it provides heating of the falling brine. The brine remaining unvaporized in the first chamber is pumped to the top of the second and flows down in the tubes. The condensate is conducted to the fresh water outlet. In an experimental plant (at Freeport, Texas) there were 12 effects in all; the brine left in the last effect was returned to the sea.

The first effect usually receives steam at a temperature that is not to exceed 250°F if deposition of scale is to be minimized. Steam enters the last effect at approximately 90°F (32°C), hence under a slight vacuum. Long tube vertical distillation was borrowed from chemical engineering practice, where it has long been used in concentrating brine or alkali.

Ways To Economize on Heat

There are other ways to heat economy than just to recover heat set free in condensation of vapor, then use it over again in evaporating a further quantity of water. Since a calorie is a definite quantity of heat, you may have been thinking that one need only count calories in reckoning heat economy and that temperature may be disregarded. Not so. Whenever heat is to be converted into other forms of energy, hence made to do work, the conversion into work is the more nearly complete the higher the temperature. This is in sharp contrast to the opposite transformation (of other forms of energy into heat), which can always be made complete, regardless of the temperature.

In brief, as heat flows down to lower and lower temperatures, its quality (the completeness with which it may be converted into work) steadily decreases. It is right here that the difference between steam-generating practice and distillation begins. A steam generator (often called a steam boiler) delivers steam at as high a temperature as is possible with the construction materials available, since the steam it produces is intended to yield mechanical work in driving the piston of an engine or in whirling the blades of a steam turbine (which perhaps drives an electric generator, thus converting a part of the energy of the steam into electric energy). The water used in a steam generator is distilled or softened in advance, hence there is no danger of scaling. The steam, after it has expended, yielding work (and usually being converted into electrical energy), is cooled in a condenser and returned to the boiler as liquid water.

Distillation, by contrast, concentrates water that is loaded with calcium and magnesium salts, hence risks deposition of scale on the walls of the still. Unless other means are taken to prevent scale, temperatures must not exceed 260°F. We have seen that distillation is best accomplished in a series of steps, each using or re-using heat at a lower temperature than the preceding one. A high initial temperature provides more stages and so uses heat more economically. Thus, even when heat is to be used as heat, in evaporating water, we may rate it as being of better quality the higher its temperature, up to the allowable maximum of about 260°F.

If heat has to be passed through a wall, the wall should be thin and of a material that is a good conductor of heat (copper, bronze, or aluminum, rather than steel or porcelain). It should be kept free from

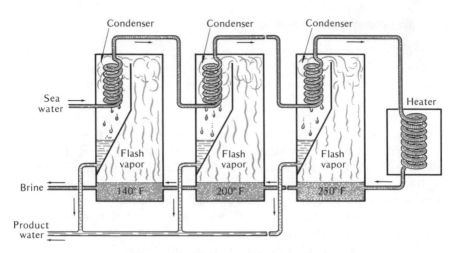

Figure 15-4. Multistage Flash Distillation

scale, which is a very poor conductor of heat. Better yet is to get rid of the wall altogether and pass heat directly from one liquid into another that does not mix with the first—from oil, for example, into water.

The transfer of heat takes place with least loss of quality when the transfer of heat is between surfaces whose differences in temperature are very small. Yet the rate of heat transfer is then very low, unless an inordinately large surface is provided. This would greatly increase the cost of the equipment. The best money economy is attained by a compromise between the very small temperature differences that transfer heat efficiently but incur an exorbitant cost of construction and larger temperature differences that do just the opposite. Here in a nutshell is the guiding principle of heat-transfer engineering.

Vacuum Flash Distillation

In vacuum-flash distillation the incoming sea water is preheated by being passed through coils that are surrounded by steam that is being condensed to liquid fresh water, yielding heat (Figure 15-4). Then the incoming stream is heated to a still higher temperature by direct heating in a steam-heated coil.

Leaving the heater at a temperature of about 190°F (82°C), the saline

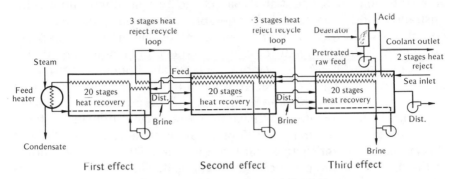

Figure 15-5. Multieffect Multistage Distillation

stream passes through several chambers in which there is sufficient vacuum to cause vigorous boiling, with flash evaporation in as many as 20 successive stages, until the temperature of the outgoing brine is reduced to about 60°C (140°F). The concentrated brine is then discarded. The heat that it carries with it is the principal loss of heat in the process.

About 90 per cent of the heat needed to heat the incoming sea water to the first flash temperature is furnished by the condensing vapor and only about 10 per cent by the heater. The whole process is conducted in a partial vacuum, that is, at temperatures below 212°F (100°C).

Vacuum flash distillation, as just described, is limited to about 20 stages, because of the slight pressure differences that are available to move the brine and distillate through each of the last few stages. Its economy comes chiefly from the fact that the heater uses waste, low-pressure steam, which is a by-product of the production of steam or generated electrical energy in several industrial processes.

Multieffect, multistage flash distillation is an improvement over the single effect process, just described. The cycle through preheating, heat input, and flash evaporation is broken up into a number of successive loops, with brine recirculation between loops, as shown in Figure 15-5. Thus evaporation is accomplished at higher temperatures than would otherwise be needed. Between loops, part of the brine is recirculated through the preceding effect. This process results in higher efficiency in the use of heat than would otherwise be attained, because more evaporation takes place at higher temperatures.

The process is still under study, and further refinements are probable. The Office of Saline Water's San Diego Test Facility set up a demonstration module (a separately operable component part of a more complex assembly). This contributed to the development of the process by furnishing complete data with respect to temperature differences, pressure differences, evaporation rates, and brine concentrations, in selected flash stages of selected effects, during long-term operation of the module. From this information, it will be possible to construct large plants that operate with maximum efficiency, producing distilled water at the rate of a million gallons a day or some round multiple of this amount. It is anticipated that there will be a 50 per cent economy in the heat needed to produce a thousand gallons of distillate, as compared with single effect flash evaporation. Along with that there may be a 20 per cent reduction in the area of heat-transfer surface.

How Corrosion and the Deposition of Scale Are Prevented

If sea water contained only sodium and potassium salts (the ions Na^+ and K^+) its purification by distillation would be much easier. The presence of calcium and magnesium salts (the ions Ca^{++} and Mg^{++}) causes scale to be deposited on the inner walls of tubes or vessels in which sea water is heated. Moreover, salts of magnesium are corrosive, since the magnesium ion is hydrolyzed (reacts with water) to form the ions $MgOH^+$ and H_3O^+. The latter, as explained in section E of the Appendix, is the typical ion of acidity.

Wherever salt is present, special precautions must be taken to prevent destruction by corrosion. Ordinary steel or iron must be replaced by special alloys, such as stainless steel or bronze. Concrete must be given special protection, for not only is it itself rapidly destroyed by acid, but in the presence of salt the reinforcing steel rods that lend it strength soon disintegrate into rust. Nor does wood last very long in a salt-laden environment, for salt holds moisture and invites attack of wood by molds, fungi, and even insects and mollusks. So the structures that house desalination projects call for almost as much engineering skill as these installations themselves.

Deposits of scale may be of two different types. Soft scale or alkaline scale may be $CaCO_3$ or $Mg(OH)_2$. It may be prevented by treating the heated, incoming saline stream with enough dilute acid to acidify it. Carbon dioxide that is set free is permitted to escape, then the liquid is made faintly alkaline (pH = 7.5). The Ca^{++} and Mg^{++} ions may also be removed by ion exchange (Chapter 9). The spent exchanger is regenerated by being treated with the concentrated brine that every desalination plant obtains as a by-product.

Hard scale is calcium sulfate, $CaSO_4$. It is most likely to be deposited at temperatures above 250°F (120°C). To decrease the risk of its being deposited on the inner walls of equipment conveying sea water, small beads (seeds) of calcium sulfate may be introduced into the incoming sea water as this is being preheated to the distillation temperature. The beads grow in size as calcium sulfate from the solution is deposited on their surface, and the concentration of that salt in the solution is correspondingly diminished.

Sea water contains too much calcium and magnesium to be economically softened by the lime-soda process, described in Chapter 9. Nevertheless, a variation of this process, in large desalination plants, is a useful preliminary to distillation. The reagents needed are $Ca(OH)_2$, which precipitates Mg^{++} as $Mg(OH)_2$, and $MgCO_3$, which precipitates Ca^{++} as $CaCO_3$. The reagents are themselves only slightly soluble, hence no great harm is done if a little too much of either is used. Removal of about two-thirds of the Ca^{++} in sea water permits heating of the partially softened residue to about 320°F without deposition of scale. The mixed precipitates can be used to regenerate a further quantity of the two reagents. Thus this softening process supplies its own reagents.

The deposition of scale may be prevented in several other ways. For example, traces of sodium polyphosphate, in concentrations too small to induce precipitation, or mixtures of the polyphosphate with lignin sulfonic acid (derived from a by-product of the paper industry) will cause Ca^{++} or Mg^{++} to separate as a non-adherent floc, instead of as scale.

Vapor Compression Distillation

We have already remarked that the vapor from saline water must be compressed if it is to be condensible at the temperature of evaporation. Compression heats it. Further compression heats it to still higher temperatures. Then it may be used to evaporate a further quantity of water.

This is the principle of vapor compression distillation. When it is once started, the energy to keep it going comes from mechanical energy put into the compressor, rather than from steam, supplied by a boiler.

As in other desalination processes that seek to economize heat, the incoming sea water is preheated to the operating temperature by exchanging heat with the hot outgoing products: desalted water and concentrated brine.

The incoming preheated sea water rises around tubes into which vapor is continuously compressed. In yielding heat to the incoming sea water the vapors are condensed to salt-free water; but the sea water, outside the tubes, boils vigorously, producing low-pressure steam (101°C, 1 atm), which is compressed and heated by the compressor to a pressure of 1.2 atm at 105°C. Comparing this temperature with that of the preheated sea water outside the tubes (about 97°C), we find a temperature difference of about 8°C, which causes a flow of heat outward from the compressed water through the walls of the tubes into the sea water. The rate at which heat flows through them, hence the rate of distillation, depends primarily on the horsepower of the compressor; but there must be enough surface, else the difference in temperature between the two surfaces between which heat is transferred will be inordinately high.

Desalting by Freezing

In desalting water by freezing (Figure 15-6), the mixture of ice and cold brine that is produced is used to precool the incoming saline water to about 37°F (2.8°C). Rapid pumping under a fair vacuum (a pressure of about 3.3 mm of mercury) supercools the liquid several degrees below its true freezing point. A part of the liquid then flash-freezes into a mixture of salt-free ice and brine.

A high degree of supercooling results in a very large number of crystal nuclei and the formation of a multitude of small crystals, difficult to separate from the brine. Moderate supercooling—to about 17°F (−3.9°C), in the case of sea water—tends to produce large crystals, readily separated from the film of adhering brine.

Since sea water may be had for the cost of pumping, its desalting by freezing is usually interrupted when about 50 per cent of it has been frozen. The 7 per cent brine that then remains is discarded. The temperature range in which desalting sea water by freezing takes place is from about −9 to −3.9°C. Continued withdrawal of heat, at lower and lower temperatures would cause sodium sulfate ($Na_2SO_4 \cdot 10H_2O$) to begin to separate from sea water at −8.33°C (17°F).

Desalting by freezing has several advantages over desalting by dis-

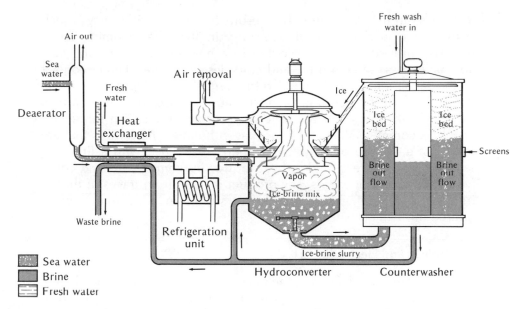

Figure 15-6. Vacuum Freezing—Vapor Compression Process

tillation: (1) There is no difficulty with scale. (2) Because low temperatures are used, corrosion is less serious. However, in the heat exchanger and sometimes also in other parts of the equipment, corrosion-resistant materials are used. (3) Cheaper structural materials may be used, since the equipment need not withstand high pressures. (4) Heat withdrawn from the water to be frozen may be applied directly to melt the ice that is produced, without interposing even a thin film of metal.

The chief handicap of desalting by freezing is that heat is transferred at low temperatures, hence with low efficiency. The ice crystals and unfrozen brine that result from partial freezing are easily separated by being pushed upward in a drainage column with perforated sides. The crystals are then washed with about 5 per cent of their own weight of desalted water and are melted by the heat that is set free when the vapor produced during pumping is liquefied by being recompressed. Since desalting by freezing is carried out at temperatures lower than that of the surroundings, provision must be made for pumping out the heat that leaks into the equipment from without.

In the method just described, heat has to pass through metallic walls in being transferred from the liquid that is being frozen into the boiling refrigerant in the evaporator. This results in a loss of efficiency, which is overcome in direct contact freezing. In this, the incoming saline stream is filtered, then is precooled in a heat exchanger by the out-flowing streams of cold brine and cold desalted water. Direct contact of the saline stream with liquid refrigerant, boiling vigorously at the temperature of the freezing chamber, causes part of the saline stream to flash-freeze into a mixture of ice crystals and brine. The refrigerant may be a commercial liquefied fuel gas, n-butane. The crystals that are formed are drained or centrifuged, then are washed with a little de-salted water and are melted by heat set free in rcompressing and lique-fying the refrigerant vapors. The product is freed from traces of the re-frigerant by stripping away refrigerant vapors in a vacuum, then is filtered through activated-charcoal.

Electrolysis and Electrodialysis

Electrolysis may be defined as the decomposition of a substance by the passage of an electric current. At the cathode, water accepts electrons and is converted into hydrogen gas and alkali (the ion OH^-). At the anode, water loses electrons and is converted into oxygen gas and acid (the ion H_3O^+). If the solution is fairly concentrated, some chlorine gas is also produced at the anode. Representing an electron (a unit of nega-tive charge) by e, these reactions are:

$$\text{at cathode: } 2H_2O + 2e \rightarrow H_2 + 2OH^-$$
$$\text{Alkali}$$

$$\text{at anode: } 3H_2O - 2e \rightarrow \tfrac{1}{2}O_2 + 2H_3O^+$$
$$\text{Acid}$$

$$Cl^- - e \rightarrow \tfrac{1}{2}Cl_2$$

Because of these difficulties, inventors, about 1950, began to develop a modified type of electrolysis, now called electrodialysis. This makes use of ion-selective materials, described in Chapter 9, except that they are formed into sheets (membranes), instead of being granular. They are called ion-selective because when they are placed in the path of moving ions they select ions of opposite sign to themselves and permit them to pass; but they repel, hence block the passage, of ions of their own sign.

An electrolytic cell, with cathode and anode of suitable materials, is

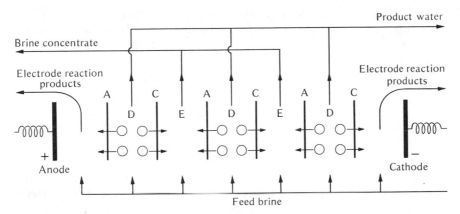

Figure 15-7 Electrodialysis

divided into a considerable number of narrow compartments by cation-selective membranes (C), and anion-selective membranes (A), arranged alternatively, as shown in cross-section Figure 15-7. When a current is passed through the cell, cations (+) in all the compartments move toward the cathode, but are stopped by the anion-selective membranes (A). Anions (—) move in the opposite direction, toward the anode, but are stopped by the cation-selective membranes (C).

Thus alternate compartments (D) are swept nearly free of both kinds of ions; in brief, are depleted. But in the intervening compartments (E) both kinds of ions accumulate, hence the solution is there enriched. Saline water, admitted to the cell, flows in parallel streams through all the compartments and emerges as two streams—one depleted, the other correspondingly enriched.

In early experiments with this method, in desalting brackish water, the membranes were soon clogged with precipitated scale. This difficulty was overcome by adding a little acid to the incoming saline water. A difficulty called polarization was also soon encountered—a sudden increase in the electrical resistance of the cell, accompanied by the production of acid and alkali in thin films adjacent to the membranes, in depleted zones. This trouble was traced to too great a flow of current for the membrane area used. The first remedy was to use a lower current or a greater membrane area, or to provide tortuous channels for the solution, to induce turbulent flow in its contact with the membrane.

Means had also to be discovered for assembling the membranes into compact membrane stacks, in which the membranes were held apart by thin separators of non-conductive materials having tortuous channels.

Within recent years, electrodialysis has been so improved that today it is used in hundreds of small- or medium-size plants throughout the world to purify brackish water. The method is not well suited for desalting sea water, because the membranes are less selective in the presence of very high concentrations of ions.

Electrodialysis is actually just the controlled electro-transport of ions. Energy is expended in moving ions of both signs through membranes, from a region of lower into one of higher concentration. True dialysis, by contrast, is spontaneous, self-energizing movement (diffusion) of ions through a membrane, from a region of higher into one of lower concentration.

Electrodialysis has been independently developed in the United States, Europe, South Africa, Japan, and elsewhere. It produces millions of gallons a day, mainly in plants that supply army camps, bottling works, and a few small cities. In the United States, brackish water desalted by electrodialysis has supplied the towns of Buckeye, Arizona, Port Mansfield, Texas, Siesta Key and Sanibell, Florida.

Figure 15-8a. Principle of Reverse Osmosis

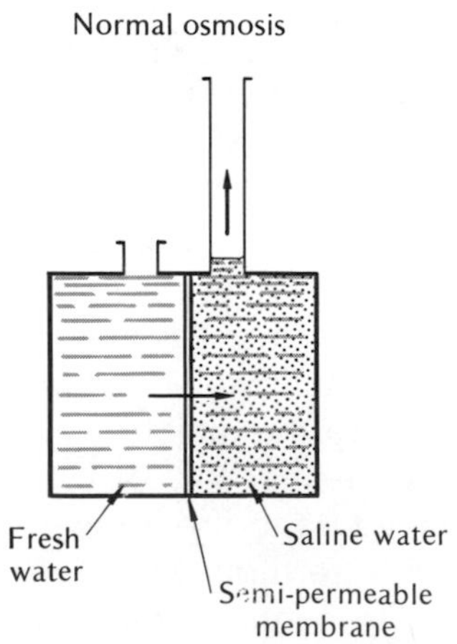

Normal osmosis   Osmotic equilibrium   Reverse osmosis

Reverse Osmosis

When pure water and a salt solution are on opposite sides of a semi-permeable membrane, the pure water diffuses through the membrane and dilutes the salt solution. This phenomenon is known as osmosis. Because of the difference in salt concentration, pure water flows through the membrane as though pressure were being applied to it. The effective driving force causing the flow is called osmotic pressure. The magnitude of the osmotic pressure depends on the concentration of the salt solution and the temperature of the water. By exerting pressure on the salt solution, the osmosis process can be reversed. When the pressure on the salt solution is greater than the osmotic pressure, fresh water diffuses through the membrane in the opposite direction to normal osmotic flow.

The principle of reverse osmosis is illustrated in Figure 15-8a. It can readily be seen how this principle can be applied in the conversion of saline water.

A diagram of the reverse-osmosis process is shown in Figure 15-8b. The salt water is first pumped through a filter where suspended solids that would damage the membranes are removed. The salt water is then raised to operating pressure by a second pump and then introduced into the desalination unit. A portion of the water permeates the mem-

Figure 15-8b. Reverse Osmosis Process

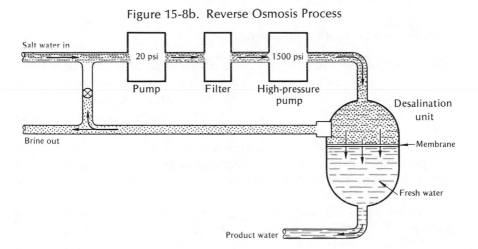

branes and is collected as product water at the bottom of the unit. The brine is discharged at the top of the unit. When desired, some of the brine may be mixed with incoming saline water and recirculated.

Operating plants carry out the reverse-osmosis principle in several different process designs such as the plate-and-frame, tubular, spiral-wound membrane module, and hollow-fiber designs. All are based on the common principle that the membrane, a flexible plastic film usually no more than 2 to 5 mils in thickness, must have a firm support to withstand the very high pressure drop across it. The preferred materials used for membranes in these process designs are cellulose acetate or polyamides which have been specially processed to make them reject salt and at the same time pass water at a reasonable rate.

Some of the important advantages of the reverse-osmosis process are: (1) Low energy consumption. Because no change of phase is involved, the only energy consumed is the electrical energy needed to drive the pumps. (2) The processing equipment is relatively simple, resulting in low equipment costs. (3) The operation of the process at normal temperatures minimizes scale and corrosion problems.

At the present time this process (as is electrodialysis), is limited commercially to desalting brackish water. However, research is being conducted to increase its effectiveness for sea water.

Currently reverse osmosis equipment is manufactured by several companies, and units are supplying desalinated water to Greenfield, Iowa—Ocean Reef Club, Key Largo, Florida, Rotunda West, Florida, other municipalities and several industries.

Desalination in Dual-Purpose Plants

We have said that heat drawn from a high-temperature source may be more nearly completely converted into other forms of energy than heat from a source of lower temperature. By contrast, desalination of sea water by distillation is limited to relatively moderate temperatures, to avoid deposition of scale on the walls of the still. This statement must have led many a reader to the idea of a dual-purpose plant, using high-temperature steam to produce electrical energy and waste steam of lower temperature to desalt ocean water, in a series of successive stages.

The success of the dual-purpose idea evidently depends on there being a good market for both electrical energy and desalted water. Southern California, with its scanty rainfall, dense population, and rapidly growing industries, would furnish such a market. Israel, in spite of earnest efforts to create industries, is still an agricultural nation, hence might not be a suitable place for dual-purpose development.

A dual-purpose plant would be essentially a distillation plant, except that a steam turbine, driving an electric generator, would intervene between the boiler and the first of several successive stages of evaporation of sea water. Steam at appropriate pressure and temperature will be taken from the suitable place in the turbine into the first stage. Steam condensed in the first stage would be returned to the boiler, and that condensed in later stages would constitute the distillate. The fuel burned under the boilers might be any of the fossil fuels (coal, petroleum, or natural gas). Yet it chanced that energy from uranium atoms was rapidly coming into use at the time dual-purpose plants were being designed, hence it has played an important part in the development of this idea.

Energy from atoms is often called atomic energy; but the name nuclear energy is better, since practically all of it is released by the splitting of the heavy, positively charged core or nucleus, at the center of the atom. Although almost any of the heavy-atomed elements, toward the end of the chemist's Periodic Table, might theoretically become the source of nuclear energy, the element uranium is the only one thus far exploited (with thorium an imminent possibility). Uranium atoms are either split or (in two successive steps) are converted into atoms of plutonium in a piece of equipment called an atomic reactor. At the same time energy is released, which finds its way into the surroundings as heat.

The first atomic reactor was set up at the University of Chicago's Stagg Field, in 1942. Its sole purpose was to show that a reaction converting uranium into other elements was self-initiating, self-sustaining, and capable of being controlled and of being stopped at will. Consequently, it was operated at such a slow rate that its temperature did not rise perceptibly above that of its surroundings. Immediately afterward, reactors were set up at Hanford, Washington, to produce plutonium for the atomic bombs that brought about the surrender of Japan, at the end of World War II. They were cooled by water from the Columbia River, which was then impounded for a time in storage basins and returned to the river.

As years passed, reactors were built that operated at higher and higher temperatures. Interest at first was confined to the possible military uses of nuclear energy. The first nuclear-powered submarine, the

Nautilus, was launched nine years after the end of the war. It used hot water under pressure, continuously recirculated, to carry heat from the ship's reactor to its steam boiler.

At about this time, the government relinquished the monopoly that it had previously held in the ownership of nuclear "fuel" (uranium). The Atomic Energy Commission then became the leader in the development of nuclear energy for peacetime civilian uses. Reactors of improved design, greater power, and operable at high temperatures were rapidly developed. At the beginning of 1968, more than 50 large nuclear-powered electrical generating plants, with a combined capacity of over 40 million kilowatts and to cost over $7 billion, were designed or being built in the United States. This was about the total capacity of all the country's hydroelectric and fuel-powered electric plants at the beginning of World War II. The nuclear-powered generating capacity of the United States is now anticipated to be roughly 140 million kilowatts by 1980.

In nuclear-powered desalination, the cost of the desalted ocean water depends on the price that may be obtained for the by-product electrical energy. Very large plants have an economic advantage. The plant designed for an island, 3000 feet offshore, at Los Angeles, was planned to produce 150 million gallons of fresh water each day at a cost of about 22 cents a thousand gallons. The associated power plant was planned to produce 1.8 million kilowatts of electric power. A considerable part of this was to be devoted to lifting the water of the California aqueduct over the Tehachapi Pass.

More realistic calculations, taking into consideration today's high interest rates and a total plant cost of well over $400 million, indicates that the cost of desalted ocean water at the plant itself would likely have been greater than 40 cents a thousand gallons.

An advantage of nuclear energy over energy from the burning of fossil fuels comes from compactness. One hears statements such as "A chunk of uranium the size of a man's head carries as much energy as a trainload of coal." This is purposely a very vague statement because the efficiency of reactors as a means for releasing energy depends on their design. A breeder reactor is theoretically possible; as an incident to releasing energy, it converts ordinary uranium into plutonium or thorium into uranium of the special kind (U-233) that is used as fuel in the reactor. Such a reactor would create its own fuel as it went along.

The different sources of electrical energy—fossil fuels, uranium, the controlled descent of water, and the hot water of thermal springs—are in active competition. Idaho is the only state in which descending water is practically the only source of electrical energy. Hot springs and geothermal energy are being actively exploited in California. Hot springs are also exploited in Italy, New Zealand, and a few other countries. The development of nuclear energy tends to be most rapid where coal is expensive—New England, for example. Yet such a localization of the different energy sources is diminished by the fact that electrical energy is itself easily transported at moderate cost over long distances by high-voltage conductors. The big generating plants in each geographical region pour their output of electrical energy into a common network or grid. Thus the individual user may be getting some of his electrical energy from each of the sources supplying his own district.

The Transport of Ions by Living Plants and Animals

The desalination methods just described include all that are important at the present moment or that seem promising for the near future. Yet many others have been suggested or studied in some detail. Living plants and animals have mastered the art of desalination in a way that seems simpler than ours. Yet their secret still eludes us, in spite of studies that are now being made of living membranes and of artificial ones that may imitate their action.

Each living creature—plant or animal, one-celled alga or billion-celled elephant or whale—must deal with salinity as best it can. Many very simple organisms are as non-selective as paper bags. Ions and simple molecules freely penetrate their walls and move in or out until osmotic equilibrium is attained. There is not the least selection or control.

Most organisms, however, have the ability to control the kinds of ions that pass through their cell walls and in some degree to control their concentrations. Plants or animals that live in salt water must absorb water, while rejecting salt. Those that live in fresh water or on land, especially land animals that use water to wash away soluble body wastes, must discard water while conserving salt.

In most animals, from roundworms up to mammals in the evolutionary scale, conserving salt is one of the functions of the kidneys. (Like most other organs, kidneys are multiple-functioned.) A human kidney consists of millions of tiny bodies called nephrons. These act as ultrafilters, holding back large molecules of fats, peptones, and other partially synthesized body materials, while permitting water and soluble materials, including salt, to filter through. Then membranes step in, to snatch back both the ions of salt. Thus the body gets rid of soluble fragments from the breakdown of proteins, indeed gets rid of practically anything whose slow accumulation in the body would do harm, but without losing much of anything that is needed or useful.

The rejection of salt by marine creatures is accomplished with the same readiness as its retention by those that live in fresh water or on land. Fish from the briniest oceans are so nearly free from salt that they must be salted when brought to the table. A frog's skin passes water and rejects salt, and continues to do so for several hours after it has been removed from the frog. Salt-tolerant plants sometime gain extra tolerance, by actively transporting sodium ion (Na^+) through the root tips from the plant into the soil.

Sea birds that spend most of their life over distant oceans are under an extra handicap. They need more water than fish do, but have only sea water to drink. Petrel and albatross and several kinds of gulls are provided with glands in their heads that concentrate salt water, then discard the concentrated brine through the nostrils. In the pelican, the brine is channeled to fall clear of the bird's beak, lest it find its way into his stomach.

Whether living membranes act to discard salt or to retain it, the salt is always moved from a region of lower into one of higher concentration. This is the opposite direction to that in which salt ions move spontaneously by diffusion. It therefore calls for a steady input of energy. In algae, this energy may be the radiant energy of the sun; but in other instances it seems to be chemical energy released in a simple chemical reaction, such as oxidation or reduction or perhaps neutralization or its opposite, hydrolysis. If it is the sodium ion, Na^+, that is primarily transported, the chloride ion, Cl^-, is dragged along, too, to maintain electrical neutrality in every part of the solution.

Living membranes do more than just transport sodium. They choose and select. Plants are able to extract potassium from a saline soil solution, while excluding most of the sodium. Crustaceans withdraw from sea water the traces of copper that they need, while rejecting most other heavy metals. There are at least two different ways for transporting alkali metal ions, one of the methods being particularly adapted to potassium, the other to sodium. Yet the capacity for selectively transporting sodium is nearly universal. Algae or root tips, kidneys, or intestinal linings, or the salt-transporting membranes of fish, frogs, or birds; the transport of sodium is the one touch of nature that makes the whole world kin.

The Office of Saline Water

In the United States, the Office of Saline Water in the Department of the Interior has been the leader of desalination research. It received and screened suggestions with regard to that art from persons of every sort, including many novices. It conducted a highly diversified and sophisticated program of investigation, not indeed in its own laboratories but under contract, in the laboratories of universities, corporations, and individual scientists. All the methods of desalination outlined in this chapter and many others are under continuous study and development. Such important incidentals as the development of corrosion-resistant materials, methods for disposing of waste brine at inland sites, and ways to prevent the deposition of scale are under constant study, too. Ion-transport through living membranes is getting deserved attention. The properties of water and brines are being determined and recorded in detail.

Desalination processes that have been found promising on a small scale always need development and testing on a larger scale before operating plants can be constructed. The Office of Saline Water has test facilities at Freeport, Texas, for the improvement of vertical-tube evaporators (VTE). Adjoining this is a test facility for testing the materials that are used in desalination, particularly with respect to their resistance to corrosion. Since about 40 per cent of the cost of most desalination methods is the original cost and replacement costs of materials, any saving brought about by the new facility will be very much worthwhile.

The Office has also operated, at Webster, South Dakota, a plant for testing desalination by electrodialysis; at Roswell, New Mexico, one for developing small plants for desalting brackish water; and at San Diego, California, one for designing and testing the component parts for plants that will ultimately produce from the ocean several million gallons of fresh water each day. In addition, there is at Wrightsville Beach, North Carolina, a 25-acre test station, at which sea water, filtered sea water, distilled water, compressed air, propane gas, high and low-pressure steam, and electrical energy are available for testing desalination equipment that has reached one of the stages of large-scale development.

The Office of Saline Water also plays a prominent part in exchange of information or development of cooperative projects with individual American states or with other Federal agencies; the Atomic Energy

Table 15-3.
Plants of 1 Million Gallons Per Day (January 1969)

Country	Location	Process	Status	Plant Capacity 1000 gpd
United States				
California	San Diego	MSF-D	O	1000
New Mexico	Roswell	VC-D	O	1000
Texas	Freeport	VTE-D	O	1000
Florida	Siesta Key	E-M	C	1200
Pennsylvania	Clairton	MSF-D	O	1440
Texas	Texas City	MSF-D	O	2160
California	San Diego	MSF-D	O	2600
Florida	Key West	MSF-D	O	2620
United States Territories				
Virgin Islands	Virgin Islands Water and Power Authority	VTE-D	C	1000
Virgin Islands	St. Thomas	MSF-D	O	1100
Virgin Islands	St. Croix	MSF-D	O	1500
Virgin Islands	Virgin Islands Water and Power Authority	MSF-D	C	2500
North America except the United States and its territories				
Mexico	Rosarita	MSF-D	O	7500
Caribbean				
Curacao	Mundo Nobo	ST-D	O	1074
Bahamas/Br.	Freeport	MSF-D	C	1267
Bahamas/Br.	Nassau, New Providence Island	MSF-D	O	1440
Curacao	Shell Petroleum	MSF-D	O	1584
Cuba	Guantanamo	MSF-D	O	2250
Aruba/Neth. Ant.	Balashi Govt.	ST-D	O	2688
Curacao	Mundo Nobo	MSF-D	O	3440
South America				
Venezuela	(Port) Cardon	F-D	O	1440
Europe (Continental)				
Netherlands	Europoort	VTE-D	C	1140
Italy	Italsider	MSF-D	O	1200
Malta	Valetta	MSF-D	O	1200
Italy	Brindisi	MSF-D	C	1320
Netherlands	Terneuzen	MSF-D	C	7650
Malta	Valetta	MSF-D	C	4400

Table 15-3. (Continued)

Country	Location	Process	Status	Plant Capacity 1000 gpd
England and Ireland				
England	Kent Oil Refinery	ST-D	O	1295
Channel Islands	Jersey	MSF-D	C	1800
Australia				
Asia				
Middle East				
Israel	Eilat A	MSF-D	O	1000
Kuwait	Shuwaikh A	MSF-D	O	1260
Kuwait	Shuwaikh C	MSF-D	O	1260
Kuwait	Shuwaikh D	MSF-D	O	1260
Kuwait	Shuwaikh B	ST-D	O	1344
Qatar	Doha	MSF-D	O	1800
Qatar	Doha Ced	MSF-D	O	2300
Kuwait	Shuwaikh E	MSF-D	O	2400
Kuwait	Shuwaikh F	MSF-D	O	2400
Kuwait	Shuaiba B	MSF-D	O	2400
Kuwait	Shuaiba A	MSF-D	O	3600
Kuwait	Shuaiba	MSF-D	C	4800
Kuwait	Shuwaikh	MSF-D	O	4800
Kuwait	Shuwaikh	MSF-D	O	4800
Kuwait	Shuwaikh G	MSF-D	C	4800
Saudi Arabia	Jidda	MSF-D	C	5000
Oman/TR.	Abu Dhabi	MSF-D	C	7200
Africa				
Morocco/Sp	Ceuta	MSF-D	O	1055
Canary Islands	Lanzarote	MSF-D	C	5284
Union of Soviet Socialist Republic				
U.S.S.R.	Shevchenco	VTE-D	O	1320
U.S.S.R.	Shevchenco	VTE-D	O	3600
U.S.S.R.	Shevchenco	VTE-D	C	31700
TOTAL	(52 Plants)			159725

Key to symbols:
    O = Operating
    C = Under Construction
VTE-D = Vertical Tube Evaporator
MSF-D = Multistage Flash Distillation
  ST-D = Submerged Tube Distillation
   E-M = Electrodialysis
   E-D = Flash Distillation

Commission, the Metropolitan Water District of Southern California, Orange County Water District, the Office of Water Resources Research, the Environmental Protection Administration, the U.S. Geological Survey, the Office of Soil Conservation and Land Development, and the Departments of Commerce, Agriculture, and Health, Education, and Welfare.

The Office of Saline Water also leads in cooperative efforts to develop desalination programs in foreign countries. Examples are aid in feasibility studies and engineering design in dual-purpose plants in Saudi Arabia, and Israel, and cooperative research and development studies with Japan. In drought-ridden lands whose prophets for ages have preached only undying hatred and unforgiving retribution, there is hope that the men of today may awake to the ancient but still unperceived truth that love is more profitable than hatred.

The opportunities presented by science in the modern world are spectacular. Let men everywhere, in spite of demogogues, tyrants, or dictators, join hands as brothers and work together to achieve a more nearly even distribution of the blessings that flow from fresh water, earth's great fountain of opportunity.

Statistics

The winning of fresh water from the ocean has developed spectacularly. In 1950, there was probably not in all the world a single plant with a capacity of over 25,000 gallons per day. As of January 1969, there were about 700, having a total capacity of about 250 million gallons per day. Approximately 50 per cent of total world capacity is for municipal needs, 48 per cent for industrial use and 2 per cent for special domestic, military, and tourist requirements. Projections indicate that by the end of 1975, the total desalting capacity in operation or under construction will reach 1.25 billion gallons per day.

Table 15-3 lists all plants of 1 million gpd capacity or greater in existence or under construction as of January 1969. The desalting plants are listed by geographical subdivision and arranged in order of size.

16

Conclusion

The Wildlife: This Is Their Continent, Too

Projects for draining swamps or damming streams have often made what developers or their engineers thought were adequate measures for the protection of wildlife. Yet sometimes these measures proved insufficient. Deer, displaced from their natural grazing grounds in the building of a dam, have sometimes found their new sites to be so deeply covered by winter snows or flooding rivers that they starved. Ducks, displaced from long-possessed nesting places by a lowered water table, have sometimes found their new sites to be alkaline or polluted by oil. Oil slicks from leaky wells or spilled oil cargoes snare helpless waterfowl and threaten valuable oyster beds and crabbing grounds.

There is danger that man's growing needs for air and water may destroy many of the scenic wonders of the continent and imperil wild creatures that should be counted among its valuable natural resources. These, the original owners of North America, possessed it in peace for uncounted centuries before humanity moved in, to remold nature's wonderland nearer to the human heart's desire—first with stone axe and bow and arrow, then with rifle, chainsaw, bulldozer, and concrete mixer. Must we permit all the "verdant, dim retreats" to be swept away, just to support an ever-increasing burden of humanity? Philosophers are not all agreed that ours is the species most deserving preservation.

The destruction of wildlife that comes from a change in the wildlife's environment is not often intentional. Most of us do not realize that many creatures of the pond, thicket, and forest depend for their existence on some very special features of their environment. Fish perish or migrate if their water no longer contains algae or near-microscopic plants on which fish depend for food, if their water becomes colder or warmer by more than a degree or two, or if it contains too little dissolved oxygen. Other species of fish thrive only in surroundings that invite insects, crustaceans, mollusks, or other animal species. Birds build their nests only in surroundings that seem to provide safety or that make their own particular type of nest building reasonably easy. Many small animals feed almost exclusively on a single species of plant. Grazing animals are often brought to the verge of starvation by being shifted to pastures where familiar herbage is missing.

Destruction of wildlife by loss of habitat may happen in many different ways: displacement by rising water in building dams, lowering of the water table in draining swamps, destruction of native vegetation in developing new agricultural areas, straightening rivers in flood control, lining canals with concrete or asphalt to decrease evaporation, controlled burning of native vegetation to improve runoff, blocking rivers to migrating or spawning fish. To this long list of ways in which wildlife may be destroyed unintentionally and needlessly may be added deliberate destruction by hunters and settlers, who have brought many valuable and interesting species to the brink of extinction and have wiped out many others forever. There are also fanatics who have a grudge against a particular species, which they try to exterminate in spite of laws for its protection. An example is the golden eagle of Texas, which lives chiefly on carrion but which sheep men believe kills many lambs.

The most needless and perhaps most deadly destruction of wildlife comes from pollution, described in some detail in two earlier chapters. There is merit in the suggestion of a sanitary barrier, about a quarter-mile wide, on both banks of every stream that may carry pollution into a larger stream or a lake. Within these areas, settlement by human beings would be forbidden. As recently recognized, this would also aid in flood control. This would be just the reverse to the method by which the continent was first colonized; for the first European immigrants settled along the rivers and only much later established homes in what was formerly timberland, or ventured to plow and irrigate the windswept prairie.

In addition to the preservation of wildlife, government agencies, and such citizen groups as the Archeological Institute of America, the American Camping Association, and various state historical societies (addresses in the latest *World Almanac*) lend a hand in the preservation of archeological or historical sites and in the development of recreational areas in which both the main divisions of outdoor enthusiasts ("Water Bugs" and "Trail Stampers") may find pleasant outings.

Appendix

A. Work, Heat, and Energy

When a force (a push or a pull) acts to change the rate of motion of a body or when it overcomes another force (as in compressing a spring) it is said to do work. Water descending a hill through a pipe that it completely fills does work in overcoming friction, and sometimes also in pushing water uphill in the next section of the pipe. The total work done is proportional to the force (f) applied and to the distance (s) through which the motion continues in the direction of force. In brief, $w = fs$. A force of 10,000 pounds, applied to the piston of a hydraulic jack, may cause the piston to move outward 2 feet. The work done by the jack is then 20,000 foot-pounds. If the force applied is insufficient to overcome opposing forces and produce motion, no work is done.

When the force overcome by a moving body is that of friction, heat is produced. Every child learns this when he first slides down a rope. The greater the force of friction, and the farther the body moves while overcoming friction, the more heat is produced, just in proportion. Thus heat, for more than a century, has been recognized as a form of motion. James P. Joule, a British investigator, was the first to prove conclusively the identity of heat and motion, which are now both measured in the same unit, appropriately called a joule.

The motion of a body, in overcoming friction, is transferred to the individual atoms and molecules that compose the body, and to those of the surface over which the body slides or rolls, or to those of the medium (gas or liquid) through which it moves. There the motion remains, indefinitely, as heat—the jostling, haphazard motion of individual atoms and molecules.

A calorie is a measure of heat. It is very nearly the quantity of heat needed to heat 1 gram of water from one temperature to another that is 1° higher on the centigrade scale. The calorie is now defined as 4.184 joules, and the 15° calorie and other units formerly used to measure heat are obsolete.

Energy is anything that can do work or produce heat. Bodies in motion have kinetic energy (energy of motion), because they can do work in changing the rate of motion of other bodies or in overcoming a force. If the force overcome is friction, the kinetic energy is converted into heat; if the force overcome is something else than friction (as in overcoming gravity in moving water uphill) the kinetic energy may be converted into potential energy. This is energy that exists because of force.[1] Potential energy may produce motion (kinetic energy) when forces temporarily held in check are permitted to act.

Energy of every kind is measured by the work ($w = fs$) that it can do or by the heat that it can produce. Kinetic energy can also be calculated from the mass and velocity squared of the moving body: $K.\,E. = \frac{1}{2}\,m\,v^2$.

In the absence of friction, which converts other forms of energy into heat, kinetic and potential energy are interconvertible without loss. When heat was recognized as being a form of energy, the statement just made was recognized as a special case of a more general principle, Conservation of Energy: Events transform one form of energy into another, without ever creating or destroying energy.

Nevertheless, as Einstein was the first to recognize, matter and energy are interconvertible. Each gram of matter converts into C^2 ergs of energy ($Co = 3 \times 10^{10}$ cm/sec, the velocity of light in a vacuum). A microgram of mass—a speck of matter barely visible to the unaided eye—is equivalent to 33.5 horsepower-hours of energy. This is the secret of atomic (better termed nuclear) energy. A few shovelsful of a nuclear fuel (uranium) would supply a large city with power and light for a century.

Some Definitions

Mass. The quantity of matter in a body, as measured by its inertia—its resistance to being set in motion by a force. Do not confuse mass

1. Do not trivially define potential energy as energy of position. A book on a table or a boulder on a mountain side has potential energy, not because of its position but because of the force of gravity, which does work in steadily increasing the rate of motion if the book falls off the table or the boulder starts to roll.

with bulk (space occupied), though bulk is also used as a measure of the quantity of matter in a body (when commodities are sold by the bushel, cubic foot, or liter).

Dyne. A very small force, nearly equal to the force of gravity on a 1 milligram mass. It is the force which, acting on a 1 gram mass that is free to move, gives that mass unit acceleration—increases its velocity by one centimeter per second (1 cm/sec) during each second that the force acts.

Erg. A unit of work or energy. It is the work done when a force of 1 dyne acts upon a gram mass while the mass moves 1 cm in the direction in which the force points.

Gram-centimeter (g-cm). The work done in lifting a mass of 1 gram a distance of 1 centimeter against the force of gravity.

Joule (j). A unit of energy of work. It is 10^7 ergs.

Calorie (cal). A unit of heat. It is 4.185 joules.

Power. Rate of doing work or expanding energy. A horsepower (hp) or kilowatt (kW) are measures of power. Energy expended (or work done) at either of these rates, steadily during one hour, is a horsepower-hour or kilowatt-hour of energy or work. So are the watt-second and kilowatt-year. 1 kW = 1000 watts = 1,000 j/sec.

B.   Temperature and Latent Heat

Since the work of Joule, more than a century ago, heat has been recognized as that part of the energy of individual atoms and molecules which can be transferred from one molecule to another, in collisions between them. When massive bodies collide (billiard balls, for example), energy always passes from the body of higher to the one of lower energy. For instance, heat always passes from a body of higher to one of lower temperature. Thus temperature is recognized as being a measure of the collision-transferrable energy of an average molecule.

When a body transfers heat to a cooler body, an average molecule of the first transfers energy to an average molecule of the second.

The first temperature-measuring instrument, a crude thermometer, was made by Galileo, the inventor of the telescope, early in the seventeenth century. The first thermometric scales were purely arbitrary, but only two of them are in use today—the Fahrenheit scale (°F), used in English-speaking countries in reporting the weather, and the Centigrade scale (°C). Water freezes at 32°F or 0°C, and boils at 212°F or 100°C.

In the Absolute or Kelvin scale (°A or °K), introduced by Lord Kelvin in 1854, temperatures are made proportional to the very thing that temperature is supposed to measure—the collision-exchangeable energy of an average molecule.[1]

Temperatures on the Absolute scale are obtained by adding 273.1 to those on the Centigrade scale. Water freezes at 273.1°A, and boils at 373.1°A, if it is under a pressure of 1 atm. Thus an average molecule of an ideal gas, at the boiling point of water, contains more heat than it does at the freezing point of water, in the ratio of 373.1 to 273.1. This is an increase in energy of about 27 per cent, in being heated from the lower to the higher temperature.

The heat that disappears in melting ice or evaporating water was formerly termed latent heat, because it reappeared as heat if the vapor was cooled until it recondensed into liquid, or if the liquid was cooled until it froze. The terms heat of fusion or of vaporization (or evaporation) are now preferred.

The heat of fusion of ice is 79 calories per gram (cal/g). That means that when ice is melted, 79 calories of heat disappear in producing a gram of liquid water, without any increase in temperature.

The heat of vaporization of water at 100°C is 540 cal., with the temperature of the vapor still at 100°C. If vaporization is at higher temperature, the heat of vaporization is less. It is zero at the *critical temperature* of water (374°C), since at the critical temperature a heat-expanded liquid is indistinguishable from the compressed vapor that is in equilibrium with it.

C.   Radiant Energy

Radiant energy includes ordinary visible light and such forms of invisible light as ultraviolet and infrared, X rays, gamma rays, and wireless waves. Regardless of how they are produced they all move in straight lines through empty space with what is probably the same velocity, 10^{10} cm/sec or 186,000 mi/sec. Through a material medium (gas, liquid, or solid) radiant energy moves more slowly. The ratio of the speed in a vacuum to the speed in the medium is called the index of refraction of the medium for that particular kind of radiant energy.

Although radiant energy may seem to be continuously emitted by the sun or any other hot object, it is actually set free as separate little packets of energy, called quanta or photons. These are flung off into space, one by one, in straight lines, like bullets from a machine gun.

1. More precisely stated, an average molecule of an ideal gas.

When they pass from empty space into matter or back again, or when they pass from one kind of matter into another they are all refracted (bent aside). Their refraction according to a definite law is evidence that the different kinds of radiant energy are of the same general nature.

Radiant energy, in its passage through matter, seems to be guided by waves of electrical force. (These waves need nothing to conduct them: they pass, quite unimpeded, through empty space; and the idea of a space-filling "ether," to carry them, was long ago abandoned.)

Each photon has a definite frequency, represented by the Greek letter ν. This is the number of double reversals each second in the direction of the wave of electrical force that guides or accompanies the photon in its flight. One may calculate the energy of a photon (in ergs) by multiplying its frequency (sec^{-1}) by a constant (Planck's constant, $h =$ 6.626 x 10^{-27} erg-sec.). In chemical reactions in which radiant energy plays a part (photochemical reactions), a photon is often represented by $h\nu$.

The journey of a photon through space may last a very small fraction of a second or several million years, all the while traveling with the speed of light. In the end it may encounter an atom, electron, or ion that is fitted to receive it (in a human eye, photoelectric cell, green leaf, or the photographic plate of a great telescope). This acceptor particle swallows the whole photon and becomes activated (energized), hence *capable of reacting,* in one or more successive steps. A fraction of a photon is never accepted, for apparently both photons and electrons remain undivided in chemical events.

Figure 1 displays different sorts of photons in the order of decreasing frequency or energy. Only a very small part of the total range of frequencies is detectible by our eyes (as visible light). Adjoining the visible frequencies on the high-frequency side are the ultraviolet rays; and on the low-frequency side are the infrared rays. Both are invisible to the human eye, but may be recorded on photographic plates that have been sensitized to radiation of that special frequency. Photons may also cause electrons to be emitted from metallic surfaces. Thus they may be detected with instruments called infrared or ultraviolet sensors. As one might expect, high-frequency or high-energy rays are more penetrating than those of lower frequency. The gamma rays, set free by atoms of the radioactive elements, are the most penetrating of all. Next most penetrating are "hard" X rays, and next to these the "softer" X rays that are used in diagnosis. Obviously the frequency, hence the

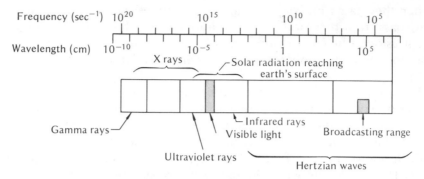

Figure 1. Different Kinds of Radiant Energy

penetrating power of the X rays generated by every X-ray machine, must be carefully regulated.

Radiant energy is often identified by its wavelength—the distance between successive crests of the wave of electrical force that guides or accompanies each photon on its flight through space. Wavelength is usually represented by the Greek letter λ. It is less fundamental than frequency, since it partly depends on the medium through which the photon is traveling, instead of being determined, once and for all, by the emitter of the photon, at the moment this is released. The product of frequency and wavelength is the velocity of the photon in the medium in which it is traveling, hence either of these two quantities may be calculated from the other. Figure 2 indicates the range of wavelengths for each of the kinds of radiant energy for which the frequency is given.

The number of photons emitted in a second by a heated surface increases very rapidly with increasing temperature. With increasing temperature, too, hot bodies become more and more like perfect radiators, whose rate of emission of radiation is a maximum for that temperature and independent of the chemical identity of the radiator. For a perfect radiator, the number of photons released every second is in proportion to the fourth power of the temperature. Thus the sun, which approximates a perfect radiator, with a surface temperature of about 6000°K, releases about $2^4 = 16$ times as many photons every second as a surface of the same area at 3000°K. Figure 2 illustrates this fact very well. (The total number of photons released each second is shown for each of several different temperatures by the area under a curve.) Observe

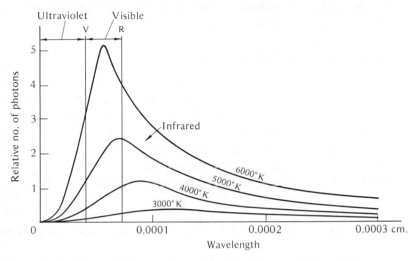

Figure 2. Emission of Photons by an Ideal Radiator at Different Temperatures

also that the higher the temperature of the emitter the greater is the proportion of photons emitted with very high frequency.

D. Operation with Very Large and Very Small Numbers

Very large and very small numbers are best expressed as powers of ten. Thus 10^8 means a 1, followed by eight zeros; and 10^{-8} means a 1 in the eighth decimal place, preceded by zeros. Prefixes, derived from the Greek or introduced in recent years, are another way of expressing such numbers:

Prefix	Abbre-viation	Meaning	Prefix	Abbre-viation	Meaning
tera	T	$\times 10^{12}$	centi-	c	$\times 10^{-2}$
giga-	G	$\times 10^{9}$	milli-	m	$\times 10^{-3}$
mega-	M	$\times 10^{6}$	micro-	μ	$\times 10^{-6}$
kilo-	k	$\times 10^{3}$	nano	n	$\times 10^{-9}$
hecto-	h	$\times 10^{2}$	pico	p	$\times 10^{-12}$
deka-	da	$\times 10$	femto	f	$\times 10^{-15}$
deci-	d	$\times 10^{-1}$	atto	a	$\times 10^{-18}$

The prefixes M to μ are by far the most frequently used.

To multiply, add exponents of the powers of ten. Thus 2.3×10^7, multiplied by 5×10^{-15} is 11.5×10^{-8} or 1.15×10^{-7}.

To divide, subtract exponents. Thus 27×10^{18}, divided by 3×10^6 is 9×10^{12}.

E.   Ions and Ionic Equations

When we speak of a soil or a solution or a plant or animal as containing sodium, calcium, magnesium, or iron, it is plain that we are not speaking of these elements in their shiny, bright "metallic" condition. Each is present in a completely altered state as a part of a salt (the principal product of the interaction of an acid and a base, in which both acid and base cease to exist in neutralizing each other).

Most salts are ionic compounds. By this we mean that they consist of ions (electrically charged atoms or groups of atoms). Most other substances (water vapor, for example) are classed as nonionic or molecular because they are composed of electrically neutral molecules, rather than of ions.

Common salt (sodium chloride), whether in the solid state or melted or dissolved, consists of equal numbers of positively charged sodium ions, Na^+, and negatively charged chloride ions, Cl^-. Since the charges on these ions are equal and opposite, and since equal numbers of the two ions are always present, common salt is electrically neutral. Water vapor, H_2O, is also electrically neutral, but for a different reason: each of its molecules is neutral.

Although common salt is often represented by the formula NaCl, this is not to deny its ionic character, but just to indicate that equal numbers of the two kinds of ions are present. Anyone who wishes to call attention to its ions may represent common salt as (Na^+, Cl^-). Na^+ and Cl^-, existing independently, yea; Na, linked with Cl to form a neutral molecule, NaCl, never.

Many ions have charges that are twice or three times the charge on the ions of common salt. Examples of salts containing such ions:

$CaCl_2$	$MgSO_4$	Na_2S	$Fe_2(SO_4)_3$	$FePO_4$	$Ca_3(PO_4)_2$
Calcium chloride	Magnesium sulfate	Sodium sulfide	Ferric sulfate	Ferric phosphate	Calcium phosphate

The ions present in these salts are:

Na^+	Ca^{++}	Mg^{++}	Fe^{+++}	Cl^-	S^{--}	SO_4^{--}	PO_4^{--}
Sodium ion	Calcium ion	Magnesium ion	Ferric ion	Chloride ion	Sulfide ion	Sulfate ion	Phosphate ion

From the formulas of the ions those of the salts may readily be found: just bring the ions together in such relative numbers that the total charge on the cations (positively charged ions) equals (hence cancels) that on the anions (negatively charged ions). The crystal, melted salt, or solution is thus electrically neutral. Check all six of the preceding formulas of salts.

Incidentally, observe that the ending -*ide* for an anion (except for an oxide or hydroxide) indicates no oxygen. The presence of oxygen in an anion is indicated by the endings -ite or -ate (with more oxygen in the latter case).

For reasons discussed in chemical textbooks, an atom of a metallic element readily loses one, two, or three electrons (negative charges of electricity). This leaves the atom (originally electrically neutral) with a surplus of positive electricity; in other words, the metallic atom is converted into a cation. But atoms or groups of atoms of non-metals are likely to gain electrons, thus becoming anions. If we represent an electron by e and remember that it is a negative charge, creation of typical cations and anions may be summarized:

$$Na - e \longrightarrow Na^+ \qquad Cl + e \longrightarrow Cl^-$$
$$Ca - 2e \longrightarrow Ca^{++} \qquad S + 2e \longrightarrow S^{--}$$
$$Al - 3e \longrightarrow Al^{+++} \qquad N + 3e \longrightarrow N^{--}$$

In addition to the cations just listed, the reader will meet the ammonium ion, NH_4^+, two ions containing iron, Fe^{++} and Fe^{+++}, and two containing manganese, Mn^{++} and Mn^{4+}. For iron, the lower and higher valence states (charges) are distinguished by calling the ions ferr*ous* and ferr*ic* ions, respectively. But because manganese and many other elements form ions with more than two valence states it is now customary to designate the valence state by a Roman numeral, enclosed in parentheses. Thus the two chief valence states of manganese are designated as Mn (IV) oxide, in MnO_2, and manganese (II) chloride, in $MnCl_2$.

In addition to the anions listed above, the reader of this book will encounter the nitrate ion, NO_3^-, and the dichromate ion, $Cr_2O_7^{--}$. A few minutes spent in learning the formulas of common ions, listed above, will greatly assist every reader.

Metallic sodium burns brilliantly in chlorine gas, forming common salt, and metallic magnesium burns brilliantly in steam, forming magnesium oxide. Taking into account the ionic character of these products, the reactions may be written:

$$Na + \tfrac{1}{2} Cl_2 \rightarrow (Na^+, Cl^-) \qquad Mg + H_2O \rightarrow (Mg^+, O =) + H_2$$

We see that what really takes place is the transfer of an electron from each atom of sodium to an atom of chlorine; or of two electrons from each atom of magnesium to an atom of oxygen (in steam). Since electrons were unknown when these spectacular experiments were first performed, the world had to wait for over a century for an explanation of what actually takes place.

One other point may be made: metallic sodium in no way resembles common salt, nor does metallic magnesium in any way resemble the white powder, magnesium oxide, that results from burning in steam. So it is evident that the transfer of electrons brings about the complete alteration of the substances that lose or gain electrons. When substances interact in such a way that their properties are completely altered, we say that they have reacted or have taken part in a chemical change or chemical reaction. (In the first of the two preceding reactions, we wrote Cl_2 to indicate that chlorine gas actually consists of molecules containing two atoms each; but we wrote ½ Cl_2 to show that only one of the two atoms is needed for each atom of sodium reacting.)

We have just observed examples of the violent reaction of metals with nonmetals or with water. In other instances (the rusting of iron, for example) the reaction occurs more slowly, but the general result is the same: the loss of electrons by metallic atoms and their transfer to nonmetallic atoms.

Nonmetals, such as chlorine or oxygen, may sometimes be dissolved in water with none or almost none of the element being chemically altered. To speak of free or elementary chlorine or oxygen is to emphasize unaltered character and electrically neutral molecules, Cl_2 or O_2. But Cl^- should be called chloride or chloride ion, not "chlorine"; and O^{--} should be called oxide or oxide ion, not "oxygen"; and similarly for other ions. To use the wrong word is to talk nonsense.

Ions often offer a very simple way to represent chemical reactions. For example, the neutralization of a solution of hydrochloric acid by sodium hydroxide may be written:

$$HCl + NaOH \rightarrow NaCl + H_2O$$

But three of the four substances here shown are ionic:

$$(H^+, Cl^-) + (Na^+, OH^-) \rightarrow (Na^+, Cl^-) + H_2O$$

We see, now, that the ions Na^+ and Cl^- have not been involved in the reaction at all. At first they were in separate solutions (of acid and base), and afterward are in the same solution (one of common salt). But bringing them together in the same solution has not made them combine to form molecules, NaCl. The essential reaction in neutralization is therefore simply:

$$H^+ + OH^- \rightarrow H_2O$$

in other words, the formation of water. (We ought to remark here that OH^- is hydroxyl ion, the typical ion of strong bases, often called alkalies.) But H^+ represents a proton (the nucleus or central core of an atom of hydrogen). The actual reactant whenever an acid neutralizes a base in the presence of water, is believed to be a hydrated proton, $H^+ \cdot H_2O$ or H_3O^+, often called a hydronium ion. Nevertheless, the symbol H^+ is often used as an arbitrary symbol for an unspecified acid. Don't call it "hydrogen." Its name is proton.

We shall give one more example of how the use of ions may sometimes simplify a chemical equation. Consider the reaction in which atmospheric carbon dioxide slowly dissolves limestone:

$$CaCO_3 + CO_2 + H_2O \rightleftharpoons Ca(HCO_3)_2$$

Calcium	Calcium
carbonate	hydrogen
(limestone)	carbonate
	(soluble)

The paired arrows, pointing in opposite directions, call attention to this as a reversible reaction. Water that has dissolved limestone in penetrating underground, may finally drip through the roof of a cave, thus relieving the solution of some of the pressure upon it. The forward (left-to-right) reaction is thus reversed and the dissolved calcium carbonate is reprecipitated as stalactites or stalagmites.

But calcium enters and leaves this reaction as calcium ion, Ca^{++} So we may leave it out of our equation and write:

$$CO_3 + CO_2 + H_2O \rightleftharpoons 2HCO_3^-$$

as the essence of what takes place when limestone is dissolved by carbon dioxide in the formation of a limestone cave.

F.   The Conductivity Test for Salt

Pure water is almost a complete nonconductor of electricity. Dissolving a little salt in it makes it a fair or good conductor, though never as good as graphite or metal of the same dimensions. If a salt solution is very dilute, its conductivity is almost in proportion to the weight of salt contained in a liter of solution. Thus we may roughly infer the concentration of salt in a dilute solution from its conductivity.

Actually, we measure the resistance of the solution, between platinum electrodes of known area and distance apart, using a high frequency alternating current and a Wheatstone bridge. (See textbooks on experimental physical chemistry.) Some salts conduct better than others; yet common salt is nearly always the predominant salt in a sample of soil or water, and its per-ion contribution to conductivity is not far from the average of other salts likely to be present. One therefore usually assumes that sodium chloride is the only salt present. This assumption should never be made in the presence of enough acid or alkali (both good conductors) to result in a pH (section H) outside the range of 6.0 to 9.0.

To test a soil for accumulated salt, moisten a sample of the soil with just enough distilled water to permit it to be stirred into a thick paste. After the past has stood for half an hour, dump it on a suction filter, separate the saturated soil extract and determine its conductance.

In the United States, state soil laboratories furnish free measurements of the accumulated salt in soils. County agricultural agents or state water resource agencies keep track of the salt concentration in important irrigation supplies and will advise about the possibility or risks of irrigation with slightly saline water.

The unit of electrical conductivity is the millimho per centimeter (mmho/cm). Water or a soil extract having a conductivity of 1 mmho/cm shows an electrical resistance of a thousand ohms, when resistance is measured between opposite faces of a cube 1 centimeter an edge. To convert millimhos per centimeter into salt concentrations in parts by weight of common salt per million by water (ppm or mg/kg), multiply by 468.

For very dilute solutions, the unit of conductivity is the micromho per centimeter. If a solution has this conductivity, its resistance, measured between opposite faces of a cube 1 centimeter on an edge, is 1 million ohms. One mmho/cm is 1000 micromho/cm.

Figure 3 shows two electrode pairs of the type usually used for testing irrigation water or saturated soil extract. Observe that the electrodes (platinum, coated with platinum black) are of measured area and fixed at a known distance apart. The type on the left is for testing solutions of low conductivity, and the other (electrodes far apart) for those of higher conductivity.

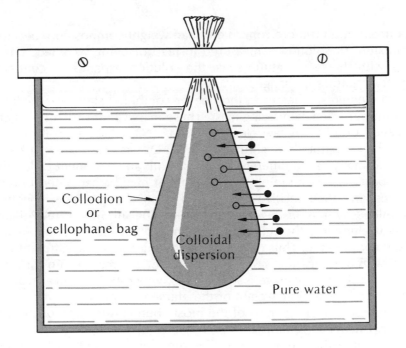

● Water molecule

○ Molecule or ion
   of an impurity

Figure 3. Purification of a Colloidal Dispersion by Dialysis

G.   Measures of Concentration and Weight Composition

The word "concentration" refers to the quantity of any component in unit volume (1 liter or 1 milliliter) of a mixture or solution. Thus we may speak of the concentration of common salt in sea water as being about 25 g/l, which is the same as 25 mg/ml.

Weight composition refers to the quantity of any component in unit weight of a mixture or solution, or the weight of any component for a stated weight of any other. Thus sea water may be described as containing a total of about 3.5 per cent by weight of dissolved salts or as containing about 30 parts (by weight) per million (30 ppm) of some heavy metal ion. This is the same as 30 mg/kg.

Concentration is more convenient than weight composition, because the mixture or solution is measured instead of being weighed; but it varies with the temperature, since the solution expands or contracts as its temperature is changed.

Most elements, whether in the free or combined state, are mixtures of atoms of somewhat varying mass. These mass variants of an element are called isotopes. A few elements (Be, F, Na, Al, P, etc.), have one stable, hence naturally occurring, isotope. Others are mixtures of several or as many as ten different isotopes. With an instrument called the mass spectrograph, a sample of any element may be separated into its isotopes, and their relative masses and relative abundance in nature determined with considerable precision. For all but a few (light-atomed) elements, the relative abundance of the isotopes in nature is fixed and definite. Thus by averaging the masses of the different isotopes, with due regard to relative abundance, one may obtain for most elements a definite average isotopic mass, which for historical reasons is still called the atomic weight of the element. Atomic weights are all in comparison with the mass of the most abundant isotope of carbon, arbitrarily taken as 12 units.

To illustrate the methods, consider the element copper. In nature, the mass spectrograph has shown that this element consists (in rounded figures) of 69.1 atoms of isotopic mass 62.93, for every 30.1 atoms of isotopic mass 64.93. Thus we may find the average isotopic mass:

$$69.1 \times 62.93 = 4348$$
$$30.9 \times 64.93 = 2006$$
$$\text{Total for 100 atoms} = 6354$$

corresponding to an average isotopic mass (atomic weight) of 63.54.

The molecular weight of an element or compound is the mass of an average molecule in comparison with that of an average atom of the most abundant isotope of carbon, taken as 12 units. (Observe that the basis of comparison is the same as with atomic weights.)

The molecular weight of every element or compound must be determined experimentally, usually by the man who first discovers or prepares it. (Fortunately, experimental methods exist for finding the molecular weights of gases and volatile liquids and substances that can be dissolved without reacting, in any common solvent.) Let us assume that the molecular weight of a compound has been determined. Then, if the percentage of each element in the compound is known and also atomic weights, one may calculate how many atoms of each element are present in a molecule of the compound. In other words, one may find a formula that represents one molecule of the compound. (See textbooks of chemistry.) From this, it is easy for anyone to find or check the molecular weight of the compound: just add the multiples of atomic weight that are shown by its formula. Thus glucose has the formula $C_6H_{12}O_6$. Adding the indicated multiples of the atomic weights:

$$(6 \times 12) + (12 \times 1.0008) + (6 \times 16) = 180$$

Similarly for ionic weights. The charges (+ or −), which represent electrons lost or gained in forming an ion do not perceptibly alter its total mass.

Moles and Equivalents

A mole is as many grams as there are mass units in the formula[1] of an atom, ion, or molecule — 60 grams of acetic acid vapor, $HC_2H_3O_2$, or 24g of magnesium, Mg^{++} for example.

When a substance is composed of ions, rather than electrically neutral molecules, it is convenient to express quantities in equivalents instead of in moles. An equivalent is the fraction of a mole of an ionic substance that corresponds to a single positive or negative charge. It is, for example, a full mole (58.45g) of sodium chloride (Na^+, Cl^-), half a mole of potassium sulfate ($2K$, SO_4^{--}) or calcium nitrate, (Ca^{++}, $2NO_3^-$), one-third mole of ammonium phosphate ($3NH_4^+$, PO_4^{---}), etc. If the formula of the compound indicates that it contains water, include this in the reckoning. (If the substance to be dissolved is to be used as an oxidant or reductant, an equivalent is defined somewhat differently; see textbooks of chemistry.)

A normal solution is one that contains one equivalent in each liter of solution. The abbreviations N, $0.1\ N$, $0.05\ N$, stand for normal, tenth normal, five-hundredths normal. They indicate the normality of these solutions.

When ionic substances react to neutralize each other or form a precipitate, equal numbers of positive and negative charges are involved, in order that the product may be electrically neutral. Consequently, equal numbers of equivalents of the two reagents are needed. If both are used as solutions of the same normality, equal volumes of the two solutions will be needed to give the same number of equivalents. But

1. In short, in recent usage, the word *mole* is often used for what used to be called a gram formula weight, and is no longer restricted to substances in which the formula actually represents a molecule.

if one solution is normal and the OTHER ONLY TENTH NORMAL, (N and O.1 N), the volume of the second solution will be ten times that of the first.

In summary: In reactions between ionic compounds, equal numbers of equivalents of the two reagents are needed. The corresponding volumes of the reagents are then either equal or are easily calculated. In any case:

$$\text{liters} \times \text{normality} = \text{equivalents}$$
$$\text{milliliters} \times \text{normality} = \text{milliequivalents}$$

(A milliequivalent is a thousandth of an equivalent; or it is as many milligrams as there are grams in an equivalent.)

H.   The pH Scale of Acidity or Alkalinity

The conductivity of ordinary tap water is decreased by distilling it, particularly if precautions are taken to prevent accidental contamination of the distillate with ionic impurities derived from the atmosphere or the glass of the still or container. Yet even repeated distillation, with all precautions taken, does not reduce the conductivity of water to zero. Instead, a definite very slight conductivity is at length attained, which depends on the temperature but is not altered by further redistillation. So it is evident that even the purest water contains a very few ions, derived from water molecules. We can account for them by assuming that an occasional water molecule transfers a proton, H + to one of its neighbors (reaction a).

H + transferred

$$H_2O + H_2O \underset{b}{\overset{a}{\rightleftarrows}} H_3O^+ + OH^-$$

This is an example of a reversible reaction, with the right-to-left reaction (b) the predominant one.

Measurements of the conductivity of the purest water that has ever been prepared, in comparison with that of dilute acids, alkalies, and salts, indicated that pure water at 25°C, contains H_3O^+ (the ion characteristics of acids) and OH^- (characteristics of base), each in a concentration of 10^{-7} equivalents per liter. Water is both an acid and a base, though very weak ones. Its concentration of H_3O^+ is that of a tenmillionth normal solution of HCl; and its concentration of OH^- is that of a ten-millionth normal solution of NaOH. Water is neutral, not because acid and alkaline ions are absent but because they are present in equal, very slight concentrations.

Very minute concentrations of H_3O^+ or OH^- are usually expressed in terms of a special scale of acidity or alkalinity, called the pH scale.

The pH[1] is the logarithm of the number of liters of solution needed to contain one equivalent of hydrogen ion, H_3O^+. For a neutral solution, the pH is 7 (the logarithm of 10,000,000).

The adjoining table will help to make the idea clear.

	Conc. of H_3O^+	pH	Conc. of OH^-
Increasing Alkalinity	10^{-14}	14	$10^0 = 1$
	10^{-13}	13	10^{-1}
	10^{-12}	12	10^{-2}
	10^{-11}	11	10^{-3}
	10^{-10}	10	10^{-4}
	10^{-9}	9	10^{-5}
	10^{-8}	8	10^{-6}
Neutral	10^{-7}	7	10^{-7}
Increasing Acidity	10^{-6}	6	10^{-8}
	10^{-5}	5	10^{-9}
	10^{-4}	4	10^{-10}
	10^{-3}	3	10^{-11}
	10^{-2}	2	10^{-12}
	10^{-1}	1	10^{-13}
	$10^0 = 1$	0	10^{-14}

1. Acidity and pH run in opposite directions. (As the concentration of H_3O^+ increases, the pH decreases.) For all acid solutions, the pH is less than 7.

2. Alkalinity and pH run in the same direction. (As the concentration of OH^- increases, so does the pH.) For all alkaline solutions the pH is greater than 7.

3. Each unit change in pH corresponds to a 10-fold change in the concentrations of both H_3O^+ and OH^-, but in opposite directions.

4. With a hydrogen electrode, pH may sometimes be measured to the nearest 0.01 unit. That corresponds to measuring the H_3O^+ concentration to within about 2.4%.

I. Colloids and High Polymers

A material is said to be in a colloidal condition when it exists as particles that are intermediate in size between ordinary atoms and molecules and particles so large that they are masses visible under the microscope. Most colloidal particles range from 1 to 100 millimicrons (mμ) in diameter. When such particles are dispersed (subdivided and scattered) through a gas, liquid or solid we have a colloidal dispersion. Some familiar examples:

China or porcelain—an opaque solid, dispersed in a transparent solid.

Fogs, mists, or steam—a liquid (droplets of water), dispersed in a gas (air).

Biscuits or cake, pumice—a gas, dispersed in a solid.

1. pH originally stood for the words potential of hydrogen, since it was measured with a hydrogen electrode.

Whipped cream—a gas (air), dispersed in a liquid, to form a foam.

Mayonnaise, milk, or butter—A liquid, dispersed in a liquid, to form an emulsion.

India ink—a solid (carbon black), dispersed in a liquid (water).

Cheese—a liquid (butterfat), dispersed in a solid (casein).

Smoke—A solid or liquid, dispersed in air to form an aerosol. Insecticides, deodorants, and disinfectants, sprayed by gas pressure from cans, belong to this class of colloidal dispersions.

We have not listed a gas, mingled with a gas, as a type of colloidal dispersion, since the intermingling of gases results in a mixture of simple molecules; in other words, forms a true solution.

All but the first of these different types of colloidal dispersions tend to be unstable: After a few minutes the dispersed material may separate out as a cream or sludge. But the addition of a very small amount of a third substance (a protective colloid) may greatly increase stability and produce a suspension or emulsion that may be stable for years. Those used as sprays for vegetables or fruits are often stabilized with soap.

Emulsifiers are substances that stabilize liquid-liquid dispersions (emulsions). Ordinary water-soluble sodium or potassium soaps disperse (emulsify) oil into soluble alkaline earth or heavy metal soaps disperse water, in small droplets, into oil.

The particles in colloidal dispersions are recognized as being of colloidal dimensions by the famous Tyndall test. If an intense beam of light is passed through the dispersion the path of the light is brilliantly illuminated, because each colloidal particle scatters a part of the light sidewise. But the path of the beam through a true solution (where the dispersed particles are ordinary molecules and ions) is almost invisible, except that it usually reveals a few particles of dust.

Substances that readily form colloidal dispersions are termed colloids. Cellulose, starch, vegetable gums, rubber, and water-soluble or insoluble proteins are examples. These are all composed of giant molecules, formed by linking simple molecules into long chains, perhaps with cross-links that convert the chains into 2 or 3 dimensional networks. Simple molecules from which colloidal particles are built are often termed monomers and the final products are called polymers and sometimes high polymers. Examples are many plastics and such synthetic fibers as nylon, acrilan, orlon, and dacron.

When placed in contact with water, many colloids produced by plants and animals absorb so much water that they are swollen to many times their original volume. Others (gums, dextrins, pectins, many proteins, and ordinary gelatin, for example) absorb water without limit and are dispersed to form viscous colloidal dispersions (incorrectly called colloidal solutions). These, on being cooled, often set to gels (sponge-like structures, traversed by interlacing sub-microscopic channels).

Plant life is dependent on the characteristics of water-imbibing colloids. When the growth of a plant begins, the stores of colloidal food-stuffs in the seed—starch, cellulose, proteins, and lipids—are swollen by water and acted upon by enzymes, themselves of colloidal nature. Thus these reserves are converted into soluble simpler materials—sugars, amino acids, and esters—and are transported in solution in water to cells in the growing root or plant shoot. There they are rebuilt into colloidal material. The mature plant consists predominantly of colloids.

Nor are plants alone thus intimately related to colloids. The protoplasm of every animal, from amoebae to men, is essentially colloidal. Large deposits of inorganic, noncolloidal material are found only in such specialized structures as the bones and teeth, and even there are in intimate association with colloids. Mineral salts also help to determine the water-holding capacity of the colloids in every living cell.

J.   Diffusion, Dialysis, Osmosis, and Osmotic Pressure

Anyone who has ever used a compound microscope has had visual evidence of the never-ceasing motion of molecules. Within the field there are always a few vibrating particles—cell fragments, specks of dust, or pollen grains. The smaller they are the wider and wilder are their oscillations.

Dust particles within droplets of liquid, enclosed in quartz crystals, have probably been in lively motion for millions of years. The motion of these microscopic particles comes from their being jostled by invisibly small molecules of water that surround them. Most of these blows come from nearly opposite directions and almost cancel out. Yet, now and then, a particularly hard blow, or several blows at once from nearly the same direction, deflect the relatively titanic mass of the visible particle, just perceptibly. So it is continuously in motion.

This direct evidence of the motion of molecules is called the Brownian movement. Almost as convincing is the spontaneous mixing of gases or dissolved substances, even when they are separated by penetrable membranes. If a colored solution is layered beneath pure water, the two will become well intermingled within a few days, in spite of all precautions; and if a cylinder of bromine vapor (which is about 5½ times as dense as air) is covered with an inverted cylinder of air, the withdrawal of an intervening glass plate will permit quick intermingling, in spite of the difference in density. Or open a bottle of ammonia or perfume in a room with quiet air and note how quickly the odor can be detected in every corner of the room.

This movement of a material from one place to another by the spontaneous, haphazard movement of its individual molecules is diffusion. A small boy, asked to explain what is meant by diffusion, showed that he had a good general idea of its nature when he answered: "It's molecules, going from where they are to where they ain't." One need not marvel that the motion of ions and molecules never ceases. The motion has become heat. It then has no other place to go. So it lingers there, indefinitely.

Diffusion is the great leveler of concentration differences, wherever they occur. In mixtures, each material moves independently of the others, from pieces in which its molecules are abundant to those where they are scarce. Each particle follows a zizag course and wanders away in a haphazard direction. The net rate of movement from one point to another, at any given temperature, is proportional to the difference in concentration between the two points. Diffusion rate increases with increasing temperature but is decreased by an increase in the viscosity of the gas or liquid through which the diffusing particles move.

The Scottish chemist, Thomas Graham, showed (1829) that the velocity of a diffusing particle at any given temperature is inversely proportional to the square root of its mass (molecular weight). Thus with oxygen gas, O_2 (mol wt 32), diffusing particles have 16 times the mass of those of hydrogen gas, H_2 (mol wt 2). The rate of diffusion of hydrogen is thus $\sqrt{16} = 4$ times that of oxygen. A thin perforated disc which will pass 100 cm³ of oxygen in a given time, gas pressures being equal on both sides of the disc, will pass 400 cm³ of hydrogen. (Note that if a gas is forced through holes or a capillary tube by applying pressure, this is not diffusion, and a different law is followed.)

The ions that compose a salt (the ions Na^+ and Cl^- for common salt) cannot diffuse independently because the solution must remain electrically neutral in every part. The net rate of diffusion of common salt is thus the geometric mean (the square root of the product) of the rates of diffusion noted with independent particles of the same mass.

Diffusion is important in the life of plants and animals, since it brings oxygen to the roots of plants and into the blood of animals. It also carries nutrients from dissolving mineral fragments in the soil solution to the root hairs through which these minerals are absorbed. Diffusion also helps determine the rate which water evaporates from moist soil or lakes, ponds and streams, and the rates at which plants get rid of carbon dioxide and water vapor in respiration and transpiration.

In industry, diffusion helps to determine the rate at which soluble substances dissolve in different solvents, the rate at which dissolved substances enter into reactions at surfaces, and the rate of propagation of flames in combustible gas mixtures.

The separation of uranium isotopes by diffusion (Oak Ridge, 1944) in the world's largest and most expensive factory, was a part of the creation of the first atomic bomb.

Purification by Dialysis

Diffusion is both a means of transport and of purification. When colloidal dispersions contain noncolloidal impurities, they are almost self-purifying. We need only bring them into contact with a water-permeable membrane, even a dead one, such as cellophane, parchment paper, or collodion (Fig. 3). Ordinary molecules and ions are relatively light; hence they move more rapidly at any given temperature and thus more frequently arrive at the surface of the membrane and pass through a pore. The massive colloidal particles, by contrast, move only slowly, hence only occasionally arrive at a pore in a membrane and pass through. A colloidal particle with a molecular weight of 300,000 has 10,000 times the mass of an ion or molecule of molecular weight 30. At any given temperature, the colloidal particle moves $\sqrt{10,000} = 100$ times as slowly as the molecule, and will that much less frequently arrive at the surface of a membrane.

Such purification of colloidal dispersions by the diffusion of noncolloidal impurities through a porous membrane is called dialysis. It is self-energizing, since it is brought about by the heat motion of the individual molecules or ions. These simply wander away from places where they are abundant to places where they are scarce. Observe that dialysis is purification brought about by a difference of mass, not by a difference in size. Thus it is not at all like purification by filtration.

Since dialysis is simple and self-energizing, it plays an important part in nature, where plants and animals must not only synthesize but also separate the products of their activities. Colloids, as long as they remain in the colloidal state, remain in the cells that produce them; but ordinary molecules and ions are lightweight midgets in comparison with colloidal particles, hence move away to distant cells and there are incorporated into colloids, or perhaps are oxidized and discarded.

In purifying colloids by dialysis (as in Figure 4) the colloidal dispersion being purified is diluted by the passage of water in the opposite direction, by osmosis. This is a handicap, which in the laboratory may be overcome, as shown in Figure 4. The dispersion to be purified is placed outside instead of inside an ion-permeable membrane. Noncolloidal impurities pass inward through this membrane and are carried away by a slow current of distilled water. The colloidal dispersion outside the membrane is meanwhile slowly concentrated by evaporation. If the liquid is slightly warmed both diffusion and evaporation are more rapid. In this way, many typical colloids, such as enzymes and proteins, have been obtained in crystalline form.

Plants and animals prevent dilution during dialysis in a way that better suits their structure. The osmotic pressure difference between neighboring cells is never very great, hence the movement of water

Figure 4. Dialysis, Combined with Concentration by Evaporation

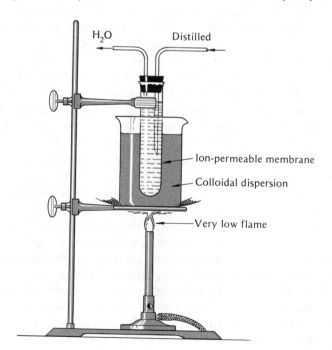

from cell to cell by diffusion is slow. Animals have veins and arteries through which a watery fluid (blood) is pumped. Plants have special channels through which water is pulled up, in a multitude of tiny threads, from roots to leaves.

Osmosis and Osmotic Pressure

We have remarked that the purification of a colloidal dispersion by dialysis is always accompanied by an inflow of water through the membrane, tending to dilute the dispersion. Actually, the flow of water is in both directions, but the inflow, from nearly pure solvent outside the membrane, is the predominant one. Such a diffusion of solvent—in this book, water—from pure solvent or dilute solution through a membrane into a more concentrated solution is called osmosis or osmotic flow. The flow of water is always from the place where water molecules are plentiful to places where they are scarcer. The same is of course true in the diffusion of any kind. The effect of osmosis is always to dilute the more concentrated solution, in other words, to diminish concentration differences. This, too, is characteristic of every sort of diffusion.

Figure 5. Demonstration of Osmosis

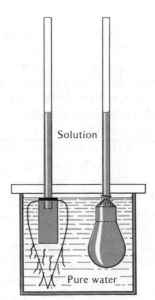

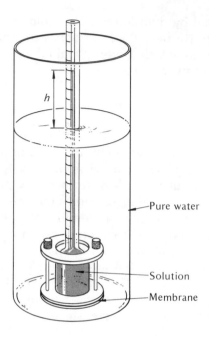

h

Pure water

Solution

Membrane

Figure 6. Measuring Osmotic Pressure of a Colloidal Dispersion

Figure 5 shows that the membrane through which osmosis takes place may be a living one—the figure shows a carrot, hollowed out to contain a solution of cane sugar or salt—or a nonliving membrane, such as a cellophane or collodion bag. The inflowing solvent sets up a pressure, called osmotic pressure, within the solution into which the water flows. This pressure may be measured by noting the pressure that must be applied to the side of the membrane that is in contact with the solution, just to stop the flow. If the solution is extremely dilute, or if the dissolved substance is a colloid, such as starch or glue, only a very slight pressure needs to be applied to stop the osmotic inflow. This pressure may be no more than the slight hydrostatic pressure caused by the slightly higher level, at which the liquid stands on the solution side of the membrane (Figure 6), when the inflow stops.

The membrane through which water diffuses in the apparatus just described may be a jelly-like precipitate (cupric ferrocyanide), electro-deposited within the pores of a porous porcelain disc. Such a membrane is strong enough to withstand the very high pressures that may be set up and is freely permeable to molecules of water, through holding back molecules or ions of dissolved substances. Such a membrane is said to be semipermeable. With this device one may readily determine the osmotic pressure of any solution by measuring, as in Figure 6, the difference of pressure that results when the other side of the membrane, instead of being in contact with pure water, is wet by a solution whose osmotic pressure has already been determined and recorded in a table.

If the term osmotic pressure is used, it is always assumed that the liquid on the other side of the membrane is pure solvent, not a dilute solution. If, by contrast, the inflow of water is from a solution, the pressure set up by the incoming solvent is usually termed diffusion pressure. This may have any value, from true osmotic pressure down to almost zero.

Readers who are just beginning to be familiar with osmosis are sometimes confused by the term *osmotic pressure,* since it seems to them to denote a pressure that would tend to drive liquid outward through a membrane, away from the solution being considered. For this reason, in Chapter 6 and elsewhere, we have sometimes used the term *osmotic pull* where osmotic pressure or diffusion pressure is meant. Of course, this term still relates to what is actually the inward diffusion of water from a more dilute solution or a pure solvent on the other side of a membrane or cell wall.

The osmotic pull is nearly disregardful of the chemical nature of the dissolved particles. At any given temperature it is determined by the particle concentration (the total number of dissolved particles, including colloidal particles, molecules, and ions) in a unit volume. Any one of these particles results in virtually the same osmotic or diffusion pressure as any other.

Osmotic pressure may be enormous. For a 5 per cent solution of common salt, for example, it is about 40 atmospheres (nearly 600 pounds per square inch). With dilute solutions, the osmotic pressure π, in atmospheres, is approximately that given by the formula

$$\pi = 0.0821 \, CT$$

in which T is the absolute temperature and C is the particle concentration (the total concentration of all particles, expressed in "moles" per liter). Remarkably, the same formula gives the pressure (atm) set up by any slightly condensible gas of the concentration C (moles per liter) at the absolute temperature T.

K. Atomic Weights of a Few Important Elements

Name	Symbol	At. No.	At. Wt.	Name	Symbol	At. No.	At. Wt.
Aluminum	Al	13	26.9815	Iron	Fe	26	55.847
Antimony	Sb	51	121.75	Lead	Pb	82	207.19
Argon	Ar	18	39.948	Lithium	Li	3	6.939
Arsenic	As	33	74.9216	Magnesium	Mg	12	24.312
Barium	Ba	56	137.34	Manganese	Mn	25	54.9380
Beryllium	Be	4	9.0122	Mercury	Hg	80	200.59
Bismuth	Bi	83	208.980	Neon	Ne	10	20.183
Boron	B	5	10.811	Nickel	Ni	28	58.71
Bromine	Br	35	79.909	Nitrogen	N	7	14.0067
Cadmium	Cd	48	112.40	Oxygen	O	8	15.9994
Calcium	Ca	20	40.08	Phosphorus	P	15	30.9738
Carbon	C	6	12.01115	Platinum	Pt	78	195.09
Chlorine	Cl	17	35.453	Potassium	K	19	39.102
Chromium	Cr	24	51.996	Silicon	Si	14	28.086
Cobalt	Co	27	58.9332	Silver	Ag	47	107.870
Copper	Cu	29	63.54	Sodium	Na	11	22.9898
Fluorine	F	9	18.9984	Strontium	Sr	38	87.62
Gold	Au	79	196.967	Sulfur	S	16	32.064
Helium	He	2	4.0026	Tin	Sn	50	118.69
Hydrogen	H	1	1.00797	Uranium	U	92	238.03
Iodine	I	53	126.9044	Zinc	Zn	30	65.37

L. Handy Conversion Factors

To convert	into	multiply by	or divide by
Linear Distance			
inches	centimeters	2.5400	0.3937
miles	kilometers	1.60935	0.62137
Area			
square feet	square meters	0.09290	10.764
square yards	square meters	0.83613	1.196
acres	square meters	4.0469×10^3	2.471×10^{-4}
acres	square feet	43,560	2.2956×10^{-4}
Volume or capacity			
cubic feet	liters	28.316	0.035316
cubic feet	U.S. gallons	7.481	0.13368
acre-feet	cubic meters	1.2335×10^3	$0.0107 \times 10^-$
acre-feet	cubic feet	43,560	0.22056
Mass			
pounds (avoir.)	kilograms	0.4536	2.2045
ounces (avoir.)	grams	28.35	0.35273
Pressure			
pounds/square inch	atmospheres	0.06805	14.695
inches of Hg (0° C)	atmospheres	0.033421	29.921
pounds/square inch	grams/square centimeter	70.307	0.014223
Work, Heat, or Energy			
horsepower-hours	kilowatt-hours	0.74569	1.3411
Btu	kilocalories	0.25198	3.9685
calories	joules	4.185	0.23894
kilogram-meters	calories	2.3427	0.42685
Velocity			
centimeters/second	miles/hour	0.02237	44.703
Volume rate of flow			
U.S. gallons/second	cubic feet/minute	8.0203	0.2468
cubic feet/minute	cubic meters/year	1459.3	6.7146×10^{-4}
cubic feet/minute	acre-feet/year	12.0748	0.0828
U.S. gallons/minute	acre-feet/year	1.6139	0.61961

Index

Absolute scale, 309–10
Aeration, and plant roots, 130
Aeration, zone of, see Zone of
    aeration
Afrika Korps, 179–80
Agriculture, 6, 155–56
Air, 57–59, 61, 63–64, 66, 68, 73;
    penetrates zone of aeration, 9;
    and joints, 10; ascending and de-
    scending, 70–71; secondary or
    minor circulations, 80–81; stable
    and unstable masses, 81–82
Alkali, 244, 247
Amazon River Basin, 90
Amazon River Valley, 65
American Camping Association, 306
American Public Health Association,
    264
American Water Works Associ-
    ation, 264
Amino acids, 125–27
Ancient times, 54, 56–57, 96–97,
    151–54, 161, 162, 178, 202
Animal life, 20, 30, 31, 34, 46, 47,
    49, 70, 92, 111, 143–45, 238; and
    plants, 141–43; osmotic equilib-
    rium, 146–47; necessary water in-
    take, 147–49; pesticides, 229–34;
    and industrial pollution, 234–36;
    and desalination, 299–300; wild-
    life preservation, 305–6
Antimony alloys, 112
Aquatic weeds, 215–16
Aqueducts, 151–53, 189–93, 194,
    195, 298
Aquifers, 14, 17, 18, 201, 208, 219;
    defined, 5; system, 6–7; zones, 9;
    flow of water in, 9–12; polluted
    water in, 19; depletion of, 51–52;
    and artificial replenishment, 52–
    53
Arabian Desert, 91
Arabian Sea, 64
Aral Sea, 26
Archeological Institute of America,
    306
Archimedes, 162
Artesian well, 7, 52–53
Aswan High Dam, 170, 197
Atchafalaya River, 182
Aztec Indians, 254

B. coli, 265
Barometric pressure, 57, 84

Bernoulli, Daniel, 167–68, 182
Boiling point, 59–60, 185, 274–75, 309
Bonneville Dam, 214
Boron, 98, 208, 246, 271
Breeder reactors, 176
Brownian movement, 325
Bureau of Reclamation, 31, 174

Calorie, 308, 309
Capillarity, 39–40; defined, 37
Carbohydrates, and plants, 124–25
Carbon dioxide, 96, 106, 138, 141–42, 260; and photosynthesis, 4, 123; and joints, 10; and formation of limestone caves, 16; in wells, danger of, 19–20; and rain-making, 89
Caspian Sea, 26
Caves, limestone, see Limestone caves
Cellobiose, 124–25
Central Valley, 52
Central Valley Project, 189–93
Centrifugal force, 84–85
Chicago River, 211
Chlorine, 96, 97, 141, 155, 210–11, 257–60, 316
Chlorine dioxide, 259–60, 261
Chlorophyll, 139
Chloroplasts, 119, 122
Cholera, 202, 203; see also Disease
Cities, modern: water sources, 154–55; and agriculture, 155–56; size, 156–58; sewage, 204–6; septic tanks, 206–7
Civil Works Program, Corps of Engineers, 186–88; see also Corps of Engineers, U.S. Army
Clay, 12, 36, 39–40
Clean Water Restoration Act of 1966, 241
Clifton Hot Springs, 218

Climatic zones, 72–74
Coast lines, 5
Cobb's seamount, 5
Cold front, 82
Colloids, 323–25
Colorado River, 28, 201
Colorado River Basin, 253
Columbia River, 197, 198, 214
Columbia River Basin, 253, 297
Conductivity, 106–7
Conservation, 29–35, 49–51, 241
Contamination, 20; wells, 18–19; vs. pollution, 200–201
Coriolis force, 74–78, 83–86
Corps of Engineers, U.S. Army, 174, 180, 181, 182, 183, 192, 194–95, 198; three principal activities, 186; hydraulic engineering, 187, 188; projects, 187–88
Coweata Hydrologic Laboratory, 34–35
Critical temperature of water, 310
Cumulostratus clouds, 88
Cytoplasmic membranes in plants, 117–18

Dalton, John, 97–100
Dams, 22, 158–60, 171–74, 181, 190–93, 197–99, 218, 225, 241–42
DDT, 232
Dead Sea, 26
Death Valley, 244
Dehydration, 39, 40, 47; moisture tension, 40–41
Deoxyribonucleic Acid (DNA), 120, 121, 122
Desalination: Office of Saline Water, 31, 277, 288, 301–4; defined, 277; methods, 277–78; costs of, 278–79, 280; demand for energy in, 279–81; purpose of, 280–81; solar stills, 281–83; multiple effect evaporation, 283–84; multistage

flash distillation, 286, 287–88, 302–3; vacuum flash distillation, 286–87; prevention of corrosion and scale deposits, 288–89; vapor compression distillation, 289–90; by freezing, 290–92; freezing vs. distillation, 290–92; electrolysis and electrodialysis, 292–94, 302; reverse osmosis, 294, 295–96; dual-purpose plants, 296–99; by plants and animals, 299–300

Deserts, 12–13; water, 12–13; precipitation, 91–92; animals in, 148–49

Detergent, 227–29

Devil's Canyon, 194, 199

Dialysis, 294

Dichromate ion, 13

Diffusion, 9, 117, 131–32, 249

Dipole moment, 103

Discharge, zone of, see Zone of Discharge

Disease, 20–21, 53, 93, 153, 178, 202–4, 265–66, 267

Dissolved oxygen, in water, 111–12, 138, 155, 200, 201, 223–25

Dolomite, 12

Dynamos, 170–71

Dyne, 309

Dysentery, 202, 203

Earthworms, and penetration of soil by water, 36–37

Electrodialysis, 292–94

Electrolysis, 292–94

Electron pairing, 100–101, 102–3, 105

Emulsifiers, 324

Environmental Protection Agency, 236, 241, 242

Erg, 309

Erosion of land, 33–35, 37, 42

Erosion control, 32–33

Eutrophication; defined, 210; and Great Lakes, 210–12

Evaporation, 49; rate of, 59–61; and precipitation statistics, 64–65; cooling effect of, 65–67; see also Vapor; Vapor pressure

Everglades, 43, 47

Extracellular water in animals, 144

Feather River, 190, 192

Federal Water Pollution Control Administration, 236

Field capacity for water, 39

Field crops, and salt, 248–49

Flood control, 179–80, 186, 189–93; Lower Mississippi River, 181–83

Fluoridation, 261–62

Food supply, see Agriculture; Plant life

Fraser River, 197

Freezing of water; freezing point, 108, 223, 274–76, 309; characteristics of, 112–13; and desalination, 290–92

Frictional loss of head, 164–65

Gila River, 218

Glaciers, 4

Glucose, 124–25

Gobi Desert, 91, 154

Gradient wind, 84

Gram-centimeter, 309

Grand Coulee Dam, 162, 172, 173

Granite, 10, 12

Gravel beds, 12

Gravitational potential energy, 166

Gravitational water, 39

Great Lakes, 22–26, 27, 141, 210–15, 241

Great Salt Lake, 244

Ground water, 12; areas of in United States, 11; in desert areas, 12–13

Gulf of Mexico, 69, 82, 179, 182,
    271, 273
Gulf Stream, 69–70
Gypsum, 245

Hadrian's aqueduct, 151
Halophytes, 250
Heat, economy of, 285–86
Heredity, 119–21
Hoover Dam, 162, 173, 174
Humboldt current, 70
Humus: defined, 29; and land ero-
    sion, 32; and irrigation, 36, 37,
    39; and moisture tension, 41; and
    water drainage, 46
Hurricanes, 67–68, 85
Hydraulics, 162, 167–68, 178–79,
    187, 188, 197–98, 226; defined,
    153
Hydroelectric energy, 162, 169–71,
    181, 193, 198–99, 225; largest
    hydroelectric developments, 173;
    production of metallic aluminum,
    174
Hydrogen, 96, 97, 99–101, 103, 105–
    6, 108, 134
Hydrogen sulfide, 268
Hydrolysis, 126
Hydrostatic balance: defined, 8; and
    water table, 8–9
Hydrostatic pressure: defined, 162–
    63; as measure of energy, 163–65
Hypochlorites and water purifica-
    tion, 257–58

Ice ages, 4–5, 21
Icecaps, 4, 102
Industry, 48, 50, 182, 185; iron and
    steel, 219; paper, 219, 220–23,
    226; see also Pollution
International Atomic Energy Agency,
    176–77

Intracellular water in animals, 144
Irrigation, 12, 37, 38, 39, 48–50, 154,
    181, 208; four chief methods, 41–
    43; salt in irrigation water, 43–44,
    156, 218, 247–48, 251–53, 280–81;
    amount necessary for crops, 44–
    45; profits and pitfalls, 45–46;
    amount of water used for, 51;
    reservoir storage, 171

Joints, 10
Joule, James P., 307
Joule, 307, 309

Kelvin scale, 309–10
Kidney, function of, 144, 149, 299–
    300
Kinetic energy, 59, 166–67, 308

Lake Baikal, 26
Lake Bonneville, 198
Lake Nyassa, 26
Lake Okeechobee, 21
Lake Sara, 158–59
Lake Tanganyika, 26
Lake Texcoco, 254
Lake Victoria, 26
Laminar flow, 165–66
Land capacity, 31–32
Lignin, 50, 220
Limestone caves, 15, 16, 209; fish
    in, 17
Limnetic zone, 138–39

McNary Dam, 197
Mass, 308–9
Meristems, 127, 128
Mississippi River, 4, 28, 30, 33, 155,
    180, 184, 185, 186, 201, 211, 240–
    41; flood control, 181–83

Mississippi River Commission, 181
Mississippi River System, 180–81
Missouri River, 33, 183, 186, 201
Multiple effect evaporation, 283–84
Multistage flash distillation, 286,
  287–88, 302–3

Nautilus, 175–76, 297–98
Nephrons, 299–300
Newton, Isaac, 83
Niagara Falls, 68, 162, 169, 173
North American Water and Power
  Alliance, The (NAWAPA), 191,
  194–95, 196–99
Nuclear energy, 54–55, 174, 175,
  193

Ocean, 9, 54, 68, 91; fresh water
  and, 3–4; and coastline, 5; level
  lowered during ice age, 5; as
  source of earth's fresh water, 21;
  currents, 69–70; currents and air
  circulation, 81; dissolved salts in,
  270–72; elements, 272–74; see
  also Desalination
Office of Saline Water, 31, 277,
  288, 301–4; see also Desalination
Ohio River, 186, 241
Oil Pollution Act of 1964, 241
Oil slicks, 305
Okobongo Swamp, 92
Oroville Dam, 190–93
Osmotic flow: defined, 276; and
  desalination, 295
Oxygen, 96, 97, 141, 149; and lakes,
  22; and fire, 35; and plants, 41,
  46; element in water vapor, 99–
  100; electrons, 100; and polarity,
  103; and water transparency, 110;
  dissolved, in water, 111–12, 138,
  155, 200, 201, 223–25; consumption by man, 149; and decay,

209; and pollution, 223–25, 226–
  27; and hypochlorous acid, 259;
  see also Photosynthesis

Paper industry, 185, 219, 220–23,
  226
Peace River, 241–42
Perris reservoir, 192
Pesticides, 229–32; see also Animal
  life; Plant life; Pollution
Photons, 311–12, 313
Photosynthesis, 4, 46, 56, 109, 122–
  23, 139–40, 141, 224, 237; defined, 4
Pitot tubes, 166–67
Planck's constant, 311
Plankton, 139–40, 209, 215, 236
Plant life, 4, 31–32, 32–33, 34–35,
  36, 207–8; strip cropping, 33; and
  irrigation, 43, 44–49, 156, 218,
  247–48, 251–53; transpiration, 44–
  45, 134–38; food supply and
  available water, 93–95; plant
  cells, 115–17, 122, 128, 132–34,
  249–50; cytoplasmic membranes,
  117–18; roots and water absorption, 127–28; root systems, 128–
  31; soil and water intake, 131–34;
  water intake, higher plants, 132–
  34; stomates, 135–36, 143; disease, 136; limnetic zone, 138–39;
  and animals, 141–43; and salt,
  156, 245–46, 247–49, 299–300;
  pesticides, 231–32; and toxic elements in soil, 246–47; see also
  Photosynthesis; Soil
Plasmolysis, 250
Platte, the, 21
Plutonium, and atomic bomb, 175,
  297
Polar molecules, 102–5
Pollution, 21, 50, 208–9, 212, 217–
  18; by human beings and animals,

18–19, 20; vs. contamination,
200–201; of lakes and ponds, 209;
salt, 218; iron and steel industries, 219; paper industry, 219,
220–23, 226; and oxygen, 223–
25, 226–27; detergents, 227–29;
pesticides, 229–34; oil, 238–39;
legislation, 239–40; national
control, 240–42
Population, 156–58
Potential energy, 59, 166–67, 308
Power, 309
Precipitation: statistics, 64–65;
transportation of energy, 67–68;
weather forecasting, 86; formation of raindrops, 87–89; rain-
making, 89–90; deserts, 91–92;
rain forests, 91–93; swamps, 92–
93; see also Wind direction
Prehistoric times, 178, 201–2
Pressure gradient force, 83–86
Protein, 126–27
Protoplasm, 114–15, 118–19, 139–40
Purification, 18–19

Quanta, 310–11

Radiant energy, 56, 67, 82, 123,
310–13; incoming and outgoing,
68–70; and water vapor, 110–11
Rainfall, conditions for, 86–89; see
also Precipitation
Rain-making, 89–90
Red Sea, 64, 270
Replenishment, zone of, see Zone
of replenishment
Reservoirs, 53, 112, 155, 186, 192;
artificial, 22, 171–74; largest, 170
Respiration, 46, 99
Re-use of water, 50
Reverse osmosis, and desalination,
294, 295–96

Ribonucleic acid (RNA), 120, 121
Rice, paddy, 46
Rio Grande, 28
Rio Grande Basin, 253
Rivers, as fresh water resources, 26–
28, 69
Rivers and Harbors Act, 187
Rodents, and penetration of soil by
water, 36–37
Roots, plant, 127–28, 128–31, 138

Sacramento River, 189, 192, 225–27
Sahara Desert, 7, 91–92, 154, 251
Sakkur Barrage, 255
St. Lawrence River, 28, 195
Saline water, 243–44, 251–53, 270–
77; see also Desalination
Salmon, in Great Lakes, 214–15, 232
San Francisco Bay, 189
San Joaquin River, 189
San Joaquin Valley, 192
Sand, 35
Sandstone, 12, 13
Satellites, and weather forecasting,
86
Sea of Galilee, 156
Searles Lake, 244
Septic tanks, 206–7
Sewage, 210; disposal, 204–6
Sierra Nevada, 189
Silt, 35–36
Silver iodide, 89
Snake River, 197
Soil: components and types, 35–36;
penetration by water, 36–38;
water-holding capacity, 38–40;
availability of moisture, 40–41;
drainage, 46–47; micronutrients,
92; penetration of root tips, 127–
28; plants and water, 131–32; salt
in, 244–45, 247–51, 253–56, 318;
toxic elements, 246–47; see also
Irrigation; Plant life

Stagg Field, University of Chicago,
    175, 297
Stationary front, 82
Stills: solar, 281–83; tilted wick,
    282; plastic covered, 282
Stomates, 135–36, 143
Stream Sanitation Commission,
    North Carolina, 240
Streamline flow, 165–66
Strip cropping, 33
Subsoil distillation, 37
Sulphur springs, 20
Sun, 67, 72; and photosynthesis, 4;
    dwindling of, 54–56; and temper-
    ate zones, 73–74
Surface tension, 108; defined, 38
Surface water: in desert areas, 12–
    13; and modern cities, 154–55
Surface wind, 84
Synergists, 231

Tehachapi Mountains, 192, 194
Thermal springs, 298–99
Thermometer, wet-and-dry bulb,
    63–64
Thermosphere, 59
Thermosphere, upper, see Upper
    thermosphere
Torrey Canyon, 238–39
Tracing water, 13–16
Transcellular water in animals, 144–
    45
Transpiration, 44–45, 134–36; rates,
    136–38
Trinity River, 185
Turbines, 169–70
Turbulence, zone of, see Zone of
    turbulence
Turbulent flow, 166
Typhoid, 202, 203–4

Underground water, 51–52, 54;
    resources of, 5–6; aquifers, 5–7,

9–12, 14, 19; uneven distribution
    of, 6; water table, 8–9; in deserts,
    12–13; tracing and measuring, 13–
    16; limestone caves, 13, 16–17,
    209; springs and wells, 17–21;
    and modern cities, 154–55; soft-
    ening of, 154
U.S. Atomic Energy Commission,
    176–77, 236, 298
U.S. Department of Agriculture,
    233–34
U.S. Department of the Interior, 31
U.S. Fish and Wildlife Service, 198
U.S. Geological Survey, 26–27, 48
U.S. Public Health Standard for salt,
    43
U.S. Soil Conservation Service, 31,
    33
University of Chicago, Stagg Field,
    175, 297
Upper thermosphere, 59

Vacuoles, 115
Vacuum flash distillation, 286–87
Vapor, 4, 38, 41, 56–57, 59–60, 88;
    transport of energy by, 67–68;
    formula of, 99–100; molecule,
    101–2; and radiant energy, 110–
    11; and desalination, 279–80
Vapor compression distillation, 289–
    90
Vapor pressure, 61–63, 274, 275–77,
    279–80
Vegetable crops, and salt, 248–49

Warm front, 82
Water balance: in adult man, 145–
    46; in livestock, 147–48; in desert
    animals, 148–49
Water-borne disease, see Disease
Water table, 10, 182; defined, 8;
    and hydrostatic balance, 8–9; and

drainage of swamps, 52
Watershed management, 33–35
Watershed protection, 31
Weather forecasting, 86
Wells, 17–21
Wheatstone bridge, 318
Wind direction, determinants of,
    83–86

Yellowstone National Park, 17
Yukon River, 198

Zone of aeration, 9
Zone of discharge, 10
Zone of replenishment, 9–10
Zone of turbulence, 57